ECO TOURS
AND NATURE GETAWAYS

To Tom —
For great trips
ahead for you —
Carole Berglie

ECO TOURS

AND NATURE GETAWAYS

A Guide to Environmental Vacations
Around the World

ALICE M. GEFFEN AND CAROLE BERGLIE

CLARKSON POTTER / PUBLISHERS
NEW YORK

To our fathers,
Thor Berglie and Joseph Geffen,
and our friends,
May Swenson and Zan Knudson

Copyright © 1993 by Carole Berglie and Alice M. Geffen, a partnership

Foreword copyright © 1993 by Allan R. Keith

Published by Clarkson N. Potter, Inc., 201 East 50th Street, New York, New York 10022. Member of the Crown Publishing Group. Random House, Inc. New York, Toronto, Sydney, Auckland

CLARKSON N. POTTER, POTTER, and colophon are trademarks of Clarkson N. Potter, Inc.

Manufactured in the United States of America

Book design by Renato Stanisic

Maps by Jason Küffer

Library of Congress Cataloging-in-Publication Data
Berglie, Carole.
    Ecotours and nature getaways : a guide to environmental vacations around the world / by Carole Berglie and Alice M. Geffen. — 1st ed.
        p.   cm.
    Includes bibliographical references and index.
    1. Ecotourism.   I. Geffen, Alice M.   II. Title.
G155.A1B4338   1993
910'.2'02—dc20   92-40761
                                                                        CIP

ISBN 0-517-88068-7
10 9 8 7 6 5 4 3 2 1
First Edition

ACKNOWLEDGMENTS

We would like to thank a number of people who have aided us in various ways. First, Roy Finamore, whose enthusiastic response to our proposal helped us land the contract, and our editor, Shirley Wohl, who supported us and encouraged us to write the best book possible.

Professional assistance was graciously provided by Jan Wolf of Abercrombie & Kent, Ron Levalley of Biological Journeys, Jan Pierson of Field Guides, Jean Warneke and Victor Emanuel of VENT, Ben King of King Bird Tours, Peter Kerkar of Cox & Kings, Edward Jackson of the Field Studies Council, Erica Frost of Quark Expeditions, Armas Hill of Focus on Nature Tours, Larry Mott of Navigations and Expeditions, Joe Van Os of TravelWild, Ginny Constance of Progressive Public Relations, Simon Ellis of BirdWatch Costa Rica, John Aspinall of Costa Rica Sun Tours, Gina Cerami of Special Expeditions, Suzie and Luis Felipa of Southwind Adventures, and Susan Hirsch and Peggy Mahoney of Continental Airlines.

Special help came from David Ramage of Oscar's Bookstore in Huntington, Long Island; Ann Smith; and Abby Frank, whose devotion to our project included the timely loan of her computer. And without our housesitters—Jeanne Laberge, Lauren Heller, and Tina Horth—we could never have left home.

CONTENTS

Foreword ix

Introduction 1

What Is Ecotourism? 1 • Taking an Ecotour 4 • Types of Tours 5 • How to Select a Trip and an Operator 8 • Safety Factors 12 • How to Prepare for Your Trip 12 • Travel in the Third World and the Tropics 13 • Traveling on Your Own 14 • Tips for a Better Trip 16 • How to Use This Book 17 Ecotours Are for Kids, Too 18

Nature Close to Home:
The United States, Canada, and Greenland 21

Northeastern United States, Canada, and Greenland 21 • Southeastern United States 28 • Texas 31 • Churchill, Southern Manitoba, and Wager Bay 33 • The Plains and Mountain States 36 • The Desert Southwest 41 California 44 • The Pacific Northwest, Including British Columbia 48 Alaska and the Yukon Territory 51 • Hawaii 62

Whales, Birds, and Fishes South of the Border:
Mexico, Central America, and the Caribbean 67

Mexico 67 • Guatemala 75 • Belize and Honduras 77 • Costa Rica 80 Panama 88 • The Caribbean Islands 90

From the Tropics to the Ice:
South America and Antarctica 105

The Galápagos 106 • Ecuador 113 • Venezuela 117 • Peru 122 The Amazon 124 • Brazil and French Guiana 131 • Bolivia 135 • Argentina and Chile 136 • Antarctica, South Georgia, and the Falkland Islands 141

Nature and Culture in One Trip:
Europe 149

Northern Europe 149 • The British Isles 154 • Western Europe 160 Central and Eastern Europe 173

FOREWORD

It is a pleasure to recommend this new book, which for the first time makes possible a broad perspective of ecotravel. The authors have produced an extremely user-friendly and well organized volume. The introduction, in particular, deserves special attention. It should be required reading for anyone considering any kind of ecotour. The sheer volume of detailed information about such a large number of tour operators and destinations is extremely impressive.

But perhaps the book's greatest contribution is in highlighting how many such travel opportunities now exist. And if history is any guide, more will be added in the years ahead. This is important because the few recent serious studies that have been done suggest that the number of people who travel to study or observe wildlife and the amount of money they spend are both much greater than heretofore suspected. In fact, ecotourism appears to be the tourist industry's fastest growing sector today. Therefore, those in government with the responsibility for developing access policy and designing facilities for parks and refuges should probably review their assumptions about who their constituency really is. For example, many agencies entrusted with public lands could do a much better job of encouraging use by wildlife hobbyists, sometimes by as simple a thing as keeping an interpretive center open on weekends.

Passive wildlife-related recreation does not consume any environmental resources, and, when appropriate facilities and services are made available, it is less concentrated seasonally than hunting and fishing. Visitors can look for birds or study plants, mammals, or insects for more of the year in most localities rather than just for a few weeks in spring or fall. As awareness grows that environmental travel is a market that can be tapped, the benefits for the local economy can lead both to improved local commitment to conservation and to better support and protection of local wildlife resources. Often this impact is accentuated in foreign countries, especially small ones such as the Caribbean islands. In such places, any incremental tourist revenue is economically significant. But more important, the economic imperative to protect the wildlife and its habitat for the future may make the difference between survival and extinction for a surprisingly large number of endemic species for which the known worldwide range may be only a few hundred acres!

To sum up, in an era when it is becoming increasingly important for visitors and host localities alike to develop an increased appreciation for the natural world, this book is both timely and effective. One hopes that it will also have an impact well beyond its authors' prospects.

Allan R. Keith, President
American Birding Association, Inc.

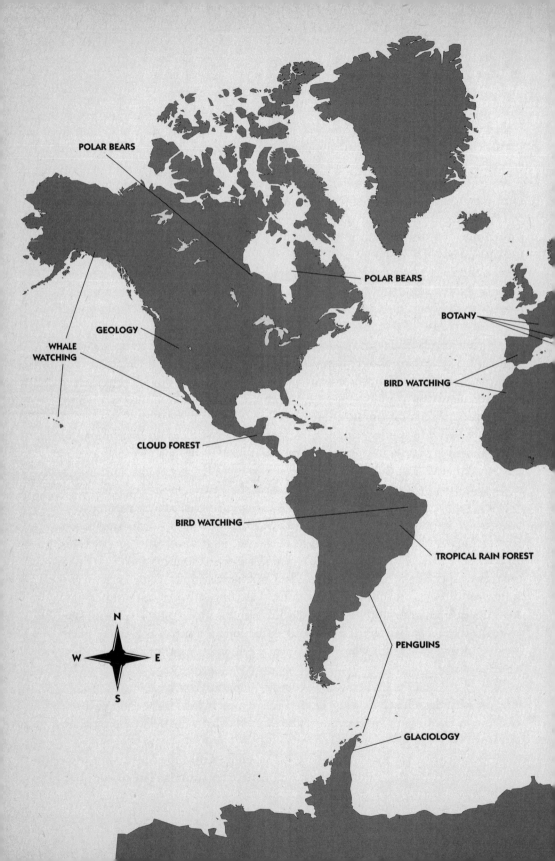

POLAR BEARS

POLAR BEARS

BOTANY

GEOLOGY

WHALE
WATCHING

BIRD WATCHING

CLOUD FOREST

BIRD WATCHING

TROPICAL RAIN FOREST

PENGUINS

N

W   E

S

GLACIOLOGY

GETTING STARTED

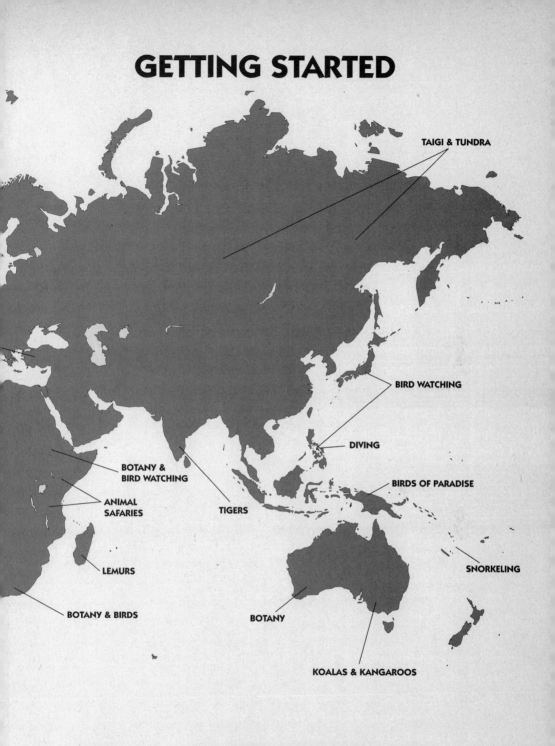

TAIGI & TUNDRA

BIRD WATCHING

DIVING

BOTANY &
BIRD WATCHING

BIRDS OF PARADISE

ANIMAL
SAFARIES

TIGERS

SNORKELING

LEMURS

BOTANY & BIRDS

BOTANY

KOALAS & KANGAROOS

INTRODUCTION

Until a few years ago, no one had ever heard of ecotourism. Many people still don't understand all of what it entails. But even without its trendy label, ecotourism is an idea and a life-style many people adopted years ago—some as far back as 1970, when the United States held its first Earth Day.

Concern for the environment around us—recycling, energy conservation, and the like—has spilled over into how we choose to spend our leisure time. In short, we look for ways to enjoy the outdoors without destroying it. So it is little wonder that nature tourism—trips to see birds, watch whales, and the like—is booming. As this book shows, there are a few hundred companies offering trips to naturalist destinations all over the world.

While contributing to an improved state of environmental affairs around the world, simultaneously you can have the time of your life hiking, biking, and snorkeling. You can work with scientists to study the behavior of an endangered species, thereby defining its requirements for preservation; or you can learn about nature through congenial bird walks or botany tours, seeking out unusual species, at the same time contributing to the world's overall knowledge about flora and fauna distribution or migration.

WHAT IS ECOTOURISM?

According to Elizabeth Boo of the World Wildlife Fund, ecotourism is nature travel that contributes to conservation. (It is called "green tourism" in Britain, but we think that sounds like you've eaten the wrong food.) The concept arose when conservationists began to see the potential benefits that could come from combining people's interest in nature with their concern for the environment. As Roger Tory Peterson noted years ago, "Nature tourism is one of the most practical ways to save the world's wildlife and wild places from more erosive forms of exploitation."

The travel and tourism industry is now the world's largest business, within which nature tours occupy a large part that is growing steadily. The situation has the following implications:

● You can select a tour operator that follows sound ecological principles and protects the environment. Over the years tourism has acquired a bad reputation, often despoiling local environments in order to construct lavish resorts, squandering critical resources, and using improper disposal methods for waste. But now you can use your vacation dollars to support responsible tourism.

● For countries like Kenya or Costa Rica, which depend heavily on income from nature tourists, maintaining their natural environment is essential to their economic survival. In other words, money speaks—loudly. Your ecotourist dollars help ensure that the Black Rhino or Mountain Gorilla is worth more alive than dead.

Unfortunately, *ecotourism* has become a buzzword, adopted by every travel company that can possibly twist its meaning to include their offerings. In this book we've tried to stick to only those companies and programs that truly contribute to conservation, that teach participants about the unique natural resources of a region, or that in some way encourage the appreciation and protection of valuable ecosystems. When you're ready to select a tour operator, read the information in Chapter 9. If you have questions, ask the operator about the company's environmental policy.

Once your tour is under way, be certain the leaders follow the guidelines of responsible tourism. If they don't, call it to the attention of the company owners. The tour companies and other organizations listed in this book have been in operation for several years, and have earned respect for their programs. They welcome your feedback and your suggestions for changes.

How Ecotourism Helps the Environment

Habitat destruction began some ten thousand years ago, when early people used simple tools to break ground and plant crops. Needing more open land to plant more crops, later generations began cutting down the brush and then the trees, damming rivers, leveling mountains, draining wetlands. Since it all began, some 2.5 billion acres of forest and woodland have been lost. And when the forests and other habitats are lost, so are the organisms that inhabit them. It is estimated that as many as one fourth of the world's plant, animal, and microbial species will disappear in the next fifty years.

Most of the world's lost habitat existed in what we know today as the Western industrial world. In fact, much of the knowledge, wealth, and comfort we take for granted is a result of that destruction. So is it any wonder that the destruction continues in the remaining countries of the world?

It is hypocritical for us simply to tell third-world countries that they must forgo economic development and leave their environments intact. We need to understand their unique situations—the pressures upon the land and the cultural background of the people—and provide ways to help them achieve economic prosperity without harming their environment.

Ecotourism is a way of reconciling economic development and species protection. It helps developing countries in the following ways.

● Trips are educational as well as fun. Tours to nature reserves and parks elsewhere in the world call people's attention to the natural beauty of other countries, acquaint them with radically different habitats, and make them aware of the plight of endangered species. Travelers become more informed about international issues and help support world conservation efforts. At the same time, people who live in those countries become aware of their natural treasures and more committed to preserving them.

● Park fees paid by nature tourists help finance antipoaching programs, pay for trail maintenance, and cover publication costs for maps and brochures. In addition, some tour operators impose a surcharge from which they make a contribution to naturalist organizations and preservation programs in the foreign countries they visit. For instance, Mountain Travel/Sobek donates a portion of its revenues to the Rainforest Action Network; Cox & Kings gives money to the Programme for Belize; and Journeys, another operator, created the Earth Preservation Fund for rehabilitation projects.

● Revenues from nature tourism often go directly into the local economy. Many operators use local agents for ground transportation, stay at small local hotels, and hire local guides. Tourists often buy local crafts made with an ecological bent. According to a recent study by the World Wildlife Fund, nature travelers spend more money in a foreign country than recreational travelers.

Ecotourists also refuse to buy products made from materials obtained from endangered species, such as ivory, black coral, or tortoiseshell, in this way demonstrating to locals a lack of interest in such items. We'd also like to think this concern will make ecotravelers hesitate before buying products at home that came into their countries illegally—like certain leather goods or tropical birds—and will discourage others from doing so as well. The United States, for example, is the largest consumer of wildlife and wildlife products in the world; if that consumption can be cut, it will end the incentive for people in developing countries to poach and export their native wildlife.

● Interest in ecotourism encourages local landowners, often with the help of international organizations, to develop low-impact facilities that double as nature reserves. For example, the Mexican group Amigos de Sian Ka'an operates a Biosphere Reserve on the Yucatán Peninsula; in Belize, a sanctuary for Howler Monkeys was established by local property owners.

Ecotourism is just as valid in the developed nations as a way of preserving the habitat we still have. Nature travel can have an immeasurable impact at home. People's awareness is increased as a result of a whale-watching trip in Monterey Bay or a hike in the High Sierras, and they return home better able to make intelligent voting decisions or pressure their representatives for policy changes.

Also, ecotourists take only photographs and leave only footprints. Indeed, nature tourists are frequently seen picking up other people's litter!

Will Success Spoil Ecotourism?

It's true—some areas are already receiving enough visitors each year. For example, there are now so many boats going to the Galápagos that rules have been established to limit visitation. Likewise, a code of ethics has been adopted for trips to Antarctica, another area with increasing tourism. In Nepal, so much of the forest has been cut to heat the trekkers' lodges that the owners have agreed to switch to kerosene.

In the United States, certain national parks are besieged with tourists, and places like Yosemite are limiting their accommodations. Backcountry trails are also restricted to a given number of hikers each day. Other park and preserve managers are looking for ways to limit access in order to preserve whatever it is that everyone comes to see. And, at Denali National Park in Alaska, park officials are fighting off recommendations by the governor to open up the park to passenger cars.

The obvious answer is strict control and encouragement to visit places less well known. In Europe, some critical preserves are not open to the public—ever. Other spots, particularly rain forests in the tropics and high peaks in alpine areas, are kept virtually inaccessible. And high park fees, especially in Africa, are a financial way of keeping the number of visitors under control. With proper safeguards, ecotourism can continue to work for conservation, not against it.

TAKING AN ECOTOUR

A nature tour, such as those discussed in this guide, is a fun-filled exploration—a naturalist's expedition in twentieth-century terms. Even if you're an independent traveler and have always avoided tours like the plague, you should consider taking a nature tour because it makes good sense.

- You are accompanied by a knowledgeable guide who can answer your questions about what you see. The guide identifies local flora and fauna, knows the location of rare species, and in the case of birds, knows their songs and can often call a bird in closer so you can see it.
- Traveling with a group means that there are more eyes looking to find what you came to see. The more experienced people on a tour generally help the less experienced, and everyone learns from one another.
- Most nature tours go to remote areas, where getting around can be difficult and often takes advance preparation, not easily done from home. The tour operator makes all the arrangements with local operators, including boat charters and

park permits. The operator also copes with last-minute changes, arranges for your meals, deals with hotel transfers, and the like.

- The trips have been researched and fine-tuned to take optimum advantage of the season of the year or to make the best use of time. If your vacation time is limited, you'll see and do more on a tour than you could on your own.

- Generally it is less expensive to travel with a group, as costs are divided among the participants. This is especially important when local flights or boat charters are involved. Also, traveling with a group represents energy savings—a minibus holding eight to twelve people is more efficient than private automobiles, ultimately decreasing our reliance on fossil fuels.

- If you are sociable, being with people of like mind is fun. Traveling by yourself or with just one other person can be isolating. You'll meet people on your trip who have taken other similar tours, so you can find out what travel to other parts of the world is like.

So what's the down side? Mention taking a tour and most people wince: "What if you don't like the people? You're stuck with them!" Of course it is possible to be with a group of people you're not compatible with, but mostly we have found that people who take nature tours are good company. The selective nature of a trip seems to eliminate the more offensive types or those interested only in shopping.

Also, taking a tour can be a bit like reverting to childhood. For the most part, you have two weeks or so when you don't have to make any important decisions and pretty much everything is taken care of for you. If you have a high-pressure job, that may be exactly what you want. Or if you haven't traveled a lot, you're apt to feel more comfortable. But it doesn't have to be this way. Most leaders fit the trip to the needs and interests of the participants. If you and the others want a more active role, just indicate that and you'll be more involved.

Any general dissatisfaction we've heard about nature trips usually involves a mismatch between participant and type of trip. If, for example, you are primarily interested in birds, don't go on a general nature tour, where the leader will know only a little about the birds and the group will want to move on rather than study a rarity. (Later in this section we'll offer some tips on how to choose the best trip for you.)

TYPES OF TOURS

The trips we've included in this book are as follows:

GENERAL INTEREST NATURE TOURS

Most trips are broad in scope, offering an overall look at a particular habitat or location, with only moderate attention to specific elements—the birds, flowers, trees, geological features, and so on. The objective is to get a general feel for the nature of the area. Tour leaders often have a specialty, with less thorough knowledge in other fields. Often these trips involve a cruise or some type of adventure travel. (We haven't included adventure trips per se; although you're bound to see some nature on a hiking or rafting trip, and the tour leaders may be familiar with some flora and fauna, generally the focus is on the adventure, not the nature.)

BIRDING TOURS

These trips are mostly designed to allow you to see as many species as possible in a given region at a particular time of year. The emphasis is usually on either resident or migrant species, depending upon the destination. Birding trips can be easygoing or hard-core, and you should check with the operator to be sure the one you want corresponds to your level of birding. Some trips are rugged or keep to a fast pace; for example, birding trips often start at dawn and end with late-night owling. Although tour leaders are keen birders, locating birds often calls for knowledge of habitat, so they are usually well versed in botany or geology as well. A birding trip is always more enjoyable and rewarding if you have studied your field guide ahead of time and know your target species—or at least the bird families you are likely to see.

BOTANY OR WILDFLOWER TOURS

Like birding trips, botany tours concentrate on one aspect of a region's biology. Leaders are knowledgeable in their field, and often know the geology as well, since it influences the soil conditions. Botany trips have the advantage of being slower paced than birding tours—birds fly but flowers stay still. The vast majority of botany trips are offered by British companies.

ANIMAL SAFARIS

Primarily, although not exclusively, offered in Africa, animal safaris usually involve going out into the bush to search for large mammals. Travel is often in four-wheel-drive vehicles, with pop-up roofs for viewing and photography. The naturalist or tour guide knows the habits and whereabouts of the game, and can also provide some cultural information on the region. These trips frequently involve both a morning and a late-afternoon drive, with midday reserved for resting or game watching from the lodge.

WHALE-WATCHING TRIPS

Although these are often one-day trips, the tours we list in this book are longer and usually involve a cruise. Successful whale watching requires being in the right place at the right time and having great patience. Tour leaders can recognize the kind of whale from the tiniest shred of evidence; they also usually know their seabirds. Don't forget your seasickness medicine.

OTHER SPECIALTY TRIPS

For people with an interest in butterflies or reptiles and amphibians, there are a limited number of such tours offered. There are also occasional trips for people interested in geology or astronomy. It's a shame that these other aspects of nature and science are not pursued more by the tour companies.

PHOTO TRIPS

There are a number of tours that provide photo opportunities and coaching to achieve better nature photos. The tour leader is usually a professional nature photographer.

CRUISES

Travel by water can often get you to places you can't otherwise reach. It can also be a very comfortable way to travel. Perhaps that's why nature cruises are so popular. Certain features are consistent: The trips are accompanied by naturalists, who provide lectures in the evening; landings in remote areas are via Zodiacs, small inflatable boats pioneered by Jacques Cousteau; and there are first-class accommodations and excellent food.

RAFTING AND CANOEING TRIPS

Most river-running trips fall into the category of adventure travel and so we haven't included them in this book. However, a slow-moving raft trip through a canyon can be an excellent way to observe the rock formations as well as plant and animal life. The raft trips we've listed feature a naturalist on board or some other aspects of nature education as part of the trip.

RESEARCH TRIPS

Not really nature tours per se, these trips offer participants the opportunity of working with scientists in the field on ecological projects. Usually the project runs for two weeks and work involves data collection. Though the actual tasks can be tedious, the idea of doing important work is stimulating. Accommodations are sometimes basic.

STUDY PROGRAMS AND WORKSHOPS

Some museums, universities, and learning centers offer study programs whereby participants learn about an aspect of nature. The programs we've listed in the book involve travel, either to a foreign setting or to a specially selected site away from home. Britain's Field Studies Council probably has the most extensive selection of such programs, both for the United Kingdom and around the world.

SERVICE TRIPS

Ever feel that it's time to give a little back to nature? If you've always enjoyed having well-marked trails or clean lean-tos, then you might want to spend your next vacation doing some of that cleanup work yourself. The Sierra Club sponsors a large majority of these trips, and they are very popular.

HOW TO SELECT A TRIP AND AN OPERATOR

By far, the most popular way of choosing a nature tour is by past experience. Almost every group we've toured with has included several people who have previously taken other tours offered by the same operator. Clients frequently become partial to one operator or develop a rapport with a particular leader, and certain naturalists have quite a following.

But if you've no experience on which to base a decision, how do you pick a nature tour operator? Word of mouth is a fine beginning, although you must always be sure that you trust the opinions of the people who are reporting their experiences. Majority opinion does help: If you've heard many people praise a tour operator, then chances are you'll be satisfied too.

There are other ways, however, to narrow your choice. If you are considering several options—different kinds of trips, to different places, at different times of the year—then you'll have a problem until you set a few parameters for yourself.

• *What kind of trip do you want to take?* Only someone with a wide range of interests would have trouble narrowing the field. Most people usually can decide whether they want a birding trip or a botany tour. But should it be a photo trip or a general nature tour? Consider your interests and how much you want to specialize in one aspect of nature. Maybe it's time to consider a study program or a workshop. If you want to relax, perhaps a cruise is more in line. Also important is whether you want to stay in one place and take short day trips or move from place to place every couple of nights. Most tours don't hop about too much, but in order to cover ground and minimize traveling they relocate several times during the tour.

● *Where do you want to go?* The possibilities are multiple but not infinite. As you'll see from this book, there are key destinations all over the world. These are the places where habitat is least disturbed and still accessible. Consider whether you like warm or cold climates, whether you want to travel to a developing country, or whether you prefer the comforts of a Western-style nation. How much traveling do you want to do? Indonesia, for example, is a twenty-two-hour flight from Los Angeles; the High Sierras are only about a seven-hour car ride.

● *When do you want to go?* Although some trips are offered year-round, most are keyed to time of year: spring or fall, wet or dry season, high or low water. Bear in mind, however, that spring and fall are reversed for the Southern Hemisphere and dry and wet are extremely variable. Tour operators plan their trips so as to be in a place at the best time. If your vacation time each year is fixed, so are your options, to some extent. However, if you can be flexible, you can find a trip to take you somewhere outstanding any time of the year. For example, if you are a birder, there's a trip leaving for somewhere in the world every week, all year long.

● *How much do you want to spend?* As you'll see from our write-ups, there is some price differentiation among the trips. But the majority of nature tours fall into the $$ and $$$ categories—$125–$200 or $200–$300 a day, respectively. Luxury cruises are, of course, more expensive, and volunteer vacations and camping trips are usually less. You can do some comparison shopping, but the type of trip and the destination are the largest factors in the cost.

If a trip involves extensive ground transportation or internal flights, that ups the price, as do high park entrance fees and the services of local naturalist guides or scientists. Although prices for most consumer items in a developing country are very low, there usually is no middle range of accommodations suitable for tourists, and therefore operators choose first-class hotels or resorts. (Although reliance on local facilities is a tenet of ecotourism, operators must ensure the safety and health of their participants; this is more easily done with superior facilities, preferably locally owned.)

In considering cost, you must also count your airfare, since tour operators usually do not include it in the cost of a trip. Airfare can be expensive, although if you can use frequent flyer miles or discounted fares, you can obtain some real bargains.

Also to be factored in is the cost of your shots and other medicine. This is not to be discounted—malaria preventive medicine, for example, can be as much as $6 a tablet, and you have to take the tablets one week before, during, and for three weeks after your trip. Injections also can cost upwards of $40 each, plus the doctor's fee. Tour operators never mention these costs, but they are quite real—and not something on which you'll want to cut corners.

Check operators' costs carefully and compare! Sometimes the same type of trip costs more with one company than with another. On a cruise to the Caribbean, we found that a museum trip cost $200 less than the same tour offered by a private company.

Once you've determined the type of trip, destination, time of year, and maximum cost, you can select from oodles of exciting options. Most tour operators are competitive—if one birdwatching trip goes to Malaysia, so does another. Get brochures and daily itineraries from both and compare. Do they go to the same places? How long do they stay in each location? Check the credentials of their leaders. Are they authors of field guides to the region or noted internationally in another way? How long have they been with the company and how long have they been leading this trip? Experience in both leadership and in the region count immeasurably. The bad reports we've heard about trip leaders all result from their lack of leadership qualities or unfamiliarity with the area.

Check the completeness of the information a company sends you about its trip. How thorough is the environmental information? How specific is it about what you'll see or do? Watch out for phrases like "we might see the elusive . . ."; read that as "only if we're really lucky." Since nothing about nature can ever be guaranteed, be wary of sure things and place your bets on what's most likely.

Also important is the number of people usually on the trip. Although we think it is a critical piece of information, not all tour operators state in their brochures how many participants are allowed on each trip, and how many leaders accompany the group. Obviously, the smaller the group the better in most cases; you have a greater chance of seeing wildlife and the group moves about with greater flexibility and speed. Generally, it also means a lower impact on the ecosystem. Large groups mean less "customization" of the tour and longer waits to get started in the morning, longer breaks for lunch or restrooms, and more involved loading and unloading of the bus or Zodiac.

There are times when a large group is unavoidable, as is certainly the case with cruises. But sometimes the disadvantages of a larger group are diminished when the number of leaders is increased. Birding tours nearly always add another leader or two when the number of participants goes up. A second or third leader means another person you can ask questions of, another pair of eyes to spot and identify wildlife, an additional guide to lead a minigroup elsewhere if participants wish to split up.

Small groups have their disadvantages as well—especially if one of the participants is disagreeable or demands special attention. Large groups (and by this we mean more than twenty) counter this problem with different social dynamics. After about the third day, personalities start to emerge and cliques begin forming; you can avoid the people you don't like by sticking with those you do. On the other hand, we agree with Mark Baker of Ecotour Expeditions that the "social aspects of a large group distract from the natural history aspects of a trip."

Next, compare the kinds of accommodations (budget, camping, first-class), number of meals covered on the trip (all meals are not always included), airport transfers, and the like. Be particularly careful about items *not* covered; some operators are fond of excluding from their responsibility costs of internal flights, park fees, and special options such as night safaris. They do this, of course, to make their trip seem less expensive. We feel these are part of the trip and should be sold as part of the package, but the shameful practice does continue among some operators. (This does not apply to extensions, however, since these are options that begin after or before the regular tour; extensions always cost more.)

If possible, speak to people who have already taken that same tour. You should be able to obtain their names from the tour operator. For example, several years ago we took Biological Journey's Sea of Cortez cruise and enjoyed it very much. Since then, BJ has given our name to people inquiring about the trip, and we've gladly supplied information and impressions. Every operator should pass on the names of people who agree to provide this service.

If you are concerned about picking the right operator, the operator in turn is concerned about you. To ensure successful trips, they all want ideal clients—physically fit, enthusiastic, self-sufficient, and agreeable. Unfortunately, not all of us may meet these requirements. So when you call tour operators to ask questions about the trip, they are listening to determine if you'll be a happy camper. A softer trip will be suggested if you seem hesitant or lacking the experience for a strenuous one. So mention your fears, and put your trust in the operator's advice.

Once you've signed on for a trip, you'll have to send a deposit to hold your space. If you decide to cancel, you should receive a full refund up to a certain point, after which you may receive a partial refund or lose your deposit.

Operators nearly always send out a pretrip questionnaire, which we think is a good idea. At this point, be sure to mention whether you have any dietary restrictions or are a vegetarian. (Keeping to a strict vegetarian diet may be difficult in some locations, but most tour operators make an attempt to be accommodating.) Tell them if you are afraid of heights or close spaces, if you can't be in the sun, or if you can't swim. Also mention whether you are greatly overweight. One operator told us about the difficulty he had fitting a 250-pound man and his 250-pound wife into standard-size hammocks on board an Amazon riverboat. Another mentioned the challenge of getting an overweight woman back into a Zodiac after she had been swimming with dolphins.

While safety is a major concern of tour operators, age is not a factor. On some trips, we've had birthday celebrations for people in their eighties. And often the older folks leave the younger ones in the dust; on a Sierra Club service trip we heard about, the retired seniors accomplished more than eighteen-year-olds!

SAFETY FACTORS

All travel necessitates some risk, however, nature travel sometimes carries a slightly higher risk factor because of the destination and nature of the activity. When the trip you are considering might entail travel to a country that has experienced recent political turmoil, or if there's an immediate threat of such an occurrence, we advise you to check with both the operator and the U.S. State Department. Operators don't want the liability risks of taking people to unsafe places, and through their local contacts usually know the situation best.

For additional travel information, the State Department's travel advisories can be helpful (phone: 202-647-5225). Listen to the recordings carefully, however, because they can be for specific locations within a country and may not apply elsewhere. Also, some of the advisories are prepared only when Americans are targeted as a group, not when violence is indiscriminate (as it can be in U.S. cities!).

For health information, the Centers for Disease Control runs a hotline (phone: 404-332-4555 or 404-639-1610). If you have questions regarding immunization, contact the U.S. Public Health Service (see your telephone book for the local phone number). This agency will provide up-to-date information on health requirements. If you would like a list of English-speaking doctors worldwide, become a member of the International Association for Medical Assistance to Travelers (IAMAT), 736 Center Street, Lewiston, New York 14092 (phone: 716-754-4883).

HOW TO PREPARE FOR YOUR TRIP

Ecotours can be expensive—on average at least $175 a day—so you want to make sure you'll enjoy your trip to the fullest. And when will you ever get back to Borneo again anyway? A little advance preparation and knowledge will help.

● Read the pretrip materials sent by the tour operator to learn as much as possible about where you are headed. If possible, get some books from the library to fill in any gaps in information. Read about the topography, the different habitats you'll be visiting, the birds, mammals, trees, and so on that you're likely to see. If you are going for birds, be sure you get a checklist. The more knowledge you bring to your trip, the more you'll see and appreciate.

● Get into as good physical shape as you can. Make sure you are up to the demands of the trip. If you have a doubt, check with the operator; there may be alternative activities for you on days that require abilities you don't have.

Also, be sure you have seen a dentist recently; you don't want to get a toothache in the jungle.

● Assemble the medicine you will need, and obtain the necessary shots. If you regularly take a particular medicine, be sure you have a supply to cover you while you are away. Check with your tour operator about what shots you will need: A tetanus shot is a must for all trips, everywhere in the world, but depending upon your destination you may also need a polio booster, gamma globulin (for infectious hepatitis), and immunization against measles or typhoid. Although a yellow fever vaccination is not required for reentry into the United States, it may be required for entry into the country you're headed for. Cholera remains a problem in some parts of South America and Central America, although tourists are not usually affected. Many hospitals in the United States have caught on to the fact that people are traveling to exotic places, and they have established travelers' immunization centers that provide information and offer the necessary shots and drugs.

● Many tour operators supply a list of suggested items: rain gear, hat, hiking boots, and other protective apparel in addition to sunscreen, bug spray, first-aid kit, and such. We have always felt that a Swiss army knife, canteen, hand wipes, clothesline and clips, and day pack are essential for every trip. If bringing binoculars or a camera, check that they are in working order. Be sure to bring plenty of film and extra batteries for your camera. Likewise, check that your rain gear is still waterproof (learn from our mistakes). Keep your luggage to a minimum; you may be toting your bags from place to place, and they gain weight rapidly. Pack your true essentials in a separate carry-on bag so that you have them should your baggage get lost during the flight.

● Check your passport to be certain it is up-to-date. Make a photocopy of your passport and pack that separately. Also, some countries require visas—again, your tour operator will inform you about these details and possibly obtain the visas for you. Leave your travel information, including a list of traveler's check numbers, with someone whom you can contact in case of an emergency.

TRAVEL IN THE THIRD WORLD AND THE TROPICS

A large number of ecotours go to third-world countries, especially in the tropics. Since travel to these countries is different from that to Europe or other industrialized countries, there are a few considerations to keep in mind.

First, don't expect everything to go exactly as planned. Local operators won't always go by the clock and might want to change plans to suit the weather or other conditions. Internal flights may leave when the plane is full, rather than at an appointed time. Realize that other people have a different concept of time and go with the flow.

Services may not be as efficient as you are used to. Telephones, mail service, plumbing, and the like are apt to be slower or less dependable. The electricity may go out for a while. The roads may be potholed or bumpy and dusty; it's all part of the adventure. Always remember that you are a guest in the country, and avoid complaints or unfair comparisons.

Water is often not potable. It is always best to drink bottled water if it is available (and it frequently is), or else use a water-purifying product such as Polar Pure (unless you are sensitive to iodine). Your trip leader will know whether you can safely drink the water at your hotel and will probably supply bottled water on day trips.

Refrigeration is often lacking, so choose your food wisely. The tour operator will have arranged for your regular meals to be safely prepared, but nonetheless be on guard against unpeeled fruit, all salads, and cooked foods that are not hot. Drink only liquids that have been pasteurized, boiled, or commercially bottled. And remember—no ice.

If you suffer from traveler's diarrhea, talk to your doctor about possibly taking an antibiotic as a preventive. Also take along bismuth liquid or tablets and/or Imodium; ciprofloxacin is very good but requires a doctor's prescription. Be prepared: you don't want to be disabled for a day and miss out on seeing that endangered species you came for.

If you are climbing to high altitudes, consider the possibility that you might suffer from altitude illness. If you take preventive medicine, you do not have to worry, so ask your doctor about it; Diamox is usually prescribed.

If traveling in the tropics, you will experience a level of heat and humidity you probably are not accustomed to, and it will take you a few days to adjust. Be sure to drink *plenty* of water—up to two and a half quarts a day—to replenish what you perspire. Also, wear tropic-weight all-cotton clothing that can breathe. If you're going to be in the jungle, opt for long sleeves and long pants; they aren't any hotter in the humidity and will afford protection from the brush or insects. And bring bug spray if there will be biting insects. If there's a chance of malaria—check with your tour operator—take preventive medicine.

And last but not least, wear a hat for protection against the sun.

TRAVELING ON YOUR OWN

Many people like either to arrive at a destination on their own and then link up with a tour, or stay on after their tour is over to travel around at their own pace. We like the latter arrangement because it gives us the best of both worlds.

For example, we followed an Abercrombie & Kent cruise in Indonesia's Sunda Strait with a week on our own in Bali. The tour operator took care of our travel arrangements for the cruise, and then we booked our stay in Bali through Aerowisata.

There are some considerations, however, in making this kind of arrangement. First, tour operators like to make your airline reservations for you. This way they can be assured that you will meet up with the group at the appointed time. In fact, they are happiest if they have been able to arrange for everyone in the group to meet at an airline hub city (such as Miami in the United States) and then fly on to the foreign destination together. This is for your benefit as well, because should a problem with the flight arise, everyone is together and the tour operator can more easily make adjustments to the schedule. Of course, the tour operator's travel agency gets the commission on the sale of your airline ticket, another reason they usually want to book your flight. So be aware that some operators impose a surcharge if you book your own flight.

If you decide to go it on your own and meet the group at the destination city, do yourself and everyone else a favor: *Arrive at least a day early.* Even in the best of circumstances, travel carries an element of chance—flight cancellations, delays, and missed connections can wreck your plans. If you arrive after the group, you may have trouble catching up with it, especially if the trip is by boat. Catch-up tales may be fun to tell afterward, but remember that you will have missed days in the field that you have already paid for.

Staying on after a tour is usually a lot easier to arrange, and the tour operator may even help you with your plans. Sometimes your group airline ticket will still be valid, too. There's also the advantage of your having gotten to know the country a little, so you probably will be more comfortable about staying on your own. This is what we did in Venezuela. Following a VENT tour to the Andes, we added on some days at a ranch in the llanos.

When making your own airline reservations, first consider your schedule, then the cost. Travel is tiring, and the more stopovers or connections, the more worn out you'll be before you even begin your trip. We've done a lot of traveling around the world and recommend most national airlines for the country that's your destination. If you wish to fly a U.S. carrier, Continental Airlines has been going all out these days with its convenient schedules and excellent service—kudos to Continental for its excellent breakfast of cereal and fresh citrus.

Here's a tip: If you have been on a rugged field trip in the tropics, and have been sweating heavily for two weeks, twenty-four hours a day, do your body and spirit a *big* favor after your tour—check into a deluxe hotel with air-conditioning and a pool. We followed a hard-core birding trip to Malaysia with a little rest and rehab at the Jakarta Hilton, and it restored our enthusiasm for more travel in the tropics.

TIPS FOR A BETTER TRIP

Once you've been on a few nature trips, you know what to expect, but if your travel has been confined to beach resorts and European capitals, there are a few things you need to know about this special brand of travel.

First, bear in mind that seeing animals in the wild is quite different from what is portrayed on television nature programs. In order to capture all that fascinating activity on camera, filmmakers spend months in the field in blinds or canopy shelters waiting for something to happen. If you take an afternoon hike through a tropical rain forest, you're not going to come face-to-face with a Tapir.

Remember that most animals are active primarily at dawn and dusk. If you want to see birds or mammals, you have to be up early and in the refuge or forest when activity is at its peak. Second, you must be quiet. Animals can hear you stomping through the woods, crushing leaves and breaking branches. Most especially, they can hear you talking, and they'll move away without your ever knowing they were there. You'll probably have more luck if you just find a promising spot and stay there. In tropical forests, it is important to wear dark clothes; bright colors will frighten away birds.

Since most trips involve riding in a minibus or walking on a narrow trail, leaders will often suggest rotating positions so that everyone gets a chance to be first. From that point, it is up to the participants to shift around every now and then. Since this is an issue that can lead to armed insurrection, be considerate of others. Besides, the person in front isn't always the one who spots the bird or animal—frequently the best place is in the rear.

If there's a decision to be made by the group—say, a choice between taking an all-day hike up a steep mountain or two shorter strolls on level ground—express your preference, but if you lose out, go along willingly unless physically you aren't up to it. No one likes a sore loser.

Traveling on a nature tour sometimes means staying at accommodations below a level you are used to, or perhaps changing your daily schedule. Remember that you are on vacation—and that means a change from your customary routine as well as a change of scenery. Be flexible, keep an open mind, and try new things. You'll surprise yourself.

Be mindful of time when you are with a group. If the leader has said you'll meet at a certain place in one hour, be sure you are there in one hour. Don't keep everyone waiting.

Be enthusiastic. Having a negative attitude can cast a shadow over the whole trip for everyone. Even if it has rained for seven of the ten days of your trip, keep going—who knows what unexpected good things your misfortune may bring? We've seen some of our best birds in the rain or snow.

All of this positive talk doesn't mean you should suffer in silence. If things aren't going as you expect on a tour, speak to the leader directly, and in private. He or she can usually find a way to satisfy your needs while also tending to those of the group. And by all means, if you feel dissatisfied with the trip, let the tour operator know when you fill out your posttrip report.

HOW TO USE THIS BOOK

We've divided the book into eight chapters covering ecotrips all over the world, plus a concluding chapter on the tour operators themselves.

Each chapter deals with a region of the world, roughly corresponding to the continents. Within each chapter are groupings of countries or regions that are visited for their naturalist interests. We introduce each region or country with a few words about its major characteristics, its biodiversity, and its environmental situation. Then follows a list of the major tours or programs for the area, listed alphabetically by tour operator.

For each tour, we've provided the following:

• *Name of tour operator.* For address, phone number, and other information, see Chapter 9.

• *Length of trip and departure months.* The number of days given for the most part corresponds with the way all tour operators describe their trips: counting from the day of departure through the day of return. However, you should realize that trips to some parts of the world—Africa, for example—involve up to four days of travel, and the actual time you will be on safari or whatever is considerably less. We think it's a bit misleading to list the return day, when you might be leaving early in the morning, as a trip day when in actuality you spend it in the airplane. Nevertheless, this is the way it is done in the industry, in part because it helps lower the per-day cost of a trip and in part because it makes the trip seem longer. The months given are the departure times, and are subject to change.

• *Cost of the trip.* The number of days for the trip has been divided into the price to give a per-day cost. Our cost figures per day are represented as follows:

$ **up to $125**
$$ **$125–$200**
$$$ **$200–$300**
$$$$ **$400 and up**

The cost reflects the operator's stated trip price plus any necessary additions such as meal supplements, park fees, and internal flights. It does *not* include airfare to the destination unless so stated. For example, "$$ (from La Paz)" means the trip begins in La Paz and you must pay the airfare to get there. This is true for the majority of trips. However, some companies, especially British ones, state their trip prices inclusive of airfare; for example, "$$ (from London)."

Also relevant to the costs of a tour, but not included in our information, is the single supplement. If you are traveling alone and wish to have your own room whenever that option is available, you are always required to pay a supplement— usually about $250 to $350 for a two-week trip. Some trips also carry what is called a "small party supplement." This means that the price could increase if only a few people sign up.

Optional extensions are not included in our cost figure, since these are additional to the program. Many times they are worth adding on if you can spare the time, since you will have already paid to get to the destination.

● *Nature of the trip.* Here, we've briefly described the trip—whether it's a birding trip, dive trip, general nature trip, and so on. We've highlighted the major elements or destinations, so you can determine if the trip is of interest to you. We've also mentioned, when applicable, if there is a maximum number of participants or if a particularly noteworthy guide is leading the trip.

The trips listed are usually offered every year or every couple of years, depending on demand. Although new trips are always initiated, our listings represent the bulk of offerings at this writing. Mostly, the popular, well-run trips continue to be offered every year. Occasionally operators will drop a trip if the political or environmental situation in a country or region changes drastically, and then reinstate it when the conditions improve, so if some trip or destination is especially appealing, contact the operator and let them know you might want to go in the future. Because of their very nature, research trips are dependent on the length of the study involved. When the data collection is completed, chances are the trip will no longer be offered.

ECOTOURS ARE FOR KIDS, TOO

Most of this book is for grown-ups, but there are some opportunities for young people. The National Audubon Society runs Ecology Camps every summer in Maine. In the Chiricahua Mountains of southeast Arizona, youngsters (ages eleven to seventeen) can explore the flora and fauna of the region with experienced naturalists at VENT's Camp Chiricahua. The National Wildlife Federation has the most comprehensive program. Its Summits all have a preschool program (ages three to four), a junior naturalist program (ages five to twelve), and a teen adventure program (ages thirteen to seventeen). In addition, you can sign up for Wildlife Camp for Kids (ages nine to thirteen). If you're a teen (ages fourteen to seventeen), you might be interested in either Leadership Training Camp or Teen Adventure.

Some tour companies run trips for families or have special activities for children. This is noted in the Tour Operators section on page 279. Many tours, although not for children, will gladly take participants over age fifteen; just ask. Kids seem to love the out-of-doors and relish learning about natural history. They are tomorrow's ecotourists; they can save our planet.

Nature Close to Home:
The United States, Canada, and Greenland

Looking for a great outdoor adventure? If you live in the United States, you don't have to go far. Some of the best naturalist vacations are right here at home. Remember that as early as 1864 the Yosemite Valley in California was designated a national park, thus serving as the forerunner of such parks around the world. In 1872, Yellowstone joined in that role, with official governmental protection. In 1891, the United States established its system of national forests. Though we can't claim to have originated the idea of conservation, the United States has played a primary role in conservation's worldwide development.

Nature travel in the United States is a major industry, and has been for many years. Close to four hundred parks and nature reserves, maintained to allow some access while preserving habitat, are a secure home for wildlife. Yes, there are some problems, especially in the buffer zones surrounding the parks. But as the trips described on the following pages show, opportunities for encounters with the natural world abound in the United States.

To an even greater extent, such naturalist opportunities lie waiting in Canada. The second largest country in the world, Canada is one of the least densely populated, so much of the land is almost devoid of people. The Canadians' goal is to set aside a full 12 percent of their land as protected areas. Let's hope they succeed.

NORTHEASTERN UNITED STATES, CANADA, AND GREENLAND

Think green—Thoreau did. Just over a century ago he left the hustle and bustle of Concord for the quiet of the Maine woods. We're suggesting you do the same. If not the Maine woods, then the northwoods of Michigan, Wisconsin, Minnesota, New Hampshire, Vermont, the Adirondacks, the Gaspé, Ontario—what is called the boreal forest. Here the loons cry at night on clear lakes, the smell of sap and resin is in the air, moose crash through the marshes, and even wolves can be heard, if not seen. Shy Indian Pipes poke up through leaf litter and Black-throated Green

Warblers flit through the trees. There are many adventures to be had in the boreal forest, from a weekend in the Adirondacks identifying plants to a week at the Audubon Ecology Camp on Hog Island (Maine) to a week tracking Timber Wolves in Minnesota with an Earthwatch research team. Here also are Sierra Club service trips along the Allagash Wilderness Waterway and birdwatching trips to Grand Manan in the Bay of Fundy.

North of the boreal forest, the world of ice prevails. The ice floes in Canada's Gulf of St. Lawrence are home to the Harp Seal, which you can visit via helicopter. Baffin Island, north of Hudson Bay, and other islands of the far north offer opportunities for observing seabirds and mammals in the rarefied atmosphere of a never-setting sun. A few trips include Greenland on their Arctic itinerary. Rich in flora, including orchids and poppies, the tundra on Greenland's west coast also supports viable populations of Arctic Fox, Arctic Hare, Caribou, and Musk Ox, in addition to White-tailed Eagle and many other birds.

TOUR OPERATORS

Adirondack Mountain Club. 3–14 days / $ (from Adirondack Park, New York) / May–October. Weekend trips emphasizing field natural history including geology, alpine flora, birds, ferns, and trees and shrubs of the Adirondacks. The Adirondack Mountain Club maintains lodges and camps in the park; most trips are run from the Adirondak Loj. Costs vary and are reduced for members.

Appalachian Mountain Club. 3–7 days / $ (from New Hampshire) / May–October. In the White Mountains of New Hampshire. Trips of varying lengths, from day and weekend hikes to longer trail service projects. Guided hikes include "Spring Wildflowers" (June), "Geology of the Presidential Range" (August), and "Wild Mushroom Hunting" (September). The AMC maintains a system of huts and lodges in the White Mountains of northern New Hampshire. Many of the daily environmental programs and guided hikes are based at these lodges. Costs vary and are reduced for AMC members.

Arctic Odysseys. 9–11 days / $$$$ (from Ottawa) / March–May, July, August. A variety of trips to the far north: dog sledding on Baffin Island, Northwest Territories (NWT), in search of Polar Bear, seals, and birds (March–May); a Baffin Island combination wildlife and cultural trip (July–August); and a general natural history trip to Ellesmere and Baffin islands (August). Small groups, native guides, flexible itineraries. The Baffin Island combo trip is good for families.

Canadian Nature Tours. 5–10 days / $$ (from various locations in Canada) / May–September. A variety of natural history trips including birding at Point Pelee

(Ontario); "Discovering Muskoka"—plants, trees, and birds; a week exploring lakes and rivers, watching loons, and botanizing; and a botany trip to Grand Manan. Some trips are designed for families.

Cornell's Adult University. 5 days / $$ (from Portsmouth, New Hampshire) / August, September. Ecology study trips to the Gulf of Maine. Based at Cornell University's Shoals Marine Laboratory on Appledore Island, you'll explore the marine mammals, birds, and biota of this rich area.

Dire Wolf. 7 days / $ (from Ithaca) / July, August. Natural history trips, with an emphasis on geology, to the Adirondacks and the Finger Lakes. Be advised that some of these tours involve traveling with large groups—30 to 40 persons!

Earthwatch

14 days / $ (from Michigan) / July. "American Forest Survey" is a research trip to study forest architecture; it is run in four areas: Warren Woods, Michigan; Puerto Rico; Mexico; and Venezuela.

13 days / $ (from North Bay, Ontario) / July, August. A research trip to study Ontario's old-growth forests. Volunteers will measure the age and size of big trees, and identify smaller trees and shrubs, in an effort to preserve the old-growth forests.

11 days / $ (from Michigan) / April–July. "Loons" is a research trip to the Great Lakes to study these endangered birds. Teams monitor the migration of loons and capture, band, and weigh them.

12 days / $$ (from Duluth, Minnesota) / April–September. "Northwoods Bears" is a research trip to study Black Bears and their behavior. Volunteers track bears, help to live-trap them, and participate in experiments designed to teach bears to leave garbage cans alone.

8 days / $ (from Isle Royale National Park, Michigan) / May, June, August. A research trip to study the interaction and relationships of moose and wolves on Isle Royale.

12 days / $ (from Hibbing, Minnesota) / July–September. "Tracking Timber Wolves" is a research trip to see what compromises wolves must make in order to live in a human-dominated world.

Field Guides

5 days / $$ (from Ottawa) / February. A winter birding trip to Amherst Island and eastern Ontario, mostly in search of owls—Snowy—Long-eared, Short-eared, Great Gray, Boreal, Saw-Whet—and Northern Hawk. Other spectacles include Rough-legged Hawks diving at Northern Shrikes—we saw this repeatedly on Amherst Island. Maximum of 16 participants, 2 leaders.

10 days / $$$$ (from Ottawa) / June. A birdwatching trip to Pond Inlet, Baffin Island, and the nearby Bylot Island Bird Sanctuary—located 400 miles north of the Arctic Circle. Though largely an expedition to see the Ivory Gull, other rarities can be seen as well, including the Common Ringed Plover. There is plenty of time to birdwatch since the sun never sets. The highlight of the trip is the four days of camping near the edge of the pack ice. Polar Bear, Walrus, and several species of whale and seal can also be seen. Shorebirds will be in full breeding plumage. Land birds include Wheatear, Lapland Longspur, Hoary Redpoll, Gyrfalcon, Snowy Owl, and Rock Ptarmigan. Maximum of 14 participants.

8 days / $$ (from Presque Isle, Maine) / July. A birding trip to the Gaspé Penin- sula. Gaspé Provincial Park is one of the few places we can think of with literally miles and miles of unbroken pine-and-fir forest. Here are the denizens of the north woods—Boreal Chickadee, Gray-cheeked Thrush, Yellow-bellied Fly- catcher, and Gray Jay. A highlight of the tour is a trip to Bonaventure Island, the most famous seabird colony on the Atlantic coast. Half a million Northern Gannets nest here, as do smaller numbers of Razorbills (relatives of the now- extinct Great Auk), Common Murres, and Black-legged Kittiwakes. In addition to its abundant bird life, the Gaspé is known for its variety of rare plants and unusual geology. Maximum of 16 participants. This trip may be combined with the 6-day Grand Manan trip, below.

6 days / $$ (from Bangor, Maine) / July. A birding trip to Grand Manan, an island in the Bay of Fundy. Grand Manan is also the jumping-off point for a visit to Machias Seal Island, known for its large nesting colonies of Atlantic Puffins (yes, those cute little guys with the big, clownlike bills), Razorbills, and Arctic Terns. You'll also visit Kent Island, where you have the chance to explore a nest- ing colony of Leach's Storm-Petrels. Maximum of 16 participants. This trip may be combined with the Gaspé trip, above.

8 days / $$ (from Detroit) / May. A birding trip to Point Pelee and north-central Michigan. Pelee is a peninsula jutting into Lake Erie, and in the spring it's loaded with birds! Tanagers and orioles fill the trees, and it's not unusual to see 100 species of birds in a day. In Michigan, you'll look for the rare Kirtland's Warbler, known to nest only in the Jack Pine forests near Grayling. Maximum of 16 participants.

Four Corners School of Outdoor Education. 8 days / $$$$ (from Min- neapolis) / January. A trip to study wolves. You'll work with the Audubon Center and the International Wolf Center, tracking wolves, inspecting kill sites, and study- ing wolf signs. Local wolf biologists provide instruction and guide field trips. Some of the time is spent in the Canadian Rockies, where you can listen to the wolves howl under the northern lights. Maximum of 20 participants.

Goldeneye Nature Tours. 8 days / $$ (from St. John, New Brunswick) / June, July. Three birding trips to Grand Manan Island. Participants can expect to see about 125 species. Two pelagic trips may yield shearwaters, storm-petrels, Northern Gannet, and several species of whale. On Machias Seal Island you'll see nesting Atlantic Puffin, Razorbill, and both Common and Arctic Terns. Maximum of 10 participants.

International Research Expeditions. 12 days / $ (from Toronto) / June–August. A research trip to the Temagami Wilderness to study old-growth forests.

Inuit Adventures. 6 days / $$$$ (from Montreal) / July–September. Photographic expeditions made by freighter canoe from Ivujivik to Digges Island, summer nesting grounds of nearly a million seabirds, then south along the coast to see Arctic flora, and on to Kuujjuaq. A different cruise (8 days) focuses on seabirds and goes, in addition, to Nottingham Island.

Labrador Scenic. 5–8 days / $$–$$$$ (from Goose Bay, Labrador) / March–September. A variety of trips, including a winter wilderness week in March and Caribou-sighting in June. Trips of any length and to suit any interest can be arranged. Native guides are used; their knowledge of the flora and fauna of the region is unparalleled.

Motmot Nature Tours. 11 days / $$ (from Halifax, Nova Scotia) / July. A natural history and cultural trip to Nova Scotia and Cape Breton Island. Pelagic and boreal birds can be seen.

National Audubon Society. 6–12 days / $$ (from Muscongus Bay, Maine) / July, August. A variety of educational and naturalist programs, including "Field Ornithology," "Marine Biology," and "Maine Coast Field Ecology." There are also Audubon camps for children and teens. In addition, there's an Audubon Ecology Workshop in Connecticut (from Greenwich). Small groups, field trips, birds, marine mammals—it all adds up to a great week!

Natural Habitat Adventures. 5–8 days / $$–$$$$ (from Halifax, Nova Scotia) / March. Trips to see the baby Harp Seals. "Whitecoats" were once hunted for their pelts; now, thanks to the International Fund for Animal Welfare, they are captured on film instead. Each spring, 250,000 Harp Seals gather in the Gulf of St. Lawrence to bear their young on the vast floating ice fields near the Magdalen Islands. Participants are taken to the ice by helicopter each day. Other outdoor activities and evening programs are offered as well. And during a moonlight hike, there's a chance of seeing the Aurora Borealis (northern lights) display.

Oceanic Society Expeditions. 6 days / $$ (from Boston) / August. Two whale-watching trips aboard the 95-foot schooner *Harvey Gamage*. Maximum of 30 passengers.

OBServ. 9 days / $$ (from Sydney, Newfoundland) / June–July. "Newfoundland and Its Seabirds" is a birding trip. Although concentrating on pelagics and alcids, you'll also go looking for Rock and Willow Ptarmigan and Boreal Chickadee.

Sierra Club. 7–14 days / $–$$ (from various locations) / January–December. The Sierra Club runs different trips each year—mostly hiking and camping, but also service trips to restore, create, and clean up trails and parks. Some recent destinations include: Sleeping Bear Dunes National Lakeshore (Michigan), Isle Royale National Park (Michigan), Acadia National Park (Maine), Adirondack Park (New York), Baxter State Park (Maine), and Forsythe Wildlife Refuge (New Jersey).

Swan Hellenic. 16 days / $$$$ (from London, England) / July. A general natural history trip to Newfoundland and Labrador. You'll visit the Avalon Peninsula for Caribou and Moose, the Northern Gannet colony at Cape St. Mary's, and Terra Nova and Gros Morne National Parks. Cultural stops include a visit to Vinland, the Viking settlement near St. Anthony. Two leaders accompany the trip.

TravelWild

5 days / $$$$ (from Toronto) / March. A trip to see the Harp Seals in the Gulf of St. Lawrence. Great photo opportunities! Maximum of 16 participants; a photo-naturalist will accompany the trip.

13 days / $$$$ (from Resolute Bay, NWT) / August. A trip to Ellesmere and Devon islands in the far Arctic. This is a trip for wildlife photographers—you'll see birds and animals, not to mention exhilarating scenery. Photo blinds are set up to shoot nesting species such as Red Knot, Baird's Sandpiper, King Eider, and Red-necked Phalarope. Marine mammals, including Narwhal, can be seen in the Alexander Fjord area of Ellesmere. Maximum of 10 participants; a photo-naturalist will lead the trip.

VENT

14 days / $$ (from Bangor) / June. A birding trip to the Gaspé and Grand Manan. Participants can expect to see up to 20 species of warblers, in addition to several northern finches, including Pine Grosbeak. But it's not all birds. Moose and Black Bear may be seen as well. From Grand Manan, you'll take trips to some smaller islands, including Kent Island (home to nesting Leach's Storm-Petrels) and Machias Seal Island, where the puffins nest. En route to the islands, sightings

of whales are not uncommon, and seals are almost certain to be seen. Maximum of 16 participants.

7 days / $$ (from Bangor) / September. A birding trip to Grand Manan to witness the wonders of fall migration of both land birds and seabirds. Maximum of 16 participants, 2 leaders.

12 days / $$ (from Halifax, Nova Scotia) / July. A birding trip to Newfoundland and Nova Scotia. Birds of the boreal forest, including Ruffed and Spruce Grouse, Rusty Blackbird, Bobolink, Black-backed Woodpecker, and breeding Mourning Warblers, make this trip—timed to coincide with the breeding season—a delight. This is also a great trip for photographing nesting seabirds, because you get very close to them at Cape St. Mary's. There are ferry trips, too, for pelagic birding; and on these you can expect to see Northern Fulmar, jaegers, shearwaters (four species), and possibly even skuas and Dovekie. As always, when out in eastern Atlantic waters, you have a good chance of seeing whales—Humpbacks, in this case. Maximum of 16 participants, 2 leaders.

9 days / $$ (from Detroit) / May. A warbler extravaganza! Point Pelee juts into Lake Erie and is a funnel of land that is used by migrating birds. On their way north in the spring, it's the first landfall they come to after crossing the lake, and the tiny tip of land becomes covered with birds. We've seen trees so full of orioles and tanagers that you would believe you're in the tropics instead of the north. Literally hundreds of warblers can be seen at Pelee every day. It's a spectacle not to be missed. In addition, this tour goes to the Jack Pine forests of north-central Michigan in search of one of our rarest birds, Kirtland's Warbler. This bird nests only in certain Jack Pines, and only in these few square miles of Michigan. There are about 500 of these lovely songsters and great care is taken not to disturb their nesting. This trip is planned to be there when the males are out singing on territory—a thrilling sight indeed.

Wildlife Conservation Society. 10 days / $$$$ (from Boston) / July. A cruise to Greenland and the Canadian Arctic aboard the 140-passenger *Illiria.* You'll see a variety of land and marine mammals, many birds, and Arctic plants. Cultural stops include Jakobshavn, birthplace of explorer Knud Rasmussen, and Thule and Inuit sites on Baffin Island. You also visit Bylot Island Bird Sanctuary and search for Narwhal in Baffin Bay. Shore excursions are made by Zodiac, and are complemented by evening lectures and slide presentations.

Wings

7 days / $$ (from St. John, New Brunswick) / August, September. Three week-long birding trips to Grand Manan, an island in the Bay of Fundy.

5 days / $$ (from St. John, New Brunswick) / January. A winter birdwatching trip to the Avalon Peninsula on Newfoundland. One of the main objectives is to

see Dovekies, a tiny black-and-white seabird that is otherwise difficult to find. Other birds to be expected include a variety of wintering gulls, Common and King Eiders, Boreal Chickadee, Willow Ptarmigan, and Bohemian Waxwing.

13 days / $$ (from Halifax, Nova Scotia) / July. A birding trip to Newfoundland, the largest eastern Canadian island. Boat trips give participants the chance to see a variety of pelagic birds, and you'll visit large seabird colonies as well.

6 days / $$ (from Port Clyde, Maine) / October. A birding trip to Monhegan Island, well-known migrant trap. Participants can expect to see about 100 species of birds.

SOUTHEASTERN UNITED STATES

With good reason, Florida—especially the southern part of the state—is a naturalist's paradise. From the famous Everglades "river of grass" to the arid Dry Tortugas, subtropical southern Florida encompasses a wide range of habitat and an equally wide variety of animal and bird life.

Several operators offer birdwatching tours to this area. Everglades National Park is a dependable spot for herons and other water birds, while on the Keys, Mangrove Cuckoo, White-crowned Pigeon, Antillean Nighthawk, and Black-whiskered Vireo are the specialties. The Dry Tortugas stretch west beyond the Keys into the Gulf of Mexico. Here Magnificent Frigatebirds hang in the air above Fort Jefferson, and on the smaller islands you can see hundreds of nesting Sooty Terns and Brown Noddies as well as rarer birds such as White-tailed Tropicbird and Masked Booby. On Florida's west coast are the famous Corkscrew Swamp Sanctuary (owned and operated by the National Audubon Society), where Wood Storks nest high in the treetops, and Sanibel Island, home of the "Ding" Darling National Wildlife Refuge.

Farther north and into Georgia, North and South Carolina, and Virginia, and west into Alabama, a variety of natural history trips take participants to the National Wildlife Refuges of the Southeast. This section of trip descriptions also covers trips to the Ozarks and the prairies of Missouri and Arkansas.

TOUR OPERATORS

Earthwatch

14 days / $$ (from Sarasota, Florida) / June–September. "Wild Dolphin Societies" is a research trip studying the relationship between dolphins' intelligence and their societies. Volunteers capture, measure, examine, and release dolphins.

10 days / $$ (from Charleston, South Carolina) / June, July. "Diamondback Terrapins" is a research trip using these amphibians to learn what keeps a salt marsh intact.

14 days / $ (from Front Royal, Virginia) / May–November. A research trip studying the wildlife of the Shenandoah, in the Blue Ridge Mountains. Volunteers mist-net birds, trap small animals, and calculate populations.

6 days / $$ (from Gloucester Point, Virginia) / May–September. "Saving the Chesapeake" is a research trip run with the Virginia Institute of Marine Science. Volunteers document the distribution, frequency, and density of tidal marsh plants.

Field Guides. 4 days / $$ (from Miami) / May. A nightbirding weekend to the Florida Keys and Dry Tortugas. Of particular interest in the Keys at this time of year is the Antillean Nighthawk.

Hawk, I'm Your Sister. 10 days / $ (from Miami) / February. Canoe trips through the Everglades Wilderness Waterway. You'll see birds, fish, marine mammals, butterflies, and all the wonderful vegetation that is the 'Glades. Some trips are for women only.

Massachusetts Audubon Society
7 days / $$ (from Jacksonville, Florida) / October. A combination birding and herpetology trip to the Okefenokee Swamp and Georgia coast. Two leaders accompany the trip.

7 days / $$ (from Miami) / January. A birding trip to the Everglades and west coast of Florida. Two leaders accompany the trip.

National Audubon Society. 7 days / $$ (from Miami) / February. Join the National Audubon Society on a field ecology workshop in the open-air laboratory of the Florida Everglades. You'll visit wet prairies, pinelands, saw grass seas, and hardwood hammocks; and meet with research biologists to learn about the Florida Panther, Manatee, American Alligator, and Bald Eagle. Colorful wading birds, owls, and the exquisite Painted Bunting all find food and shelter in this amazing ecosystem. A nature photography course is also given.

National Wildlife Federation. 6 days / $ (from Asheville, North Carolina) / July. An ecology summit at the YMCA Blue Ridge Assembly. Participants can explore the diverse life zones along the Blue Ridge Parkway, observe the devastating effects of acid rain atop Mount Mitchell, and study aquatic ecology—or go hiking and birdwatching. Ideal for families; cost reductions for children and teens.

Oceanic Society Expeditions. 5 days / $$ (from Orlando, Florida) / January. Swim with the Manatees! Yes, for three full days, participants get to snorkel and swim with these fascinating marine mammals—the real mermaids. Each winter, Manatees migrate north from the Gulf of Mexico to these warmer, spring-fed waters. Other activities will include birdwatching and snorkeling with tropical fish. The trip is based at Crystal River National Wildlife Refuge.

Sierra Club. The Sierra Club offers a variety of nature-related hikes, river trips, and service trips. Destinations change from year to year, but some recent trips went to the Everglades, Okefenokee Swamp (Georgia), Joyce Kilmer Wilderness (North Carolina), and southeastern National Wildlife Refuges (Alabama, Florida, and Georgia).

TravelWild. 5 days / $$ (from Fort Myers, Florida) / January. Photo workshops on Sanibel Island. The J. N. "Ding" Darling National Wildlife Refuge offers great opportunities for bird photography. Maximum of 20 participants, 2 leaders.

VENT

10 days / $$ (from Miami) / April. A birding trip to South Florida. You'll visit a variety of habitats, from Lake Okeechobee to the Everglades to Key West, from pinelands favored by Bachman's Sparrows to ponds full of Roseate Spoonbills to hardwood hammocks where Mangrove Cuckoos skulk. Maximum of 16 participants, 1 leader.

4 days / $$ (from Key West) / April, May. Birding weekends to the Dry Tortugas in search of rarities such as Sooty Terns and Brown Noddies. Highlights of past tours include White-tailed Tropicbird, Black Noddy, and Masked Booby. The tour can be taken in conjunction with the South Florida trip, above.

7 days / $$ (from Jacksonville, Florida) / April. A birding trip to Georgia: the Okefenokee Swamp and Cumberland Island. Participants can expect to see about 150 species of birds, including Prothonotary and Yellow-throated Warblers, Swallow-tailed Kite, and Red-cockaded Woodpecker. Maximum of 16 participants.

10 days / $$ (from Springfield, Missouri) / May. A birding trip to the Ozarks and prairies of Missouri and Arkansas. Greater Prairie Chickens boom in the early mornings, Scissor-tailed Flycatchers perform acrobatic feats, and Henslow's Sparrows nest in the tallgrass prairies. And the wildflowers! Tickseed Coreopsis, Prairie Blue-eyed Grass, Shooting Star, and Wood Betony, just to name a few. Maximum of 16 participants.

Wings

9 days / $$ (from Charleston, South Carolina) / April. A birding tour to South Carolina's Low Country. Many historical sites, plantations, and gardens will also be visited. Participants can expect to see about 125 species of birds, including Barred Owl, Pileated Woodpecker, Red-cockaded Woodpecker, and one of our most gifted songsters, Bachman's Sparrow.

11 days / $$ (from Miami) / April. South Florida and the Dry Tortugas is a birdwatching trip. You'll look for parakeets, mynas, and other exotics in Miami,

then go on to the prairies of southwestern Florida for Snail Kite and Red-cockaded Woodpecker. Before heading for the Everglades, you'll stop at National Audubon's Corkscrew Swamp Sanctuary, where you'll see Wood Storks nesting. Finally, you'll spend three days in the Dry Tortugas, searching for Black and Brown Noddies, Sooty Tern, White-tailed Tropicbird, and Masked Booby. NOTE: The Tortugas portion can be taken separately.

TEXAS

Texans are boastful about their state, and when it comes to natural history, they are certainly justified. This is a magnificent destination, especially for birdwatching.

The Rio Grande Valley is a must for any birder, but it will also appeal to other naturalists. Our very own subtropics is home to hundreds of birds, some found nowhere else in the United States: Crested Caracara, White-tailed Hawk, Ringed and Green Kingfishers, Brown and Green Jays, Buff-bellied Hummingbird, Audubon's and Altimira Orioles—the list could go on. Hook-billed Kites make regular trips across the river from Mexico, while the Ferruginous Pygmy Owl has nested for several seasons near the Falcon Dam. There are many birding trips to this special place.

The Texas Gulf Coast is famous for its wintering Whooping Cranes, a magnificent species that is being brought back from the edge of extinction. The area around Rockport is especially rich in birdlife.

Most birdwatching trips also spend several days in the wildflower-rich Texas Hill Country searching for special species such as the Black-capped Vireo, Green Kingfisher, Cave Swallow, and Golden-cheeked Warbler, and also visit the Davis Mountains in search of the Montezuma Quail.

A variety of birdwatching and river-running companies go to Big Bend, the most remote of our national parks. With deserts, mountains, and canyons, it's a special place, especially to see otherwise uncommon birds, including Gray Vireo and Lucifer Hummingbird. The Chisos Mountain Range is the only place in the United States where one can find the rare Colima Warbler. For river trips, a variety is offered by Far Flung Adventures, from a one-day trip through Colorado Canyon to a seven-day whitewater trip through the lower canyons (east of the park). Other canyons visited are Santa Elena, Mariscal, and Boquillas, the longest and most tranquil. Stunning landscapes and geologic features as well as a variety of wildlife are routinely observed on all trips.

TOUR OPERATORS

Earthwatch. 9 days / $$ (from San Antonio) / March, April. "Big Bend Volcanoes" is a research trip studying how extinct volcanoes can help us predict future eruptions. Volunteers perform gravity and magnetic surveys, collect rock samples, and map the landscape.

Far Flung Adventures. 3–8 days / $–$$ (from Rio Grande Village or Terlingua) / March, April, October, November. Raft trips down the Rio Grande include some that concentrate on wildflowers, some that are general naturalist trips, and some that are photo-naturalist trips. Trips range greatly in difficulty. All are led by professional guides.

Field Guides

8 days / $$ (from Corpus Christi) / February. A birding trip to the Rio Grande Valley and the Gulf Coast for the Whooping Cranes. Rarities are frequently seen in the Valley—past tours have seen Golden-crowned Warbler and Masked Tityra. Participants can expect to see about 200 species of birds, including the specialties of South Texas. Maximum of 16 participants.

9 days / $$ (from San Antonio) / May. A birding trip to Big Bend and the Davis Mountains. Big Bend is noted for Lucifer Hummingbird and Colima Warbler; other specialties include Gray Vireo, Crissal Thrasher, and Hepatic Tanager. In the Davis Mountains, you'll be looking for Montezuma Quail. Two days are spent in the Hill Country searching for Black-capped Vireo and Golden-cheeked Warbler. Maximum of 16 participants, 2 leaders.

4 days / $$–$$$ (from Harlingen or Amarillo) / March, April. Two birding weekends, each with a specialty. The March trip is a nightbirding weekend, searching for owls and nightjars. The April weekend is devoted to the Lesser Prairie Chicken, one of our five endemic birds. Maximum of 16 participants.

Goldeneye Nature Tours. 8 days / $$ (from Corpus Christi) / February. A birding trip to South Texas to see Whooping Crane and other wading birds. You'll also visit the Sabal Palm Sanctuary in Brownsville, Bentson, and the Falcon Dam. Maximum of 9 participants.

Hawk, I'm Your Sister. 10 days / $ (from Big Bend National Park) / March. A river trip through the lower canyons of the Rio Grande. Wildflowers will be in bloom.

National Audubon Society. 7 days / $$ (from Big Bend) / April. Audubon Ecology Workshop in Texas. You'll explore the landscape and discuss the conservation issues that are so much a part of its future.

The Nature Conservancy. 4 days / $$$ (from Corpus Christi) / October–April. Birding weekends to Matagorda Island. The trip is run from the local field office. Cost includes a contribution to the Conservancy.

VENT. The most comprehensive birding tour program in the state; no less than nine full tours and innumerable weekends are offered. "Grand Texas" is a 15-day overview of the upper Texas coast, Edwards Plateau, and the Valley. There's a 10-day trip to Big Bend; a trip to see the Whooping Cranes and visit the enormous and very birdy King Ranch; a winter trip to the Rio Grande Valley (6 days); and spring, autumn, and New Year's trips to South Texas. Costs vary depending on trip chosen. All trips are limited to 14 to 16 participants, and most have 2 leaders.

In addition, a birding workshop is offered for people who want to learn more about birds. Field trips are complemented by evening lectures and slide shows. The 4-day workshop, in December, costs $495 (from Corpus Christi).

Wings

21 days / $$ (from Houston) / April. A comprehensive birding tour of the state, visiting the hardwood swamps and pine forests of the east, the Gulf Coast, the Rio Grande Valley, the Edwards Plateau, and the Chisos Mountains (Big Bend). Specialties are looked for. The trip is offered in three sections and can be taken as a whole or in part.

7 days / $$ (from Corpus Christi) / January. A winter birding workshop in South Texas. Identification problems with raptors, waders, and sparrows are covered. An optional extension to see Whooping Cranes is available. Maximum of 10 participants.

CHURCHILL, SOUTHERN MANITOBA, AND WAGER BAY

Nature travel isn't confined to the tropical rain forests. In North America, there is also a world of ice and snow, and, curiously, these cold northern waters are the richest in nutrients. They are also home to many marine mammals and invertebrates. Although plant life is sparse, birds and animals flourish during the brief sunny summers. Long days, when the sun never sets, mild temperatures, and a reliable food supply provide just the right conditions for these creatures of the north.

Surely the Polar Bear is the emblem of this environment, and many tours go to observe and photograph these handsome creatures in the fall. In fact, Churchill, Manitoba, is known as the Polar Bear Capital of the World, and deservedly so: Where else can you see a 1,500-pound iceberg walking down Main Street? But springtime, when tussock grass pushes its way up and bird song softens the harshness of the far north, is also a popular time to visit. That's when you can see shorebirds singing from the treetops and whales swimming in the Churchill River; while up in Wager Bay, Polar Bears are on the prowl.

Southern Manitoba—an overlap zone for eastern and western species—is a popular birding destination and is frequently combined with a trip to Churchill. The wetlands, wide-open prairies, and native grasslands are filled with wildflowers and birds. Sought-after species include Connecticut Warbler, Yellow Rail, Sprague's Pipit, Baird's Sparrow, and Great Gray Owl.

TOUR OPERATORS

Arctic Odysseys. 9 days / $$$$ (from Winnipeg) / August. A trip to Wager Bay that emphasizes viewing Polar Bears in their natural habitat. From boats—with native guides— the close-up views are superb.

Birdquest. 19 days / $$$ (from Winnipeg) / May. A birding trip to southern Manitoba, Churchill, and the Canadian Rockies. Participants can expect to see about 225 species of birds in a variety of habitats. Maximum of 16 participants, 2 leaders.

Canadian Nature Tours. 4 days / $$$$ (from Winnipeg) / November. A Polar Bear–watching trip. Maximum of 15 participants; a nature photographer accompanies the trip.

Churchill Wilderness Encounter. A variety of trips in and around Churchill, ranging from a 1-day boat trip on the Churchill River to see the Beluga Whales (June 21–September 1) to a 6-day birding tour of Churchill (May–mid-July) to Polar Bear–watching trips (October 10–November 4). On the birding tour, participants can expect to see about 100 species. Cultural tours can also be arranged. Costs vary with program selected. All tours are guided by a local naturalist.

Field Guides. 12 days / $$ (from Winnipeg) / June. A birding tour to southern Manitoba and Churchill. Nesting shorebirds are at the height of courtship display at this time, and the mouth of the Churchill River can be literally jammed with Pacific and Red-throated Loons and masses of scoters and eiders, too. Recent tours have seen upwards of 200 species, including Willow Ptarmigan, Spruce Grouse, Yellow Rail, Great Gray Owl, Smith's Longspur, and LeConte's Sparrow. A great number of animals can also be seen—Moose, Black Bear, Beaver, and Lynx. Maximum of 16 participants.

Flora and Fauna. 8 days / $$ (from Winnipeg) / June. A birding trip to southern Manitoba and Churchill. Participants have a chance to see Beluga Whales in the Churchill River.

International Expeditions. 8 days / $$$ (from Winnipeg) / October. Three Polar Bear–watching expeditions.

Massachusetts Audubon Society

11 days / $$ (from Winnipeg) / June. A birding trip called "Winnipeg to Churchill" includes the famous train ride from which the group often sees Willow Ptarmigan, Sandhill Crane, Northern Hawk Owl, and Moose and Caribou. Maximum of 11 participants; an ornithologist leads the trip.

6 days / $$$$ (from Winnipeg) / November. A Polar Bear–watching trip in the well-known Tundra Buggies.

Natural Habitat Adventures. 6–9 days / $$$ (from Winnipeg) / October. Polar Bear–watching trips aboard the Tundra Buggies. Maximum of 26 participants.

North Star Tours. 1–14 days / $$ (from Churchill) / May–November. A variety of nature programs exploring Churchill's tundra, taiga, and tidal environments: Polar Bear–watching on the Tundra Buggies; boat tours on the Churchill River to see the Beluga Whales; birdwatching trips; photo-naturalist tours; and scuba diving in the Churchill River. All trips are accompanied by local naturalist guides.

TravelWild

11 days / $$$$ (from Winnipeg) / July. "Arctic Wildlife of Wager Bay" is a trip to observe and photograph Polar Bears. Participants will see other animals and birds as well. Maximum of 16 participants; a professional photographer accompanies the trip.

7–12 days / $$$ (from Winnipeg) / October, November. Joe Van Os pioneered these Polar Bear–watching trips in 1981. The trips use Tundra Buggies—specially designed vehicles that get you close to the bears without harassing them. You really are *with* them, which is pretty exciting. On some tours you get to live out on the tundra (in the Bunkhouse, a sort of movable motel) for a few days. Arctic Fox are regularly observed, as are several species of birds, including Snowy Owl, Gyrfalcon (the rare white phase, if you're lucky), Willow Ptarmigan, and Northern Goshawk. Maximum of 19 participants; a naturalist-photographer accompanies the trips.

6 days / $$$$ (from Winnipeg) / June. "Bird Photography in Churchill." On the shore of Hudson Bay, Churchill is probably the most accessible tundra in North America. And tundra in June means nesting shorebirds and blankets of colorful wildflowers. Photo blinds are set up for close-ups. Maximum of 16 participants; a photo-naturalist leads the trip.

Tundra Buggy Tours. 1–8 days / $–$$ (from Churchill) / June–August, October–November. Spring and summer tundra tours to see nesting birds, wildflowers, and animals. The October and November trips are to watch Polar Bears. In November, at the end of the season, there is a week-long trip aboard the Bunkhouse out to Cape Churchill. Trips are led by owner Len Smith, who designed and built the Tundra Buggy and Bunkhouse. (He leases them out to other tour operators.)

VENT

14 days / $$$$ (from Winnipeg) / July. A birding, animal, and photography tour to Wager Bay, on the north of Hudson Bay, about 50 miles south of the Arctic Circle. Mammals include Polar Bear, Ringed and Bearded Seals, Barren Ground Caribou, and Arctic Hare. As for the birds, there are large colonies of Black Guillemots and Thayer's Gulls; Rock Ptarmigan, Lapland Longspur, and several raptors are also to be seen. Maximum of 11 participants.

13 days / $$ (from Winnipeg) / June. Two birding trips to southern Manitoba and Churchill. Participants can expect to see over 200 species of birds. Maximum of 16 participants, 2 leaders.

Wings. 10 days / $$ (from Winnipeg) / June. Two birding trips to southern Manitoba and Churchill. Participants can expect to see over 200 species of birds.

THE PLAINS AND MOUNTAIN STATES

The plains of North America extend from Alberta and Saskatchewan in Canada south to northern Texas. Their grassland habitat exists in partnership with the mountains and plateaus that lie just to the west. Together, this west-central part of the continent is an area of contrast and convergence. Biologically speaking, the West begins at the 100th Meridian—the dividing line between eastern and western species. And as with all borders and dividing lines, there is an intriguing mixture of ecosystems and species.

Most birding tours visit the plains to see the prairie chickens and grouse, or to observe the large flocks of Sandhill Cranes gathering along the shores of the Platte River. But with mountainous terrain relatively close, they often look for passerines as well.

The Canadian and American Rockies are a dramatic chain of mountains that beckon nature travelers, who come each year as much for the plants and mammals as they do for the birds. Banff and Jasper National Parks in Canada, and Grand Teton and Rocky Mountain National Parks in the United States are prime destinations, as are Yellowstone and the Great Basin to the west. This part of the continent fits every naturalist interest—botany, geology, astronomy, ornithology, and zoology.

Yellowstone is our oldest and largest national park. Most people expect to see Old Faithful, but there's lots more—Moose, Elk, Bison, and, being reintroduced, Wolf. Although originally established to protect the geologic features (the geysers and the Grand Canyon of the Yellowstone), these two-plus million acres are a complete ecosystem. Yellowstone nearly abuts another national park—Grand Teton, with a fabulous range of mountains, many peaks well over 12,000 feet.

TOUR OPERATORS

Birdquest. (See the section on Churchill, Southern Manitoba, and Wager Bay, page 34.)

Cornell's Adult University

6 days / $$$ (from Lewiston, Idaho) / August. Two river dory (wooden boats) trips—one on the Upper Salmon and one on the Lower Salmon. The trips combine the excitement of white water and the magnificent scenery of this relatively pristine wilderness. With a geologist and naturalist along, travelers learn about the plants, wildlife, weather, and night sky. A physically active but not strenuous program.

10 days / $$ (from Lander, Wyoming) / June. "The Wind River Expedition" is a natural history hiking and camping trip into the Wind River Wilderness. You can try your hand at wildlife identification and field botany. Packhorses carry the heavy equipment; participants hike several miles a day and camp each night.

Denver Museum of Natural History. The museum has a varied travel program. Past trips have included a week in Yellowstone to learn about winter wildlife and geology and a hiking trip into the Wheeler Geological Area (Colorado). Contact the museum for its current program.

Earthwatch

10 days / $ (from Yellowstone National Park) / January–March, May. "Yellowstone Coyotes" is a research trip studying the role of these animals in the park and how that role might change when wolves are reintroduced.

8 days / $$ (from Pocatello, Idaho) / January, February, June–August. A research trip studying Mountain Lions. Winter teams help find lions and radio-collar them; summer teams use vans to track the collared lions. All volunteers document kill sites.

14 days / $ (from Gunnison, Colorado) / June, July. "Rocky Mountain Wildflowers" and "Alpine Wildlife" are two research trips run from the Rocky Mountain Biological Laboratory. Wildflower volunteers monitor the flowering of Glacier Lily and Larkspur, and help observe and collect insect pollinators. Wildlife volunteers help band birds and assist in a 19-year hummingbird study.

Focus on Nature Tours

8 days / $ (from Denver, Colorado) / June. A birding trip to the Pawnee Grasslands and the Rocky Mountains. Birds to be looked for include Sage Grouse, White-tailed Ptarmigan, Mountain Plover, Black Swift, Lewis' Woodpecker, and McCown's Longspur. Among the mammals you'll see are Elk, Bighorn Sheep, and Pronghorn Antelope. Maximum of 12 participants; an ornithologist leads the tour.

6 days / $ (from Omaha, Nebraska) / March, April. Four birding trips to east and central Nebraska. You'll witness the displays of Greater Prairie Chicken, Sharp-tailed Grouse, and American Woodcock, plus half a million Sandhill Cranes amassed in the Platte River. The April tours may see migrating Whooping Cranes as well. Maximum of 10 participants.

Foundation for Field Research. 14 days / $ (from Great Falls, Montana) / August. "Project Prairie Dog" is a research trip to study the impact that Prairie Dogs and cattle have on vegetation. Work is done in the Charles M. Russell National Wildlife Refuge in northern Montana.

Four Corners School of Outdoor Education. A winter Wolf trip to Minnesota and the Canadian Rockies. (See the section on Northeastern United States, Canada, and Greenland, page 24.)

Goldeneye Nature Tours. 8 days / $$ (from Pocatello, Idaho) / May. A birding trip to southern Idaho. In early summer, the Great Basin has considerable bird activity. You'll visit a variety of habitats—from sagebrush desert to mountains. Owls are the main focus, with searches for Short-eared, Long-eared, Burrowing, and Great Gray. You'll also see grouse, nesting waterfowl, and shorebirds. Maximum of 9 participants. A "Great Gray Owl Weekend" is offered in June, and an "Idaho Grouse Weekend" in April.

High Desert Museum. 3–10 days / $$ (from various locations) / April–July. The museum offers a variety of natural history programs, mostly weekends to such destinations as the Great Basin (for bird migrations, in April), the Snake River (for birds of prey, in May), and Yellowstone National Park.

International Research Expeditions. 8 days / $ (from Denver) / May, June. A research trip to survey canyon country for nesting Peregrine Falcons. This project helps the Forest Service better manage lands as falcon habitat. You'll be working in the Dark Canyon Wilderness area and along the San Juan River.

Motmot Nature Tours. 7 days / $$$ (from Bozeman, Montana) / August. A birding trip to Yellowstone, home to some 240 species of birds. You'll also see

Moose, Bison, and Bighorn Sheep on this luxury, tented camping trip. Two leaders accompany the trip.

National Audubon Society

7–12 days / $ (from Denver) / June–August. Seven-day and 12-day field ecology sessions at the Audubon Camp in the Wind River Mountains of Wyoming.

4 days / $$ (from Jackson, Wyoming) / June. Nature photography in Yellowstone and the Grand Tetons. Professional photographers accompany the trip.

8 days / $$ (from Gardiner, Montana) / January. Winter ecology and nature photography workshop in Yellowstone. You'll study how plants and animals adapt to snow and cold, the geology of fire and ice, animal social systems, winter photography techniques, the politics of endangered species, and the future of the Yellowstone ecosystem.

National Wildlife Federation. 7 days / $ (from Big Sky Resort, Montana) / August. "Big Sky Summit" is a conservation workshop on all aspects of nature. You'll be just 40 miles north of Yellowstone, in southwest Montana. Activities include a trip to Yellowstone; wildlife classes on animals; geology; birdwatching; and nature hikes. Ideal for families; reduced costs for children and teens.

Sierra Club. The Sierra Club runs a variety of naturalist hiking, river-running, and service trips in this area. Recent destinations have included: Salmon River (Idaho), Bob Marshall Wilderness (Montana), Jedediah Smith Wilderness (Wyoming), Wind River Range (Wyoming), Glacier Park (Montana), and Vermilion Cliffs Wilderness (Utah).

The Nature Conservancy. 6 days / $$ (from Pine Butte, Montana) / May–September. A variety of natural history workshops at the Conservancy's Pine Butte Guest Ranch, located 80 miles south of Glacier National Park, adjacent to an 18,000-acre preserve. Mammal tracking, birdwatching, and studying Grizzly Bears are just a few of the programs offered.

TravelWild

8 days / $$ (from Jackson, Wyoming) / September. A photo-naturalist trip to the Grand Tetons and Yellowstone. Leaves are changing color, Elk are rutting, and birds are migrating. Maximum of 16 participants; 2 professional photographers accompany the trip.

6 days / $$$ (from Gardiner, Montana) / February. Two photo safaris to Yellowstone in winter—a splendid time to observe and photograph wildlife. The crisp, icy air enhances the ethereal effect of the park's geothermal activity. Bison and Elk come in close. Maximum of 16 participants; 2 professional photographers accompany the trips.

8 days / \$\$\$ (from Calgary, Alberta) / July. A general nature and photography trip to Banff and Jasper National Parks in the Canadian Rockies. You may encounter Bighorn Sheep, Moose, Elk, Mountain Goat, and Black-tailed Deer here, among some of the most magnificent mountains in the world. Maximum of 16 participants, 2 leaders.

VENT

9 days / \$\$ (from Pueblo, Colorado) / April. A birding trip concentrating on grouse: the Sharp-tailed and Sage, and Greater and Lesser Prairie-Chickens. The latter is one of our five endemic birds. Other species you may see include Ferruginous Hawk, Mountain Plover, Curve-billed Thrasher, and Chestnut-collared and McCown's Longspurs. Maximum of 16 participants, 2 leaders.

5 days / \$\$ (from Omaha, Nebraska) / March. Birding on the Great Plains and along the Platte River. The annual gathering of half a million Sandhill Cranes along the river is a staggering sight. Huge numbers of migrating waterfowl will also be seen.

Wings

10 days / \$\$ (from Edmonton, Alberta) / June. A birding trip exploring a variety of habitats from willow river valleys to alpine meadows. Includes a day at Elk Island National Park, where the southern edge of boreal forest makes contact with prairie sloughs. You'll visit Jasper and Banff National Parks, stopping on the way at the awesome Columbia ice field, the largest glacier south of Alaska. Participants can expect to see about 200 species of birds, including Harlequin Duck, Varied Thrush, Three-toed Woodpecker, Mountain Bluebird (the bluest of all blue birds), Bohemian Waxwing, Spruce Grouse, and MacGillivray's Warbler. Moose, Elk, Hoary Marmot, and Coyote are among the animals regularly spotted.

7 days / \$ (from Denver) / June. A birding trip to the mountains and adjacent prairies of Colorado. You'll see a good cross section of birds, including grassland (longspurs and Lark Bunting), boreal (Spruce Grouse and flycatchers), and tundra (White-tailed Ptarmigan) species.

8 days / \$\$ (from Jackson, Wyoming) / June. A birding trip to Yellowstone, the Grand Tetons, and the surrounding area. Includes an evening raft trip down the Snake River. Participants can expect to see about 150 species of birds plus many mammals.

6 days / \$ (from Omaha, Nebraska) / March. A birding trip to the Platte River and south-central Nebraska. In addition to the vast numbers of Sandhill Cranes and waterfowl, you'll see a variety of raptors, and displaying American Woodcock, Sharp-tailed Grouse, and Greater Prairie-Chickens.

THE DESERT SOUTHWEST

Mention the Desert Southwest and most people think of sand. But in fact there's hardly any sand to speak of. Oh, sure, there's the Painted Desert, but most of Arizona and New Mexico is mountains and forests, lakes and rivers. Southeastern Arizona, in particular, is a prime birding spot. At the Nature Conservancy's Mile Hi Ranch in Ramsey Canyon, for instance, there are more species of hummingbirds— nearly twenty—than anywhere else in the United States. And the canyons in the nearby Huachuca Mountains are breeding locales for several Mexican species that wander just this far north. South of Tuscon, in Madera Canyon, are several different owls and nightjars, some of which also are Mexican vagrants. The grasslands along the Mexican border are the wintering grounds for many species of sparrows. Other border canyons harbor specialties, too.

The American Museum of Natural History has its famous Southwestern Research Station in Cave Creek Canyon, in the Chiricahua Mountains in the extreme southeast corner. This is an area of wide biodiversity, and the research station is home to several scientists, all working on various scientific projects. Over 300 species of birds have been recorded here, along with 29 fish, 67 reptiles, 17 amphibians, 95 mammals, and 1,880 plants. Cave Creek is also the center of the Thick-billed Parrot reintroduction program.

Farther north, the mighty Colorado River cuts through the grandest geological extravaganza in the United States—the Grand Canyon. There are many ways to travel down the river, and in the process experience the power of the water as it has cut through layers of history. Some of the trips are for thrills; others are more leisurely, with a greater emphasis on the river-level ecology. The Grand Canyon is just one in a series of canyons, including Zion and Bryce, in southwestern Utah. In fact, all of southern Utah is called Red Rock Country, and there are many national parks and monuments preserving these unique geologic features: Canyonlands, Arches, Cedar Breaks, and Capitol Reef.

TOUR OPERATORS

Birdquest. 22 days / $$ (from Tucson) / May. A birding trip to southeast Arizona and California. In Arizona you'll visit the Arizona Sonora Desert Museum in Saguaro National Monument. Other birding hot spots include Madera Canyon, Patagonia, the Huachuca Mountains, and the Chiricahuas. Participants can expect to see about 150 species of birds during the 9 days in Arizona, with additional species in California. Maximum of 16 participants.

Colorado River & Trail Expeditions. 5–12 days / $–$$ (from Denver, Salt Lake City, or Las Vegas) / May–September. A variety of river-running trips, many with natural history emphasis. The "Grand Canyon Geology Expedition" (June–July) goes from Lees Ferry to Whitmore Wash. A geologist explains volcanic activity as well as river erosion and the formation of the canyon. "Grand Canyon Natural History Expedition" (June) has naturalists on board to explain about the plants, animals, and environments of the canyon. College credit is available at extra cost.

Field Guides. 10 days / $$ (from Tucson) / May. A birding tour to southeast Arizona. You'll visit all the hot spots, including Madera Canyon and the Chiricahuas. The highlight of the trip is the time spent searching for nightbirds. Southeast Arizona boasts no fewer than 11 species of breeding owls! Maximum of 16 participants, 2 leaders. In addition, Field Guides runs two weekend trips to this area: a nightbirding weekend (May), and a winter weekend (January). The winter trip has produced some Mexican vagrants, including Ruddy Ground-Dove, Rufous-backed Robin, and Aztec Thrush.

Focus on Nature Tours. 7 days / $ (from Tucson) / August. A birding trip to southeast Arizona. From Cave Creek in the Chiricahuas (where you stay at the American Museum of Natural History's Southwestern Research Station) to Madera Canyon. You'll see lots of birds. August is especially good for hummingbirds, and the trip includes a stop at Ramsey Canyon Mile Hi Ranch, famous for hummers. Maximum of 12 participants.

Foundation for Field Research. 5 days / $ (from Phoenix) / December. A research trip to study wildlife at the Sears Point archaeological site in southwest Arizona. Volunteers live-trap animals and mist-net and band birds.

Goldeneye Nature Tours. 8 days / $$ (from Tucson) / May, December. Birding tours to southern Arizona. The May trip is for nightbirds such as owls and nightjars; participants can expect to see about 150 species of birds. The December trip focuses on wintering raptors, waterfowl, and sparrows. In addition, two "Hummingbird Weekends" are offered (August, September). You stay at the Mile Hi in Ramsey Canyon, where about 12 species of hummers can be seen.

Grand Canyon Dories. 5–19 days / $$ (from Flagstaff, Bright Angel Creek, or Las Vegas) / March–October. Geology close up! River trips down the Colorado in a wooden dory à la John Wesley Powell. The pace is slower than in a motorized raft. Short trips down tributaries of the Colorado are also offered. In addition, there is a 47-day re-creation of Powell's trip from the Green River in Wyoming to the Virgin Arm of Lake Mead. This is an excellent way to see the most spectacular canyons as well as to trace the gradual taming of the West's greatest water source.

(The trip may be taken in 8-to-17-day segments, and is a benefit for Friends of the River.)

Grand Canyon ExpeditionS Company. 8 days / $$ (from Las Vegas) / April–September. Special-interest raft trips for those interested in astronomy, ecology, geology, and nature photography. Maximum of 14 passengers; naturalists accompany these trips.

Hawk, I'm Your Sister. 11 days / $ (from Moab, Utah) / August. A women's canoe trip on flat water through Utah's Canyonlands National Park.

International Research Expeditions. 7 days / $ (from Tucson or Phoenix) / June–September. The "North America Four Corners Projects" include archaeology, astronomy, and ecology research trips to the Grand Canyon, San Juan Mountains, and Lake Powell. There is also a botany program based in the Sonoran Desert, where volunteers will study legumes.

Motmot Nature Tours. 7–12 days / $ (from Tucson) / February, April. Birding trips to southeast Arizona. In February you'll see wintering species, while April is for breeding birds.

National Audubon Society. 7 days / $$ (from Tucson) / May. An ecology workshop based at the American Museum of Natural History's Southwestern Research Station. The key topic is biodiversity, and participants focus on the incredible variety of plant and animal life in the Chiricahua Mountains and surrounding area. You also learn about the Thick-billed Parrot reintroduction program.

Sierra Club. The Sierra Club runs a variety of natural history hiking, river-running, and service trips to this area. Some recent destinations include Kofa Wildlife Refuge (Arizona), Arches Park (Utah), Chiricahua Wilderness (Arizona), and Pecos Wilderness (New Mexico).

VENT
11 days / $$ (from Tucson) / May, August. Birding trips. The August trip offers an optional 4-day extension to the White Mountains, where boreal birds such as Spruce Grouse, Gray Jay, and Lewis' Woodpeckers can be seen. In southeast Arizona, the concentration will be on nightbirds and hummingbirds. Maximum of 16 participants, 2 leaders.

5 days / $$ (from Tucson) / August. A hummingbird trip to Madera Canyon, Cave Creek Canyon, and Ramsey Canyon. Maximum of 16 participants.

8 days / $ (from Tucson) / May. "Arizona Nightbirds." Participants may see over 10 species of owls and several nightjars. Daytime birding could turn up such

species as Strickland's Woodpecker, Buff-breasted Flycatcher, Mexican Chickadee, and Red-faced Warbler. Maximum of 16 participants.

12 days / $ (from Tucson) / June, July. "Camp Chiricahua" is for children between the ages of 11 and 17. Campers do not have to be experienced, but they must be interested in birds and nature. This is a rare chance for young birders and naturalists to be in the field with expert leaders. Maximum of 16 participants, 2 leaders.

Wings

12 days / $ (from Phoenix) / September. A birding trip to southwestern Utah and northern Arizona. Visiting the canyons, rivers, and forests of the Colorado plateau, including the Grand Canyon, Bryce and Zion canyons, the Vermilion Cliffs, Painted Desert, Monument Valley, and the Petrified Forest. Participants can expect to see about 150 species of birds, including several *Empidonax* flycatchers, Canyon Wren, Mountain Bluebird, Lazuli Bunting, Clark's Nutcracker, Gila Woodpecker, and Townsend's Solitaire. Some historic and cultural sites will be also be visited.

9 days / $ (from Tucson) / May, July, August. Three birding trips to southeast Arizona, each at a different season, and each with its own specialties. May is better for owls, July is good for studying grassland sparrows, and August is best for hummingbirds.

7 days / $$ (from Tucson) / July, August. Five birding trips. Participants are based at the Crown C, a working cattle ranch located a few miles south of Sonoita, in southeastern Arizona. Ideally suited for families. Noted naturalist Rich Stallcup leads the trips.

8 days / $ (from El Paso) / April. A birding trip to southeastern New Mexico. You may see lekking Lesser Prairie-Chickens in shortgrass prairie as well as Cave Swallows at Carlsbad Caverns. You'll go to the Guadalupe Mountains, where the endemic Faxon Yucca can reach a height of 20 feet; and at Rattlesnake Springs, near Carlsbad, you can hear both Brown and Curve-billed Thrashers singing while you admire the brilliant Vermilion Flycatchers. In the Sacramento Mountains you'll search for Red-naped Sapsucker, Pygmy Nuthatch, Virginia's Warbler, and other montane species.

9 days / $$ (from San Diego) / January. "Deserts in Winter" is a birding trip. (See the section on California, page 47.)

CALIFORNIA

A state of ecological contrasts, California is a world unto itself. Its northern coast is perpetually damp. The low-lying desert is as scorching and dry as the Sahara, while the peaks of the Sierras are Arctic. The long coastline is mostly mountainous, often losing land to the ocean. The fertile Central Valley arcs for 450 miles north-south through the center of the state and is an agricultural workhorse for the nation. Skyscraper-high Redwoods and other conifer forests characterize the northern part of the state.

Interest in the environment is strong here, so it is no surprise that there are trips to suit every temperament and interest. Pelagic birding trips—setting out to sea to look for birds that never come in to shore—always encounter shearwaters and their avian relatives, but also are good for spotting marine mammals—dolphins, otters, and seals are drawn to the nutrient-rich offshore waters. Coastal land ecosystems are equally rich, attracting migrating shorebirds as well as a host of resident birds that are the focus of so many nature trips. The river valleys and mountain regions are destinations for botany, birding, and mammals trips.

As the most populous state in the nation, California must find a way to reconcile the disparate needs of its people and also preserve its remaining wilderness. Much of the state is already paved over; the paradise that attracted so many people is disappearing. How Californians solve their ecological dilemma will set the tone for the nation.

Tour Operators

Biological Journeys/Dolphin Charters. 3–5 days / $$$ (from Berkeley) / March–October. Natural history trips up the San Joaquin and Sacramento rivers. Located in a mix of rural and wildlife areas, the rivers and their deltas acquaint travelers with the history of the region as well as its environment. Also offered are 1-day trips in the San Francisco Bay area: In April you'll be looking for Gray Whales; in March you'll visit the seabird rookeries of the Farallones Islands.

Birdquest. 22 days / $$ (from Tucson) / May. The second half of a birding trip to Arizona and California. This part of the trip starts in San Diego, then visits the Salton Sea, Yosemite National Park, and Monterey, where you'll take a pelagic trip. Participants can expect to see 150 to 200 species of birds on this leg, including waders, thrashers, quail, warblers, flycatchers, and California's only endemic bird, the Yellow-billed Magpie. Maximum of 16 participants, 2 leaders.

Earthwatch
11 days / $ (from San Francisco) / March–May. "A Tale of Two Parks" is a research trip to Marin Headlands, in California, and Ile d'Ouessant, in France. Both are United Nations Biosphere Reserves. Volunteers identify plants, map habitats, catch and document animals, and examine past and current uses of the land.

14 days / $$ (from Santa Cruz) / January–December. "Sea Lion Language and Behavior" is a research trip. Volunteers feed and care for the animals; census dolphins, sea otters, and seals by boat; and help perform cognitive experiments.

12 days / $ (from San Francisco) / July, August. "Bobcat and Fox" is a research trip in Golden Gate National Recreation Area to study these animals and how the two species interact. Volunteers help capture Bobcats and Gray Foxes, affix radio collars, and then track the animals.

11 days / $ (from Reno) / June–September. A research trip to determine how root disease is harming our forests. Volunteers locate sites of suspected root disease, sample root sections, and help with studies in plant physiology. All this in the spectacular Lassen and Modoc National Forests in northern California.

14 days / $ (from Reno) / June, July. "Spotted Owl Alert" is a research trip studying the Northern Spotted Owl in the Sierra Nevadas. Volunteers identify tagged animals and dissect owl pellets to learn more about what owls eat.

Field Guides. 12 days / $$ (from Los Angeles) / May. A springtime birding trip that begins around the Los Angeles area. Participants first search for the California Gnatcatcher, then travel up the coast to catch late-migrating shorebirds. Later they head inland to Mt. Pinos and the lower San Joaquin Valley, and then go north into the Sierras and Yosemite National Park. The final day is a pelagic trip on Monterey Bay. Maximum of 16 participants. An optional 3-day pretour extension to the California deserts is offered. Also offered are birding weekends: San Francisco Bay area (January) and Santa Barbara (September).

International Research Expeditions. 7 days / $$ (from Moss Landing) / September, October. A research trip to study the distribution, abundance, and behavioral ecology of the White-sided Dolphin in Monterey Bay.

Marin Discoveries. 1–7 days / $ (from Marin County) / January–December. A varied program of natural history trips—including botanical trips, birding, animal tracking, mushrooming, and astronomy—in various parts of the state. There are also outdoor programs for the disabled. Some trips are designed for families.

Massachusetts Audubon Society. 9 days / $$ (from Los Angeles) / April. A natural history exploration of Death Valley and the eastern Mohave Desert.

National Audubon Society. 7 days / $$ (from San Francisco) / April. "California Wetlands" is an ecology workshop that visits the Monterey coast tidal wetlands at the peak of shorebird migration as well as San Francisco Bay National Wildlife Refuge to explore the complexities of saving wetlands in an urban area. You also see wildflowers and herons at Audubon Canyon Ranch, then visit riparian wetlands in the Central Valley.

National Wildlife Federation. 6 days / $ (from Monterey) / June. A conservation summit at Asilomar Conference Center. Activities and field trips focus on the wildlife and habitats that are found on this scenic coastal area. From birding walks to tide pool explorations, you'll discuss and learn about a variety of natural history concerns.

Shearwater Journeys. 1–3 days / $ (from Monterey) / January–December. Day and weekend pelagic trips into Monterey Bay in search of seabirds and marine mammals. Each season has its specialties. All trips are accompanied by several experienced naturalists.

Sierra Club. California is the home of this environmental organization, and most of its trips are to wilderness areas in the state. An extensive program is offered each year. In addition, the club maintains the Clair Tappaan Lodge in the Sierras, near Norden. Environmental workshops are held at the lodge during the summer.

VENT

13 days / $$ (from San Francisco) / August. A birding tour of northern California—from the Central Valley to the Sierras to Mono Lake. The grand finale is a pelagic trip out of Monterey Bay. Participants can expect to see about 250 species of birds, including flycatchers, warblers, quail, Western Tanager, Bushtit, Burrowing Owl, Lazuli Bunting, Calliope Hummingbird, White-headed Woodpecker, and Sage Grouse. On the pelagic trip, be on the lookout for Black-footed Albatross. Maximum of 16 participants, 2 leaders.

8 days / $$ (from Monterey) / November–December. A birding trip to the central California coast, beginning with a pelagic trip in Monterey Bay. You then proceed south along Highway 1 to Big Sur and Morro Bay, the winter home of more than 200 species of birds. On the arid Carrizo Plains you'll look for wintering Sandhill Crane, Mountain Bluebird, and Lewis' Woodpecker, as well as Prairie Falcon and other raptors. Maximum of 16 participants.

Wings

15 days / $$ (from San Diego) / September. A birding trip beginning with a southern California pelagic trip. You'll then spend a day looking for the California Gnatcatcher and other specialties before traveling on to the Salton Sea, where sighting the Yellow-footed Gull is a good possibility. The trip then goes north to the Owens Valley, Mono Lake, and Yosemite, and ends with a pelagic trip in Monterey Bay. Participants can expect to see about 300 species of birds.

9 days $ (from San Diego) / January. A birding trip to the deserts of California and Arizona. Waterfowl, raptors, woodpeckers, and sparrows will be among the birds seen. In dry washes, Crissal Thrasher and Gray Vireo are possible. The San Rafael Grasslands are home to wintering Sprague's Pipit and Baird's Sparrow.

10 days / $$ (from Arcata) / May. A birding trip to northern California and southern Oregon. Redwood forests, seabird colonies, and migrating shorebirds are among the highlights of this trip, which also takes you to Klamath Basin wetlands and the alpine forests near Crater Lake.

THE PACIFIC NORTHWEST, INCLUDING BRITISH COLUMBIA

The Pacific Northwest states of Oregon and Washington, and Canada's coastal province of British Columbia, boast some of the most dramatic landscapes in North America. The contrasts are striking: lush and moist rain forest, arid desert, snow-capped mountains, rocky shoreline. Wildflowers fill the alpine meadows; owls, eagles, and other birds of prey hunt at the margins of vast stands of trees.

A goodly number of the trips in this region are for whales and seabirds. The waters from Vancouver Island to the Queen Charlotte Islands especially form a rich biological area with vast seabird colonies as well as seals, otters, and sea lions. Orcas and Minke Whales feed in the channels and bays between the islands and the mainland. Still seemingly remote, the Pacific Northwest is a siren call for nature lovers.

TOUR OPERATORS

Biological Journeys

3–9 days / $$$$ (from Vancouver) / May, June, September, October. Several trips aboard the 10-passenger *Delphinus* to see Orcas, Dall's Porpoises, and seals and sea lions. Go with the experts! BJ pioneered these northwestern whale-watching trips. Four of the trips cruise the Inland Passage. In addition to the marine mammals, you may see Rhinoceros Auklets, Tufted Puffins, Common Murres, and both Bald and Golden Eagles.

7 days / $$$$ (from Vancouver) / July. Photo trips to Johnstone Strait aboard the 7-passenger *Blue Fjord.* This strait is known as one of the major areas for Orcas in the entire Northern Hemisphere. A professional photographer accompanies the trips.

Earthwatch. 10 days / $$ (from Friday Harbor, San Juan Island, Washington) / June–September. "Orca" is a research trip to study killer whales. Volunteers photograph and identify Orcas, recording behavior and vocalizations.

Field Guides. 10 days / $$ (from Portland) / August. A birding trip concentrating on the rugged Oregon coast for shorebirds (over 30 species), plus a pelagic trip for seabirds. Participants then go into the Cascades for woodland birds, and some time is spent at Malheur National Wildlife Refuge for high-desert birds. Maximum of 16 participants, 2 leaders.

International Research Expeditions. 10 days / $ (from Olympic National Park, Washington) / May–September. Research trips to study hawk migrations and botany. Volunteers write up field notes from observations, photograph and sketch in the field, and assist in the mounting of plants and the compilation of a flora guide emphasizing unusual or threatened plant communities.

National Audubon Society. 7 days / $$ (from Portland) / August. A workshop that explores the complex ecosystem of old-growth forests in Oregon. There's also investigation of the complex political and economic factors at work here, with discussion of forest management practices and wildlife conservation.

Nature Expeditions International

8–15 days / $$ (from Portland) / July–September. An "Ancient Forest Seminar" combining scientific study and hiking. The shorter trip concentrates on the central and coastal Cascades; the longer trip also visits central and southern Oregon, and has more emphasis on hiking. The seminars feature guest lectures and field presentations in forest ecology, which complement the field trips.

16 days / $$ (from Portland) / July–September. An in-depth study of the ecology of the Pacific Northwest. Highlights include the Columbia River Gorge, Mount Hood, Crater Lake, Olympic National Park, and Mount St. Helens.

15 days / $$ (from Victoria, BC) / July, August. Two expeditions to Vancouver and the Queen Charlotte Islands of the Inside Passage. Participants may see Bald Eagle, Black Bear, Otter, and porpoises. Cultural stops to Haida Indian villages are included.

Nature's Touch. 6 days / $ (from Campbell River, BC) / July, August. Eight canoe trips in the Esperanza Inlet. These are slow trips with stops to study the intertidal zone and marine wildlife on the west coast of Vancouver Island. Natural history guides accompany all trips.

Oceanic Society Expeditions

6 days / $$$ (from Port Hardy, Vancouver Island) / August. "Killer Whales" is a cruise aboard the 68-foot sailboat *Island Roamer* to Robson Bight, where Orcas, Dall's Porpoises, and Minke Whales feed. Birds, deer, and bear are also likely. Naturalists on board interpret whale behaviors. Maximim of 16 participants.

5 days / $$ (from Victoria, Vancouver Island) / September. Minke Whales, Steller Sea Lions, Harbor Seals, and Dall's Porpoises feed in the waters of the Juan

de Fuca Strait, around the San Juan and Gulf islands. A shore excursion to Mandarte Island, an ecological preserve, offers close-up looks at Pelagic and Double-crested Cormorants. The 68-foot ketch *Island Roamer* takes up to 16 participants.

Outer Edge Expeditions. 8 days / $$ (from Vancouver Island) / July–September. Three sea kayaking trips—"Orcas Galore"—taking paddlers alongside Orcas. You get to listen to them with a hydrophone. Shoreline stops include hikes into evergreen forests. Bald Eagles are fairly common. Maximum of 8 participants.

Questers. 12 days / $$ (from Seattle) / June, August. A general natural history trip to the Pacific Northwest. From Seattle, the trip visits San Juan Island via ferry, watching for Orcas, eagles, and puffins. You continue to Vancouver Island, visiting the Dominion Astrophysical Observatory and Butchart Gardens, then cross the Juan de Fuca Strait to Olympic National Park, where you have a chance to see subalpine wildflowers, Hoary Marmot and Mountain Goat, and various birds. The tour goes on to Mount St. Helens for a study of volcanic activity and to Mt. Rainier to see glaciers, wildflowers, and montane birds. Maximum of 20 participants.

Sierra Club. A number of nature-oriented hikes, river trips, and service trips to Oregon and Washington. Recent destinations include Eagle Cap Wilderness (Oregon), and San Juan Islands and Olympic National Park (Washington).

Special Expeditions. 8 days / $$$ (from Portland) / April, May, September, October. "In the Wake of Lewis & Clark" is a luxury trip down the Columbia and Snake rivers aboard the 70-passenger M. V. *Sea Lion* and the M. V. *Sea Bird* (a twin vessel). You'll cruise among the peaceful wooded islands of the spectacular Columbia River Gorge. Side trips include a jet-boat ride into Hell's Canyon and a Zodiac trip in the narrow canyon of the Palouse River. The boats pass through the locks of the Bonneville Dam, where migrating salmon can be observed, and on to Astoria for a visit to the Columbia River Maritime Museum. NOTE: These ships are often chartered by natural history museums and organizations that run an identical program.

VENT. 14 days / $$ (from Seattle) / September. A birding trip to a variety of habitats within Washington State. You'll visit Mount Rainier and Olympic National Parks and take a pelagic trip as well. Participants can expect to see upwards of 200 species of birds, including such regional specialties as Brandt's Cormorant, Black Oystercatcher, Surfbird, Black Swift, Eurasian Skylark, and Chestnut-backed Chickadee. Maximum of 16 participants.

Wings. 10 days / $$ (from Seattle) / July. A birdwatching trip to Washington and British Columbia. You'll visit the Olympic Peninsula, Vancouver Island, and the

British Columbian mainland east to Manning Provincial Park, concentrating on resident bird populations. Some species to be expected are Vaux's Swift, Gray Jay, Rosy Finch (Gray-crowned Race), Barred Owl, Mountain Bluebird, and Lewis' Woodpecker. Ferry rides enable you to add some pelagics to your list, such as Rhinoceros Auklet and Marbled Murrelet.

ALASKA AND THE YUKON TERRITORY

America's last frontier, Alaska is the untamed part of us, the unpredictable, unmanaged side of our collective personality. And this is why so many people tell us they are eager to get to Alaska. It is the one large chunk of America that hasn't yet been paved over.

Alaska is so big and so diverse that generalizations are absurd. Few people see all of it, especially in one trip. This is a place you come back to again and again; the glacier bays of the southeast, the upland grasses and tundra of the central portion, the rugged barren ground of the far north—all command you to return, and perhaps just begin to uncover the multiple mysteries of "Seward's Folly."

We've divided Alaska into three basic areas: southeast, south and central, and north. Cruises along the Inside Passage are covered in the southeast section. Although birdwatching trips generally visit more than one area of the state, most of their time is concentrated in south and central Alaska, so they are listed in that section.

Southeast Alaska and the Yukon

Sometimes called the "Alaska panhandle," southeast Alaska stretches in a stepping-stone collection of islands and a narrow strip of mainland south from Skagway and Haines almost to Prince Rupert, British Columbia. It's a place of glaciers and fjords, of Orcas and eagles.

The scenery is spectacular—calving glaciers drop their mammoth icebergs into shimmering water; the mist from the fjords floats gently over forests of Sikta spruce, hemlock, pine, and cedar. This is one of the last coastal rain forests left in the world, with 11,000 miles of pristine shoreline. Multiple inlets and bays hold nutrient-rich waters that nourish such marine mammals as the Humpback Whales that migrate here each summer from Hawaii and Mexico. Bald Eagles, Peregrine Falcons, Grizzly Bears, seals, and otters are often visible from boats, as are views of snow-capped peaks, waterfalls, and glacial valleys.

For many people, particularly seniors, this is accessible Alaska: Comfortable cruise ships ply the waters, wending their way northward from Seattle or Vancouver to Ketchikan, Wrangell, and Petersburg; around Kootznahoo (Admiralty) Island, to Sitka and Juneau; perhaps on to Haines or Skagway; and finally to

Glacier Bay National Park. On our cruise through the Inside Passage, we whiled away the time counting Bald Eagles perched in the treetops along shore—their bright white heads shone like beacons. But remember that the 27 million acres that make up this part of Alaska (only 7 percent of the state's area) has the highest density of eagles in North America—more than the lower forty-eight states combined.

Cultural stops along the way include viewings of totem poles in Ketchikan or Wrangell; gold-rush history and lore in Haines, Skagway, or Whitehorse; the Norwegian influence in Petersburg and the Russian influence in Sitka. At Glacier Bay, trips into the rain forest offer hikes through woods webbed with moss and dripping with dew. Higher elevations offer alpine wildflowers and broad vistas.

It seems that almost every major museum or natural history organization offers a cruise to Southeast Alaska at one time or another. The trip is usually accompanied by a naturalist who will answer questions and offer evening lectures on the birds, glaciers, or marine mammals. Add to this the large number of trips run by private cruise companies, and it is clear that there are lot of choices here. We've limited our listing to the museum trips and trips run by regular naturalist outfitters. When comparing trips, check the size of the boat (smaller boats with shallow drafts can get into the narrower channels and come closer to the glaciers or shoreline) and number of passengers (offloading into Zodiacs or other small craft can take a lot of time when many people want to go ashore). If comfort is a big factor, you'll find some boats more luxuriously equipped than others; prices are a reliable indicator. Price also depends on deck level, with higher prices for upper decks. If getting naturalist information en route is important, ask the tour operator about the qualifications of the accompanying naturalists—some specialize in glaciology or birds, for example. Don't forget your binoculars, and remember to bring warm clothing; although this point may seem obvious to some, we've seen many travelers shivering in shirtsleeves as they looked at glaciers.

There are ways other than luxury cruises to see the multiple wonders of this part of the world. Of particular note is the Tatshenshini River, in Canada just north of Haines, Alaska. The "Tat" is a wild and scenic river. Though protected at its lower end, it is threatened by mining and logging interests at its source. Another popular southeast destination is the Chilkat River, where large flocks of Bald Eagles gather in the fall to catch and eat the salmon that pass downstream.

Some general natural history trips include Glacier Bay, but that's just one of many stops. Look for these trips in the next section, South and Central Alaska.

TOUR OPERATORS

Alaska Wildland Adventures. 5 days / $$$ (from Juneau) / May–September. Aboard the 90-passenger *Sheltered Seas,* an inland passage cruise. You sail up Tracy

Arm National Monument (be on the lookout for Black Bear and Mountain Goat), then pass in sight of North and South Sawyer glaciers, and on to LeConte Glacier. All sailing is done during the day; nights are spent ashore in Petersburg.

American Museum of Natural History. Aboard the M.V. *Sea Lion* (see the "Special Expeditions" listing in this section).

Arctic Edge

9–11 days / \$\$ (from Haines) / June, August. "Tatshenshini/Alsek River Rafting Trip." The river's whitewater canyon in the St. Elias Mountains cuts through an area populated by Mountain Goat, Dall Sheep, Grizzly Bear, and Moose, while Bald Eagles, Beaver, and Otter are seen on the river margin. The white water is class IV— exciting but safe. Maximum of 12 participants; the raft is skippered by 3 experienced guides.

6 days / \$\$ (from Whitehorse, Yukon) / August, September. A raft trip down the rarely traveled Alsek River, through the heart of the Yukon's Kluane National Park—a dry, interior, steppe ecosystem between two great mountain ranges.

12–21 days / \$\$ (from Whitehorse, Yukon) / July, August. A variety of canoe trips down some famous wild rivers: the Snake, Keele, Liard, Mountain, and South MacMillan. Animals and birds can be seen on all trips, along with spectacular scenery.

6–13 days / \$ (from Whitehorse, Yukon) / July, August. Treks in Kluane National Park, an amazingly varied landscape—alpine meadows, tundra, nonpolar ice fields—with many productive habitats. You'll see bears, goats, sheep, and, if lucky, wolves.

Biological Journeys. 6–9 days / \$\$\$ (from Juneau, Petersburg, or Ketchikan) / June–September. A variety of whale-watching trips aboard the 10-passenger *Delphinus*—a lovely small yacht. These are natural history and photography cruises and will get you up close to Humpback Whales and Grizzly Bears. One trip goes only to Glacier Bay; other trips combine Glacier Bay with Frederick Sound. The "Southeast Alaska Explorer" (July) aboard the 40-passenger *Wilderness Explorer* goes to Glacier Bay and Kootznahoo (Admiralty) Island. Some trips are accompanied by a professional photographer.

Denver Museum of Natural History. Aboard the M.V. *Sea Lion* (see "Special Expeditions").

International Oceanographic Foundation. Aboard the M. V. *Sea Bird* (see "Special Expeditions").

Intersea Research. 10 days / $$$ (from Juneau) / June–August. Six trips aboard the diesel yacht *Acania*. Participants on this research expedition enjoy cruising Frederick Sound, Stephens Passage, and Chatham Strait while they learn about research on marine mammals. The focus here is on Humpback, Killer, and Minke Whales and Steller Sea Lions, though the ship's scientist also explains about other animals and plants of the sea and land. Evening presentations include slide shows or discussions about the research, marine mammals, birdlife, and other aspects of natural history. There's time for fishing, hiking, bathing in hot springs, and the like. Travelers choose their own level of participation, from collecting and identifying samples to documenting whale behavior. Maximum of 14 participants. One departure is run jointly with Oceanic Society Expeditions.

Journeys. 9 days / $$ (from Juneau) / June–August. "Southeast Alaska Wildlife Odyssey" is a general natural history trip aboard the M.V. *Wilderness Explorer*. You'll visit Glacier Bay, Icy Strait, and Kootznahoo (Admiralty) Island, where you can see abundant wildlife including Tufted Puffin, Bald Eagle, whales, sea lions, and seals.

Massachusetts Audubon Society. Aboard the M.V. *Sea Bird* (see "Special Expeditions").

Motmot Nature Tours. 7 days / $$$ (from Whitehorse, Yukon) / July. A birdwatching tour based at Oldsquaw Lodge, near Mac Pass in the Yukon. Over 130 species of birds have been seen here, including Oldsquaw, Gyrfalcon, Willow Ptarmigan, Wandering Tattler, and Smith's Longspur. Animals include Caribou, Moose, and Grizzly Bear.

Mountain Travel/Sobek. 10 days / $$ (from Juneau) / June–September. Four departures. These are kayak trips to Glacier Bay and Kootznahoo (Admiralty) Island. Participants can expect to see whales, seals, and seabirds at Glacier Bay; Brown Bears and Bald Eagles on Kootznahoo. Other river trips are also offered, including a raft trip down the Tatshenshini.

Oceanic Society Expeditions

10 days / $$$$ (from Prince Rupert, BC) / August. Aboard the 68-foot sailing vessel *Island Roamer*. You'll explore Misty Fjords National Monument, Wrangell Island, and Frederick Sound, known for its Humpback Whales. Maximum of 14 participants.

10 days / $$$ (from Juneau) / July. Participate in a research project to study Humpback Whales at their feeding grounds. This trip is cosponsored by Intersea Research, and is conducted aboard the 14-passenger *Acania*. You visit Baranof

Island, Frederick Sound, and Kootznahoo (Admiralty) Island. Maximum of 14 participants.

30–91 days / $$$ (from Juneau) / August–November. An Arctic research expedition beginning in Juneau and heading north. Maximum of 14 participants. You may take the entire trip or sign up for 30-day segments.

Outback Expeditions

7 days / $ (from Petersburg) / June–August. "LeConte Glacier Explorer" is a kayak trip from Petersburg across Frederick Sound to the mainland. The route skirts the coastline, passing the uplifted Horn Cliffs and snow-fed Moonshine Creek on the way to LeConte Bay, a fjord cut into the Coastal Mountain Range. From a base camp, travelers explore the rain forest, see waterfalls and coves, and possibly witness the birthing of Harbor Seals or the spawning of salmon. You return through the Dry Straits to Petersburg. Low-impact camping. Guides have extensive knowledge of the area's natural history.

7 days / $$ (from Petersburg) / June–August. A paddle float down one of the last navigable wilderness rivers in North America, the Stikine. You'll visit Great Glacier, Alpine Creek, and enjoy the waters of Chief Shakes Hot Springs.

Sierra Club. The Sierra Club runs many nature-oriented trips to the forty-ninth state. These include hiking/backpacking trips, river-running (kayak, canoe, and raft) trips, and service trips. Recent destinations in Southeast Alaska have included Glacier Bay, Misty Fjords, Kootznahoo (Admiralty) Island, and the Tatshenshini River.

Special Expeditions

10 days / $$$$ (from Sitka, Alaska, or Prince Rupert, BC) / August. "Exploring Alaska's Coastal Wilderness" is a luxury cruise aboard the 70-passenger M.V. *Sea Lion*. The itinerary includes visits to Sitka, Kootznahoo (Admiralty) Island, and Tracy Arm, a spectacular fjord with an active glacier at its end. You then continue to Glacier Bay National Park, explore LeConte Bay and Petersburg, and finally visit Misty Fjords National Monument. Travelers see whales, sea lions, seals, bears, eagles, and a host of other animals and birds in their natural habitats. Trips are accompanied by a geologist and other naturalist guides.

14 days / $$$$ (from Vancouver, BC) / June, August. "To the Land of the Eagles" is a luxury cruise aboard the 70-passenger M.V. *Sea Bird*. The itinerary includes traveling through the Johnstone Strait, recognized as one of the main areas for Orcas. You then visit the Queen Charlotte Islands, Misty Fjords National Monument, Kootznahoo (Admiralty) Island, the Tracy Arm, Sitka, and Glacier Bay National Park—a good place for Humpback Whales. You may even see a calving glacier crash into the sea. Cultural stops include an old Haida Indian village

on Anthony Island, and Norwegian and Russian heritage sites in Petersburg and Sitka. Several naturalists accompany all the trips.

TravelWild. 6 days / $$$ (from Haines) / November. "Bald Eagles of the Chilkat River" is a photo safari to see (and photograph) the spectacular gathering of more than 3,000 Bald Eagles as they congregate each fall along the Chilkat River. This is the last major salmon run of the year, so the birds flock to it from hundreds of miles away. They wade into the water and snatch the dead or dying fish, dragging them ashore onto snowy gravel bars. Maximum of 16 participants.

Wildlife Conservation Society. Aboard the M.V. *Sea Lion* (see "Special Expeditions").

South and Central Alaska and the Aleutian and Pribilof Islands

How they arrange the itineraries may differ, but a large number of trips to Alaska hit the "highlights": Denali National Park and the Alaska Range, Prince William Sound, the Kenai Peninsula and Cook Inlet, and sometimes Katmai National Park or Kodiak Island. Some trips include a visit to Glacier Bay, too. This is the Alaska sampler, and though it frequently means only brief experiences in each location, it is a good way to get a true taste of this vast and varied state.

Denali National Park is larger than the state of Massachusetts, a high mountain area with access to the upland tundra and possible observations of the wildlife it supports: Grizzly Bear, Moose, Caribou, Dall Sheep, Arctic Fox, Wolf, and Golden Eagle. Only 200 miles south of the Arctic Circle, the park seems to be in a race against time—there are just two months of fair weather for the plants and animals to reproduce and prosper before winter sets in again. There are 450 species of plants, 37 mammals, and 130 birds supported by this fragile environment.

Prince William Sound is a name that should be familiar to everyone by now. It has only been a few years since the *Exxon Valdez* tragedy, and it will take many more years for this region to come close to being the rich ecological place it once was. With Chugach National Forest and the sound's many islands, this region is a mosaic of green and blue. Seacoast glaciers, mountain trails, and high mountain lakes are among its many features.

The Kenai Peninsula hangs down from south-central Alaska between the Columbia Glacier and Cook Inlet. Half of the area makes up Kenai National Wildlife Refuge, a 2-million-acre spot of incomparable beauty. With lowland spruce and birch forests, crystal-clear lakes fed by glaciers, and the towering Kenai Mountains rising to 6,600 feet, the refuge is a prime area for Moose, Dall Sheep, Caribou, Wolf, Grizzly Bear, Lynx, Wolverine, Beaver, and more—plus

146 species of resident and migratory birds, including the lovely Trumpeter Swan. This is also the spawning ground for four species of Pacific salmon.

Katmai National Park, on the Alaskan Peninsula, is where glacial ice and volcanic fire meet—where the volcanoes of the Aleutian Range are fringed with coniferous forest, alpine streams, and salmon-filled rivers. The Valley of the Ten Thousand Smokes, as a part of Katmai was once known, is the remnant of a violent volcanic eruption in 1912. Now a river cuts through the thick layer of fine ash to reveal the stains of fumaroles, some of which are still smoking. The park also provides prime habitat for twenty-seven species of land mammals, including shrews, hares, voles, Porcupine, Red Fox, Wolf, Brown Bear (Grizzly), Moose, Lynx, and Wolverine.

The Aleutian Islands stretch 1,100 miles off the end of the Alaska Peninsula toward Asia, forming one of the largest units of the Alaska Maritime National Wildlife Refuge. They are largely of volcanic origin, windswept and treeless.

Whereas the Aleutians are largely uninhabited, the Pribilof Islands are home to the Aleut people, brought there in the 1700s by Russian fur traders to harvest the seal pelts. Today, the Pribilofs are equally famous for their seabird colonies. Many birds nest on the grass-covered rocky cliffs, and Fur Seals breed each spring on the beaches. Most of the major birding tours spend several days on the Pribilofs, enjoying the abundant birdlife.

Tour Operators

Alaska Wildland Adventures. 7–12 days / $$$ (from Kenai Airport) / May–September. A variety of wildlife trips, including a visit to Denali and a boat excursion on the Kenai River. All trips include hiking, camping, and animal viewing. A special "Senior Safari" (8 days, no camping) is also offered.

Attour. 14–21 days / $$$ (from Anchorage) / May, June, September. Attu is the easternmost island in the Aleutians, the most remote and rarely visited place in the United States. Some of the rarest birds in North America can be found here, and there is also a good chance of seeing Asian vagrants. Waterfowl and buntings are more likely on the first trip; flycatchers and cuckoos on the second trip; shorebirds, pipits, and wagtails on both. The September trip is timed for the middle of fall migration. Optional extensions to Nome and Gambell are available. Maximum of 30 participants.

Betchart Expeditions. (See "Massachusetts Audubon Society," below.)

Earthwatch. 14 days / $ (from Fairbanks) / May–October. "Muskoxen and Caribou" is a research project that studies the nutrition of these two species. Volunteers will monitor captive animals on different diets.

Field Guides. 18 days / $$$ (from Anchorage) / June. A birdwatching tour to Denali National Park, the Pribilof Islands, Seward (including a boat trip to Kenai Fjords National Park), Nome, Barrow, and the Anchorage area. Participants can expect to see about 250 species of birds, including many northern specialties. The trip can be taken in either of two shorter (9-day) segments. Maximum of 16 participants; 2 leaders.

International Expeditions. 10 days / $$$ (from Seattle) / July, August. A general wildlife trip to Denali and the Kenai Fjords. Optional extension to Glacier Bay.

Massachusetts Audubon Society. 11 days / $$$ (from Anchorage) / July–August. A natural history trip to the Kenai Peninsula (where you can see Beluga Whales and Bald Eagles), Kenai Fjords National Park (home to thousands of nesting seabirds), Nome and the Seward Peninsula, and Denali National Park. Two leaders accompany the trip. This trip is being run jointly with Betchart Expeditions.

Mountain Travel/Sobek. 9 days / $$$ (from Anchorage) / June–August. Wildlife safaris to the Kenai River, Kenai Fjords, Chugach National Forest, and Denali National Park. You'll see Caribou, Moose, Grizzly Bear, and lots of glaciers, marine mammals, and birds. Six departures.

Natural Habitat Adventures
11 days / $$$$ (from Anchorage) / July. "Alaska and Brown Bears of Katmai" is a wildlife trip that includes a visit to Denali, Prince William Sound, Kenai Fjords, and Katmai.
11 days / $$$ (from Anchorage) / June. "Alaska Wildlife Watch" visits Prince William Sound, the Kenai Fjords, and Denali National Park.

Nature Expeditions International. 15 days / $$$ (from Anchorage) / June–August. "Alaska Wildlife Expedition" is ideally suited for the first-time visitor. This trip visits the most beautiful areas of Alaska, and those with the richest wildlife habitats: Glacier Bay, Katmai, and Denali National Park. Historical sites include Sitka, Anchorage, and Fairbanks. Maximum of 16 participants.

Oceanic Society Expeditions. 30–91 days / $$$$ (from Juneau) / August–November. An Arctic research expedition to study and collect baseline data on marine mammals and seabirds. Bowhead, Gray, Beluga, and possibly Narwhal Whales as well as Sea Otters and Walrus are among the mammals likely to be encountered. Highlights on the northbound portion (from Juneau) include many of the Aleutian Islands, the Kuskokwim and Yukon River delta areas, Nunivak Island, Nome, the Diomede Islands, Point Barrow, and Provideniya (Siberia). Southbound, the boat will call at St. Lawrence Island, the Pribilof Islands, Attu, the Aleutians, and Kodiak before returning to Juneau. Participants may sign up for the entire expedition or join it for 30-day segments.

Questers. 17 days / $$$$ (from Juneau) / June, July. A general natural history trip, beginning with a cruise on Glacier Bay to see seabirds, then to Denali with a stay at the North Face Lodge, in full view of Mount Denali. The trip continues to the Seward Peninsula, Katmai National Park, and Anchorage.

Sierra Club. The club runs a variety of nature-related trips, including hiking and backpacking, river-running, and service trips. Recent destinations have included Katmai, Denali, and Prince William Sound.

TravelWild

7 days / $$$$ (from Anchorage) / July. A photo trip to Afognak Island, in the Gulf of Alaska. The world's largest concentration of Sea Otters and several Steller Sea Lion colonies are found here. Numerous Bald Eagles nest in the island's dense forests of Sitka Spruce, and Horned and Tufted Puffins breed on offshore islets. Maximum of 12 participants; a professional photographer accompanies the trip.

12 days / $$$$ (from Anchorage) / July. "The Best of Alaska" is a photo trip to Glacier Bay, Denali, and the Kenai Fjords. Maximum of 16 participants; a naturalist and a professional photographer accompany the trip.

5 days / $$$$ (from Anchorage) / June, July. "Brown Bears of Katmai National Park." Four photo tours to Katmai, well-known for its large concentrations of Brown Bears. Maximum of 18 participants; naturalists and photographers accompany the trips.

6 days / $$$$ (from Anchorage) / July. Three photo trips to St. George in the Pribilof Islands. Here you can get up close to several species of nesting seabirds and Northern Fur Seals. Wildflowers are also in bloom at this time. Maximum of 7 participants.

VENT

16 days / $$$ (from Anchorage) / June. A birdwatching trip visiting a variety of habitats: Nome, where you might find a Slaty-backed Gull or Harlequin Duck; Anchorage, where Bohemian Waxwings are in backyards; Kenai Fjords, for alcids; the Pribilof Islands, and Denali. An optional extension (3 days) goes to Barrow. Participants can expect to see about 200 species of birds. Maximum of 16 participants, 2 leaders. This trip can be combined with the trip to Gambell, St. Lawrence; see their trip to North Alaska, page 62.

12 days / $$ (from Anchorage) / June. A shorter birding tour, for those with limited time. You visit Kenai Fjords, Denali, and Nome. An optional extension to Barrow is offered. Maximum of 16 participants, 2 leaders.

Voyagers International. 9 days / $$$$ (from Anchorage) / July. A photography trip to central Alaska, including Denali and Kenai Fjords. An optional extension to the Pribilof Islands is offered. A professional photographer accompanies the trip.

Wings

20 days / $$$$ (from Anchorage) / May. A birding tour from Nome and Gambell to the Pribilofs, Denali, the Kenai Peninsula, and Seward. Participants can expect to see about 200 species of birds, including Asian vagrants in Gambell, Red-legged Kittiwake and Red-faced Cormorant on the Pribilofs, and auklets and murrelets off Kenai. In Denali, there will also be lots of animals. Two leaders accompany the trip.

20 days / $$$$ (from Seattle) / June. A birding trip to Glacier Bay, the Pribilofs, Kenai Peninsula, Denali, Resurrection Bay (near Seward), Nome, and Barrow. This trip is less strenuous than the one in May (see above). Participants will still see a good many birds, and also lots of animals (Denali) and marine mammals (off Kenai). Two leaders accompany the trip.

14 days / $$$$ (from Anchorage) / August. A birding trip focused on coastal Alaska: Homer, the Pribilofs, Nome, and St. Lawrence Island (Gambell). Breeding birds will still be present and fall migration will have begun, so this is a good time to bird the coastal regions. A 3-day extension to the confluence of the Kelly and Noatak rivers, northwest of Kotzebue, for the Siberian Tit is available at extra cost. Two leaders will accompany the trip.

North Alaska: Nome, St. Lawrence Island, the Brooks Range, and Barrow

Located on the southern side of the Seward Peninsula, Nome is practically within spitting distance of Siberia. The Bering Land Bridge National Preserve, on the north side, is a bare 100 roadless miles from Nome. Nome, of course, is best remembered for the gold rush, a time when men were sleeping in tents and standing elbow to elbow on the beach, panning for gold. Today it's the finish line of the Iditarod—a 1,049-mile dogsled race beginning in Anchorage that retraces the historic diphtheria serum delivery of 1925. Because it is also a top birding spot, most tours spend at least two or three days here. Beyond the treeline, the tundra can be alive with wildflowers and birds.

Gambell is an Eskimo village on the westernmost tip of St. Lawrence Island, only eighteen miles from the Date Line (and forty miles from Siberia). Famous for its Asian strays, it's a top birding spot and many tours spend several days there, albeit in somewhat less than luxurious conditions. But, for the dedicated bird-watcher, the birds more than make up for the discomforts.

The central and western Brooks Range is home to a variety of wildlife, including Moose, Caribou, Dall Sheep, Grizzly and Black Bears, Wolverine, and Lynx, plus many migratory birds that nest here in summer. Gold attracted people to this region in the nineteenth century, oil in the twentieth. Though parts of the Brooks Range show the scars of oil exploration and development, the region surrounding Bettles remains virtually undeveloped.

The eastern Brooks Range is part of the vast Arctic National Wildlife Refuge, which at present preserves a largely undisturbed portion of this environment. Its unique scenic wilderness is home to Musk Oxen, Caribou, Wolf, and Grizzly Bear. This area is threatened, however, by possible development and oil and gas exploration. It recently got a reprieve, but the pressure will undoubtedly be turned on again in the near future. Enjoy it while you still can.

Barrow, the "top of the world," is infrequently visited, but there are some birding tours that get all the way up. Sea ducks—Steller's Sea Eider and Spectacled Eider—can be seen.

TOUR OPERATORS

Hallet and Harper. 12 days / $$$$ (from Anchorage) / May. A birding trip to Anchorage, Nome, and Gambell (on St. Lawrence Island). A feature of the trip is a tundra search for Bristle-thighed Curlew and Bluethroat. Four days are then spent at Gambell looking for seabirds, shorebirds, and Siberian vagrants. An optional extension to Juneau for the Steller's Sea Eagle is available. Maximum of 7 participants, 1 leader.

Innerasia Expeditions. 14 days / $$$$ (from Anchorage) / July–August. A rigorous adventure that visits both sides of the Bering Sea. The trip starts in Anchorage, then on to Kotzebue and the Seward Peninsula, St. Lawrence Island, and over to Provideniya (Siberia), on the other side of the Bering Strait. Here, you'll spend a week in the center of Chukchi culture and make whale- and walrus-watching excursions.

Mountain Travel/Sobek. 7–11 days / $$–$$$ (from Fairbanks) / June, August. River-rafting trips on the Sheenjek and Kongakut rivers in the Brooks Range area of the vast Arctic National Wildlife Refuge. You'll have an opportunity to see Moose, Grizzly Bear, and many other animals and birds as you glide unobtrusively through their environment. Experienced guides accompany all trips.

Oceanic Society Expeditions. (See the section on South and Central Alaska, pages 58–59, for information about their three-month research trip.)

Sierra Club. A variety of nature-oriented hikes, river trips, and service trips to the far north. Recent destinations included Arctic National Wildlife Refuge and Gates of the Arctic Park and Preserve.

Sourdough Outfitters. 7–21 days / $–$$ (from Beetles) / February–April, June–September. A variety of hiking, canoeing, and float trips in and around the Brooks Range, Gates of the Arctic National Park, Noatak River, and Arctic National Wildlife Refuge. Most trips last for 1 week. Canoe and float trips on remote rivers give participants a true sense of wilderness, and often you can see animals up close. In the winter, dogsledding trips are run in Gates of the Arctic Park.

VENT. 7 days / $$$ (from Anchorage) / June. A birding trip to St. Lawrence Island (Gambell). When not looking at Asian strays, participants can enjoy the hordes of murres, puffins, and auklets that nest east of the village. Maximum of 16 participants. This trip can be combined with the June "Grand Alaska" trip, see the section on South and Central Alaska, page 60.

Wings. 14 days / $$$$ (from Anchorage) / May. A birding trip concentrating on St. Lawrence Island. Though a few days in Gambell is included on the regular Alaska tour, this trip offers keen birders more time here, where birdwatching varies from excellent to incredible. You'll see local breeding birds, seabirds in migration, and possibly Asian vagrants. Three leaders accompany the trip.

HAWAII

Captain James Cook landed on Kauai Island on January 20, 1778, opening up these Pacific islands to trade, whaling, and Western settlement. Our fiftieth state, Hawaii comprises eight major islands and 124 small islets, forming a crescent that extends 1,500 miles in the Pacific. The main islands for tourism are Hawaii (the big island), Maui, Oahu, and Kauai. Hawaiian Islands National Wildlife Refuge encompasses numerous small islands and reefs northwest of Kauai.

Lying 2,400 miles from the nearest continental land mass, Hawaii's volcanoes emerged from the ocean devoid of plant and animal life. Hawaii (like New Zealand) has no native reptiles, amphibians, or terrestrial mammals (other than the Hawaiian Hoary Bat). The evolution of Hawaii's birds has been remarkable. Most spectacular was the development of the unique family of Hawaiian honeycreepers, *Drepanididae*—with at least twenty-three species (and twenty-four subspecies) evolving from a single ancestral species. There are more than seventy native birds and a group of more recently introduced species. But Hawaii's endemics are at risk. In the two centuries since people have colonized the islands, at least twenty-three species have become extinct, and another thirty are in danger.

Hawaii is a living laboratory for volcanologists. Kilauea (in Hawaii Volcanoes National Park) just won't quit. Recently it sent streams of lava down to the sea, enlarging the island and wiping out a village in the process. Many of Hawaii's other volcanoes are also considered active. You can climb Haleakala, a dormant volcano on Maui, where the rare and endemic Silversword grows in the crater. This beautiful plant takes fifteen years to produce a six-foot bloom, then it dies. On Kauai, the Alakai Swamp is home to some of Hawaii's rarest plants and birds. Many trips include a visit to the Nature Conservancy's Waikamoi Preserve, one of the wildest places left in the state and a great spot for finding endemic birds and plants.

Most nature tours include whale-watching and pelagic trips as part of their programs. A lot of the research on Humpback Whales is done in these waters. And some of the small islets are the nesting grounds for pelagic birds such as the Laysan Albatross. Of course, all these warm waters and reefs make for good snorkeling as well. Hundreds of corals, tropical fish, and sea plants can be seen, even by a beginner.

TOUR OPERATORS

Break Away Adventure Travel. 6–14 days / $$ (from Molokai or Kauai) / January–December. A variety of hiking and sailing trips. On the sails you'll snorkel. Hikes visit Waimea Canyon and the Na Pali coast on Kauai, Haleakala volcano on Maui, and Hawaii Volcanoes National Park.

Cornell's Adult University. 10 days / $$$ (from Honolulu) / October. "Natural History of the Hawaiian Islands" is a study program exploring the vegetation and marine life produced by the favorable climate and warm waters of the archipelago. It also covers the volcanic development of the islands. Visits Oahu, Maui, Hawaii.

Earthwatch
12 days / $$ (from Kona, Hawaii) / January–March. A research trip to study the Kohala coast population of Humpback Whales. Volunteers track whale pods in order to age, sex, and identify as many individuals as possible.
14–28 days / $$ (from Honolulu) / January–December. "Dolphin Intelligence." Since 1969, scientists have been trying to discover the limits of dolphin intelligence. Volunteers help to train dolphins, and care for and work with the animals.

Eye of the Whale
7 days / $$ (from Kona, Hawaii) / January–December. "Earth, Fire, and Sea" is a natural history trip focusing on Hawaii's wilderness. You'll explore the Big Island's forests, coral reefs, offshore tropical waters, and volcanic activity, and hike across the crater of Kilauea, the world's most active volcano. A highlight of the trip

is a 3-day voyage on a 42-foot sailing yacht along the Kona Coast for whale-watching and snorkeling. Maximum of 6 participants.

5 days / $$ (from Kona, Hawaii) / January–March. "Whale Tales." Sailing off the Big Island between Kawaihae and Kealakekua Bay, you'll use marine mammal biology and research techniques to locate and study Humpback Whales in their winter breeding grounds. Maximum of 6 participants.

10 days / $$ (from Kauai) / January–December. A general natural history hiking trip to Kauai, Molokai, and Hawaii. You'll visit the Na Pali Coast and Waimea Canyon (Kauai), Halawa Valley (Molokai), and Volcanoes National Park and endemic montane rain forest (Hawaii). Maximum of 10 participants.

NOTE: Other tour operators book these trips, and offer them under their own auspices.

Geo Expeditions. (See "Eye of the Whale," above.)

International Expeditions. 14 days / $$ (from Kona, Hawaii) / January, February, August, November. A natural history and cultural trip to three of the islands—Hawaii, Maui, and Kauai—to explore rain forests, tide pools, coral reefs, volcanic activity, and Polynesian mythology.

Intersea Research. 10 days / $$$ (from Kona, Hawaii) / November–March. Sailing on the classic brigantine *Varua,* participants help with ongoing research on Humpback Whales, either in Kawaihae Harbor and Cook's Bay on Hawaii, or among the islands of Maui, Molokai, and Lanai.

Journeys. (See "Eye of the Whale," above.)

National Audubon Society. 10 days / $$ (from Honolulu) / March. A natural history workshop to four islands: Hawaii, Oahu, Maui, and Kauai. Program studies the critical conservation problems challenging Hawaii while also offering opportunities to see birdlife, including Maui Parrotbill, Palila, Akepa, Hawaii Creeper, Hawaiian Hawk, and Akiapolaau; there's a visit to a newly established Laysan Albatross colony on Kauai. Participants will have time to snorkel, whale watch, and look for active lava flows at volcanic sites while learning about many rare native plants.

Nature Expeditions International. 15 days / $$ (from Honolulu) / January, March, August, September, December. A general natural history exploration of Maui, Kauai, Oahu, and Hawaii. Humpback Whales are a special focus for the winter trips.

Oceanic Society Expeditions. (See "Eye of the Whale," pages 63–64.)

Questers. 14 days / $$$ (from Honolulu) / November–March. A luxury-level general nature tour that visits Oahu, Hawaii, Maui, Lanai, Molokai, and Kauai, exploring the geological, biological, and ecological aspects of this archipelago. Maximum of 20 participants.

See & Sea. 7 days / $$$ (from Kona, Hawaii) / January–December. Live-aboard diving trips off the Kona Coast. Here you can dive lava formations spattered with brilliant color and thronged with clouds of reef fish.

Sierra Club. The club usually runs about four or five trips to Hawaii each year. These differ, but generally include a family trip, a service trip, and a couple of hiking/backpacking trips.

The Nature Conservancy. 7 days / $$$ (from Honolulu) / May. The Hawaii chapter of the Conservancy offers a study of Hawaiian flora and fauna at its preserves around the state. Cost includes a contribution to the Hawaiian Conservancy. Maximum of 7 participants; a Conservancy representative accompanies the trip.

VENT. 15 days / $$ (from Honolulu) / October. A birding trip to Oahu, Maui, Hawaii, and Kauai. You'll visit The Nature Conservancy's Waikamoi Preserve, the seabird colonies of Kilauea Point National Wildlife Refuge, and search for the rare Nene Goose at the summit of Haleakala. A pelagic trip off Oahu for seabirds and marine mammals is included. Participants will see a high percentage of native land birds as well as many marine species. There will even be time for snorkeling. Maximum of 16 participants.

Voyagers International. 7–14 days / $$–$$$ (from Honolulu or Kona) / April, June–August, October, November. Various natural history and birdwatching programs, some run for universities or natural history organizations such as the American Birding Association.

WHALES, BIRDS, AND FISHES SOUTH OF THE BORDER: MEXICO, CENTRAL AMERICA, AND THE CARIBBEAN

In the United States we are lucky indeed to have such easy access to the biological richness just south of our border. Mexico, Central America, and the Caribbean constitute a gigantic reservoir of biological diversity at our doorstep. Short and frequent flights, comfortable accommodations, and multiple types of nature tours make getting to this part of the world easy and not too costly. Being a good neighbor to this developing part of the world means getting to know and appreciate the natural as well as cultural features of these countries. Indeed, ecotourists can help shape the future for species in the tropical and desert regions, using tourist dollars to buy interest in preservation and to counter the destructive force of ill-planned developments. We urge you to visit our neighbors to the immediate south.

MEXICO

Our southern neighbor, Mexico is a vast country with extraordinary physical variety. Its 761,600 square miles represent a transition from our temperate climate to the tropical zone of the Caribbean. Thus, with the Tropic of Cancer cutting Mexico virtually in half, the country's northern region is largely desert terrain, while its southern region is tropical.

Even a quick trip to Mexico City is enough to acquaint you with the environmental problems here. Air pollution, water contamination, overpopulation, and land degradation are major issues. However, the government has begun to institute some controls on industry and there have been some attempts to curb auto emissions.

Beyond the major population centers lie the prime destinations for nature lovers. Our section on Mexico is divided regionally, presenting opportunities for whale watching, snorkeling, birding, or botanizing, occasionally with time for visiting cultural sites as well.

Baja California and the Sea of Cortez

Baja California is a rough, rugged finger of land that juts south from southern California. Originally it was part of mainland Mexico, but that's ancient history. Today, Baja is much more like California than Mexico. It's mostly deserts, mountains, and beaches. Vast stretches are uninhabited, and the Sea of Cortez holds dozens of people-free islands. The main attraction of Baja and the Sea of Cortez is whales. Whales can be seen around the entire peninsula, from Scammon's Lagoon on the Pacific Coast all the way around to Bahía Concepción in the Sea of Cortez. Every winter, hundreds of Gray, Humpback, Blue, and Finback Whales migrate from the cold Arctic to these warmer waters. In the protected lagoons of the Pacific, Gray Whales mate and calve, while Blue Whales (the world's largest mammal) relax in the Sea of Cortez. Countless dolphins, sea lions, and many species of seabirds also spend the winter months here.

There are many trips to this area. Some specialize in whale watching, some search for a particular species of whale, some are diving trips (including live-aboards), and some are general natural history trips that do a little bit of everything. Choose carefully the type of trip that best suits you.

TOUR OPERATORS

American Museum of Natural History. 12 days / $$$$ (from Loreto) / February. Aboard the 37-cabin M.V. *Sea Lion*, this cruise features close encounters with several species of whales including Gray, Blue, Finback, and Humpback. Numerous naturalists accompany the trip.

Baja Expeditions. 4–7 days / $$–$$$ (from Los Angeles or Tucson) / January–April. Whale watching, natural history cruises, and scuba trips (year-round) are offered.

Biological Journeys. 7–12 days / $$ (from La Paz) / January–May. Biological Journeys runs several whale-watching trips to Baja, including a Blue Whales trip, a trip to see and interact with Gray Whales, and a general natural history trip. We were particularly pleased with "Blue Whales of the Sea of Cortez." Although the trip concentrated on this magnificent leviathan (and indeed we had great looks at a mother and her calf), there was still time for other natural history pursuits such as snorkeling and birdwatching.

Earthwatch. 14 days / $ (from San Diego) / May–July. "Baja Island Communities" is a research trip studying predators on islands in the Sea of Cortez.

Foundation for Field Research. 7+ days / $ (from San Diego) / June–October. The foundation sponsors several research projects in Bahía de Los Angeles, a bay in the Sea of Cortez. Projects are ongoing. Contributions are $700 for the first week, less for additional weeks. The foundation also sponsors research projects on Isla de Cedros, off the western coast of Baja near Guerrero Negro. Costs are comparable to the other Baja projects.

International Oceanographic Foundation. 11 days / $$$$ (from Loreto) / February. This is a general natural history cruise aboard the 70-passenger M.V. *Sea Bird.*

Massachusetts Audubon Society. 11 days / $$$$ (from Loreto) / January. Aboard the M.V. *Sea Bird.* Daily Zodiac trips take you up close to the whales; then you travel on to the Sea of Cortez for some botanizing, birdwatching, and snorkeling.

Mingan Island Cetacean Study. 7 days / $$ (from Loreto) / March. Research teams invite guests to join them on day sails out of Loreto. The study primarily involves photographing and studying Blue Whales. This work is supplemented by studies of Bryde's, Humpback, and Finback Whales.

Natural Habitat Adventures. 7 days / $$$ (from Los Angeles or Tucson) / January. Two whale-watching trips aboard the *Don Jose* are offered, one from La Paz to Cabo San Lucas, the other concentrating on Magdalena Bay.

Nature Expeditions International. 9 days / $$ (from San Diego) / April, November. A motor yacht trip in the Sea of Cortez exploring the bird, plant, and animal life of the islands. Maximum of 16 participants.

Oceanic Society Expeditions. 8 days/ $–$$$ (from San Diego) / December–May. Eight boat-based trips are offered, most of which concentrate on whale watching and general natural history. There is also an 8-day land-based natural history trip in May, which includes daily boat excursions. Maximum of 16 participants.

Pacific Queen. 10 days / $$ (from San Diego) / January–April. The *Pacific Queen* is owned and operated by Captain Eddie McEwen. Six expeditions, some run in conjunction with the San Diego Natural History Museum, some with local universities. The trips follow the path of Gray Whales as they migrate along the coast of Baja California.

Scripps Aquarium-Museum, University of California. 7–9 days / $$ (from San Diego) / February, October. The February trip is an expedition down the west coast of Baja to the San Ignacio Lagoon. The October trip is a diving and collecting expedition in the Sea of Cortez. Participants must be members of the aquarium and be certified divers.

See & Sea. 7 days / $$ (from La Paz) / May–October. Live-aboard dive trips on a 16-passenger boat.

Sierra Club. 7 days / $–$$ (from various locations) / December–March. The Sierra Club runs several (members only) kayaking and general natural history trips to the Sea of Cortez.

Special Expeditions. 8 days / $$$$ (from Loreto) / January, December. Aboard the twin vessels M.V. *Sea Bird* and M.V. *Sea Lion,* these are general natural history cruises in the Sea of Cortez. Daily excursions are made by Zodiac. (Both ships are used by various natural history museums and zoological societies.)

Wildlife Conservation Society. 9 days / $$$$ (from Loreto) / March. This trip circumnavigates Baja aboard the 70-passenger M.V. *Sea Lion.* Frequent Zodiac excursions are made to various small islands.

World Wildlife Fund. 9 days / $$$$ (from Loreto) / January. This trip travels along the coast of Baja aboard the 70-passenger M.V. *Sea Lion.*

Western Mexico

Here is a rich and varied habitat along the eastern side of the Sea of Cortez and down along Mexico's Pacific slope. Travelers to this part of the country experience tropical weather, flashy birds, and captivating scenery. Though the Mexican states of Colima and Jalisco are smaller than many counties in the United States, their complex topography offers a wide spectrum of life zones and habitats—from sea level to more than 10,000 feet in elevation—making this a prime destination for birding trips. Also, the Pacific coastline is a key nesting spot for sea turtles.

TOUR OPERATORS

Earthwatch

14 days / $ (from Buenavista) / January–May. This is a research trip to study one of North America's most active volcanos: Colima. Volunteers take samples of

mercury-laden soil and radon gas on the volcanic cone and surrounding caldera. Part of the trip involves camping on the volcano's saddle (at 11,000 feet).

14 days / $ (from Puerto Vallarta) / April, May. "American Forest Survey" is a study of four deciduous forests (the others are in Puerto Rico, Michigan, and Venezuela). Teams lay out transects, study plots, and identify trees.

Field Guides. 9 days / $$ (from Manzanillo) / March, November. These are bird-watching tours to the states of Colima (lowlands) and Jalisco (highland habitats). You can expect to see about 300 species, including Wagler's Chachalaca, Banded Quail, Lilac-crowned Parrot, Amethyst-throated Hummingbird, Citreoline Trogon, Russet-crowned Motmot, White-striped Woodpecker, White-throated Magpie Jay, Happy Wren, Golden Vireo, Blue-hooded Euphonia, Red-headed Tanager, Collared Forest-Falcon, Long-tailed Wood-Partridge, Rufous-necked Wood-Rail, and Red-breasted Chat. Nightbirding may produce Eared Poorwill, Balsas Screech-Owl, and possibly Stygian Owl. Maximum of 14 participants.

Foundation for Field Research. 7–14 days / $–$$ (from Lazaro Cardenas Airport, Michoacan) / December–February. Based in Michoacan, between Puerto Vallarta and Acapulco, this research expedition studies the giant Leatherback Turtles of Mexiquillo Beach. Volunteers carry newly laid turtle eggs from the nests (which might be disturbed) to a protected nursery area. When the eggs hatch, the hatchlings are released into the open sea.

VENT. 9 days / $$ (from Manzanillo) / October. A birdwatching tour to the states of Colima and Jalisco. At least 300 species can be seen, including more than 30 endemics. Special effort is made to find the Orange-breasted Bunting, Red-breasted Chat, and Rosy Thrush-Tanager. One evening will be devoted to the Balsas Screech-Owl. Maximum of 14 participants.

Wings. 14 days / $$ (from Manzanillo) / March. Species seen on this birding trip are largely the same as on other tours. The trip is a few days longer than most, however, allowing more time to hunt for the endemics.

Northern Mexico

Stretching across a 1,300-mile border with the United States, the northern Mexican states of Sonora, Chihuahua, Coahuila, Nuevo Leon, and Tamaulipas offer exciting and varied ecovacation possibilities. In Sonora—farthest west—are now-extinct volcanoes that testify to a dramatic past. In Chihuahua is Mexico's famed Copper Canyon—the Barranca del Cobre—a massive gorge incised one mile into the rugged western side of the Sierra Madre Occidental. The trans–Sierra Madre train line is spectacular, crossing no less than thirty-nine bridges spanning vast gaps in the terrain. And in the east, only 300 miles south of Brownsville, Texas, is a region of tropical cloud forest.

TOUR OPERATORS

VENT

10 days / $$ (from Los Mochis) / April. This birding tour begins on the west coast of Mexico, in the lowlands, but most of it is spent at the higher elevations of the Sierra Madre Occidental. Here you can see Military Macaws and Thick-billed Parrots as well as rarer species such as the Eared Trogon. Trip includes Copper Canyon train ride. Maximum of 14 participants.

11 days / $$ (from Harlingen, Texas) / August. This birdwatching camp at Rancho Cielo Cloud Forest is an excellent introduction to neotropical birding for teenagers. Several species—Red-crowned Parrot, Crimson-collared Grosbeak—are found nowhere else in the world except this corner of Mexico. Other Mexican endemics to be seen include Spotted Wren, Blue Mockingbird, and Rufous-capped Brush-Finch. Maximum of 18 participants, 3 leaders.

Central and Southern Mexico

Though dominated by Mexico City, central Mexico and the regions to the south and east have some extraordinary destinations for naturalist activities. Listed here are trips that visit the fir forests of Michoacán, the diversified habitats of Oaxaca, and the cloud forest of El Triunfo in Chiapas.

Michoacán

When the weather turns cool in northern regions, millions of Monarch Butterflies migrate south, arriving in the Transvolcanic Mountains of Michoacán. Stretching westward from Mexico City, Michoacán is noted for its charming villages and some natural areas.

TOUR OPERATORS

TravelWild. 6 days / $$$$ (from Houston) / February. This photo safari to the Monarch Butterfly wintering area offers both outstanding photo opportunities and in-depth natural history interpretation. In addition, the trip sponsor directly aids local environmental education to preserve butterfly habitat. Maximum of 14 participants; a professional photographer accompanies the group.

Oaxaca

In addition to the famed pre-Columbian ruins and the colorful markets and crafts of the local Indians, Oaxaca offers a surprising range of habitat from the cactus-covered foothills of the Oaxaca Valley to the rugged mountains, oak-pine woodlands, and cloud forest. Many species of birds can be found in this southern part of Mexico.

TOUR OPERATORS

Earthwatch. 14 days / $ (from Oaxaca) / January, February. "Encyclopedia Botanica" is a research trip to survey the trees and shrubs of the cool, mountain habitats of southern Mexico. Volunteers set up study plots, then map, measure, and collect plant specimens.

VENT. 10 days / $$ (from Oaxaca) / December. Although this is a birding tour, some time is spent enjoying the famous holiday celebrations. Maximum of 14 participants.

Wings

9 days / $$ (from Oaxaca) / December. A birdwatching tour, but some time is spent visiting ruins and enjoying the holiday festivities. Maximum of 14 participants.

16 days / $$ (from Oaxaca) / March. "Oaxaca and Chiapas" more fully explores the birdlife of this rich region. (This trip may be taken in sections: 8 days for the Oaxaca section; 8 days for Chiapas.)

El Triunfo

In the high mountains of southern Mexico is a beautiful valley. The abundant rainfall and fertile soil of this region have produced one of the world's most remarkable cloud forests, where ferns reach the height of trees, and the trees are laden with orchids. Birds are everywhere. A Biosphere Reserve, El Triunfo is home to the Horned Guan, without question one of the rarest and most endangered of our birds.

TOUR OPERATORS

Earthwatch. 14 days / $ (from Veracruz City) / January–March, July, August. "Vanishing Rain Forests of Mexico" is a research trip whose mission is to find out how big a forest must be in order for animals to survive there. Volunteers, based at

Los Tuxtlas Biological Station, help determine which forest fragments are supporting the greatest number of species. At least 320 bird species, 90 mammal species, 100 reptile species, and 600 tree species live within the reserve.

Field Guides. 12 days / $$ (from Mexico City) / February. This is a camping and birdwatching trip. Well over 300 species of birds can be seen, although a special effort is made to find the Horned Guan. The cost includes a $100 tax-deductible donation to El Triunfo. Maximum of 12 participants, 2 leaders.

Foundation for Field Research. 14 days / $ (from San Diego) / December–January, April. There are two research projects: "Howler Monkeys of the Chiapas," which is based in Tuxtla Gutiérrez; and "Quetzal Quest," which is actually based in El Triunfo.

VENT. 10 days / $$ (from Cancun) / March. This is a camping and birdwatching trip. Well over 300 species of birds can be seen. The cost includes a tax-deductible contribution to El Triunfo. Maximum of 14 participants, 2 leaders.

The Yucatán Peninsula

Flat and rocky, dry and covered with brush, the Yucatán Peninsula juts north from the lowlands of southeastern Mexico. Ten endemic species of birds make their home here, while on nearby Cozumel Island (perhaps best known for its beach resorts) there are three additional endemics: the Cozumel Wren, Cozumel Thrasher, and Cozumel Vireo. In addition, the coastal village of Celestun is home to a colony of 6,000 flamingos.

Most birdwatching trips also visit Palenque, located at the foot of the Yucatán Peninsula, just inland from the vast marshes of the Usumacinta River. Palenque's magnificent Mayan ruins are set against a backdrop of tropical forest where North American warblers and other migratory birds share the trees with neotropical residents including toucans, parrots, and antbirds.

TOUR OPERATORS

Far Flung Adventures. 10 days / $$ (from Villahermosa) / January–April. A raft trip down the Usumacinta River. Surrounded by North America's largest remaining tropical rain forest, the Usumacinta is home to Howler Monkeys and Scarlet Macaws. This is a Class III trip, 105 miles in length.

Massachusetts Audubon Society. 10 days / $$ (from Miami) / February. This is a general natural history trip with an emphasis on birding.

Motmot Nature Tours. 11 days / \$\$\$ (from Cozumel) / January. A birdwatching trip to the Yucatán and Palenque. Special attention is given to searching for endemics.

Questers. 15 days / \$\$\$ (from Mérida) / October, December–February. General natural history trips with some sight-seeing.

VENT. 14 days / \$\$ (from Cozumel) / February. "Palenque, Yucatán, and Cozumel" is a birdwatching trip. Special efforts are made to find the endemic species. In addition, the tour visits three of the finest Mayan ruins: Chichen Itza, Uxmal, and Palenque. Maximum of 14 participants, 2 leaders.

Wings

8 days / \$\$ (from Villahermosa) / November. "A Week at Palenque" is a birdwatching trip. Participants regularly see over 200 species of birds. Maximum of 7 participants per leader.

15 days / \$\$ (from Mérida) / January. "Palenque and the Yucatán" is also a birding trip. Owing to more varied habitats and a longer stay, more species can be expected on this tour. The ruins of Chichen Itza, Uxmal, and Palenque are visited. Maximum of 7 participants per leader.

GUATEMALA

A culturally rich country, Guatemala is small (about 42,042 square miles, or the size of Ohio), although it is the third largest of the Central American republics. Mountains divide Guatemala into four regions: the Petén, the central highlands, the Atlantic littoral, and the southern coast. The Petén is the large "panhandle" between Mexico and Honduras, similar in habitat to the Yucatán Peninsula, and with the major Mayan ruin of Tikal. (Some trips to Belize include a trip to Tikal. For those, see the section on Belize and Honduras, page 77.) The central highlands are a series of mountains and high plateaus, with an imposing chain of volcanos and picture-perfect lakes such as Atitlán. The coastal regions are lowlands, dissected by numerous streams.

Environmentally, the country retains a large percentage of its forests, although there is steady cutting to provide farmland for the country's growing population. At present there remains an incredible diversity of species and exceptional natural history opportunities.

It is fitting, then, that this Latin American country proudly sports its national bird—the Resplendent Quetzal. A magnificent bird, the quetzal is emerald green, with a crimson breast and three-foot-long tail streamers—nearly twice the size of the bird's body! In pre-Columbian times, the cult of Quetzalcoatl flourished. Even today, images of the quetzal are everywhere—in legends, in movies, and on textiles. The country's currency is the quetzal; Quezaltenango is a major city. Yet, ironically, the quetzal is endangered. It has nearly been extirpated from Mexico—a few survive in El Triunfo (see the section on Mexico, page 67). In Guatemala, they receive some protection; it's illegal to kill them, at least, and the Biotopo del Quetzal—a refuge—has recently been established.

TOUR OPERATORS

Field Guides

9 days / $$ (from Guatemala City) / March. This is a birdwatching trip to the highlands, where many rare birds can be found. Two days are spent at the Biotopo del Quetzal, the cloud forest habitat of the Resplendent Quetzal. You then go to volcano-ringed Lake Atitlán, where the extremely local Belted Flycatcher is seen and Flame-colored Tanagers sing on the hillside. A stop is made at the famous handcraft market in Chichicastenango before going on to Quezaltenango. In the cloud forest just south of the city flocks of Pink-headed Warblers are easily seen as well as various thrushes and hummingbirds. The Resplendent Quetzal is often here, too, flying back and forth in the gorge. Other unusual birds spotted on this trip include Highland Guan, Rufous-browed Wren, Spotted Nightingale-Thrush, and Prevost's Ground-Sparrow. Maximum of 14 participants, 2 leaders.

7 days / $$ (from Guatemala City) / March. A birding trip to Tikal, though it may be taken in conjunction with the Guatemalan Highlands trip (above). Maximum of 14 participants, 2 leaders.

Focus on Nature Tours. 9 days / $$ (from Guatemala City) / April. This is a birdwatching tour to the highlands and Tikal. Birds of particular interest (seen on past tours) include Barred Forest-Falcon, Ocellated Turkey, Scarlet Macaw, Fulvous Owl, Resplendent Quetzal, Northern Royal Flycatcher, and Prevost's Ground-Sparrow.

International Research Expeditions. 14 days / $ (from Tikal) / May–July. This is a research trip to Tikal. Teams record the vocalizations of the more than 300 species of birds to be found here. A week-long canoe trip down the Monkey River concludes the expedition.

Questers. 16 days / $$ (from Houston) / November, December, February, March. A combination cultural and general natural history trip to the highlands, Tikal, and Copán.

Sierra Club. 14 days / $$ (from Guatemala City) / February. All Sierra Club trips are for members only. Guatemala is a frequent destination of the Sierra Club;

recent trips have included a trip to the highlands, with a visit to the Biotopo's cloud forest where the Resplendent Quetzal can be seen. Cultural sites and markets are also visited.

VENT. 14 days / $$ (from Belize City) / March. This is a birdwatching trip by raft, 200 miles down the Usumacinta, a tropical river that flows by numerous Mayan ruins in the heart of the largest remaining lowland rain forest in Central America, in Guatemala's Petén region. Be on the lookout for Scarlet Macaw, White-whiskered Puffbird, Rufous-tailed Jacamar, Blue-crowned Motmot, Black-headed Trogon, and Thrushlike Manakin, among many other species. Maximum of 16 participants.

BELIZE AND HONDURAS

From reefs to rain forests, the tiny country of Belize offers a wide variety of natural history experiences. The coral reef that extends along the country's entire Caribbean coast is the second longest in the world and is recognized as one of the finest diving and snorkeling sites.

There's a wild side to Belize as well. Inland, in the jungle, a frequent destination of many birdwatching trips is Chan Chich (which means "little bird" in Mayan) Lodge. One of the best-known conservation efforts is the Programme for Belize. Established as a nonprofit Belizean company, it has protected—and continues to protect—the country's tropical forests, home to jaguars, hundreds of species of birds, and a wide variety of flora and fauna. Most trips to Belize divide their time between the rain forest and the reef; a few concentrate on one or the other.

Nearby Honduras is also becoming an ecotour destination. There's good snorkeling on its extensive Caribbean coast, and a number of marine mammals can also be seen there.

TOUR OPERATORS

American Museum of Natural History. 10 days / $$$$ (from Belize City) / February. This is a cruise aboard the 41-cabin *Polaris* visiting the Yucatán (Mexico) and Honduras coast in addition to Belize. A marine biologist accompanies the trip.

Betchart Expeditions. 11 days / $$$ (from Belize City) / January, November. This is a general natural history trip visiting Crooked Tree Wildlife Sanctuary, Chan Chich, and Ambergris Caye (on the reef); a visit is also made to nearby Tikal (in Guatemala).

Biological Journeys. 11 days / $$$ (from Belize City) / March–April. Bird-watching and snorkeling are combined on this trip.

Birdquest. 14 days / $$$ (from Belize City) / March. This is a birdwatching trip with most of the time spent inland. About 300 species of birds can be expected, including many tanagers, orioles, wrens, parrots, and hummingbirds. Two days are spent at both Chan Chich and Tikal. At the end of the trip, participants go to Saint George's Caye out on the reef for shorebirding and snorkeling. Maximum of 16 participants, 2 leaders.

Caligo Ventures. 8 days / $$$ (from Belize City) / January. A general natural history trip, including a stay at Chan Chich Lodge. Visits are also made to Mayan ruins.

Cox & Kings. 14 days / $$$ (from London, England) / January–December. General natural history trips to study the birds, mammals, butterflies, marine life, and plants of Belize. An extension to Chan Chich is offered. A donation is made to the Programme for Belize for each participant.

Earthwatch. 12 days / $ (from Dangriga, Belize) / February, March. "Belize's Barrier Reef" is a scientific expedition that seeks to understand the community structure of the reef. The trip focuses on Moray Eel and Squirrelfish, two nocturnal predators.

Field Guides. 8 days / $$$ (from Belize City) / May, July. This is a birdwatching trip to Chan Chich Lodge, where over 300 species of birds can be seen. An optional 2-day extension to look for the Keel-billed Motmot is offered. Maximum 14 participants.

International Expeditions. 5–14 days / $$ (from Miami) / January–December. International Expeditions offers a variety of natural history trips that visit the rain forest, reef, and some Mayan ruins as well. Extensions to Chan Chich, the Cockscomb Basin Jaguar Preserve, and Copán (in Honduras) are also available.

International Oceanographic Foundation. 9 days / $$ (from Belize City) / August. This is a general natural history trip run by Mountain Travel/Sobek for the IOF. Several days are spent at the jungle lodge Chan Chich.

International Zoological Expeditions. 7–14 days / $–$$ (from Belize City) / January, March, April, August, December. This company specializes in tours to

Belize, offering a variety of birding, diving, and natural history trips. Extensions to Tikal are included.

Journeys

9 days / $$ (from Belize City) / February–April. General natural history trips with visits to Chan Chich and the Cockscomb Jaguar Reserve. Extensions to the ruins at Tikal and/or Copán (Honduras) are available.

7 days / $$ (from Belize City) / January–December. A "Marine Mammal Odyssey" to Honduras. You stay at the Institute for Marine Sciences in Roatan. The trip includes an opportunity to swim with dolphins at Bailey's Key. This trip is ideally suited for families.

Massachusetts Audubon Society. 9–11 days / $$–$$$ (from Miami) / February. This is a natural history trip with an emphasis on birdwatching. A visit is also made to Tikal.

Mountain Travel/Sobek

10 days / $$ (from Belize City) / January–December. Suitable for families, this trip features walks in the jungle and visits to the Ix Chel Mayan herb farm and Mayan ruins.

9 days/ $$ (from Belize City) / January–April. "Belize Barrier Reef" is a snorkeling expedition, via sea kayak, to various locations on the 175-mile-long reef. A local fisherman accompanies the trip, sharing his knowledge of the sea and local culture.

Nature Expeditions International. 10 days / $$ (from Belize City) / February, April, December. Natural history trips concentrating on the mammals and birds of the Cockscomb Reserve and the marine life of the barrier reef. A visit is made to the Mayan ruins of Xunantunich.

Oceanic Society Expeditions. 8 days / $$ (from Belize City) / April, June, November. This snorkeling trip to Lighthouse Reef atoll includes visits to the nearby Half Moon Caye Natural Monument, a bird sanctuary. You also visit the Blue Hole, made famous by a Cousteau documentary for its unique stalagmites. Maximum of 15 participants.

See & Sea

7 days / $$ (from Belize City) / January–December. A live-aboard dive trip to Lighthouse Reef atoll, where you'll dive among lovely coral gardens with rays, turtles, and big schools of colorful fish.

7 days / $$ (from Belize City) / January–December. A live-aboard dive trip in the waters of Roatan Bay, Honduras.

Sierra Club. 9 days / $$ (from Belize City) / February. For members only. This is a general interest trip with a visit to Tikal included. Time is spent snorkeling on the reef and learning about local conservation issues.

The Nature Conservancy. 7 days / $$$ (from Miami) / June. This is an ecology workshop on the barrier reef, run by International Expeditions. A Nature Conservancy representative accompanies the trip, and costs include a tax-deductible contribution to the Nature Conservancy. A 13-day, general natural history trip is available at comparable cost.

VENT. 7 days / $$ (from Belize City) / February, July, November, December. VENT runs about six birding trips a year to Chan Chich Lodge, a comfortable lodge set in a private reserve surrounded by tropical forest.

Voyagers International. 10 days / $$$ (from Belize City) / April. This is a diving, snorkeling, and natural history trip.

Wildlife Conservation Society. 8 days / $$$$ (from New York) / April. This is a general natural history trip including visits to the Baboon Sanctuary, Cockscomb Jaguar Reserve, Ambergris Caye, and Chan Chich. An optional extension to Tikal is available. Maximum 16 participants; a NYZS naturalist accompanies the trip.

Wings. 7–13 days / $$ (from Belize City) / February–April. Birdwatching tours to either Belize and Tikal or to Belize and Chan Chich Lodge. Birdwatching weeks at Chan Chich Lodge are also offered.

COSTA RICA

Nature lovers have been going to Costa Rica for years; in fact, this tiny country (about the size of West Virginia) practically pioneered ecotourism. With approximately 12 percent of its land set aside as preserves, Costa Rica has made conservation and wildlife protection a top priority. Owing to its position on the isthmus and its diversity of habitat, Costa Rica is home to about 8 percent of the world's flora and fauna: 12,000 species of plants, including 1,500 orchids; 350 reptiles; and over 830 birds. Ten percent of the world's butterflies are here, too. Trips to Costa Rica focus on the country's natural wealth, with birding tours of variable length, as well as research trips and naturalist treks.

The national park system consists of forty-five separate areas, with at least one example of each of twelve ecosystems represented. For instance, Santa Rosa, the first park to be established, covers 260 acres near the Pacific Ocean and protects ten different habitats, from beaches and mangroves to dry forests and wooded savannahs. The wildlife includes monkeys, anteaters, coatimundis, peccaries, and deer. Hiking trails are marked through the savannah and to a seacoast sanctuary for the Ridley Pacific Turtle. At 716-acre Manuel Antonio National Park, on the Pacific coast, the beach vegetation is inhabited by Iguanas and Squirrel Monkeys. Tortuguero National Park on the Caribbean coast protects the nesting grounds of the endangered Green Sea Turtle and serves as home for Two- and Three-toed Sloths, Manatee, and Crocodile. One of the most popular parks is Poas Volcano National Park, which provides visitors the opportunity to explore a live volcano. Add to these the parks and lodges in the higher elevations and you have an extensive network for naturalist adventures.

In the lowland tropical forest of the northeast is La Selva Biological Reserve, a field station. Selva Verde Lodge is nearby and offers comfortable accommodations. Both the lodge and the reserve have extensive trails and are favorite stops for many birding tours. Less well-known but equally rewarding is Tiskita Jungle Lodge with its 400 acres including a biological station and a tropical fruit farm. On the southwestern Pacific Coast, Tiskita has over 250 acres of virgin rain forest, with an extensive trail system. In addition to 285 species of birds, there is the chance to see the endangered Squirrel Monkey. Many trips also visit the 4,000-acre Monteverde Cloud Forest, a private biological reserve that is a primary spot for seeing the Resplendent Quetzal. In addition, there are several private lodges in the rain forest, some of which are visited by the tours listed here.

TOUR OPERATORS

American Museum of Natural History. 14 days / $$$ (from San Jose) / February. On this natural history trip you'll have the chance to see the wildlife of Costa Rica—from coral reefs at Cahuita National Park to the Resplendent Quetzal of Monteverde. A museum naturalist accompanies the trip.

Betchart Expeditions. 13 days / $$ (from San Jose) / December, January. An introduction to the wildlife of Costa Rica.

Birdquest. 21 days / $$ (from San Jose) / August. An intensive birdwatching trip visiting all the major reserves and parks as well as the farm of Dr. Alexander Skutch, the dean of Costa Rican ornithology. Maximum of 16 participants.

BirdWatch Costa Rica. 7–21 days / $–$$ (from San Jose) / January–December. Personalized trips to various lodges in all the major regions of Costa Rica—from Tiskita Lodge on the Pacific Coast to Monteverde to the Arenal Observatory Lodge. Some trips have preset itineraries, others are customized.

Caligo Ventures. 9 days / $$ (from San Jose) / March. A general natural history trip visiting Poas, Monteverde, and Manuel Antonio National Park.

Caribbean Conservation Corporation. 10–17 days / $$ (from Miami) / March–September. This is the famous volunteer research program at Tortuguero National Park. From March through June volunteers work with Leatherback Turtles, while Green Sea Turtles are tagged by teams from July through September. The program is administered by the Massachusetts Audubon Society. A portion of the cost is tax-deductible.

Canadian Nature Tours. 14 days / $$ (from Toronto) / April. A natural history trip to the forests of Costa Rica.

Cheeseman's Ecology Safaris. 15 days / $$ (from San Jose) / March. Two trips are offered, both covering the major ecosystems. Over 300 species of birds, 4 species of monkey, plus other mammals including armadillos, sloths, and coati-mundis can be seen. Maximum of 10 people, 2 leaders.

Cox & Kings. 10 days / $$ (from San Jose) / January–April (southern); July–December (northern). Three trips are offered: the "Eco Explorer Cruise" is aboard the *Temptress*; "Southern Eco Explorer" and "Northern Eco Explorer" are general natural history trips. Different regions of Costa Rica are covered: The southern trip focuses on the national parks, while the northern trip provides excellent opportunity for divers and concentrates on marine life.

Denver Museum of Natural History. 11 days / $$ (from San Jose) / July. A comprehensive overview of the natural history and ecology of Costa Rica. The tour includes a 2-day symposium on rain forests at the museum.

Earthwatch

14 days / $ (from Monteverde) / March–June. "Dancing Birds" is a study of the Long-tailed Manakin and its courtship behavior. Teams mist-net and radio-track the birds, locate nests, and observe males on dance perches (from blinds).

14 days / $ (from San Vito) / March–May. "Tropical Forest Invaders" studies deforestation and the effects that exotic (nonnative) species of plants have on the rain forest. Teams select and prepare experimental sites and measure damage from herbivores, as well as monitor hummingbirds—a prime pollinator. Based in southern Costa Rica, this area is home to a troop of White-faced Capuchin Monkeys and many spectacular birds including trogons, manakins, motmots, parrots, and toucans.

14 days / $ (from Guanacaste) / January, February. "Tropical Dry Forest" is based in Guanacaste, on the Pacific slope of northwestern Costa Rica. Here,

volunteers help scientists understand how the forest copes regularly with six months of drought. Teams moniter soil and tree moisture content. The dry season is an ideal time to view this region's beautiful flowers and abundant wildlife, which includes monkeys, tapirs, peccaries, and over 100 bird species.

14 days / $$ (from Golfito) / January–December. "Costa Rica Dolphins" teams search for dolphins from a boat and record their behavior with a video camera in a effort to study how these marine mammals survive in such a harsh environment.

Escapes Unlimited. 7 days / $$ (from Los Angeles) / January. This is a general natural history trip, visiting the ocean, cloud forest, and volcanos. Suitable for families; limited to 20 participants.

Field Guides

16 days / $$ (from San Jose) / March. On this birdwatching trip, participants may expect to see nearly 500 species of birds including Wrenthrush, Highland Tinamou, Sunbittern, Vermiculated Screech-Owl, 35 or more species of hummingbirds, Prong-billed Barbet, and the Resplendent Quetzal. A feature of the trip is a visit to Los Cusingos, Dr. Alexander Skutch's farm.

10 days / $$$ (from San Jose) / December. "Holiday Costa Rica" is also a birding trip. Somewhat different species are seen.

Focus on Nature Tours

9 days / $$ (from San Jose) / March. A birding tour to southern Costa Rica, including a stay at Tiskita Jungle Lodge, Corcovado National Park, and Las Cruces Biological Station. Four species of monkey can be seen along with over 300 species of birds, some endemic to southern Costa Rica and adjacent Panama. Maximum of 14 participants.

7 days / $ (from San Jose) / January–December. A birding tour to Rara Avis, a lodge in the north, and Tiskita Lodge, on the Pacific coast in the south. Over 300 species of birds can be seen. English-speaking guides at the lodges accompany you.

10 days / $–$$ (from San Jose) / March, April. A birding tour to northern Costa Rica. You'll visit Tapanti and Cano Negro Wildlife Reserves, Laguna del Lagarto, and Los Angeles Cloud Forest Reserve, where Resplendent Quetzal can be seen.

Geo Expeditions. 10 days / $$ (from San Jose) / February, March, August, December. General natural history trips to Poas Volcano National Park, Monteverde Reserve, and Corcovado National Park on the Osa Peninsula. Included is a day trip to Isla del Caño, which has the largest concentration of coral-building organisms along the Pacific. Maximum of 15 participants.

Geostar. 10 days / $$ (from San Jose) / March–December. In addition to running trips for the Nature Conservancy, Geostar takes other groups to Costa Rica. The

"Explorer" is a general nature trip to various parks and reserves; other trips are offered as well.

Holbrook Travel. 8 days / $$ (from Miami) / January–December. Holbrook runs various natural history trips to Costa Rica. Its "Rainforest, Mangroves, Beaches, and Cloud Forest" trip departs weekly throughout the year and includes a stay at the Selva Verde Lodge.

Innerasia Expeditions. 10–16 days / $$ (from San Jose) / January–March, July, September–November. "Costa Rican Wildlife" includes visits to the Monteverde Cloud Forest Reserve and Manuel Antonio, Corcovado, and Tortuguero National Parks.

International Oceanographic Foundation. 10 days / $$$ (from San Jose)/ April. The trip concentrates on observing and identifying sea life and visits Monteverde, Volcan Poas, and Santa Rosa National Park as well.

International Research Expeditions. 10 days / $ (from San Jose) / March, June–August. This is a research project focusing on bird vocalizations. Volunteers assist with acoustic sound-recording equipment, binocular identification, and notetaking.

Journeys. 10 days / $$ (from San Jose) / January–December. Journeys runs monthly trips to Costa Rica, including some that are specially designed for families. The "Tropical Trails Less Traveled" program is for independent travelers. The "Tropical Odyssey" is an 11-day trip offered from December to April, while the "Tortuguero Jungle Odyssey" (10 days in July and August) features midnight beach walks to see turtles. The 10-day "Family Odyssey" is offered year-round (there is a discount for children).

Massachusetts Audubon Society

10–13 days / $$$ (from Miami) / February, March. Three trips are offered, each with a different point of view: One is a general natural history trip, one concentrates on birdwatching, and the third specializes in marine life. Local guides assist MAS naturalists.

9 days / $$$$ (from San Jose) / December. A cruise through the Panama Canal and on to the tropical rain forest of Darién (Panama) and Costa Rica's Marenco Biological Reserve, Poas, and Manuel Antonio National Park. Aboard the 80-passenger M.S. *Polaris*.

Michael Snow. Michael Snow specializes in guided tours of Costa Rica's national parks and wildlife preserves. There are both fixed and custom itineraries visiting the Atlantic slope, Guanacaste, the central Pacific coast, and the southern Pacific coast. All trips have a maximum of 10 participants. Birds and butterflies are Snow's specialty, and he is quite willing to work at night to find owls and turtles as well. A visit to Dr. Alexander Skutch's private reserve can be arranged. Costs vary considerably, depending on accommodation chosen and length of trip desired. Two days at Selva Verde can run to about $150 per person, including all meals; hotels and pensions at Monteverde range from $30 to $60 a day, including meals.

Motmot Nature Tours. 12 days / $$ (from San Jose) / January, March. Two birding trips, both of which include visits to the Tapanti Biological Reserve, Cerro de la Muerte (a good place to find the Resplendent Quetzal), the Carara Biological Station, Los Cusingos, and several of the major national parks. Local biologists assist the (U.S.) leaders.

Mountain Travel/Sobek. 9 days / $$ (from San Jose) / December–July. "Natural History of Costa Rica" visits the major parks and reserves. In Monteverde Cloud Forest Reserve an effort is made to find the Resplendent Quetzal. The trip concludes with a visit to Poas Volcano and its bubbling geysers.

National Audubon Society. 9 days / $$$ (from Miami) / January. This is an International Ecology Workshop. Costa Rica is the perfect backdrop for studying the dynamics of tropical forest systems and the conservation problems associated with these highly threatened ecosystems. The program covers several major conservation issues including preservation of tropical forests and wetlands, the problems posed for migratory birds, and the role of ecotourism in the environmental movement.

Nature Expeditions International. 15 days / $$ (from San Jose) / January, March, July, December. These are wildlife trips that visit nature reserves and national parks.

Nature World Explorations. 11 days / $$ (from San Jose) / August, December. This company specializes in natural history trips to Costa Rica, with an emphasis on birdwatching. On a Christmas tour, it would not be unusual to see 50 or more birds in a single tree. A feature of the Christmas trip is a visit to Dr. Alexander Skutch's farm, where Fiery-billed Aracaris and Bay-headed Tanagers can be seen in the yard. In August, a 3-day extension to Marenco Biological Station is offered (extra cost). Maximum of 16 participants, 2 leaders.

New Jersey Audubon Society. 14 days / $$$+ (from New York) / March. NJAS offers a cruise of both the Caribbean and Pacific shores of Costa Rica and Panama aboard the 138-passenger *Yorktown Clipper*.

Oceanic Society Expeditions. 14 days / $$ (from San Jose) / April. A natural history trip visiting Poas Volcano, Monteverde, La Selva Biological Preserve, Tortuguero National Park, and other parks and reserves. This trip is cosponsored by Golden Gate Raptor Observatory and is limited to 20 participants.

Overseas Adventure Travel. 8 days / $$ (from San Jose) / February–April, July, August, November, December (some departures are for singles only). Monteverde Reserve and Tortuguero National Park are among the destinations visited. A longer trip, including 3 days of whitewater rafting, is also offered.

Questers. 15 days / $$ (from San Jose) / November–March. Natural history trips visiting Tortuguero, Palo Verde, Santa Rosa, and Braulio Carillo National Parks as well as Monteverde Reserve. Participants will see birds, turtles, and mammals as they explore this country's twelve life zones.

See & Sea. 10 days / $$$ (from San Jose) / January–December. This is a diving trip (on a 12-to-14-passenger live-aboard) to Cocos Island, located in the Pacific off the coast of Costa Rica. You'll dive among schools of hammerheads numbering in the hundreds, and have a good chance of seeing White-tipped Shark, Marbled Ray, Manta, Sailfish, Wahoo, and even Whale Shark.

Sierra Club. 14 days / $$$ (from San Jose) / June. This trip (for members only) allows you to experience three different endangered tropical ecosystems: the cloud forest at Monteverde, a Pacific dry forest (also in Costa Rica), and the Cuyabepo Nature Reserve, an Amazon rain forest in Ecuador. Local ecology is studied, and you also observe and discuss the impact of human population on these areas.

Smithsonian. 12 days / $ (from San Jose) / July, September. This is a research trip to study Arenal Volcano. Volunteers monitor Arenal twenty-four hours a day; they also collect ash samples and plants.

Temptress Cruises. 6 days / $$$ (from San Jose) / (northern route) June–September; (southern route) November–March. A 174-foot, 33-cabin cruise ship tours the Pacific coast of Costa Rica, visiting different national parks on each of the routes. Daily landings are made, and local naturalists lead walks through a variety of habitats. Many birds and mammals are routinely seen. The northern cruise is good for observing a wealth of marine life. Participants on the southern cruise can expect to see Scarlet Macaw, Wood Stork, and Golden-hooded Tanager, as well as all four species of Central American monkeys.

The Nature Conservancy

7 days / $$$ (from Miami) / June. A rain forest ecology workshop at Tortuguero National Park, handled by International Expeditions. A Conservancy representative accompanies the trip.

10–16 days / $$$ (from San Jose) / June, November. Two general natural history trips, handled by Geostar (see above). A Conservancy representative accompanies trips. Costs include a contribution to the Nature Conservancy; all trips include visits by local conservation experts as well as the services of a trained in-country naturalist.

University Research Expedition Program, University of California at Berkeley. 14 days / $ (from San Jose) / June. This is a study trip to Lomas Bar-budal, a dry forest in northeastern Costa Rica. Participants observe, track, and record the behavior of birds and insects found there.

VENT. 10–18 days / $$ (from San Jose) / January, March–May, July, December. There are five birdwatching trips: "Grand Costa Rica," which visits the four major regions of the country; "Short Costa Rica," which goes to Monteverde and La Selva; "Costa Rica Highlands," and a New Year's and summer trip as well. Each trip produces different birds—quetzals, guans, barbets, cotingas, wrens, and hummingbirds. Maximum of 14 participants, 2 leaders.

Voyagers International. 10–16 days / $$–$$$ (from Miami) / December–March. Voyagers offers many trips, including an ecology trip with a special refor-estation project, a horticulture workshop sponsored by Harvard and Cornell universities, and a trip focusing on geology and marine biology.

Wilderness Travel. 9–14 days / $$ (from San Jose) / December–March, July, August. "Costa Rica Wildlife" is a two-week natural history trip visiting Tor-tuguero Park, La Selva Biological Reserve, and the Monteverde Cloud Forest Reserve. A rafting and rain forest trip are offered as well.

Wings. 7–21 days / $$–$$$ (from San Jose) / February, March, October. These are birdwatching trips, and one can expect to see about 350 species of birds on a two-week trip. A special feature of the Wings trips is a visit to Dr. Alexander Skutch, the dean of Costa Rican ornithology, at Los Cusingos. All the important parks and reserves are visited as well.

Wonderbird Tours. 8–15 days / $$ (from New York or Miami) / June. Two bird-ing tours that cover nearly all the habitats and biological regions of the country.

At least 400 species of birds are regularly seen. Maximum of 12 participants, 2 leaders.

Woodstar Tours. 9–14 days / $$–$$$ (from Miami) / January–March. Bird-watching tours. The guides are residents of Costa Rica and are extraordinarily familiar with the avifauna of their country. Participants visit rain forest, cloud forest, beaches, and active volcanos, and take the famous jungle train in Poas Volcano National Park.

World Wildlife Fund. 14 days / $$$ (from Miami) / April. On this general natural history trip you'll have the opportunity to learn firsthand about WWF's twenty-eight-year involvement with conservation in Costa Rica. From Poas Volcano to Monteverde, from Santa Rosa National Park to Carara Biological Reserve—all the major parks and reserves will be visited.

Zegrahm Expeditions. 14–17 days / $$$+ (from San Jose) / April, September, October. General natural history cruises offered in conjunction with Clipper Adventure Cruises to Costa Rica and Panama (or Costa Rica and Mexico).

PANAMA

For many Americans, Panama is only a canal, a shipping shortcut that has lost much of its relevance, especially now that the United States no longer controls the canal. But the canal cuts through only part of the 375-mile-long country that is Panama—a land of tropical rain forests, upland forests, savannahs, and coastal mangroves. As the VENT catalog explains: "Tiny Panama [is] the land bridge where the fauna and flora of two great continents intermingle. . . ."

With that in mind, it is easy to see why for years Panama was a favorite destination for naturalists. After all, it is home to 900 species of birds, 1,500 species of trees, and 10,000 species of plants. And now that the political situation has stabilized, there are increasing numbers of people heading for the lowland forests of the former Canal Zone, as well as the more formidable jungle of Darién and the heights of the Pirre Mountains.

TOUR OPERATORS

Caligo Ventures. 9 days / $$ (from Panama City) / February. A general natural history trip visiting the highlands of Chiriqui, the cloud forest of Baru Volcano, and Amisted National Park. An extension to the San Blas Islands is offered.

Field Guides

9 days / $$$ (from Panama City) / December. A birdwatching trip to Cerro Pirre and the highland habitats of Darién. Be sure to look for the Viridian Dacnis

and Black-tipped Cotinga in the flowering Immortelle trees. This trip involves some camping. Maximum of 14 participants.

16 days / $$ (from Panama City) / March. A birding trip that traverses the country from the rain forests of the former Canal Zone to the peaks in the highlands of Chiriqui. About 500 species of birds can be expected, as well as mammals such as the Kinkajou, Olingo, and various sloths. Among the birds are a dozen species of parrots, 30 hummingbirds, 9 trogons, 6 toucans, and 40 tanagers. Three-wattled Bellbird, Resplendent Quetzal, and Snowy Cotinga can also be seen. Maximum of 14 participants.

International Expeditions. 10 days / $$ (from Miami) / January–March. Four general natural-history trips. A visit to the Panama Canal is included.

Massachusetts Audubon Society. (See the section on Costa Rica, page 84.)

Mountain Travel/Sobek. 10 days / $$ (from Panama City) / January, March, October, December. Here's a chance to become knowledgeable about one of the decade's foremost challenges: the maintenance of our delicate ecosystems. ANCON, a local nonprofit conservation organization working with the Nature Conservancy, and the Smithsonian Tropical Research Institute, which is based in Panama, are working to save this environment. The trip will include visits to their research sites, including a marine biological laboratory and a nature reserve.

VENT. 9 days / $$ (from Panama City) / January. A birdwatching trip to the lowlands of Panama. Participants may expect to see about 400 species of birds, including Blue Cotinga, Red-capped Manakin, Ornate Hawk-Eagle, White-throated Crake, Great Jacamar, and Yellow-eared Toucanet. Many species of shorebirds, hummingbirds, and tanagers will also be seen. Mammals include several species of sloths, Marmoset, Kinkajou, and Howler Monkey. Maximum of 14 participants.

Woodstar Tours. 8 days / $$ (from Panama City) / January–April. Birdwatching trips. Highlights include a visit to Soberania National Park, home to 230 species of birds; a visit to the Smithsonian Tropical Research Institute; a look at the Panama Canal; and a trip to Isla Barro Colorado—a 12,000-acre national monument that is the oldest tropical forest reserve in the Western Hemisphere. Barro Colorado has Tapir, Black Howler Monkey, and many other animals, as well as 300 species of butterflies and hundreds of birds. A representative of the Panama Audubon Society accompanies the trip. An optional 2-day pretour extension to the San Blas Islands is available.

THE CARIBBEAN ISLANDS

The playground of North America, the Caribbean Sea and its islands have attracted tourists for centuries. Most people come to enjoy the warm waters and balmy breezes, relishing the escape from wintertime blues and snow. But beyond the beaches are mangrove lagoons, tropical rain forests, and highland valleys that hold botanical and zoological treasures.

The islands were far richer many years ago. At the time of Columbus, there were nearly thirty species of endemic parrots, for example; now only about twelve remain. The causes for such a decline include loss of habitat, conflicts with exotic (nonnative) species, harvesting for the pet trade, and natural disasters (mostly hurricanes—Hurricane Hugo, in 1989, wiped out half the population of the Puerto Rican Parrot). Nevertheless, many of the Caribbean islands are well worth a natural history trip.

Bahamas and Turks and Caicos Islands

Barely a hop from Florida's south coast, the Bahamas stretch southeastward toward Haiti and the Dominican Republic. At the tip of the Bahamas are the Turks and Caicos Islands.

The tours listed here mostly ply the waters around the less visited Bahama Islands. Along with the Turks and Caicos, these are well-known for their lush coral gardens and many species of tropical fish. Birdwatchers should note that the Bahama Parrot is found only on Great Abaco and Great Inagua islands.

TOUR OPERATORS

Bottom Time Adventures. 5–10 days / $$ (from Fort Lauderdale) / May–December. The *Bottom Time II,* a 30-passenger (live-aboard) catamaran, specializes in dives at remote locations in the Bahamas. Featured are video dives, dolphin swims, dolphin dives, and wall diving in the Near Bahamas. Stops are frequently made in Bimini as well.

Canadian Nature Tours. 7 days / $$ (from Fort Lauderdale) / February, November. This is part of the Ottawa Canada Banding Group's bird-banding project in the Bahamas. Based on Andros Island, the study group works from the Forfar Field Station. Resident bird populations are documented, but a special effort is made to search for wintering Kirtland's Warbler. Maximum of 10 participants.

The Dream Team. 7 days / $ (from West Palm Beach) / January–December. Diving trips on the 12-passenger, live-aboard M.V. *Dream Too.* Participants are offered four to five dives a day, and the boat's standard areas of operation are the reefs in the Little Bahama Bank, north of Grand Bahama Island. Divers regularly encounter dolphins, several species of sea turtles, sharks, octopus, rays, and large schools of fish. Most reefs are healthy with live corals and colorful sponges.

Earthwatch

10 days / $ (from San Salvador, Bahamas) / July, December. "Underwater Meadows" is a research trip on San Salvador Island, Columbus's first landfall (according to some scholars) in October of 1492. Scientists are now monitoring oceanic pollution by studying the great undersea meadows of sea grass. Snorkelers collect sea grass samples, while onshore team members wash and sort the samples by species.

11 days / $$ (from Bimini Islands) / June–August. "Lemon Sharks" studies how sharks live. Little is known about the lives of sharks; this project attempts to answer the most fundamental questions by studying basic shark physiology. Teams track the sharks ultrasonically. All this takes place in the clear waters of Bimini Lagoon.

14 days / $ (from Andros Island) / January–March, May–June. "Bahamas Blue Holes" are found off Andros Island. Here, in these deep caverns, participants study the endemic freshwater Mosquitofish. Because it thrives in so many different habitats within a relatively small area, it serves as a perfect subject for the study of the evolutionary and ecological factors that shape its life history. Team members are based at the Forfar Field Station.

10 days / $$ (from Hope Town, Elbow Cay) / April, May. "Whales of the Bahamas" studies the various species of whales that live in and around the Bahamas. Teams use small outboards to photograph and record vocalizations of any sighted whales or dolphins.

International Research Expeditions. 7–14 days / $ (from Andros Island) / February, November. IRE also involves participants in the Ottawa Canada Banding Group's bird-banding project on Andros Island.

Oceanic Society Expeditions. 7 days / $$ (from the Bahamas) / May–August. The society sponsors "Bahamas: Project Dolphin," a research swim with dolphins. Travel and accommodations are aboard a 70-foot schooner. Under the guidance of a researcher, participants collect data on dolphin family and social structure, behavior and habitat requirements, and communication.

See & Sea. 7 days / $$ (from various locations in the Bahamas) / January–December. Several live-aboard diving trips are offered. The 50-foot, 6-passenger *Aquanaut* takes divers out to the reefs of the Turks and Caicos, while the somewhat larger (20-passenger) *Coral Star* plys Bahamian waters.

The Greater Antilles and Cayman Islands

South of Florida and almost directly eastward are the Greater Antilles—Cuba, Jamaica, Hispaniola (Haiti and the Dominican Republic), and Puerto Rico. Generally the islands are characterized by a central range of mountains, with long spurs that stretch toward the coast and deep valleys between them. Lagoons and mangrove swamps are common on the coast, with some area of plains inland.

Nearly all these islands have been cleared for cultivation—historically, sugarcane. Nevertheless, all have some endemic birds and other features that attract naturalists.

Situated south of central Cuba are the coral islands of Grand Cayman, Little Cayman, and Cayman Brac. They are low-lying rocky reefs, originally called Las Tortugas by Christopher Columbus because of their numerous turtles. Today, they are primarily a diving destination.

Cuba

The largest of the Antilles, Cuba has the greatest species diversity and the greatest number of endemic species, including a giant shrew, a rare crocodile, and blind cave fish. It is the last stronghold of the Ivory-billed Woodpecker, now extirpated from the United States. According to the *Environmental Almanac,* Cuba until recently had the lowest deforestation rate of any Latin American country. Of course, the situation may change now that Cuba has fallen on hard times.

Although Americans are permitted to go to Cuba, at present it is not possible to fly there from the United States; one generally flies from Canada.

TOUR OPERATORS

The Great Auk. 7 days / $$ (from Toronto) / January–April. The Great Auk specializes in birdwatching trips to Cuba, home to 388 species of birds, of which many are endemic. The trip focuses on the Zapata swamp and peninsula, a 4,000-square kilometer area that surrounds the Bay of Pigs. Of the 162 species recorded here 17 are endemic, including Gundlach's Hawk, Blue-headed Quail Dove, Cuban Parakeet, Cuban Trogon, Zapata Rail, Zapata Wren, and the tiny Bee Hummingbird, the world's smallest bird. Arturo Kirkonnell, of the National Museum of Natural History in Havana, is the Cuban ornithologist guide. Maximum of 15 participants.

Jamaica

This 4,243-square-mile island (smaller than the state of Connecticut) harbors 25 species of endemic birds—more than any other Caribbean island—and is the most productive birding area in the Antilles. It has 20 endemic lizards, 82 endemic ferns, and 784 endemic flowering plants as well. The Blue Mountains, in the east, and the

John Crow Mountains and the Cockpit Country, to the west, are among the last remaining sectors of primary growth on the island, supporting breeding Jamaican hutias, snakes, tree frogs, giant swallowtail butterflies, and many birds. Happily, the 193,260 acres of the Blue Mountains are due to become a national park, a move that may help offset the effects of general habitat destruction and pollution.

TOUR OPERATORS

Field Guides. 6 days / $$ (from Montego Bay) / April. On this birdwatching trip, the search for Jamaican specialties takes you far off the beaten tourist track—from Montego Bay and Falmouth to Cockpit Country, and finally to the Blue Mountains (famed for their coffee) in eastern Jamaica, where, in some of the island's original montane forest, you can see the Blue Mountain Vireo and the peculiar Jamaican Blackbird. There's even a chance of finding the Crested Quail-Dove along the forest's edge. Nocturnal birding may turn up the Jamaican Owl.

Field Studies Council. 14 days / $$$ (from London) / January. This is a course of special interest to geologists. The dramatic effects of weathering in the Cockpit Country as well as the fascinating metamorphic and richly fossiliferous sedimentary rock sequences are studied. Some days are spent botanizing or birdwatching.

Sunbird. 11 days / $$$ (from London) / December. A Christmastime birdwatching trip. From the Blue Mountains and the Holywell Forest Reserve to Portland Ridge (home to the irresistibly cute Jamaican Tody) and Marshall's Pen, this tour covers the island. In Cockpit Country you'll be on the lookout for Yellow-billed Parrot, Jamaican Lizard-Cuckoo, Rufous-tailed Flycatcher, and a host of other specialties. On the grounds of the hotel in Montego Bay you might see Vervain Hummingbird and Antillean Palm-Swift.

VENT. (See the section on Puerto Rico, page 95.)

Wonderbird Tours. 7 days / $$ (from New York or Miami) / April, July, September, December. These are birdwatching tours; the December trip includes an opportunity to participate in the Jamaica Christmas Bird Count. (The Christmas Bird Count is an annual event throughout the United States and in some Latin American and Caribbean countries as well. The censuses provide us with invaluable information about the status of thousands of species of birds.)

Dominican Republic

With over 800 miles of coastline, a central mountain range—the Cordillera Central—that reaches 10,000 feet, and a large valley in the north, the Dominican

Republic offers a pleasing diversity of habitat even though it does not claim endemic species.

TOUR OPERATOR

Massachusetts Audubon Society. 12 days / $$ (from Miami) / March. A general natural history trip with an emphasis on birding. The extensive coastline along both the Atlantic Ocean and the Caribbean Sea provides important resting grounds for migrating shorebirds. This trip travels the length of the island, visiting a variety of habitats and getting to know their flora and fauna.

Puerto Rico

Few countries in temperate climates can claim to have a tropical rain forest, but the United States can: The 28,000-acre Caribbean National Park—El Yunque—is a lush region in the rugged Luquillo Mountains, complete with epiphytic ferns, orchids, vines, and lianas, even a mist-enshrouded elfin forest. Puerto Rico is the tropics in our own backyard.

Although densely populated in parts, Puerto Rico has excellent reserves for flora and fauna—6,000 acres of which are under the control of the Conservation Trust of Puerto Rico. Its newest reserve—Las Cabezas de San Juan Nature Park—is on a peninsula in the northeast and includes mangroves, coastal forest, scenic beaches, coral gardens, and a phosphorescent lagoon.

TOUR OPERATORS

Earthwatch

14 days / $ (from San Juan) / January–March. "American Forest Survey" is a research trip to study forest architecture, and is run in four areas: Puerto Rico, Mexico, Michigan, and Venezuela. Volunteers lay out transects, study plots, and identify, tag, and map trees.

9 days / $$ (from Mayagüez) / January, May. This is a research trip to study the Caribbean Mongoose at Cabo Rojo Wildlife Refuge in western Puerto Rico. Although originally imported from India to control rats in the sugarcane plantations, the mongoose has wreaked havoc with many island species. One problem with mongoose control is that we know very little about the animal's biology, including its life span and its reproductive success. Team members study these and other aspects of mongoose behavior by trapping and examining them. After biologist Roy Horst implants microchips, volunteers return the animals to the wild and begin collecting data that will provide important clues to the success of these predators. Two teams also go to St. Croix, in the U.S. Virgin Islands.

Focus on Nature Tours. 9 days / $$ (from San Juan) / April. A birdwatching trip to Puerto Rico and Saint Lucia (in the Lesser Antilles). Special effort is made to find endemics, including Puerto Rican Lizard-Cuckoo, Nightjar, and Screech-Owl; Yellow-shouldered Blackbird; and Elfin Woods Warbler. A variety of hummingbirds can be seen as well. On Saint Lucia you'll visit the Edmond Forest Reserve for specialties such as the White-breasted Trembler, Rufous-throated Solitaire, and St. Lucia Parrot. In the northeastern part of the island you'll look for the rare St. Lucia Wren.

VENT. 11 days / $$ (from San Juan) / April. A birdwatching tour to Puerto Rico and Jamaica that offers an opportunity to see 38 endemic species of birds! On Puerto Rico, where the trip begins, habitats vary from rain forest to dry scrub. Participants can expect to see all 13 endemics including Puerto Rican Bullfinch, Tanager, Vireo, Lizard-Cuckoo, Parrot, Emerald (a hummingbird), Screech-Owl, Nightjar, and Tody. The Puerto Rican Tody is almost unbelievable: a four-inch Day-Glo emerald-green bird with a pink bill, pink sides, and a yellow breast. There's a similar tody on Jamaica, where the tour continues. All 25 endemics on this island are generally seen as well. The national bird—the Streamertail Hummingbird—is common and will even sit on your fingers! Maximum of 14 participants.

Cayman Islands

Although at present primarily a dive destination, the Cayman Islands offer other naturalist opportunities as well. The Cayman Islands National Trust is building the Cayman National Botanic Park on Grand Cayman, where 80 percent of its sixty acres is native growth. Part of this park will also be a release area for the trust's program to save the endangered Blue Iguana.

On Cayman Brac, the Cayman Brac Parrot (*Amazona leucocephala hesterna*) has been declared an endangered species. In December 1991, the Cayman Brac Parrot Reserve was established to help protect the 100 or so remaining individuals of this species.

TOUR OPERATORS

See & Sea. 7 days / $$ (from the Cayman Islands) / January–December. These are live-aboard dive trips to the Cayman Islands, just south of Cuba.

The Lesser Antilles

The smaller islands of the West Indies include the Virgin Islands, the Leeward and Windward islands, and the islands off the northern coast of South America.

Many are traditional stops for cruise ships or are beach resorts. Some of the less touristy islands, however, are good nature-tour destinations.

Virgin Islands

A group of about 100 small islands and cays extending in a sixty-mile arc east of Puerto Rico, the Virgin Islands comprise both British and U.S. territories. On the U.S. islands, St. Croix's Sandy Point National Wildlife Refuge is one of only two nesting sites for the Leatherback Turtle in the United States. Of special note: U.S. Virgin Islands National Park occupies more than half of St. John, and is heavily forested—home to mongooses, hermit crabs, turtles, snakes, and many birds.

TOUR OPERATORS

Break Away Adventure Travel. 8 days / $$ (from the Virgin Islands) / January–December. Sailing trips in the British Virgin Islands. Snorkeling and diving equipment is carried on board.

Earthwatch
   10 days / $$ (from St. Croix) / April–July. This is a research trip to St. Croix to monitor the nesting and hatching of critically endangered Leatherback Turtles. Since 1982, nearly 600 Earthcorps volunteers have spent more than 46,000 hours walking 56,000 kilometers to help the highly endangered Leatherbacks. Over a five-year period, teams have ensured the emergence of nearly 35,000 hatchlings. Earthcorps volunteers have helped test a new method for identifying individual Leatherbacks. Night patrols find and record data from nesting mothers, measure nest temperatures, move erosion-prone nests, and chaperone hatchlings to the sea.
   9 days / $$ (from St. Croix) / January, May. This is the second part of the Caribbean Mongoose research program, which is based both here and in Puerto Rico (see the section on Puerto Rico, page 94).

World Nature Tours. 7 days / $ (from St. Thomas) / March. This is a general natural history cruise, with an emphasis on birdwatching. On board the 95-foot *Harvey Gamage,* a two-masted schooner, you sail through the U.S. Virgin Islands. Shore excursions take you into dry mountains and tropical rain forest. There are about 160 species of birds to be seen, including White-tailed Tropicbird, Bahama Duck, Brown-throated Parakeet, Loggerhead Kingbird, Troupial, and Antillean Crested Hummingbird. Special efforts are made to see the Caribbean Elaenia, Lesser Antillean Bullfinch, and Bridled Quail-Dove. There may be an opportunity to stop at Green Cay National Wildlife Refuge, a 20-acre islet off the coast of St. Croix, where the very rare St. Croix Ground Lizard remains.

The Leeward and Windward Islands

Dropping southward in a curve like a comma off Puerto Rico, the Leeward and Windward islands are a long chain of small tropical islands. The Leewards stretch from the Virgin Islands to Guadeloupe (some sources include Dominica); the Windwards are from Martinique to Grenada.

One of the more unspoiled islands, Anguilla, recently created an artificial reef for divers by recycling shipwrecks, and has also formed a National Trust to preserve the island's natural areas. Saba has just completed restoration of hiking trails that trace old donkey tracks across the island. Dominica and Grenada both retain a large percentage of forestland. Although some of the Leeward and Windward islands are traditional tourist destinations, a few are indeed gems for the naturalist. We've grouped all the tours to these islands together here, with the exception of Dominica and Grenada, which are primary nature destinations.

TOUR OPERATORS

American Museum of Natural History. 10 days / $$$$ (from Antigua) / January. A cruise aboard the 35-cabin *Sea Cloud* to various islands. The leader of the expedition is Art Cooley, a founder of the Environmental Defense Fund. Ports of call include St. Lucia, Grenada, Dominica, Anguilla, and Antigua. Several museum staff members, including a marine biologist, accompany the trip. You may expect to see a wide variety of birds and marine mammals and to enjoy snorkeling opportunities as well.

Focus on Nature Tours. Birding trip to St. Lucia and Puerto Rico (see section on Puerto Rico, page 95).

See & Sea. 7 days / $$ (from various locations) / January–December. These are multi-island, dive-cruise combinations to St. Maarten and Saba on a live-aboard. Unusual tube worms, sponges, and other invertebrates can be seen in the shallow reefs, while the deeper pinnacles around Saba feature huge fans, schooling jacks, and exciting encounters with rays, sharks, and barracuda. Snorkelers are also welcome.

Dominica

The largest of the Windward Islands, Dominica is commonly known as the "nature island." It is home to 162 species of birds, including the Imperial Parrot (endemic), and 80 percent of the island is virgin rain forest. In fact, there is more acreage under protection here than under cultivation. Dominica National Park (a.k.a. Morne Trois Pitons) is a 16,000-acre region with hiking trails to lakes in the interior.

TOUR OPERATORS

Cox & Kings. 15 days / $$$$ (from London) / August. This is a botany tour. There is a variety of Caribbean vegetation with several very distinct and interesting habitats to visit, including elfin woodlands, montane thickets, mangrove swamps, seasonal forests, and rain forests. Dominica's rain forest is the finest in the Caribbean, with a multitude of species. Beginning with a visit to the Botanical Gardens, participants then go on to see Freshwater and Boeri lakes, drive to the foothills of Morne Diablotin, and walk into the rain forest to look for the Imperial Parrot—the national bird of Dominica (and an endemic). You'll visit the Emerald Pool in Morne Trois Pitons National Park, where you will see giant trees such as the Gommier and Bois Bande. A boat ride up the Indian River is also part of the program. Among the plants you may expect to see are a range of Filmy Ferns and Tree Ferns, a very large Gentian with cream flowers, two Bromeliads, and other endemic plants and trees.

Denver Museum of Natural History. 8 days / $$$$ (from Denver) / February. This natural history trip studies island ecology, birds, and marine life. A local naturalist accompanies the trip. Many habitats are visited, including extinct volcanos, the Indian River mangrove swamp, the Emerald Pool, Scotts Head (for snorkeling), and Freshwater and Boeri lakes (the tour price includes a donation to the museum).

Earth Tours. 7 days / $$ (from Dominica) / June–December. On this hiking and general natural history trip, half the time is spent in rain forest guest houses, the other half in beachfront cottages. A trip up the Indian River through mangroves is a feature. Local guides are employed in addition to Earth Tours personnel. A trip for seniors (or the less active) is also offered. Travel is by van (instead of on foot) and the major rain forest areas and waterfalls are visited.

Massachusetts Audubon Society. 9 days / $$$ (from Miami) / February. This is a general natural history trip to Dominica and St. Lucia. One of the trip's main objectives is to find the three endemic *Amazona* parrots: Imperial, Red-necked, and St. Lucia. This is an excellent introduction to tropical birding.

Nature Expeditions International. (See the section on Trinidad and Tobago, page 102.)

Oceanic Society Expeditions. 7 days / $$ (from Dominica) / March. A whale-watching and birding trip cosponsored by Seafarers Expeditions. The main focus is to observe the Sperm Whales near Dominica. Other sightings may include Pilot, Humpback, and False Killer Whales. From the boat, the 62-foot *Bruur,* participants use a hydrophone to record the sounds of these marine mammals. Island hikes into the lush interior focus on finding Imperial and Red-necked Parrots, among other birds. Maximum of 18 participants.

World Wildlife Fund. 8 days / $$$ (from Dominica) / February–March. A general natural history trip to explore the greatest expanse of rain forest in the Caribbean.

Grenada

The southernmost of the Windward Islands, Grenada is at present underdeveloped as a nature-tour destination. Nevertheless, this mountainous three-island nation has designated 13 percent of its land as national parks, the largest being Grand Etang in the heart of the main island. Grenada boasts 453 species of flowering plants; an endemic fern (*Danaea* species), an endemic tree (*Maytenus grenadensis*), and an endemic cabbage palm (*Oreodoxa oleracea*); 150 species of birds, including the critically endangered Grenada Dove and Grenada subspecies of the Hook-billed Kite; 4 species of amphibians and 8 species of reptiles (none poisonous), including the endangered Hawksbill Turtle; and 4 species of native mammals. The beautiful Mona Monkey, originally from Africa, is endangered also.

Grenada's Grand Etang National Park is an exceptionally lush tropical rain forest rich in flora and fauna, including the Rufous-breasted Hummingbird; trails developed with the help of the Peace Corps provide access into the rain forest, including the elfin forest. A new national park is being developed in the mangrove swamp of Levera, in the northeast; this is the northernmost roosting area for the Scarlet Ibis. On Carriacou (one of the smaller islands), High Point National Park is to be developed on the northern coast.

TOUR OPERATORS

Foundation for Field Research. 7+ days / $–$$ (from Grenada) / June, July. The foundation sponsors several research trips to Grenada, including "The Lost Parrot of Grenada," an expedition to search for the Gray Parrot, and a study of the Grand Etang Forest. Also offered are "Environmental Impact," a project studying the effects of landfills in mangrove swamps; "Christmas Bird Count," to track fluctuating bird populations; and "African Monkeys in the Caribbean," a study of the Mona Monkeys.

Curaçao and Bonaire

Off the coast of Venezuela, Curaçao and Bonaire are familiar tourist destinations, particularly noted for diving. Bonaire was the first Caribbean island to prohibit the taking of coral and instructs divers on ways to protect the underwater ecosystem.

TOUR OPERATORS

Earthwatch. 13 days / $$ (from Bonaire) / May–July. A research trip to map the distribution of organisms of the deep reefs off Bonaire. Up to 40 percent of a coral reef is space—a series of cavities that house snails, sponges, and a host of other animals. Despite their small size, these creatures have a major effect on the structure of the entire ecosystem. By boring into or encrusting reef cavities, they gradually change the reef's size and shape. Diving twice a day, teams record distributions of reef dwellers.

See & Sea. 7 days / $$ (from Curaçao or Bonaire) / January–December. Live-aboard dive trips to Curaçao and Bonaire. The boat anchors at reef sites, so you can dive whenever you want—at dawn, at night, or any other time.

Smithsonian. 14 days / $$ (from Curaçao) / January. This is a research trip to study the giant land turtles that formerly inhabited Curaçao. Similar to those found in the Galápagos today, these extinct animals lived here 10,000 to 20,000 years ago. Volunteers excavate the bones as part of an ongoing study to determine the cause of their extinction.

Trinidad and Tobago

Two islands in the southernmost part of the Caribbean, just off the coast of Venezuela, the independent state of Trinidad and Tobago is a primary destination for nature lovers. In character, the islands are quite different from one another. Trinidad is only ten miles from the South American mainland and, physiographically, is an extension of that mainland. For instance, the mountains of its Northern Range are the counterpart of the Cadena del Litoral Oriental in Venezuela. Culturally, Trinidad seems South American as well.

Trinidad in particular is the choice of many birders unfamiliar with neotropical avifauna, since it is considered by some to be more characteristic of South America—with its great diversity and abundance—than of the Caribbean. The Asa Wright Nature Centre, famous for its comfort and the variety of birds that can easily easily be seen from its veranda, is also a great base for visiting nearby marshes, swamps, savannah, and forests. All birding trips to Trinidad include a boat trip to the Caroni Swamp, where hundreds of Scarlet Ibis fly in at dusk to roost, making the green trees alive with red flashes.

Tobago, although also an extension of the Venezuelan coastal range and only about twenty miles from Trinidad, seems more like a Caribbean island. Its people, its pace of life, and its landscape resemble islands of the West Indies. Tobago's beaches and coral reefs, especially Buccoo Reef, are world famous. Nevertheless, many trips also visit Tobago for its seabirds—as well as for several other species of birds that are not found in Trinidad.

Trinidad and Tobago is a relatively prosperous country, providing its people with a good way of life. In addition, it has been able to successfully manage its forests and has established eight coastal or marine parks. Three percent of its land is under protection. Although there is an increasing environmental problem from general tourism development, ecotourism has a limited impact on the environment.

NOTE: Cruises to the lower Caribbean and Orinoco River of Venezuela—a popular combination—are to be found in the section on Venezuela (page 117).

TOUR OPERATORS

Caligo Ventures. 7–10 days / $$ (from New York or Miami) / January–December. Caligo is a travel agency and the booking agent for the Asa Wright Nature Centre and Lodge in Trinidad. It also offers package birding tours to either Trinidad or Tobago, as well as combination trips. The combination tour is 10 days; single-island trips are a week. You have the opportunity to join in the Christmas bird count at Asa Wright. Some of the trips are unguided.

Canadian Nature Tours. 7 days / $$$$ (from Toronto) / March. This is a general natural history trip to Tobago. Participants live aboard a 72-foot yacht and take day hikes on the island. Activities include snorkeling, birdwatching, stargazing, and nocturnal searches for nesting Leatherback Turtles. Maximum of 6 participants.

Field Guides. 9 days / $$ (from Trinidad) / December. This birdwatching trip is an excellent introduction to many neotropical bird families: motmots, jacamars, toucans, woodcreepers, ovenbirds, antbirds, and manakins. The tour is based at Asa Wright (while on Trinidad), where a half day is spent exploring the cave roosts of the Oilbird—a fruit-eating relative of nighthawks and nightjars. Found only in Trinidad and Venezuela, these large brown birds are the sole representative of their family, Steatornithidae. On Tobago, you'll search for species not found on Trinidad, such as the Rufous-vented Chachalaca and the beautiful Blue backed Manakin. There will also be a boat trip to Little Tobago, where Red-billed

Tropicbirds nest. You might expect to see about 200 species of birds. Maximum of 14 participants.

Motmot Nature Tours. 12 days / $$ (from Trinidad) / February. A birdwatching tour to Trinidad and Tobago. Visits to the lek of the White-tailed Sabrewing (a hummingbird), the Little Tobago seabird colonies, Nariva and Caroni swamps, and the Arena Forest are features of the trip. On Trinidad, you'll be based at Asa Wright. Noted author Richard ffrench leads the trip.

National Audubon Society. 11 days / $$ (from Miami) / June. An ecology workshop in Trinidad focusing on biodiversity and tropical forest and wetland preservation. There is special emphasis on coral reef ecology and conservation as well. Field trips include a visit to a freshwater swamp to view wading birds and anaconda, the Caroni Swamp for the Scarlet Ibis, and an evening excursion to see Leatherback Turtles nesting. Lectures are presented by experts from the Trinidad Audubon Society and by other leading environmentalists working on Caribbean issues.

Nature Expeditions International. 10 days / $$ (from Trinidad) / January, March, December. Nature study trips to Trinidad, Tobago, and Dominica.

New Jersey Audubon Society. 10 days / $$ (from New York) / June. A birding trip to Trinidad and Tobago. On Trinidad you stay at the Asa Wright Nature Centre and make excursions to various locales, including Dunston Cave (the Oilbird roost) and Caroni Swamp. On Tobago, expeditions are made to the Gilpin Trace and Buccoo Reef. Maximum 10 participants.

New York Botanical Garden. 7 days / $$$ (from New York) / February. "Plants and Birds of Trinidad" is a natural history tour based at the Asa Wright Nature Centre. Day trips are taken to various sites on the island, but time is spent at the center as well, where 50 or more species of birds can be observed from the veranda of the main house. Professional biologists from the NYBG accompany the trip. A $300 tax-deductible donation is included in the price.

Questers. 11 days / $$$ (from Trinidad) / November. This general natural history trip includes a trip to the Caroni Swamp to see the spectacle of the Scarlet Ibis roost. While on Trinidad, you stay at the Asa Wright Nature Centre, high up in the mountains of the Northern Range. The second half of the trip is on Tobago and includes a day trip to Little Tobago Island to look at the cliffs where the Red-billed Tropicbirds nest. A snorkeling excursion is made to Buccoo Reef.

VENT. 10 days / $$$ (from Miami) / December. A birdwatching trip to Trinidad and Tobago. While on Trinidad, you'll stay at the Asa Wright Nature Centre, where field trips and discussions are supplemented by lectures. In addition to bird identification, this tour emphasizes the natural history of animals and plants of Trinidad. Several days on Tobago provide an interesting contrast to the rain forests of Trinidad. About 200 species of birds can be expected; while on Tobago, participants have an opportunity to go snorkeling on the famed Buccoo Reef. Maximum of 12 participants.

Wings. 9 days / $$ (from Trinidad) / January. Participants on this birdwatching trip are based at Asa Wright Nature Centre, from where daily field trips are taken. A 4-day extension to Tobago is offered (extra cost). Participants can expect to see upwards of 200 species, including the spectacular Scarlet Ibis, Oilbird, several species of hummingbird, and the Channel-billed Toucan.

Wonderbird Tours

6–10 days / $–$$ (from New York or Miami) / January–December. Several bird-watching trips are offered, including a birding combination to both Trinidad and Tobago and a December trip that gives participants the opportunity of participating in the Tobago Christmas Bird Count.

6 days / $$ (from New York or Miami) / February, October. This is a research trip with participants assisting with ongoing ecological studies of stream fish communities in Trinidad (some vigorous work is involved).

7 days / $$ (from New York or Miami) / March, May, August. There are over 700 species of butterflies in Trinidad and Tobago. On this "Tropical Butterfly Expedition" you'll visit localities where the Iridescent Blue Morpho and the Great Owl Butterfly are found, and will also have the opportunity to see Glasswings, Swallowtails, the Blue Pierella, and many others. Backlighting is possible for those interested in moths, beetles, and other nocturnal creatures.

FROM THE TROPICS
TO THE ICE:
SOUTH AMERICA AND ANTARCTICA

With its coasts on either side higher than its interior, South America presents a peculiar topographic profile. Instead of flowing to the sea, most of the rivers merge into long and mighty channels that keep the interior moist and lush. Over 80 percent of the continent lies within the tropics, but because the Andes are so extensive and so high, there are large regions of temperate or cold climate near the Equator. Thus, you have a diversity of environment unequaled in the world.

Here is the neotropics in its full glory; owing to its geological development, largely in isolation, its flora and fauna reflect the strongest biological originality in the world. The figures on plant endemics are awesome: 25 families and 3,500 genera found in tropical and temperate rain forests, deciduous woodlands, savannahs and pampas, and alpine meadows.

And animal life is just as diversified. South America boasts 2,700 species of freshwater fish, 1,500 in the Amazon Basin alone. There are over 85 families of birds and 2,700 species—more than are found in Africa or Asia. Endemic to the continent are entire families of birds such as rheas, curassows, hoatzins, and Oilbirds, while other species—hummingbirds, motmots, jacamars, manakins, and toucans—have their largest representation here. Land mammals include marsupials, sloths, anteaters, armadillos, monkeys, and tapirs. And there is equal diversity in the sea: dolphins, whales, seals, and marine iguanas.

South America has two primary ecotourist destinations: the Galápagos and the Amazon Basin. Because each has an identity markedly different from that of the country to which it belongs, we have listed both separately. Also, trips to the Amazon may visit either Peru or Brazil. All other trips to South America, however, are listed by country.

NOTE: Since most trips to Antarctica leave from South America, we have included those trips in this chapter.

Most travelers find the South American Explorers Club to be helpful. Their offices are: 126 Indian Creek Road, Ithaca, NY 14850 USA (tel. 607-277-0488); Casilla 3741, Lima 100, Peru (tel. 5114-314480); and Apartado 21-431, Quito,

Ecuador (tel. 5932-566076). There's a clubhouse in Lima at Avenida Portugal 146, Breña, open Monday to Friday, 9:30 to 5:00; in Quito, the clubhouse is at Toledo 1254, La Floresta.

THE GALÁPAGOS

"Here, in both space and time, we seem to be brought somewhat near to that great fact—that mystery of mysteries—the first appearance of new beings on this earth." So wrote Charles Darwin in his *Voyage of the Beagle* (1845). Discovered in the early sixteenth century, these volcanic islands became, in the nineteenth century, a popular stopover for whaling ships. Here the sailors replenished their water tanks and captured tortoises for their meat. In fact, the islands were named for these reptiles: *Galápagos* is the Spanish word for "giant tortoises."

Herman Melville thought the islands looked like "heaps of cinders dumped here and there." It's true—at first sight they are not very attractive, not lushly green like Tahiti or postcard-pretty like Hawaii. As with so many other things in nature, you must look closely to see the marvels: the quiet elegance of the Swallow-tailed Gull, the sleek gracefulness of a swimming Sea Lion, the silent determination of a bristling Lava Cactus.

The Galápagos are the birthplace of evolutionary theory. More than 150 years ago, a small research vessel anchored here and a young naturalist named Charles Darwin began his exploration of this remarkable chain of some 400 islands and islets—an archipelago of active volcanos and arid, rocky terrain. For years, sailors had spoken of the giant tortoises, and of the birds that could not fly, of dragonlike lizards, and of iguanas that swam in the sea. Darwin looked at what was on the islands and asked the questions that eventually led to his *Origin of Species by Means of Natural Selection,* published twenty-five years later.

In particular, Darwin was fascinated by the small differences he observed among the thirteen separate species of finches that lived on the islands—differences that he later surmised were adaptations to varying food sources on each island. Seeing all the Darwin Finches is a goal of many birdwatchers who visit the islands today.

Because these volcanic islands rose from the ocean floor in isolation from the mainland, they developed a unique flora and fauna. Many of the plants and all of the reptiles (except one species of gecko) are found nowhere else. Of particular interest are the land iguanas, the marine iguanas, and the giant tortoises, which are now rare. Sea mammals include the common Galápagos Sea Lion and the scarce Galápagos Fur Seal. The near-total absence of predators allowed the animals and birds to evolve remarkably tame, making the islands a nature lover's dream.

The Ecuadorian Park System maintains a strict program of preservation on the islands to prevent disruption of fragile plant and animal life. Visitors are allowed to visit only certain islands; boats may land only in designated areas; and travelers are restricted to marked trails and must be accompanied by certified local guides.

Most travelers fly to Quito and then to Guayaquil, Ecuador, where they connect with a flight to the islands. Upon landing at Baltra, they are transferred to their boat, which serves as both transportation between the islands and as accommodation. There are seventeen major islands in the archipelago, and depending on the length of the trip, most boats call on at least six. There is no end to the types of trips that are offered: volcano hiking, birdwatching, diving, and general natural history combinations. Although there are plenty of generalist trips offered as well, it's hard to miss anything in the Galápagos.

Nearly every nature club and natural history touring company offers some type of trip to the Galápagos. In addition to taking your special interest into account, you should also consider: (1) the boat you'll be on; (2) the size of the group; (3) the length of time you will spend at each site; (4) whether the boat travels by day or by night; and (5) which islands you will visit.

There are many regulations relating to travel in and around the islands. The Ecuadorian Park Service determines all cruise itineraries in the Galápagos and reserves the right to change an itinerary at any time. Tour participants must stay on established trails, and you may not pick up anything—rock, shell, feather—to take home as a souvenir. These rules are strictly enforced by your guide. All boats must have a licensed Galápagos National Park guide on board. We've found that the better boats get the better guides, and in this case especially, the guide can make or break the trip. We suggest a small boat (such as one of the motor yachts or trimarans: *Cachalote, Andando, Encantada, Isabela, Isabela II, Sulidae,* and *Lammer Law*) and a two-week trip. On such a trip you can reasonably expect to visit ten to thirteen islands; see nearly all the birds; snorkel with sea lions, sea turtles, sharks, and penguins; hike a volcano; and, with luck, see dolphins and whales. We also recommend choosing a boat that travels at night. This maximizes the time you have to spend ashore or in the water, and in addition will give you the unbeatable thrill of seeing bioluminescence—the light given off by an organism, a shimmering phosphorescence that makes the water seem alive with light. Dophins, swimming up to the boat, look like giant, starry ghosts. One of the advantages of the smaller boats is that your group is small—generally no more than ten to twelve people. Besides enjoying the obvious advantages of a smaller group, you should know that large groups are not allowed to visit all the sites in the Galápagos. Some of the most spectacular places are classified as "intensive"—for small groups only.

Although the Galápagos Islands are on the Equator, ocean currents keep the islands cool. The warmest season is from January to April; June to September is the *garua*, or rainy season, though it's more of a mist than rain. The water is rarely rough, but there may be fog in September and October. If you want to see the Waved Albatross, be sure to go between March and December.

Casual, comfortable clothes are best; no one dresses up. Extra sneakers are always useful, particularly for walking on lava beds. A reef vest is handy for keeping warm while snorkeling. Be sure to bring snorkeling equipment if your boat doesn't provide it. And you will need lots and lots of film; it's hard to come by on the islands, even if you go to town. There are a couple of small towns, but don't expect too much. Bring some money to buy souvenirs, but *please do not buy any black coral*; the black coral is seriously endangered. There are great T-shirts for sale both in Puerto Ayora (on Isla Santa Cruz) and at the Charles Darwin Research Station, also on Santa Cruz. And Mrs. Jacqueline de Roy makes stunning silver jewelry, for sale at her studio.

TOUR OPERATORS

Abercrombie & Kent. 11–14 days / $$$$ (from Quito) / January–December. These are general natural history cruises on board the *Isabela II* and the *Lammer Law*. Pretour and posttour extensions to other South American destinations are available.

Betchart Expeditions. 8 days / $$$$ (from Miami) / January, August, November. Aboard the *Beagle III, Encantada, Isabela II*, or M.V. *Santa Cruz.* Some trips include 3 days in mainland Ecuador; a 6-day extension to Peru is offered (extra cost).

Biological Journeys. 14– 21 days / $$$ (from Quito) / January, March–August. BJ offers birding trips, general natural history trips, and a Sperm Whale special (in January) on small boats such as the *Sulidae, Cachalote,* and *Andando.* On the bird-watcher's special, an effort is made to find all 26 endemic species, including the 4 mockingbirds and 13 finches. Especially delightful are the rosy pink flamingos on the lava beds of Floreana. There are daily snorkeling excursions; and while you're on Santa Cruz, a day hike to see the giant tortoises and a trip to the Charles Darwin Research Station are offered. Twelve to fourteen islands are visited, including Tower, Santa Fe, San Cristóbal, Española, Isabela, North Seymour, Fernandina, Floreana, South Plazas, and Bartolomé. Optional extensions to La Selva, a jungle lodge in the Ecuadorian rain forest, are available.

Birdquest. 12 days / $$$$ (from Quito) / April. This is an intensive birdwatching tour spent hunting up the 26 endemics while enjoying close looks at frigatebirds, boobies, warblers, flycatchers, shorebirds, and other birds as well. A day hike into the humid highlands of Santa Cruz enables participants to see the giant tortoises in their natural habitat. Snorkeling excursions are also part of the tour. You will be using a small motor yacht with twin-berth cabins. Maximum of 15 participants.

Canadian Nature Tours. 9–16 days / $$$$ (from Toronto) / February, November. Aboard the *Andando*. Maximum of 11 participants.

Cheesemans' Ecology Safaris. 14 days / $$$ (from Baltra) / June. A general natural history trip aboard the *Andando*. A 4-day extension to La Selva in the Amazon Basin is offered (extra cost). Maximum of 12 participants.

Field Guides. 12 days / $$$ (from Guayaquil) / July. A birdwatching exploration of the islands timed to coincide with the nesting season of both the Waved Albatross and the Great Frigatebird. All the important islands, including Tower, Isabela, Fernandina, Española (Hood), Floreana, Santiago, Santa Cruz, North Seymour, and South Plaza, are visited. A trip to the highlands of Santa Cruz to see the Galápagos Tortoises in the wild is included. A birding guide accompanies the trip in addition to the park guide. Maximum of 7 participants.

Field Studies Council. 12 days / $$$$ (from London) / July. A general natural history trip on board the *Andando*; in addition, several days are spent exploring the mainland.

Focus on Nature. 8 days / $$$ (from Baltra) / January–May, July, August, November. Aboard the 110-foot yacht *Coral* (20 passengers), you'll visit ten islands, including Española, Floreana, Santa Cruz, Tower, Isabela, Fernandina, Santiago, and Bartolomé.

Galápagos Holidays. 7+ days / $$$$ (from New York) / January–December. This company has specialized in tours to the Galápagos since 1982. A variety of tours is available, ranging from 7-day trips aboard the large boats to longer trips on smaller yachts, such as the *Isabela*. Passengers can choose between a package tour or a tailor-made trip using their preferred vessel. The agency donates $25 per passenger to the Charles Darwin Research Station; the contributions are currently being used to eradicate feral pigs from Santiago Island.

Galápagos Travel. 10–14 days / $$$ (from Baltra) / January–December. Natural history and photography tours calling on thirteen of the islands. There are daily shore excursions as well as two snorkeling sessions a day. Informal discussions about the natural history of the Galápagos are held in the evenings.

Geo Expeditions. 10 days / $$$ (from Baltra) / January–December. General natural history cruises to the Galápagos aboard the *Nortada* or the *Resting Cloud,* both small motor yachts. Maximum of 10 participants. (Combination Galápagos-Amazon and Galápagos-Peru trips are also available.)

Holbrook Travel. 10–14 days / $$$ (from Miami) / January, March. Several Galápagos trips are run every year. Most combine 7 days in the islands with several days on the mainland. Islands visited include Santa Cruz, Floreana, Bartolomé, Santa Fe, and Española, though itineraries vary. Maximum of 12 to 14 participants.

Inca Floats. 10–18 days / $$$ (from Baltra) / January–December. Inca Floats specializes in trips to the Galápagos and offers probably the widest variety of Galápagos combos—from the 10-day "Essential Galápagos" to the 18-day "Galápagos Adventures." It also offers private charters and diving charters. As you might expect with such a variety of trips, several different yachts are used, though all are small (10 to 16 participants). The 10-day trip (8 days on the islands) usually visits Bartolomé, Floreana, Española, Santiago, Santa Cruz, and Sante Fe; boats used are the *Lammer Law, Reina Silvia,* and *Coral.* The 18-day "Galápagos Adventures" offers a hike and camp-out on Alcedo Volcano, where you can see Galápagos Tortoises. Departures are weekly for the shorter trips; the 18-day trip goes in April.

International Expeditions. 10–16 days / $$$ (from Miami) / January–December (except March and June). General natural history trips to the islands.

International Journeys. 10 days / $$$ (from Miami) / January–December. The trip visits Española, San Cristóbal, Santa Cruz, Santa Fe, and Floreana. Snorkeling and hiking excursions daily. A biologist accompanies the trip in addition to the park guide.

International Research Expeditions. 11 days / $$ (from Baltra) / January, March, May, August. A research trip to the Galápagos to study Darwin's Finches. The purpose of the project is to record bird songs and calls and, using audio playback, determine territory size, song type, and mate selection.

Journeys. 11–18 days / $$$ (from Baltra) / January–December. All trips to the Galápagos are aboard small (12 to 20 passengers) yachts such as the *Cachalote, Encantada, Lobo del Mar,* and *Reina Silvia.* The 18-day trip includes 14 days cruising the islands. A special attraction is an optional 3-day backpack trip to the tortoise sanctuary inside Alcedo Volcano on Isabela. Special group departures for families can be arranged, and charters are available as well. Extensions to mainland destinations are another option.

Massachusetts Audubon Society. 10 days / $$$ (from Miami) / February, March. Both a birdwatching trip and a general natural history trip are offered aboard the *Cruz del Sur,* a 16-passenger motor yacht.

Mountain Travel/Sobek. 7–14 days / $$$ (from Baltra) / January–December. General interest cruises aboard motor yachts. Extensions to La Selva Jungle Lodge (extra cost) can be arranged.

Natural Habitat Adventures. 10 days / $$$ (from Miami) / June, August, November. A cruise among Española, Floreana, South Plaza, Santa Fe, Santa Cruz, Tower, and North Seymour islands aboard the 20-passenger *Galápagos Adventure*. Snorkeling expeditions are made frequently, and there is a visit to the Charles Darwin Research Station.

Nature Expeditions International. 7–14 days / $$$$ (from Baltra) / January–December. One- and 2-week cruises to the islands aboard a motor yacht. The 2-week tour is led by an NEI biologist in addition to the park guide. A combination trip to Ecuador and the Galápagos is also offered.

Naturetrek. 20 days / $$$ (from London) / August, December. Naturetrek incorporates two weeks in the Galápagos as part of its 20-day exploration of Ecuador. An effort is made to find all 26 endemic bird species, and there is a 2-day trek up Alcedo Volcano (on Isabela) to see the Galápagos Tortoise in the wild. Frequent snorkeling expeditions, where you have the opportunity to swim with seals and penguins along with a host of tropical fish, round out the program. Maximum of 15 participants.

New Jersey Audubon Society. 14 days / $$$ (from Miami) / April. A 2-week birdwatching trip to Ecuador and the Galápagos, a week of which is spent on the islands. In addition to the park guide, the trip will be led by Paul Greenfield, author of the forthcoming field guide to the birds of Ecuador. Maximum of 14 participants.

Oceanic Society Expeditions. 7 days / $$$$ (from Miami) / February, August. A general natural history exploration of the islands including Bartolomé, North Seymour, Santa Cruz (including the Charles Darwin Research Station), Santiago, Floreana, Barrington, Santa Fe, South Plaza, and Española. An Oceanic Society naturalist accompanies the trips in addition to the park guide. Maximum of 16 participants.

Quark Expeditions. 16 days / $$$ (from San Cristóbal) / July–August. A diving expedition aboard the *Lammer Law*. Islands visited include Floreana, Española, Santa Fe, Daphne, Bartolomé, Darwin, Wolf, Tower, and San Cristóbal. Although this is a dive trip, there are some onshore excursions as well. Maximum of 18 participants; a dive master accompanies the trip in addition to the park guide.

Questers. 17 days /$$$ (from Miami) / January, February, October. An 8-day cruise as part of a 17-day natural history tour of Ecuador. Aboard the M.V. *Santa Cruz* you'll visit Floreana, Española, Santa Cruz (including the Charles Darwin Research Station), South Plaza, Santiago, Bartolomé, Tower, Isabela, and Fernandina.

See & Sea. 17 days / $$$ (from Baltra) / January–December. Dive trips aboard the *Encantada,* a 70-foot staysail schooner and the best boat for divers. Groups have had encounters with whales, Loggerhead Turtle, Ocean Sunfish, Manta Ray, Orca, and other species. Be on the lookout for the rarer species, too, such as Wrasse-assed Bass, Red-bellied Batfish, Golden Grouper, or Red Horse Conch. One third of the inshore marine species are endemic to the islands. Over twenty major dive sites are visited, and participants will enjoy the bird and animal life of the islands as well. Special underwater photography trips are also available.

Southwind Adventures. 8 days / $$$ (from Baltra) / January–December. A cruise to San Cristóbal, Española, Santa Cruz, South Plaza, North Seymour, Rabida, and Bartolomé aboard a 12- or 16-passenger yacht.

Sunbird. 14 days / $$$$ (from London) / April. This British birdwatching company offers a cruise to the Galápagos either separately or as part of its comprehensive tour to Ecuador. All the major islands are visited, and a special effort is made to find all the endemic birds. Highlights include the Red-footed Booby nesting colony on Tower, breeding Waved Albatross on Española, and a trip into the highlands of Santa Cruz to see Galápagos Tortoises. Maximum of 14 participants, 2 leaders.

The Nature Conservancy. 7 days / $$$$ (from Miami) / June, August, November. The Conservancy offers a few Galápagos trips, run by either Geostar or International Expeditions (see above). All trips are hosted by a representative of the Conservancy in addition to the park guide.

TraveLearn. 7 days / $$$$ (from Miami) / 8 departures yearly. The cruise to the Galápagos is part of a two-week trip to Ecuador. TraveLearn is a contributor to the Charles Darwin Foundation for the Galápagos Islands.

Voyagers International. 10–14 days / $$$ (from Miami) / November–July. Voyagers runs several trips to the Galápagos: a two-week trip including a hike up Alcedo; a special birdwatching trip led by Paul Greenfield, a leading ornithologist; photography trips; and general natural history cruises. Many trips combine other Ecuadorian and South American destinations with the Galápagos cruise, or offer them as extensions.

Wilderness Travel. 7–14 days / $$$$ (from Miami) / January–December. Various trips to the Galápagos are offered. Often these can be combined with a hiking and camping trip up Alcedo Volcano. Boats used are all 8-to-12-passenger motor yachts such as the *Encantada, Sulidae, Cachalote,* and *Andando.* A Galápagos cruise is also offered as part of a general natural history trip to Ecuador (see page 117). In addition, Wilderness Travel can arrange private charters in the Galápagos.

Wildlife Conservation Society. 7 days / $$$$ (from New York) / May, November. Aboard the 20-passenger *Coral,* participants cruise among the islands, calling at South Plaza, Española, Floreana, Santa Cruz (including a visit to the Charles Darwin Research Station), Tower, Isabela, and Bartolomé. A representative of the Zoological Society accompanies the trip in addition to the park guide.

Wings. 12 days / $$$$ (from Quito) / March. This is a birdwatching trip. Highlights include the world's largest nesting colony of Red-footed Boobies on Tower, breeding Waved Albatross on Española, and a good chance of finding all 13 species of finches plus the 4 mockingbirds. A 6-day pretrip extension to La Selva is offered (extra cost).

World Wildlife Fund. 12 days / $$$$ (from Miami) / June. Aboard the 34-passenger *Isabela II,* this cruise visits all the major islands. A WWF representative accompanies the trip in addition to the park guide. A 6-day pretrip extension to the Amazon Basin is available (extra cost).

Zegrahm Expeditions/Eco Expeditions. 10 days / $$$ (from Baltra) / April, May, June, July. The cruises visit San Cristóbal, Española, Floreana, Santa Cruz, Isabela, Fernandina, Bartolomé, Santiago, Tower, and South Plaza. Highlights include snorkeling at Devil's Crown and a visit to the Charles Darwin Research Station. Day hikes to seabird colonies and opportunities to swim with sea lions and penguins are sure to please everyone. Well-known naturalists Peter Harrison and Shirley Metz accompany the trips in addition to the park guide. Maximum of 18 participants.

ECUADOR

One of the smaller countries in South America, Ecuador comprises 110,000 square miles—about the size of Great Britain. The country straddles both the Equator and the Andes, thus the diversity of its landscape: mountains, páramo grassland, cloud forest, rain forest, and coastal lowlands. The Galápagos Islands, about 580 miles from the mainland, are also part of Ecuador.

The Andes are actually two lines of peaks twenty-five to thirty miles apart. The Cordillera Occidental (western range) is generally lower in elevation than the Cordillera Real (eastern range). Many peaks are active or dormant volcanoes.

Between the two mountain ranges lie the highlands of the central valley, which vary in elevation from 6,000 to 10,000 feet. Much of the valley is under cultivation. The Pacific coastal plain was once tropical forest, but now also is mostly cultivated. East of the eastern range is the area called the Oriente, site of Ecuador's cloud and rain forests.

Ecuador boasts more plant species than any other South American country, and is second only to Peru in having the most bird species in South America—about 1,500. There is a corresponding variety of freshwater fish, and all major groups of reptiles, as well as unique insects such as phosphorescent beetles.

Although deforestation is a major problem, especially in the Costa—an area noted for its especially high number of plant endemics—a recent debt-for-nature swap has encouraged environmental protection. At present, a full 38 percent of the country's land has been put under protection.

NOTE: Galápagos trips are described separately at the beginning of this chapter; some of the following mainland tours also visit the Galápagos.

TOUR OPERATORS

Biological Journeys. 10–12 days / $$ (from Quito) / July, December. "Birds, Butterflies, and Orchids" explores the Andean cloud forests of the west slope, the Amazon Basin's rain forest, and the highlands—Cotopaxi National Park. (The 10-day July trip is timed so it can be taken following the July Galápagos cruise.) Maximum of 7 participants, 1 leader (July); 14 participants, 2 leaders (December).

Birdquest. 17 days / $$$ (from Quito) / July. A birding trip that visits the major habitats in search of such specialties as the Andean Condor, Andean Cock-of-the-Rock, Amazonian Umbrellabird, and Gray-breasted Mountain-Toucan. In addition, participants can be assured of a dazzling array of tanagers, hummingbirds, jays, and macaws. Participants can expect to see about 400 species of birds. Maximum of 16 participants, 2 leaders.

Cox & Kings. 14 days / $$$$ (from London) / March–December. General natural history trips, including a 4-day cruise to the Galápagos.

Earthwatch. 11 days / $$ (from Quito) / June, July. "Sex in the Rain Forest" is a research trip to study Arctiidae moths. The first two teams set up and maintain a colony each of various arctiid moth species; teams three and four then videotape moth courtship and record the serenades of mating moths.

Ecotour Expeditions

16 days / $$ (from Quito) / March. "Cotopaxi to Coca" is an expedition to all the biomes of Ecuador—from the alpine heights of the Andes to the lowland forests of the Ecuadorian Amazon. Travel (never more than an hour or two a day) is by minibus and small boats; scientists accompany the trip. Maximum of 15 participants.

11 days / $$ (from Quito) / February, April, June, August, November. A general natural history exploration of the Ecuadorian Amazon rain forest, the Napo Refugia. Days are spent on forest hikes and short boat trips. In the evenings there are optional walks to observe the fabulous variety of frogs that are endemic to this region. Maximum of 15 participants.

Field Guides. Offers four intensive birdwatching trips to Ecuador (plus a trip to the Galápagos, see page 109). These trips go to different regions: Amazonian Ecuador and the Cuyabeno Reserve for 10 days in August; northeastern Ecuador for 15 days in February; southern Ecuador for 17 days in January and February; and the general Ecuador tour for 18 days in August. All trips are limited to 14 participants and have 2 guides. Each trip has its specialties, and you can expect to see at least 300 species on any of the tours. Costs range from $2,500 to $3,600, depending on the trip chosen.

Focus on Nature. 11 days / $ (from Quito) / February, July. A birding tour with 7 days at La Selva Lodge, deep in the Amazonian Basin. Other days are spent searching out rarities such as the Giant Conebill. One day you'll go to the Nono Mindo Road, a good spot for Toucan Barbet, Andean Cock-of-the-Rock, Lyre-tailed Nightjar, as well as hummingbirds and tanagers.

Geostar. 18 days / $$$ (from Miami) / July. A natural history trip that includes the Galápagos, Andes, and Amazon (Cuyabeno Reserve). The leader is Oswaldo Muñoz, noted conservationist, ecologist, and biogeographer. Maximum of 18 participants.

International Oceanographic Foundation. 14 days / $$$ (from Miami) / September. Abercrombie & Kent runs this trip to Ecuador and the Galápagos for the IOF. Half the time is spent cruising the archipelago aboard the *Isabela II,* the other half exploring the mainland.

Journeys. 11 days / $$ (from Quito) / January, February, April, May. An Andes and Amazon odyssey with an emphasis on wildlife, hiking, and indigenous cultures. Time is spent equally in the mountains, cloud forest, and jungle. This trip can be combined with a trip to the Galápagos.

Nature Expeditions International. 17 days / $$$ (from Quito) / February, July, November, December. A natural history trip to Ecuador that includes a trip to the Galápagos.

Questers. A 17-day tour of Ecuador and the Galápagos; time is spent in the Andes and on the islands (see also the Galápagos section, page 112).

Southwind Adventures

12 days / $$ (from Quito) / February–November. An in-depth exploration of the rain forest at the Cuyabeno Wildlife Reserve. Some time is spent camping. You're accompanied by a Siona Indian guide as well as a resident biologist while you learn about the plants, birds, and the symbiotic relationships that exist in tropical rain forests.

10 days / $$ (from Quito) / March–November. A wildlife odyssey from the páramo highlands to the Amazon Basin, featuring nature hikes through the Pululahua, Cotacachi-Cayapas and Pasochoa Reserves, and a day trip to Cotopaxi National Park. Four days are spent in the rain forest of Cuyabeno Wildlife Reserve. Local guides accompany the trips.

Sunbird. 18 days / $$$ (from London) / April. This British company offers a birdwatching trip to the high Andes and the Amazon lowlands. Participants may expect to see 300 to 400 species, from hummingbirds on Pichincha Volcano (just northwest of Quito) to antbirds along the Rio Napo. This trip may be combined with their Galápagos trip (see the Galápagos section, page 112).

University Research Expeditions Program

14 days / $ (from Quito) / June, July. A research trip to study the rain forest of the Maquipucuna Reserve, on the western slope of the Andes, north of Quito. The project will continue a detailed inventory of plant species in the reserve. Ecuadorian scientists and students work with the team.

14 days / $ (from Quito) / June, July. An ecotourism project in partnership with Capirona, an indigenous Quichua community in Ecuador, to develop a small-scale nonintrusive ecotourism program. The village of Capirona is located in a remote part of the lowland Amazon Basin region of Ecuador's Napo province.

VENT

14 days / $$ (from Quito) / March, August. "The Best of Ecuador" is a birdwatching trip that visits both the Andes of northern Ecuador and the Amazonian region, a top combination for one's first birding trip to Ecuador. Participants may expect to see an assortment of hummingbirds, antbirds, tanagers, and the spectacular Andean Cock-of-the-Rock—a knockout bird with an orange head that seems to glow from inside!

14 days / $$ (from Quito) / July. "Southern Ecuador" is a birdwatching trip led by Paul Greenfield, an expert on the birds of Ecuador. You'll visit the montane areas of the south, where you are likely to see a number of endemics. An entire day will be devoted to searching for the El Oro Parakeet, a very local endemic described as new to science by Robert Ridgely and Mark Robins in 1988. Maximum of 14 participants.

Voyagers International. 14 days / $$ (from Miami) / November. A birding trip run in conjunction with the American Birding Association; you'll visit the Andes and the Amazon Basin. A 7-day extension to the Galápagos is available for an additional $1,400. Other general natural history and photography trips to Ecuador are available, some with Galápagos extensions.

Wilderness Travel. 16 days / $$ (from Quito) / April, August. The "Natural History of Ecuador" is a 16-day trip that combines a stay at La Selva Lodge in the Amazon Basin with a cruise to the Galápagos. A longer trip, adding a few days in the Andes, is also offered.

Wildlife Conservation Society. 8 days / $$$$ (from New York) / December. Two natural history trips to the Ecuadorian Amazon. An optional 4-day trip to the Galápagos can be combined with the tours. Maximum of 16 participants; a NYZS naturalist accompanies the trips.

Wings

19 days / $$ (from Quito) / July. A birding trip to all the major habitats: volcanos in the Andes, páramo grasslands, and Amazonian rain forest. Participants may expect to see 300 to 400 species, including the Andean Cock-of-the-Rock, Amazonian Umbrellabird, White-edged Oriole, Speckle-breasted Wren, Bronze-winged Parrot, Golden-headed Quetzal, Sword-billed Hummingbird, and hosts of others. A 5-day (optional) extension to the coastal area around Guayaquil is available.

11 days / $$ (from Quito) / January. A birding trip to the Amazonian rain forest, staying at the comfortable La Selva Lodge.

VENEZUELA

Venezuela is about twice the size of California, with substantial energy, mineral, and other natural resources. Thirty-five large national parks protect about 10 percent, or nearly 25 million acres, of the land (the United States protects about 9 percent of its land). These parks include fifteen distinct ecosystems.

Venezuela can be roughly divided into several regions. The Caribbean coast is to the north. The dry flatlands, called the *llanos,* and the rain forest occupy most of the interior. The Andes angle along the west; a feature of these mountains is the cold, tropical, alpine grasslands known as páramo habitat, which is home to several endemic birds such as the Paramo Pipit and Paramo Wren, and is characterized by its dominant plants, most notably the more than 40 species of *Espeletia* (called *frailejon* in Spanish). The Orinoco River (1,600 miles long) bisects the country and eventually flows southward to the Amazon Basin. South of the Orinoco, in *Green Mansions* country, the Tepuis dominate the landscape. *Tepuis* is the Indian word for the spectacular, isolated, sandstone tabletop mountains that are found scattered throughout the southeast.

Seasons in the tropics are different from ours—instead of summer and winter there is wet and dry (or wet and less wet!). Along the coast there are two rainy seasons: October to December and May to July. The rest of the country is mostly dry from December to May, although in the rain forests of the south it may rain at any time. In the llanos the contrast between wet and dry is remarkable. The Arauco River, for example, is a good ten feet lower in the dry season!

There are 1,300 species of birds in Venezuela; nearly half of all South American bird species can be found here. And there are countless butterflies, wildflowers, bromeliads, ferns, and trees. Mammals include the Capybara (world's largest rodent), Gray (River) Dolphin, Giant Anteater, Jaguar, Ocelot, Red Howler Monkey, White-tailed Deer (like ours, only smaller; it may be a separate species), and Red Squirrel. Spectacled Caiman, Matamata Turtle, Llano Side-necked Turtle, Iguana, and Anaconda are representative of the reptile and amphibian life. Many species of fish are found in the rivers of Venezuela along with Piranha, which, curiously, don't eat birds or animals—we were told they don't like the feathers or fur—while colorful tropical fish ply the Caribbean waters.

TOUR OPERATORS

Birdquest. 22 days / $$$ (from Caracas) / December. A birdwatching trip covering the country from Henri Pittier National Park to the llanos, from the Andes to the Tepuis. Endemic and specialty birds are sought. Participants can expect to see upwards of 400 species. Maximum of 16 participants, 2 leaders.

Caligo Ventures. 8 days / $$ (from Caracas) / March, December. A general natural-history trip from Henri Pittier National Park to the llanos.

Earthwatch. 14 days / $ (from Caracas) / August, September. One part of the four-part "American Forest Survey." Volunteers lay out transects, study plots, and identify trees. (The other teams study forests in Michigan, Puerto Rico, and Mexico.)

Field Guides. This operator offers six birding tours to Venezuela: "Venezuela," for 15 days in January, visits three distinct areas: the Andes near Mérida, the northern range along the Caribbean, and the llanos. "Venezuelan Tepuis" is a 10-day trip to the eastern highlands, where participants can expect to see more than 25 endemic species. "Tachira, Venezuela" is an 8-day trip to this small western state on the Colombian border. "Amazonas and Falcón" concentrates on the humid lowland forest along the Rio Ventuari (staying at Junglaven Camp) and the arid coastal zone of northwest Falcon. "Venezuela Short" is a one-week trip in November to two of the most productive birding areas: Hato Piñero (a ranch in the llanos) and Henri Pittier National Park. "Caumara" is a week spent at a lodge near the Rio Caura, one of the Orinoco's large tributaries, where you can see a mix of everything from the common and colorful to the obscure and drab. All trips are limited to 14 participants and have 2 leaders. Costs: $1,500 to $2,600 (from Caracas), depending on the trip chosen. Some trips may be combined for a savings on the total price. All trips, except the last two (which may be combined), go in January or February.

Focus on Nature. 10 days / $$ (from Caracas) / June. A birding trip to Henri Pittier National Park, the llanos, and the Andes. Easily over 300 species of birds may be seen, including such specialties as Bearded Helmetcrest (a hummingbird) and the spectacular Andean Cock-of-the-Rock.

International Expeditions. 10 days / $$$ (from Miami) / January, February. A general natural history trip that concentrates on mammals, visiting the llanos, Morrocoy and Henri Pittier National Parks, and the coral reefs of the Caribbean coast. An optional extension to Angel Falls is available (extra cost).

International Oceanographic Foundation. 11 days / $$$$ (from Miami) / November. Aboard the 84-passenger M.S. *Polaris,* this is a cruise on the Orinoco River from Ciudad Guayana down to the Caribbean and on to Trinidad, Islas los Roques, Bonaire, Curaçao, and Aruba. A flight to Angel Falls, deep in the heart of the setting for Arthur Conan Doyle's *The Lost World,* is included.

International Research Expeditions. 10 days / $$ (from Caracas) / April, May, August–December. These are research trips to study tropical birds: Caribbean Grackle breeding behavior; relationships among five species of flycatcher; and the Red-capped Cardinal and Pied Water Tyrant. Volunteers are based at a research station in the llanos.

Journeys. 11–15 days / $$ (from Caracas) / February, April, July, August. "Wildlands Odyssey" visits the llanos, Andes, Morrocoy National Park, and Angel Falls. An 11-day camping safari to the Tepuis and Henri Pittier National Park is also offered.

Lost World Adventures. Specializes in trips to Venezuela. From trips in and around the Andes to Angel Falls; from Doña Barbara Lodge in the llanos to Kawaik Lodge in the Tepuis; and from an Amazonas river trip to Morrocoy National Park—just about every natural history destination in the country is visited. Doña Barbara is a 95,000-acre cattle ranch that doubles as a wildlife sanctuary for nearly 300 species of birds as well as Red Howler Monkey, Gray Fox, Ocelot, Capybara, and Spectacled Caiman. All trips include the services of a guide. Cost: $540 for a 5-day, 4-night trip to Doña Barbara, from Caracas; a 7-day river trip is $1,700, from Puerto Ayacucho. Trips go year-round, most with weekly departures.

Massachusetts Audubon Society. 11 days / $$$$ (from Miami) / November. Aboard the M.S. *Polaris,* the "Exploring the Orinoco and Lower Caribbean" trip follows the same itinerary as the one sponsored by the International Oceanographic Foundation.

Motmot Nature Tours. 14 days / $$ (from Caracas) / January. A birding trip from the Tepuis to Henri Pittier National Park to the llanos. Participants may expect to see 300 to 400 species. Six-day trips to the llanos and Henri Pittier are also offered; departures in December, February, March.

Mountain Travel/Sobek. 14 days / $$ (from Caracas) / March, June, December. "Venezuela Natural History" visits the Andes, llanos, and coral reefs. Two days are spent at the Matiyure Wildlife Sanctuary, where participants can birdwatch and take Jeep and river excursions to observe Caiman, Capybara, and other fauna. Three days are spent camping in the Orinoco delta.

National Audubon Society. 10 days / $$ (from New York or Miami) / March–April. This is an international ecology workshop. The first part is spent in the llanos at a private wildlife sanctuary where wetlands and wet grasslands are studied. The second part of the workshop is held at a 150,000-acre jaguar refuge deep within the Orinoco River basin. Key individuals from the Venezuela Audubon Society present lectures.

New York Botanical Garden. 7 days / $$$$ (from New York) / January. A botanical tour to the cloud forests and llanos. Birds and mammals can also be viewed, including Crab-eating Fox, Red Howler Monkey, Giant Anteater, Capybara, and river dolphins. Cost includes a donation to NYBG.

Questers. 14 days / $$$ (from Miami) / January, February, November. General natural history trips visiting the Andes, llanos, Caribbean coast (at Henri Pittier National Park), and Angel Falls.

Southwind Adventures. 14 days / $$ (from Caracas) / February–September. "Wildlife Adventure" is designed with nature lovers and photographers in mind. You'll visit the Matiyure Reserve in the llanos, Henri Pittier National Park, and triple-tiered Para Falls—reached via a 4-day canoe expedition on the Caura River. Local naturalist guides accompany the trips.

Sunbird

13 days / $$$ (from London) / February–March. A birding exploration of Henri Pittier National Park and the llanos (staying at Hato Piñero). The variety of habitats ensure a large number of species.

14 days / $$$ (from London) / March. "The Tepuis and the Andes" is really an extension of the previous trip, and together they give a full picture of Venezuelan birdlife. Maximum of 14 participants, 2 leaders.

TravelWild. 12 days / $$$ (from Caracas) / February. "Natural Wonders of Venezuela" is a general natural-history trip. Most of the time is spent at Hato Piñero, a ranch on the llanos, where it's possible to see Ocelot. A few days are spent in the Andes as well. Maximum of 16 participants.

VENT. There are seven birding trips to Venezuela. "Grand Venezuela" covers the whole country, while other trips, such as "Rancho Grande" and "Hato Piñero" concentrate on a particular part of the country. The Venezuelan Andes trip is particularly rewarding to both those with and without experience birding in the tropics. A variety of habitats from the llanos near Barinas to the páramo grasslands of Pico Aguila guarantees a wealth of bird species. Participants may expect to see 350 species on the Andes trip. Some of the trips are scheduled so that they may be combined for a fuller experience. Sample costs (from Caracas): $3,100 for "Grand Venezuela," 19 days, January; $2,000 for "Junglaven," 10 days, December; $1,600 for "Eastern Venezuela," 11 days, January; $1,700 for "Venezuelan Andes," 11 days, January. All trips have a maximum of 16 participants; most have 2 leaders.

Wings. 25 days / $$ (from Caracas) / February. A birdwatching trip visiting the llanos (staying at Hato Piñero), the Caribbean coast and Rancho Grande (Henri Pittier National Park), the Andes and Sierra Nevada National Park, and the Tepuis. Specialties and endemics are sought. A shorter (10-day) trip is offered at Christmastime; participants will visit Hato Piñero Ranch and Henri Pittier National Park.

Woodstar Tours. 16 days / $$ (from Caracas) / January, March, May, July, November. A birding tour led by top-notch Venezuelan birder Gustavo Rodriguez. Itinerary includes Hato Piñero (or Hato El Cedral) in the llanos, Los Frailes, Mérida, Henri Pittier National Park, Morrocoy National Park, and Canaima National Park (Angel Falls and the Tepuis).

World Nature Tours. 10 days / $$$ (from Caracas) / March. A birding tour to Venezuela. You'll visit Henri Pittier National Park on the Caribbean coast, Doña Barbara Ranch in the llanos, and then spend 3 days in the high-elevation Andes. Participants may expect to see about 300 species of birds. Two leaders accompany the trip.

PERU

Twice the size of France, Peru is South America's third largest nation. Its entire Pacific seaboard is a profound desert; from here the Andes rise steeply, studded with massive peaks and gouged by deep canyons. The mountains in the east are deeply forested and ravined. Eastward from these mountains lies the vast jungle of the Amazon Basin and the headwaters of one of two major tributaries of the Amazon River.

Tourism is not a new phenomenon for Peru. People have been visiting the extraordinary Inca ruins at Machu Picchu since their discovery in 1911. But for the past few decades people have also been coming because of Peru's outstanding biodiversity. More types of birds have been recorded in Peru than anywhere else in the world, let alone South America—about 1,700 in 88 families. The country's high peaks and cloud forests, grasslands and deserts, and tropical and subtropical forests are also habitat for multiple species of insects, including brilliantly colored butterflies. Unique reptiles and amphibians are no less represented. And the Humboldt Current, which passes along Peru's coast, provides the food for the most dense concentration of marine avifauna on earth. Plants are equally diversified, many species unique to the region, especially orchids and bromeliads.

This section focuses on trips to the coast (Ballestas Islands and Paracas Peninsula), and to Manu National Park (designated by the United Nations as a Biosphere Reserve) and Tambopata Nature Reserve—both in the southeast. Trips to (and in) the Amazon Basin are discussed in the Amazon section, page 124.

TOUR OPERATORS

Birdquest. 22 days / $$$ (from Lima) / July. A serious birdwatching tour visiting the major habitats, including Machu Picchu, Explorer's Inn, and the Ballestas Islands. Endemics and rarities are sought after.

CanoAndes Expeditions. A variety of trips ranging from a 3-day stay at Explorer's Inn to a 2-week exploration of Manu National Park. Cost: $155 to $2,000, plus airfare, depending on the trip chosen. Explorer's Inn can be visited anytime; the Manu trip departs twice a month from April to November.

Earthwatch. 14 days / $$ (from Iquitos) / August. A research trip to study the camouflage and biodiversity of Amazon katydids.

Field Guides. 23 days / $$$ (from Lima) / June. A birdwatching tour to Manu National Park. In addition to the many birds, participants may expect to see numerous mammals, including 10 species of monkeys, Giant Otter, Capybara, Brazilian Tapir, and Jaguar. The trip may be divided into sections and either part taken. Maximum of 14 participants, 2 leaders. A trip to Iquitos is also offered; see the Amazon section, page 127.

Journeys. 14 days / $ (from Lima) / January–December. General natural history trips to Manu National Park and the Tambopata Nature Reserve.

International Research Expeditions. 14 days / $$ (from Iquitos) / February, March, May, June, August–November. "Jungle Monkey" is a research trip studying the Uaraki, a monkey that inhabits the Peruvian rain forest. Among the 30 species of primates that inhabit the jungle, this monkey is unique for its red facial coloration and short tail. Volunteers travel by canoe up small Amazon tributaries on the Brazilian border and assist scientists in mapping Uaraki territories, censusing populations, and recording behavior.

Mountain Travel/Sobek. 12 days / $$$ (from Lima) / May, July, September. "Manu Wildlife Adventure" visits both the cloud forest and the rain forest, and includes a river trip as well as easy hikes. Some of the time you'll be based at a comfortable lodge on the upper Madre de Dios River, where you can observe the hundreds of parrots and macaws that gather daily to feast at a salt lick. A naturalist accompanies the trip.

Oceanic Society Expeditions. 7 days / $$$ (from Lima) / July, August. A week in Manu, staying at the Manu Lodge. Easy day trips on foot and by boat to see birds and animals. Maximum of 15 participants; a local biologist and a naturalist from the Oceanic Society accompany the trip. A 6-day extension to the Tambopata River basin is available (extra cost).

Outer Edge Expeditions. 16 days / $$ (from Lima) / May, June, August. "Amazon Jungle Adventure" is a trip through Manu National Park by dugout canoe. Far from civilization, participants may expect to see a host of wildlife, including up to 13 species of monkeys, hundreds of birds, Giant Otter, both White and Black Caimens, and possibly a Jaguar. The trip continues to Machu Picchu. Maximum of 7 participants.

Southwind Adventures

12 days / $$ (from Lima) / May–October. A combination cultural-natural history trip including several days at Manu National Park, Cuzco, and Machu Picchu. Some travel in Manu is by dugout canoe, and there are nature hikes as well. Local guides accompany the trips.

17 days / $$ (from Lima) / April–November. A combination natural history trip to the Andes and the Amazon. While in the Andes you'll raft the Urubama River and trek along the Inca Trail to Machu Picchu. In the Amazon, you'll spend time at the confluence of the Napo and Amazon rivers where guided nature hikes, a visit to the Amazon Center for Environmental Education and Research (ACEER) canopy walkway, and an overnight trek to a macaw salt lick provide excellent bird and wildlife viewing, as well as a better understanding of this region.

VENT. 17 days / $$$ (from Lima) / July. A birdwatching trip to Manu National Park, based at Manu Lodge, on the Manu River. More species of birds have been recorded here than in any park in the world. Maximum of 12 participants; Steve Hilty, senior author of *A Guide to the Birds of Colombia,* leads the trip. A 5-day "Cloud Forest Extension" is available (extra cost).

Wilderness Travel. A variety of trips is offered: "Peru Adventure" is a combination cultural and natural history trip of 8 days, 2 of which are spent at Explorer's Inn. "Peru Explorer" is also a combo trip; some of its 16 days are spent on the coast and visiting the Ballestas Islands, home to large seabird colonies. "Manu Wildlife Expedition" spends 9 days in Manu National Park. All trips are limited to 15 participants. Costs: $2,500 to $3,000, plus airfare, depending on the trip chosen. Frequent departures. Several treks (varying levels of difficulty) in and around Peru are also offered.

THE AMAZON

In the past few years, we have all been hearing and reading a great deal about the environmental destruction of the Amazon rain forest. Largely owing to the work of groups such as the Rainforest Action Network and Conservation International, we've become familiar with the role of this vast tropical wooded area in supplying the world's oxygen. We've heard too about the acres of forestland clear-cut each day to provide more pastureland for cattle, a practice that continues to expand in order to supply our hunger for cheap beef. The forest's species of flora and fauna are also disappearing before they have even been discovered and named by scientists, let alone valued for their uniqueness, beauty, or potential medicinal properties. And our sympathy has been aroused for the indigenous forest tribes whose cultures are rapidly being wiped out as their lands are taken from them.

We suppose that is why, when we recently returned from a trip to the Amazon River, the question most commonly asked us was, "Did you see much destruction? Were there any trees left?" We're not disputing the validity of the environmentalists' fears; destruction of the Amazon rain forest is a critically important world problem. But the immensity of the Amazon River basin is beyond the scope of one's understanding. Know that when you take a tour to the Amazon, you are seeing but one drop of moisture in a rainstorm, one small leaf on a towering tree.

The Amazon River stretches approximately 3,900 miles, from its beginning in the glacier-fed lakes of Peru to its outflow near the Equator on Brazil's Atlantic coast. In length it is second only to the Nile, but in terms of volume and area of drainage it is the tops. In Peru, the upper stream that passes down to Iquitos technically is called the Marañon, and from there on, the Amazon. In Brazil, the Amazon begins at Manaus, where the Rio Solimões (from Iquitos) joins the Rio Negro at what's called the meeting of the waters. But call it what you will, about one fifth of all the fresh water that runs off the earth's surface is carried by the Amazon. When it meets the Atlantic, it is discharging 170 billion gallons of water an hour.

The more than 1,000 tributaries that contribute to the Amazon flow from the Guiana Highlands, the Brazilian Highlands, and the Andes. Some of these tributaries are significant in their own right, with the Madeira more than 2,000 miles long and the Negro, Orinoco, Jurua, Tocantins, and Xingu each a good 1,000 miles in length. These rivers drain an area comprising about 2.7 million square miles, including most of Brazil and parts of Venezuela, Colombia, Equador, Peru, and Bolivia. They flow from and through diverse habitat, from cloud forest to grassland. Since the level of the river fluctuates widely between the dry and rainy seasons (on a par with the Bay of Fundy's tidal shift), there is a wide and fertile flood plain called the *varzea*, which is farmed during periods of low water. The waters themselves are rich with fish species, including the legendary piranha, but they also support electric eels, giant water snakes such as the Anaconda, stingrays, shockingly large caiman, turtles, Amazonian Manatee, dolphins, Nutria, Capybara, and Brazilian Tapir.

The immense forestland dominates the ecological system, however, from the cacti-spotted dry meadows of the Andes to the mangrove swamps near the coast. Mostly it is tropical rain forest, varying in its degree of wetness but almost always characterized by a high diversity of plant species. In fact, over 25,000 species of plants have been identified. The fauna of the forest is likewise mind-boggling, with more than 8,000 species of insects alone. These forests have been home to nearly one third of the world's 9,700 known species of birds. Even discounting the species that have been lost, there are well over 1,000 kinds of birds to be seen here.

We already know about the destruction on all fronts in the Amazon Basin. Some improvements in the situation are under way, including the establishment of reserves for native peoples, debt-for-nature swaps, and attempts to change poor agricultural practices. But here, too, is a place where the sensitive ecotourist can make a difference by focusing on the natural wealth of the area and affirming its lasting value through tourist dollars directed to the right sources.

NOTE: Tours going to the Amazon fall into three basic groups—those that leave from Iquitos, those leaving from Manaus, and those leaving from Belém.

Tours from Iquitos (Peru)

Iquitos, in northern Peru, is a frontier town, bustling with ecotour and naturalist activity. With its modern conveniences, it serves as a gateway to Amazon jungle adventures. Down the Amazon from Iquitos are a few lovely camps and lodges where you can stay overnight in the midst of the rain forest. Amazon Camp is at the Momon River, only thirty minutes from Iquitos. Club Amazonia, also at the Momon River, is an hour from Iquitos. Explorama Inn, one of the most luxurious, is two hours away on the Amazon, while Explorama Lodge and Amazon Lodge are farther downriver. Explornapo Camp, on the Napo River, is one of the more adventurous overnight spots. Pacaya-Samiria National Reservation, located south of Iquitos, is bisected by the Yavari River. There is a comfortable lodge amid this area of lowland tropical rain forest.

Cruises on the river generally travel downstream, utilizing a variety of wooden riverboats, some with air-conditioned cabins. More intimate travel up small tributaries is via motorized dugout canoe. The river is generally lowest from June to January, and highest from February to May. There's no predicting which months will be the wettest.

TOUR OPERATORS

Amazon Outreach. 16–21 days / $$ (from Miami) / March–December. A 700- or 1,700-mile raft trip aboard a replica of *Kon-Tiki,* which explores the lush Peruvian Amazon with visits to Indian tribes, fishing, and nature treks into the jungle. For the adventurous. Local guides accompany the trip.

Amazon Explorers. 12 days / $ (from Lima) / January–December. Begins with a tour of Lima, then a flight to Pucallpa and a visit to an Indian village by canoe. The flight to Iquitos, with transfer to Amazon Camp, is followed by a river cruise on the 50-passenger *Rio Amazonas* riverboat. The boat sails to Leticia, with visits to Monkey Island, Indian villages, and jungle walks.

Amazon Tours & Cruises. This operator offers a variety of short tours and itineraries using riverboats of varying size, and runs the Amazon Camp and Club Amazonia lodges. This company is the local operator for several U.S.-based tour companies. Cost: $250–$500, depending on trip, from Iquitos.

CanoAndes Expeditions. Several river cruises, varying in comfort level and price, from Iquitos to Leticia and Tabatinga. Cost: $240–$545 from Iquitos. Also offers stays at any of several camps and lodges.

Earthwatch. (See the section on Peru, page 123.)

Field Guides. 10 days / $$ (from Iquitos) / December. A birdwatching trip. Participants stay at two lodges in the Peruvian Amazon, from where over 500 species of birds have been recorded. Possible rarities include Nocturnal Curassow and Black-necked Red-Cotinga. Maximum of 14 participants, 2 leaders.

Hawk, I'm Your Sister. 19 days / $ (from Miami) / February. Women's expedition to the Amazon region, with the Amazon's only woman guide. Trip is based at Pacaya-Samiria National Preserve lodge, and a primitive jungle camp upriver from Iquitos while exploring slow-moving rivers and blackwater lakes and lagoons. Includes learning Indian crafts, swimming with dolphins, tree climbing, and birdwatching.

International Expeditions
8 days / $$ (from Miami) / March. "International Rainforest Workshops" bring you together with an international team of scientists in the Amazon rain forest of Peru, enabling you to learn more about these habitats that are so vital to the well-being of our global ecology. In addition, some participants will witness firsthand the construction of the ACEER site and canopy walkway. ACEER, located on 250,000 acres of virgin rain forest, is being built of local materials. When completed, it will house both expedition participants and researchers. The canopy walkway is to be a 1,250-foot walkway suspended among the massive trees of the rain forest. Its benefits to scientists (and visitors) are expected to outweigh the difficulties of its construction, which happily will not damage the trees.
8 days / $$ (from Miami) / January–December. A general interest trip that stays at Explorama Lodge and Explornapo Camp while exploring life on the river via dugout canoe and rain forest hikes. Machu Picchu extension available (extra cost).

International Journeys. 9 days / $$$ (from Miami) / January. A general natural history trip accompanied by a biologist from the Museum of Comparative Zoology at Harvard University and a Peruvian naturalist guide. You'll travel aboard a 90-foot wooden riverboat with air-conditioned cabins from Iquitos to Tabatinga. Trip includes side trips either on foot or by motor launch, and tributary trips in a dugout canoe.

Mountain Travel/Sobek. 7 days / $$ (from Iquitos) / March–September. Cruise on a twin-decked wooden riverboat, with day hikes into the rain forest.

Oceanic Society Expeditions

7 days / $$$ (from Miami) / June. Participants will swim with Pink Dolphins (*Boutus*)—the largest of the river dolphins—learning about their biology, habitat requirements, and behavior. You'll stay in a jungle lodge near the Pacaya-Samiria Reserve. Nature walks, accompanied by a resident wildlife biologist, provide opportunities to see butterflies, birds, flowers, and mammals such as sloths, monkeys, and tapirs. Maximum of 16 participants.

7 days / $$ (from Iquitos) / June, July. "Rainforest, Dolphins, and Birds" is a natural history trip aboard the 7-cabin *Marguerita* to Pacaya-Samiria Reserve. The itinerary includes easy nature hikes into the rain forest and a stop at an Indian village. Maximum of 14 participants, 2 leaders.

7 days / $$$ (from Miami) / July. The "Amazon Dolphin Project" is a research trip to study Pink Dolphins—both above and below—in a protected "clearwater" lake in the Amazon. The concern is that the dolphins are at high risk from growing human use of their environment. Participants must know how to swim. Maximum of 12 participants.

Outer Edge Expeditions. 15 days / $$ (from Iquitos) / July, August. Hiking, rafting, canoeing, and jungle exploration, with a stay at a remote jungle lodge, if desired.

Special Expeditions. 8 days / $$$$ (from Iquitos) / October. You'll explore the upper Amazon in luxury aboard the M.S. *Polaris.* Daily Zodiac excursions are made up side streams or to small villages.

Southwind Adventures. (See the section on Peru, page 124.)

Tours from Manaus (Brazil)

The Rio Negro, flowing south from the Guiana Highlands, and the Rio Solimões, flowing eastward from Iquitos, join at Manaus. The two major rivers—the former with its acidic, dark water and the latter with its sweet, muddy beige water—slowly merge in what is called the meeting of the waters. At Manaus, you are still 930 miles from the mouth of the Amazon, yet the river has grown wide and full. Oceangoing steamers can come upriver as far as Manaus, and indeed, this is the upstream destination of some luxury river cruises. Some tours operating out of Manaus cruise up the Rio Negro rather than the Rio Solimões, largely because the mosquito problem is so severe on the Solimões. On the other hand, the tannic waters of the Negro mean there's less wildife to see. The Solimões is more densely settled with river people farming the *varzea,* whereas the Negro's shores are darkly forested, with some of the islands set aside as wildlife preserves. Seeing a little of each river is your best bet. However, to get into any substantive virgin forest, you must travel upstream for at least five days.

There are lodges in the area that provide modern conveniences in a rain forest setting, including the Guanavenas Lodge on the Amazon, Amazon Village on Puraquequara Lake, Ariau Jungle Tower Lodge on the Rio Negro, and Janauaca Jungle Lodge on Janauaca Lake.

TOUR OPERATORS

Brazil Nuts. 3–7 days / $–$$ (from Manaus) / January–December. "Ecological River Safaris" are run using typical Amazonian-style riverboats—the 10-cabin *Tuna* or the 5-cabin *Fagra*. Programs at Ariau Jungle Tower, Amazon Village, and Amazon Lodge are also offered. At Amazon Lodge, a one-week paddling expedition is an option, using the lodge as a base and spending some nights at remote campsites.

CanoAndes Expeditions. A variety of trips based on different levels of experience and providing various levels of comfort. An ecological safari aboard the 20-passenger *Tuna* riverboat is a 3-day tour, costing $500 from Manaus. Expedition boats offer 4- to 10-day trips on the Amazon, Rio Negro, Carabinani, and Unini River; costs range from $455 to $1,200 (from Manaus). The "Tapajos River Safari" is a 5-day trip from Manaus to Santarem; the cost is $780. CanoAndes also offers stays in local lodges, and Jeep, canoe, and foot explorations of the Negro and Orinoco rivers. A 22-day marathon kayaking expedition down the Amazon from Manaus to Belém is run in an attempt to draw attention to the need for better preservation of the Amazon rain forest. Expect to paddle up to 40 miles a day.

Ecotour Expeditions

14 days / $$ (from Manaus) / May, August, December. "Igapo Flooded Forest" consists of several days' travel on the Rio Negro, visiting the *igapo,* or black-water flooded forest. You'll make stops in the Analvilhanas Archipelago, the Lago Januari Ecological Park in the delta of the Negro, and the white-water rivers near the Rio Branco. Boat trips up tributaries, nature hikes in the rain forest, and optional camping round out the trip. Maximum of 12 participants.

14 days / $$ (from Manaus) / July, September, November. "White Waters and Black" is an exploration of the *varzea,* the white-water-flooded forest of the Solimões and Amazon. As with all Ecotour expeditions in the Amazon, participants visit river settlements in addition to taking day hikes in the rain forest. You'll see plenty of plants, especially orchids, bromeliads, and lianas, as well as birds and animals. Maximum of 12 participants.

14 days / $$ (from Manaus) / July. "Igarape and Terre Firme" explores one of the small streams, or *igarapes,* along the northern bank of the Rio Negro. Daily walks observing and identifying plant and animal life, early morning birdwatching expeditions, and evening talks by a scientist are features of the trip. Most nights are spent camping. Maximum of 12 participants.

Field Guides. (See the section on Brazil and French Guiana, page 133.)

Navigations and Expeditions. 7–14 days / $$ (from Manaus) / September–December. Riverboat cruises on both Rio Solimões and Rio Negro, with most of the time spent on the Negro, up to the archipelago and back. Participants sleep in hammocks on deck. Trips include stops on the shore for jungle walks and visits to river settlements. Good emphasis on water system ecology. The 2-week trip offers optional camping, longer jungle treks, and overnights with families of river people. Maximum of 12 participants, 2 leaders.

New York Botanical Garden. 14 days / $$ (from Miami) / June. Special emphasis is placed on observation of the jungle's lush plant life. Some of the complex plant-animal interactions that exist in the tropics are explained during walks. Participants are based aboard a small Amazonian riverboat; daily excursions are made by canoe, and hikes into the rain forest round out the program. Cost includes a contribution to NYBG.

Quark Expeditions. 10 days / $$$ (from Miami) / September. A natural history trip aboard a 16-passenger riverboat, the M.S. *Cichla Ocellaris*. You'll travel from Manaus to Lake Janauaca and its tributaries, the Rio Negro, the Analvilhanas Archipelago. Hoatzins and Horned Screamers are among the many species of birds you can expect to see.

Tours from Belém (Brazil)

The Amazon empties into the Atlantic in a wide, wide delta that includes Marajo Island, a savannah the size of Switzerland. Belém is the port city, so to speak—it is about eighty miles upstream from the coast—where the larger cruise vessels enter the Amazon and begin their trips. Shortly, they enter a region of a thousand islands, where the passage through is known as the narrows, and where you can get pretty close to shore. The next major stop after this is Santarem, at the confluence of the Tapajos River and the Amazon.

TOUR OPERATORS

Nature Expeditions International. 15 days / $$ (from Belém) / March, June, August, November. An exploration of the Amazon from the Atlantic coast to the Peruvian jungle. You travel by plane, riverboat, dugout canoe, Jeep, and on foot to discover an amazing variety of plant and animal life.

Special Expeditions. 15 days / $$$$ (from Belém) / October. Aboard the M.S. *Polaris*, you travel "Two Thousand Miles up the Amazon." Daily Zodiac excursions are made as you travel from Belém to Iquitos.

BRAZIL AND FRENCH GUIANA

Brazil is the fifth largest country in the world, and eighth with regard to population. Its mass covers almost half of the South American continent. The Amazon River basin accounts for a substantial part of the country, and we discuss this in the previous section (see page 124). For the ecotraveler, however, there's more to Brazil than just the Amazon.

In fact, smack-dab in the very center of South America is one of the world's largest wilderness areas: the vast Planalto Central, or central plateau, a high, gently rolling plain with a grassy campo, seasonal marshes, and riverine forests. Slightly to the west is Brazil's best-kept secret: a vast wetland teaming with wildlife, a part of which is known as the Pantanal. And rather than having to fight your way through dense jungle—and scaring away all the living creatures in the process— you can see and photograph everything beautifully.

Along the Atlantic coast, in southeastern Brazil, a section of coastal rain forest was cut off from the rest of tropical Brazil and many unique species evolved. This tropical forest was once a vast area; however, it has been hacked away over the years and is now but a remnant. Nevertheless, many tours visit the region in search of its unique species, representing the most endangered continental flora and fauna on earth. There are other parts of Brazil, of course, but they aren't heavily visited by nature tours.

The Guianas comprise three small countries—Guyana (formerly British Guiana), Suriname (formerly Dutch Guiana), and French Guiana—tucked into the South American continent just north of Brazil. (When questioned, many people tend to place them in Africa, instead.) They have never been considered part of Latin America, in part because the Spanish conquistadors found no wealth there. Nevertheless, these countries represent a swath of coastal plain and tropical rain forest. At present there are no nature tours to Guyana. Suriname, though at one time a favored destination for birding tours, is currently suffering government unrest and therefore it is not advisable to go there. Right now there is only one trip to this area—a research trip to French Guiana.

French Guiana rises from a wide coastal strip to higher slopes and plains or savannahs, eventually to forested hills and valleys. The climate is tropical, with heavy rainfall.

The following are trips to Brazil (apart from the Amazon) and French Guiana. Some of the Brazil trips include brief stops in the Amazon Basin or offer Amazon River cruise extensions.

TOUR OPERATORS

Abercrombie & Kent. 16 days / $$$$ (from Miami) / September. A luxury cruise from Barbados to Trinidad, then partway along the Orinoco River

(Venezuela), down the coast of South America to Devil's Island and French Guiana, and up the Amazon River to Manaus.

Betchart Expeditions. 15 days / $$$ (from Rio de Janeiro) / September. A general natural history tour to Brazil, including visits to Manaus and the Anavilhanas Ecological Station on the Amazon, the Pantanal, and three special reserves for the conservation of highly endangered primates: Caratinga (Wooly Spider Monkey), Rio Primate Center (rare marmosets), and Poco das Antas (Golden Lion Tamarins). You'll also visit Emas National Park for Maned Wolf, Anaconda, and Brazilian Tapir. An extension to Iguazu Falls is offered (extra cost).

Birdquest. 24 days / $$$ (from Rio de Janeiro) / September. This is a birding trip to the coastal rain forest reserves of Nova Lombardia and Sooretama, Emas National Park in the Mato Grosso, the Pantanal, and Iguazu Falls. At the end of the trip there is a 3-day visit to Itatiaia National Park, back on the coast. A feature of the trip is a visit to the estate of the late Dr. Augusto Ruschi, where many species of hummingbirds can be seen close-up. Each area visited holds its own special birds such as tanagers, antbirds, tinamous, toucans, woodpeckers, nightjars, and flycatchers.

Brazil Nuts. 4 days / $$ (from Cuiaba) / January–December. Various trips are offered: a river trip on a small boat on the Cuiaba River, using canoes to explore smaller creeks and including a drive through the Transpantaneira, a dirt road into the Pantanal; a 4-day Jeep safari across the Pantanal; and short trips to Iguazu Falls, the Atlantic rain forest, and Itatiaia National Park.

Cox & Kings. 14 days / $$$$ (from London) / April–October. General natural history trips that include a cruise on the Rio Negro (Amazon) and a visit to the Pantanal, with a stay at Pousada Caiman, a lodge with protected forest and savannah.

Earthwatch. 16 days / $ (from São Paulo) / May, September. "Island Rain Forest" is a research expedition to study Brazil's dwindling coastal rain forest. The Mata Atlantica is the number-two biodiversity hot spot on earth (after Madagascar). Ilha do Cardoso Park serves as a research center to study the island's ecosystem. Teams search for caiman nests, observe animal behavior, map landforms, and enter data into computers.

Ecotour Expeditions. 9 days / $$ (from Cuiaba) / April, July, August, October. South of the Amazon is the Matto Grosso, an area of lowland rain forest, tropical dry-deciduous forest, semiarid plateau, and a huge flooded savannah known as the Pantanal. The Pantanal covers 89,000 square miles, an area half the size of California. This tour explores the Pantanal and Planalto Central by minibus, traveling no more than an hour or two a day. Among the many birds you'll see is the world's largest and most spectacular parrot—the Hyacinth Macaw. The tour also visits Chapada dos Guimaraes National Park. Maximum of 12 participants; a scientist accompanies the trip.

Field Guides

11 days / $$$ (from Manaus) / September. A birdwatching tour based in Manaus at the meeting of the waters. This—the Amazon lowlands—is the heartland of the South American tropics. Over 600 species of birds can be seen here. A feature of the tour is time spent at the tower—125 feet high above the canopy. Be on the lookout for Crimson Fruitcrow and Harpy Eagle, both of which are regularly seen here. Maximum of 14 participants, 2 leaders.

16 days / $$ (from Rio de Janeiro) / September. This is a birding tour to central Brazil, concentrating on the Pantanal and central plateau, with a visit also to Serra da Caraca, an isolated range in Minas Gerais that supports several endemics. Lots and lots (400+) of species of birds can be seen on this trip, and special attention is paid to searching out rarities and endemics. A 5-day extension to Emas National Park is offered (extra cost), and the entire trip may be combined with the Manaus trip (see above). Maximum of 14 participants, 2 leaders.

23 days / $$$ (from Rio de Janeiro) / September. A birding trip to southeastern Brazil that concentrates on seeing the endemic birds of this area. You'll visit the Atlantic coastal forest; mountainous Serra do Mar, including Itatiaia National Park; the Araucaria forest and grasslands of Rio Grande do Sul; and forest reserves in São Paulo and Santa Catarina. Of the approximately 160 endemic bird species, participants may expect to see at least 130, perhaps more. Optional 5-day extension to Iguazu Falls (extra cost). Maximum of 14 participants, 2 leaders.

Field Studies Council. 17 days / $$$ (from London) / August–September. A botany learning vacation to the Pantanal, Iguazu Falls, and the Amazon Basin. Participants have opportunities to explore the vast array of plants and flowers, birdlife and animals. Ground transportation is by bus, Jeep, and boat.

Focus on Nature. 8 days / $$$ (from Cuiaba) / August. A birding trip to three different habitats: the Pantanal, the highlands of Chapada dos Guimaraes National Park, and a region of Amazonian forest. An optional extension (3 days) to Iguazu Falls is available.

International Research Expeditions. 6 days / $$ (from Rio de Janeiro) / July, October, November. "Brazilian Leaf-cutting Ants" is a research trip.

Volunteers determine population density and study the relationship of ants to their tropical forest.

Journeys. 16 days / $$ (from Rio de Janeiro) / July–October. Trans-Brazil wildlife safaris traverse the country by air and use four-wheel-drive vehicles to explore the savannahs of the central highlands, marshes of the Pantanal, and coastal rain and cloud forests of the Atlantic highlands.

Motmot Nature Tours. 13 days / $$$ (from Manaus) / September. A birding tour to the Amazon, the Pantanal, and the Chapada dos Guimaraes gives participants a good chance of seeing a wide variety of birds.

Mountain Travel/Sobek. 15 days / $$ (from Rio de Janeiro) / February, April, June, August, November. A general natural history trip to Brazil's Atlantic coastal rain forest. Even though only 5 percent of the original area remains, it still exhibits some of the world's greatest diversity and highest levels of endangered species. Day hikes and boat excursions allow travelers to discover the fertile richness of this rain forest on the coast. You'll also visit Superagui National Park and Guaraque-caba Ecological Station, and end with a day at Iguazu Falls.

New York Botanical Garden. 14 days / $$ (from Cayenne, French Guiana) / September. This is a research expedition studying the pristine rain forest. The work is to culminate in a book on the flora of an area proposed as a national park as well as another book on tropical botany. Work includes collecting and processing specimens, studying pollination and seed dispersal, mapping a new trail, and preparing a natural history guide to the trail. Stay is in a rustic homestead.

Questers. 16 days / $$ (from Manaus) / February, April, July, October. A general natural history tour. Participants visit a variety of habitats—including the savannah of Marajo Island, the Amazonian rain forest, the *varzea,* and *igapo* (permanently flooded forest)—in search of sloths, tapirs, monkeys, reptiles, and birds. Some nights are spent in jungle lodges.

Sierra Club. 10 days / $$$ (from Rio de Janeiro) / December. A camping vacation on the beaches of Rio's Ilha Grande and in mountainous Itatiaia, Brazil's oldest national park. Moderate-level hikes through coastal rain forest and strolls in high-altitude meadows.

Southwind. 8 days / $$ (from Cuiaba) / March–November. A general nature tour featuring a 4-day cruise into the Pantanal, a day trip in Chapada dos Guimaraes, and 2 days in Manaus. Local guides accompany the trips.

Swan Hellenic. 18 days / $$$ (from Rio de Janeiro) / May, October. A general natural history tour. Participants visit Itatiaia National Park, the Ouro Preto National and World Heritage Site, Caratinga Biological Research Station—home to four primate species—the Pantanal, and Iguazu Falls. Two leaders (including a local ecologist) accompany the trip.

Turtle Tours. 17 days / $$ (from Rio de Janeiro) / September–April. Combo natural history trip to Pantanal and the Valdez Peninsula (Argentina). Includes a visit to Iguazu Falls.

VENT. 23 days / $$ (from Rio de Janeiro) / October. This is a birding trip to southeastern Brazil, visiting the coastal rain forest (Sooretama and Nova Lombardia reserves), the cloud forest at Itatiaia National Park, and the rich pampas and marshes of Rio Grande do Sol. You then head inland, passing from rolling grasslands into *Araucaria* forest and finally reaching the immense Iguazu Falls. A special feature of the trip is a visit to the estate of the late Dr. Augusto Ruschi, a famed hummingbird expert. Here, on the grounds, participants have close-up looks at more than a dozen species of hummingbirds. Special attention is paid to rarities and endemics, and you can expect to see about 400 species of birds on the trip.

BOLIVIA

Although Bolivia straddles the Andes, within its borders lie diverse regions: plains, Amazonian rain forests, Andean peaks, and the altiplano. Lake Titicaca, at the northern end of the altiplano, is an inland sea; at over 12,500 feet, the highest navigable lake in the world. Vicuña, Chinchilla, and Red Fox are the main wild animals. Over 40 percent of South American birds—1,300 species—can be found in this landlocked country. Vegetation includes 14 kinds of palms and 11 varieties of resinous trees.

For the most part, Bolivia is unexplored by tourists.

TOUR OPERATORS

Bird Bonanzas. 21 days / $$ (from Santa Cruz) / May. A birding tour of Bolivia visiting all the major regions in search of as many birds as possible. Participants may expect to see about 450 or more species, including several endemics and rarities such as the Ochre-cheeked Spinetail, Scarlet-headed Blackbird, Scissor-tailed Nightjar, and Giant Conebill.

Birdquest. 22 days / $$ (from Rio de Janeiro) / August. A birdwatching tour planned to coincide with the beginning of spring in Bolivia. From Andean Condors and rheas to antpittas and tanagers, from seedsnipes and ground-tyrants, to the bizarre Bolivian Earthcreeper, special efforts are made to search out endemic birds (17 species). Maximum of 16 participants, 2 leaders.

Field Guides. 19 days / $$ (from Santa Cruz) / March. An intensive birdwatching tour. Of the 17 endemics, you can expect to see 10, along with 100 or more other species that are rarely seen outside of Bolivia. Black-hooded Sunbeam and Black-throated Thistletail can be seen on the humid eastern slopes of the Andes— if you're not too distracted by Crested Quetzals or Red-necked Woodpeckers. Participants may expect to see upwards of 400 species of birds. Maximum of 12 participants, 2 leaders.

VENT. 18 days / $$ (from Santa Cruz) / August. A birding trip to eastern Bolivia, one of the last untraveled wilderness regions in South America. Participants have the opportunity to visit some remote and beautiful areas and also to see terrific birds and wildlife, including some species that few have seen before. You'll visit grasslands, gallery forests, *chaco* (a desert scrub habitat), and the eastern slopes of the Andes. Mammals include some large cats, Tapir, and Maned Wolf. Special birds that might be seen are Red-throated Piping-Guan, Horned Sungem, Rusty-necked Piculet, Snow-capped Manakin, and Tooth-billed Wren. Maximum of 14 participants; noted ornithologists Steve Hilty and Ted Parker lead the trip.

ARGENTINA AND CHILE

Argentina is the second largest country in South America, bordered on the west by the Andes and on the east by the Atlantic Ocean. There are four main geophysical areas: the Andes, the North and Mesopotamia, the Pampas, and Patagonia. The Andes run from the high and dry Bolivian altiplano to the low and deeply glaciated region in the Patagonian south. The North and Mesopotamia region contains the vast forested plains of the Chaco. The Pampas are the central, flat, rich heartland. And Patagonia, in the south, is a land of arid, windy plateaus. About 4 percent of Argentina comprises parks and preserves.

Chile is a ribbon of land—2,700 miles long, but nowhere wider than 150 miles—sandwiched between the Andes and the Pacific Ocean. The southern part of Chile is often paired with Argentina and known as Patagonia. Tierra del Fuego—"the land of fire"—is actually an island at the extreme southern tip of the continent and is shared by both countries. Much of Chile (16 percent) has been set aside as national parks and protected areas.

Popular tourist destinations include Patagonia and the Lake District (both Argentine and Chilean), Iguazu Falls (northernmost Argentina), the Valdes Peninsula (eastern Argentina), Torres del Paine National Park (southern Chile), and Tierra del Fuego.

TOUR OPERATORS

Betchart Expeditions. 14 days / $$$ (from Buenos Aires) / November. An exploration of the Lake District of Argentina and Chile, including a visit to the Valdes Peninsula, home of many marine mammals and Magellanic Penguin. The trip ends at Iguazu National Park.

Birdquest. 28 days / $$$ (from Buenos Aires) / November. A birdwatching exploration of Argentina—from the altiplano of the high Andes on the Bolivian border to the subantarctic coasts of Tierra del Fuego. Penguins by the millions, all three species of rhea, a great variety of seabirds, most of South America's waterfowl, Andean Condor, and an amazing variety of thrushes, parrots, hummingbirds, cotingas, and warblers can be expected. A day at San Clements, for example, can easily produce 100 or more species of birds. Maximum of 16 participants, 2 leaders (one of whom is an Argentine).

Denver Museum of Natural History. 14 days / $$$$ (from Denver) / November. A combination wildlife-culture trip to Argentina and Chile, visiting the Valdes Peninsula and Tierra del Fuego. The cost includes a donation to the museum. Maximum of 30 participants.

Field Guides

17 days / $$ (from Buenos Aires) / November. "Northern Argentina: The Pantanal, Chaco, and Northern Andes" is a birdwatching tour. The Chaco is a center of avian endemism, and you'll look for such seldom-seen specialties as Brushland Tinamou, Spot-winged Falconet, Blue-tufted Starthroat, Scimitar-billed Woodcreeper, Chaco Earthcreeper, and Many-colored Chaco-Finch. Other rarities and endemics will be searched for as well. Maximum of 16 participants, 2 leaders.

18 days / $$ (from Buenos Aires) / December. "Southern Argentina: The Pampas, Patagonia, and Tierra del Fuego" is also a birding trip and, happily, is designed to complement "Northern Argentina" (see above). You'll see penguins, rheas, and wren-spinetails, as well as marine mammals. Participants on either tour may expect to see 300 to 400 species, including many endemics. Maximum of 16 participants, 2 leaders.

Focus on Nature

14 days / $$ (from Buenos Aires) / October. A birdwatching tour from the Beagle Channel to the Bolivian border. The trip includes a pelagic trip on the Beagle Channel, where three species of penguin can be seen in addition to other oceanic birds and marine mammals.

14 days / $$ (from Buenos Aires) / November. A birdwatching tour of northern Argentina, including a trip to Iguazu Falls. This trip may be combined with the preceding one. An optional 4-day extension to Chile is offered.

11 days / $$ (from Santiago) / November. A birdwatching tour to a variety of habitats all the way down to Tierra del Fuego. A pelagic trip is included. Specialties that will be sought after include Andean Condor, Magellanic Woodpecker, Diademed Sandpiper-Plover, as well as rheas, tapaculos, and other austral species. An optional 3-day extension to the north includes another pelagic trip.

Geo Expeditions. 19 days / $$ (from Buenos Aires) / January, November. "Patagonia Wildlife" is a general natural history trip visiting the Valdes Peninsula to see Sea Lion, Elephant Seal, and penguins; Tierra del Fuego and the Beagle Channel; and several national parks. A 22-day Patagonia trek is also offered; maximum of 10 participants. Both trips use local leaders and guides.

Geostar

14 days / $$$ (from Santiago) / December. "Wildflowers and National Parks of Southern Chile" takes you to La Compania to see the largest remaining stands of the Chilean Wine Palm (*Jubaea chilensis*). In Villarrica National Park (location of a unique *Araucaria* forest) two new species of Southern Beech can be found; while endemic conifers are to be found on Volcán Chillán. Other unusual plant communities are visited as well, and representative bird and animal life include Guanaco, Lesser Rhea, and Magellanic Penguin. Maximum of 14 participants; a botanist accompanies the trip.

18 days / $$$$ (from Los Angeles) / February. A trip to southern Chile, including a 6-day cruise among the fjords. While on land, you visit Torres del Paine, Perito Moreno Glacier, and Punta Arenas. There's great birding and spectacular scenery.

Innerasia Expeditions. 15–19 days / $$ (from Buenos Aires or Santiago) / February, March, November, December. Treks in Argentina and Chile, concentrating in Patagonia. There is a 15-day rigorous trek in the Torres del Paine National Park. A 19-day general natural history trip to Patagonia offers a stay at the Estancia Cristina, an exclusive ranch.

International Expeditions. 10–14 days / $$$ (from Miami) / November–February. General natural history trips to the Argentine: Pampas, Patagonia, and the Andes, including visits to various national parks. You can expect to see a variety of mammals including Guanaco, Mara, Elephant Seal, and Southern Right Whale as well as many land- and seabirds. Ten-day cruises of the Chilean fjords are also offered.

Journeys. 17–19 days / $ (from Buenos Aires) / January, February, October. The "Argentina Wildlife Odyssey" begins in Tierra del Fuego National Park, goes on to

Glacier National Park, then to the Valdes Peninsula, and ends at Iguazu Falls. A "Patagonian Wildlands Safari" that visits both Argentina and Chile is also offered. Local naturalists accompany the trips.

Motmot Nature Tours. 16 days / $$ (from Buenos Aires) / March. A natural history trip to Argentina and Chile with an emphasis on birdwatching. A highlight of the trip is a visit to Lago Argentino and the austral Andes of Chile. There is a day's outing to Perito Moreno glacier, the only glacier in the Western Hemisphere that is actively growing.

Nature Expeditions International. 19 days / $$$ (from Buenos Aires) / January, March. Expeditions to Patagonia explore forests, glacial lakes, and the Andes. Participants visit Tierra del Fuego and the penguin and sea lion colonies on the Valdes Peninsula.

Oceanic Society Expeditions

10 days / $$$ (from Miami) / October. "Marine Mammals and Penguins" focuses on the Peninsula Valdes Reserve and the penguin rookery at Punta Tombo. Maximum of 16 participants; Stephen Leatherwood, author of the *Sierra Club Handbook of Whales and Dolphins,* leads the trip.

17 days / $$$ (from Miami) / November. "Patagonia and the Andes; Wilderness and Whales" is also led by Leatherwood. This trip visits the Valdes Peninsula, Punta Tombo, Tierra del Fuego, Lago Argentino, and the Perito Moreno Glacier; then crosses into Chile to visit Paine National Park and see Guanacos. Maximum of 16 participants.

Questers. 21 days / $$$$ (from Miami) / January, November. General natural history trips to Patagonia and Tierra del Fuego, home to 500 species of flowering plants. By visiting various habitats—glaciers, forests, and coastline—participants will see a variety of plant and animal life, including many birds. The rookery at Punta Tombo, for instance, is home to half a million Magellanic Penguins, while marine mammals can be found around the Valdes Peninsula, and Capybara and Pampa Deer can be seen near San Clemente.

Southwind Adventures. 23 days / $$ (from Buenos Aires or Santiago) / October–March. "Nature Discovery Tour" is an overview of Argentina and Chile, and features excellent marine wildlife viewing at Valdes Peninsula, Punta Tombo, and Tierra del Fuego. You'll get up-close views of glaciers at Perito Moreno. There is a visit to Iguazu Falls as well. Other trips, including hut-to-hut hiking in the Andes, are also offered.

Swan Hellenic. 21 days / $$$ (from Buenos Aires) / February, November. A natural history tour of Patagonia. You'll visit the Valdes Peninsula, Perito Moreno Glacier, Lago Argentino, Torres del Paine National Park, and Ushuaia and the Beagle Channel.

TraveLearn. 14 days / $$$ (from Buenos Aires) / February. An educational trip to Argentina and Chile, including a 7-day cruise through the Straits of Magellan. An optional extension to Easter Island is available.

Turtle Tours. 17 days / $$$ (from Buenos Aires) / March, October. "Argentinian Wildlife Adventure" visits Tierra del Fuego, the Valdes Peninsula, and Iguazu Falls—home to birds, orchids, and over 25 species of butterflies. At nearby Esteros de Ibera, a marshland, you can see Capybara, monkeys, and wading birds. A combination Valdes Peninsula and Pantanal trip is also offered (see the section on Brazil and French Guiana, page 135).

The Nature Conservancy. 14 days / $$$ (from Miami) / October. Run through International Expeditions, the Conservancy trip goes to Argentina. This trip is hosted by a Conservancy representative, and includes visits by local conservation experts as well as the services of a trained in-country naturalist. You'll visit the Valdes Peninsula, Tierra del Fuego National Park, and the Beagle Channel. An optional extension to Iguazu Falls is available.

VENT. 32 days / $$ (from Buenos Aires) / October. This is a three-part birdwatching exploration of Argentina: 11 days in the northwest as a pretrip; 16 days in the pampas, Valdes Peninsula, Tierra del Fuego, and Glacier National Park; and a 5-day extension to Iguazu Falls. Participants can expect to see over 400 species of birds, including many endemics and specialties. There are also opportunities for viewing marine mammals. Maximum of 16 participants; 2 leaders.

Wilderness Travel. 14–24 days / $$ (from Buenos Aires) / October–March. Various general natural history and hiking trips to Patagonia are offered. "Patagonia Natural History" is a 17-day trip to Iguazu Falls, the Valdes Peninsula, and Torres del Paine National Park (in Chile). A 2-week "Chilean Fjords and Glaciers" trip is another option. Maximum of 15 participants.

Woodstar Tours. 21 days / $$$ (from Buenos Aires) / November. A birdwatching tour that includes a boat ride in the Beagle Channel. Accompanied by Alejandro Ronchetti Corvalan, one of Argentina's top field ornithologists, you'll visit Iguazu Falls, the Gran Chaco, Punta Tombo, the Valdes Peninsula, Lago Argentino and the Perito Moreno Glacier, and Tierra del Fuego. Participants may expect to see 300 to 400 species of birds, as well as Guanaco and marine mammals.

World Wildlife Fund. 17 days / $$$$ (from Buenos Aires) / October. A trip to see Southern Right Whales, Elephant Seals, and Magellanic Penguins. From Tierra del Fuego to the snow-capped Andes to Iguazu Falls, you see lots of birds, animals, and butterflies.

ANTARCTICA, SOUTH GEORGIA, AND THE FALKLAND ISLANDS

"It appears out of the fog and low clouds, like a white comet in the twilight." So begins Stephen Pyne's book *The Ice: A Journey to Antarctica.* "Ice is the beginning of Antarctica and ice is its end. As one moves from perimeter to interior, the proportion of ice relentlessly increases. Ice creates more ice, and ice defines ice." Antarctica is "The Ice," a term of endearment used by the increasing numbers of people enchanted by this cold, dry, windy world.

Ranked fifth in the earth's hierarchy of continents, Antarctica comprises approximately 6 million square miles—fully one tenth of the world's land mass. More meaningfully, it holds in solid form over 60 percent of the world's freshwater reserves. Formed over millions of years by the slow accumulation of snow, the ice cap that tops Antarctica has an average depth of 6,500 feet. It is so heavy that it has depressed the continent almost 2,000 feet, yet Antarctica remains the world's highest continent, with an average altitude of between 7,000 and 8,000 feet (Asia averages only 3,000 feet).

Beneath all that ice is an almost circular island divided by the Transantarctic Mountains into two unequal parts: East Antarctica is the larger, an area of mountains and plains; West Antarctica is an extension of the Andes that, with the ice cap gone, would simply be an archipelago curving southward from the tip of South America.

A cold desert, Antarctica is almost completely devoid of noticeable vegetation. Although there are about 800 plant species, most of them are lichens. Land fauna are limited to invertebrates, including two species of beetles. But the nutrient-rich waters and many islands in the region support large populations of fish, marine mammals, and seabirds.

The Antarctic Convergence is an oceanic boundary north of the continent where warm subantarctic waters meet cold polar waters—roughly 60 degrees south latitude. Though many of Antarctica's birds and sea mammals cross the convergence to feed, some species breed exclusively on one side or the other. For example, only the Fur Seal breeds in Antarctica itself; the Weddell Seal, Crabeater Seal, Leopard Seal, Ross Seal, and Southern Elephant Seal frequent Antarctica's cold waters but breed amid the warmer waters of the South Georgia, Kerguelen, and Macquarie islands. Though some whales won't even cross the convergence, many do, including Orca, Sperm, Bottle-nosed, Southern Right, Humpback, Blue, Fin, Sei, and Minke. The Pygmy Right Whale is endemic to Antarctic and sub-antarctic waters.

Most trips to Antarctica leave from Punta Arenas in Chile, then cross the rough waters of the Drake Passage to the Antarctic Peninsula. Some visit the Falkland Islands and a few also call at South Georgia Island. The Falklands are windswept islands with a British flavor. They are home to the endemic Falkland Steamerduck and the Falkland Islands Fur Seal. In addition, 61 species of birds breed here, and it is a stopover for migrants as well. On the Falklands, you can see five species of penguin: King, Gentoo, Magellanic, Macaroni, and Rockhopper.

South Georgia is wilder. Once a whaling station, it is now inhabited by millions of seabirds. Among the twenty-nine species of breeding birds are five penguins (Macaroni, Chinstrap, King, Gentoo, and Rockhopper) and four albatrosses (Wandering, Black-browed, Gray-headed, and Light-mantled). Also here are Snow Petrel, Kelp Gull, Blue-eyed Shag, Brown Skua, and Snowy Sheathbill.

An international treaty signed in 1959 has assured that Antarctica will be used for only peaceful purposes. Over the years, the treaty has been expanded to provide protection for whales, seals, and living marine resources (krill and fish). Though new issues keep arising, such as oil and mineral rights, it remains in the world's best interests to safeguard this special part of the globe. The most recent treaty institutes rules on marine pollution, waste disposal, and protection of flora and fauna. At present, there are no rules regarding tour operations.

Will tourism ruin Antarctica? Almost 4,000 people now visit Antarctica annually, making their way via luxury cruise ship to the Antarctic Peninsula, where Zodiacs take them ashore for close encounters with wildlife. Ron Naveen, a long-time expedition leader and founder of Oceanites, a nonprofit educational organization devoted to raising the public's awareness of the oceans and their resources, has been monitoring the effect of tourism on Antarctica. He reports that beginning in the 1989–90 season, tour operators have seriously been trying to keep their trips "clean and green." According to Naveen, "they have made a concerted effort to collect or compact all inorganic waste for proper disposal at home ports. . . ." Nevertheless, there is concern that tourists get too close to the animals or trample fragile mosses. Naveen and a few other Antarctic naturalists prepared a Traveler's Code, which has been distributed to all tour operators and is reproduced here. It is similar to the guidelines for visiting another fragile ecosystem—the Galápagos.

TOUR OPERATORS

Abercrombie & Kent. 15–22 days / $$$$ (from Santiago, Chile) / November–March. A & K uses the 98-passenger *Society Explorer* to offer four different cruise itineraries: "Project Antarctica" is 15 days and visits the Antarctic Peninsula; "Pro-

The following Antarctica Visitor Guidelines have been adopted by all U.S. ship tour operators; passengers will be expected to adhere to them.

1. *Maintain a distance of at least 15 to 20 feet from penguins, nesting birds, and crawling (or true) seals, and 50 feet from fur seals.* Most of the Antarctic species exhibit a lack of fear, which allows you to approach closely; however, please remember that the austral summer is a time for courting, mating, nesting, and rearing young. If you approach the animals or birds too closely you may startle and disturb them sufficiently that they will abandon the nesting site, leaving eggs or chicks vulnerable to predators. And even from the recommended distance you will be able to obtain fantastic photographs. You should also remember that wild animals, especially seals, are extremely sensitive to movement and a person's height above the ground in relation to their size. Approach wildlife slowly when preparing to take photographs. And it is important to remember that your photography is not over when the shutter clicks—make your retreat from the subject in the same way you approach. The key point to remember is not to cause the animals any distress. You should be careful to avoid altering their natural behavior.

2. *Be alert while you are ashore!* Watch your step in order not to stumble upon an aggressive fur seal or a nesting bird that is unaware of your presence. And pay attention to the behavior of flying birds, as well as those on the ground. For example, when a tern or skua becomes excited or agitated and starts "dive-bombing" you, it is a good indication that you are walking too close to its nest, though you may not have spotted it.

3. *Do not get between a marine animal and its path to the water, nor between a parent and its young.* Never surround a single animal, nor a group of animals, and always leave them room to retreat. Animals always have the right of way!

4. *Be aware of the periphery of a rookery or seal colony, and remain outside it.* Follow the instructions given by your leaders.

5. *Do not touch the wildlife.* The bond between parent and young can be disrupted, and the survival of the young jeopardized.

6. *Never harass wildlife for the sake of photography.* Our intention is to observe wildlife in its natural state.

7. *Keep all noise to a minimum in order not to stress the animals.*

8. *Avoid walking on, stepping on, or damaging the fragile mosses and lichens.* Regeneration is extremely slow and the scars from human damage last for decades.

9. *Take away only memories and photographs.* Do not remove anything, not even rocks or limpet shells. This includes historical evidence of human presence in Antarctica, such as whalebones seen at some sites, which resulted from the whaling industry's activities.

10. *Return all litter to the ship for proper disposal.* This includes litter of all types, such as film containers, wrappers, and tissues. Garbage takes decades to break down in this harsh environment.

11. *Do not bring food of any kind ashore.*

12. *Do not enter buildings at the research stations unless invited to do so.* Remember that scientific research is going on, and any intrusion could affect the scientists' data. Be respectful of their work.
13. *Historic huts can only be entered when accompanied by a specially designated governmental representative or properly authorized ship's leader.*
14. *Smoking is prohibited when ashore!*
15. *When ashore stay with the group and/or one of the ship's leaders.* For your own safety, do not wander off on your own.
16. *Listen to the expedition leader, lecturers, and naturalists.* They are experienced and knowledgeable about Antarctica. If you are not sure about something, please don't hesitate to ask your leaders and guides.

ject Antarctica and the Falklands" is also 15 days, spending 2 days on the Falklands. A 22-day trip adds either South Georgia or the Chilean Fjords. Day visits to penguin colonies and historical sites are made by Zodiac landing craft.

Adventure Network International/Quark. 12–20 days / $$$$ (from Punta Arenas or Santiago, Chile) / November–January. ANI offers hiking and climbing trips on The Ice as well as photo-safaris and more traditional natural history cruises. Cruises are aboard a 38-passenger Russian oceanographic research vessel, the *Molchanov.* A 19-day circumnavigation of South Georgia and the Falkland Islands is aboard the 75-passenger *Akademik Sergey Vavilov.* On a 2-week photo-safari to photograph breeding Emperor Penguins, participants are flown from Punta Arenas, Chile, to the base camp at Patriot Hills in the Ellsworth Mountains, and from there to the rookery near Halley Bay. You'll spend 5 days camped near the rookery, accompanied by an ornithologist. This trip is run in conjunction with Eco Expeditions and Zegrahm Expeditions. Maximum of 8 participants.

American Museum of Natural History. 14 days / $$$$ (from Buenos Aires, Argentina) / January. Uses the 70-cabin *Illiria* to visit the 700-mile Antarctic Peninsula. Museum naturalists, including an ornithologist and a geologist, accompany the trip in addition to the shipboard naturalists. Day excursions are made by Zodiacs.

Birdquest. 23 days / $$$$ (from Santiago, Chile) / January. This is a birding trip beginning in Santiago, Chile, where 3 days are spent looking for such South American specialties as the Andean Condor, the endemic Moustached Turca, and the Diademed Sandpiper-Plover. You then fly to Punta Arenas to board your ship and sail to the Falkland Islands, South Georgia, the South Orkneys, and Antarctica. Maximum of 16 participants.

Clipper Cruises. 15–21 days / $$$$ (from Miami, Florida) / December, February. Three cruises to Antarctica; one also goes to the Chilean Fjords, another to the Falkland Islands. All trips are aboard the 130-passenger *World Discoverer.* At least 4 naturalists accompany the trips.

Discovery Charters. Operators of the S.V. *Tradewind,* a 123-foot, two-masted topsail schooner. Trips are made to the subantarctic islands of Campbell, the Snares, and the Auckland Island group as well as to South Georgia, the Falklands, and Antarctica. This is one of the few non-cruise-ship trips to The Ice. The subantarctic islands trips are 18 days from Dunedin, New Zealand; January and February departures. Cost: $3,500, plus airfare. The Antarctic trip leaves from Ushuaia, Argentina; it is 21 days; January departure. Cost: $4,450, plus airfare. A trip to the Falklands and South Georgia, 28 days, in February, is $4,450, plus airfare.

Eco Expeditions. (See "Zegrahm Expeditions," page 147.)

Field Studies Council. 14 days / $$$$ (from London, England) / December. A trip to the Falkland Islands to study animals, birds, plants, and the ecology of the islands. Participants stay at guest houses in Port Stanley.

Innerasia Expeditions. 17–21 days / $$$ (from Santiago, Chile) / December, January. A trip to the Antarctic Peninsula, sailing from Punta Arenas aboard the Chilean vessel M.V. *Pomaiare* (10 days on board). Also offered is a 21-day trip into the Scotia Sea to visit the Falklands, South Georgia, and the South Sandwich Islands, which have the largest penguin population—an estimated 10 million. In conjunction with the Scotia Sea voyage, a small expedition crosses South Georgia Island, following the route taken by Ernest Shackleton in 1916.

Mountain Travel/Sobek

14 days / $$$$ (from Ushuaia, Argentina) / January, February. Aboard the *Illiria* or the *Molchanov,* a general natural history exploration of Antarctica (some trips also go to the Falkland Islands). Day excursions are made by Zodiacs. There are 7 naturalists on board. A special family rate is available.

18 days / $$$ (from Santiago, Chile) / January. A general natural history tour of the Falkland Islands and Patagonia. On the Falklands you'll travel by Land Rover and on foot, coming, at times, within a few feet of nesting penguins or cormorants. Maximum of 16 participants.

Quark Expeditions

28–31 days / $$$$ (from Cape Town, South Africa, or Fremantle, Australia) / November–February. Three journeys to the "Far Side of Antarctica" aboard the 115-passenger Russian icebreaker *Kapitan Khlebnikov.* The November trip visits the Crozet and Kerguelen islands, and participants have the opportunity to see Emperor, King, and Adélie Penguins. The December trip, from Fremantle, recreates Mawson's Great Antarctic Banzare Expedition of 1930–31, and visits many subantarctic islands as well as the West Ice Shelf. The January voyage is "In the Footsteps of Scott, Shackleton and Mawson," and visits Cape Royds, the Ross Ice Shelf, and the subantarctic islands of New Zealand. At least 6 naturalists and scientists accompany the trips.

15–19 days / $$$ (from Ushuaia, Argentina) / November–February. Twelve trips to the Antarctic Peninsula, and 1 to South Georgia and the Falkland Islands aboard the *Professor Molchanov* or the *Akademik Sergey Vavilov.* Naturalists accompany all the trips, and these are among the few non-cruise-ship Antarctic voyages. The South Georgia and Falkland Islands trip circumnavigates South Georgia. Participants can expect to see 6 species of penguin, 5 species of albatross, numerous other seabirds, and many marine mammals during the dozen or so land excursions. In addition, South Georgia is full of history—you land at the very spot where Sir Ernest Shackleton beached his lifeboat before crossing to the then-active whaling station at Stromness Bay.

Sea Quest. 27–29 days / $$$$ (from Hobart, Tasmania, and Bluff, New Zealand) / December–February. This operator uses the *Frontier Spirit* for a variety of trips, all of which include day excursions to natural history and historical sites as well as evening lectures and films. The ship has several naturalists on board. "Ross Sea and Antarctica" leaves from Hobart, Tasmania, Australia, and visits Macquarie Island, the Ross Ice Shelf, McMurdo Sound, Cape Evans (visit Scott's hut), Cape Royds (visit Shackleton's hut), the subantarctic islands of New Zealand, and lands at Bluff, New Zealand. This is a 24-day trip; January and February departures; cost: $11,100 (and up), plus airfare.

Swan Hellenic. 18 days / $$$$ (from Santiago, Chile) / January. A cruise to Antarctica and the Falkland Islands aboard the *World Discoverer.* Day trips to islands and locations on the peninsula are made by Zodiac—two or three landings a day are planned, depending on weather conditions. Scientific research stations are visited as well.

TravelWild. 21 days / $$$$ (from Buenos Aires, Argentina) / January. A photo-safari to Antarctica, South Georgia, and the Falkland Islands. Day excursions are made in Zodiacs. A photographer accompanies the trip in addition to the shipboard naturalists.

VENT. 15–22 days / $$$$ (from Santiago, Chile) / January, November. Birdwatching trips aboard the *Society Explorer.* The 15-day trip visits the Antarctic Peninsula; the longer trip also visits South Georgia and the Falkland Islands. Both trips feature day excursions by Zodiac landing craft to natural history sites. An optional 7-day Chilean pretrip is offered (for the November departure only). Bird possibilities include Diademed Sandpiper-Plover, Magellanic Woodpecker, Des Murs Wiretail, Elegant Crested-Tinamou, and Tawny-throated Dotterel, among many others. Maximum of 28 participants; 1 leader in addition to the ship's naturalists.

Voyagers International. 14 days / $$$$ (from Santiago, Chile) / December–February. Cruises to the Antarctic Peninsula aboard the *Illiria*. Day excursions are made in Zodiacs.

Wildlife Conservation Society. 14 days / $$$$ (from Buenos Aires, Argentina) / December. A natural history cruise aboard the M.V. *Illiria*. Day excursions are made by Zodiac landing craft. A NYZS naturalist accompanies the trip.

Woodstar Tours. 14 days / $$$$ (from Santiago, Chile) / December. Acting as agents for Croisieres Polaires Internationales, Woodstar offers a birdwatching trip to Antarctica and the Falkland Islands.

World Nature Tours. 14 days / $$$ (from Punta Arenas, Chile) / January. This is a birdwatching trip to the Falkland Islands. Five species of penguin, including the King Penguin, breed on the Falklands, as do seabirds such as Hall's Giant Petrel, Southern Fulmar, Snowy Sheathbill, and Common Diving-Petrel. In all, there are 152 species of birds on the Falklands list, of which 61 breed. Visitors may also expect close encounters with a variety of marine mammals, and many unusual wildflowers can be seen as well. Although there are no native trees, the giant Tussac Grass grows on offshore islands up to a height of ten feet and offers shelter for several breeding birds. The trip is timed to coincide with the height of summer.

World Wildlife Fund. 14 days / $$$$ (from Santiago, Chile) / February. Uses the *Illiria*. Day excursions are made in Zodiacs to natural history and historical sites. Evening lectures and slide programs are presented. Naturalists, including a representative from the WWF, accompany the trip.

Zegrahm Expeditions
15 days / $$$ (from Christchurch, New Zealand) / December. "Subantarctic Islands Down Under" is a general natural history trip run in conjunction with Southern Heritage Tours. These cruises—aboard the 20-passenger M.V. *Pacific Ruby*—visit Stewart, Auckland, Campbell, Snares, Bounty, and the Chatham Islands with their hordes of penguins and seabirds.

19 days / $$$ (from Ushuaia, Argentina) / November. "Circumnavigation of the South Georgia and Falkland Islands" does just that, aboard the 75-passenger *Akademic Sergey Vavilov*. This is a great trip for viewing penguins!

15–22 days / $$$$ (from Montevideo, Uruguay; Puerto Williams and/or Punta Arenas, Chile) / December–February. Three general natural history cruises aboard the 130-passenger *World Discoverer*. The 2-week trip is to Antarctica only; the longer trips go to the Falkland Islands and/or South Georgia. Peter Harrison, author of *Seabirds,* is among the naturalists on board.

14–20 days / $$$$ (from Punta Arenas, Chile) / November. "Emperor Penguin Photo Safari" is a trip to find and photograph nesting Emperor Penguins. This trip is run in conjunction with Eco Expeditions and Adventure Network International. Noted naturalist Peter Harrison leads the trip.

30 days / $$$$ (from Capetown, South Africa, and/or Fremantle, Australia) / November–January. "Antarctica Far Side"—three trips aboard the 115-passenger *Kapitan Khlebnikov,* an icebreaker. The cruises go to several seldom-visited sub-antarctic islands, including Crozet, Kerguelen, Heard, and St. Paul. Participants have an excellent chance of seeing Emperor Penguins, which are not normally seen on trips to the Antarctic Peninsula.

NATURE AND CULTURE IN ONE TRIP: EUROPE

Ecotourism in Europe? Yes, Europe is not just palaces and museums, fancy shops and wonderful restaurants. Beyond the cities there is still plenty of nature left, even in Western Europe. Great Britain has an extensive network of preserves—and the public's strong interest in aspects of nature. France has a vast scheme of natural reserves, forests, and parks; and Switzerland and Greece are far from paved over, with montane forests and alpine meadows their particular strengths. Among the Western European nations, Spain is the least developed—its national parks rival ours in scope and level of sophistication.

Eastern Europe has even more potential for the ecotourist. Although Americans have heard about the environmental destruction there, and indeed some parts of some countries are badly affected, much remains that is wild and virtually pristine. The plains of eastern Hungary are famous for their rare birds, while bison and wolves still stalk the forests of Poland. And that's just a start.

Many British tour companies specialize in nature tours to Europe—mostly focusing on either birds or botany—that visit countries on the continent as well as different parts of Britain. A few U.S. companies also run tours to Europe, especially birding tours, or coordinate their tours with British companies. On the continent, there's no question that British companies have the edge, providing comfortable, economical tours using knowledgeable guides.

NORTHERN EUROPE

Iceland

Iceland, which lies astride the great crack in the earth's crust that is known as the Mid-Atlantic Ridge, is well-known for its active volcanos, geysers, and glaciers. In fact, it has been estimated that Iceland has produced one third of the total lava flow from the earth since 1500.

This island country in the North Atlantic—the westernmost country in Europe—is also home to large colonies of nesting seabirds, including puffins, fulmars, gannets, and shearwaters. Inland, Lake Myvatn in the north is host to the world's largest and most varied group of ducks.

On a vegetative border between tundra and coniferous forests, Iceland boasts considerable bogs and moors. Since the country is sparsely populated, except for Reykjavik, there is little threat to existing wildlife.

The few tours that visit Iceland go for the seabirds and the geology.

TOUR OPERATORS

Field Studies Council. 15 days / $$ (from Glasgow) / June. "Land of Ice and Fire" is a general interest expedition. You'll make a complete circuit of the island (by road), exploring the lava deserts of Mount Hekla, the Eastern Fjords, Lake Myvatn, and the Snaefellsnes Peninsula, with its spectacular bird cliffs and ice-capped volcanos. Participants will learn about the geology of Iceland and also do quite a bit of birdwatching.

Questers. 16 days / $$$ (from New York) / June, August. A general natural history trip. In addition to driving around the island—with many stops for birds, plants, and geological features—you'll visit the bird-rich Westman Islands, off Iceland's southern coast. Seven million Atlantic Puffins nest here, along with Black-legged Kittiwakes, Northern Fulmars, and Black Guillemots. The boat brings you up close to the sea stacks, where the birds nest; while at sea, good views of Northern Gannets and Manx Shearwaters are likely. You might even see seals and whales. On land, you explore glaciers, volcanos—some still active—and lava fields, marshes and heathlands, fjords and valleys.

Swan Hellenic. 13 days / $$$$ (from London) / July, August. A combination cultural–natural history tour exploring the geology and birdlife as well as folk art and modern architecture. Participants walk across lava fields, visit hot springs, and see nesting Red-necked Phalarope, among many other birds. You also visit the Westman Islands and the seabird colonies there.

Norway

No other country in Western Europe has such large areas of almost untouched wilderness—in fact, over 15 percent of the land, including seabird colonies, wetlands, and forests, is protected. Trips to Norway focus mainly on the fjords, where steep glacial slopes drop sharply to crystalline waters. Inland, at higher altitudes, dense forests of mostly spruce and pine fill glacial valleys, the ground carpeted by leafy mosses and heather. Lower down, birch forests predominate, followed by willows. Reindeer, Wolverine, Lemming, and other Arctic animals exist in mountain regions, while Elk and Red Deer are in the conifer forests.

NOTE: Unfortunately Norway has said it plans to resume harvesting Minke Whales in violation of international agreements.

TOUR OPERATORS

Cal Nature Tours. 16 days / $$$ (from Amsterdam) / May, July, October. "Arctic Adventure" (to northern Europe and Scandinavia) is a combination cultural–natural history trip. It includes 5 days exploring the marshes, woodlands, and Dutch islands; 5 days in Norway enjoying spectacular river valleys and fjords; 3 days of nature trekking in Denmark; and a 3-day trip aboard the M.S. *Nordbrise* cruising along the coastline of the "Seven Icebergs" and onward to Moffen Island, where Walrus and Polar Bears may be sighted.

Earthwatch. 15 days / $ (from Tromsö) / July, August. "Glaciers in a Greenhouse" is a research trip to study glacial advances and retreats, and to find out how these actions are linked to climate changes. Volunteers help map a glacier, track its speed, and measure snow densities.

Massachusetts Audubon Society. 16 days / $$$$ (from Bergen) / July. "Beyond the North Cape" is a natural history cruise aboard the 80-passenger M.S. *Polaris,* traveling from Bergen to Spitsbergen, far above the Arctic Circle. One of the highlights of the trip is a stop at Bear Island in the Barents Sea, host to tens of thousands of seabirds—guillemots, kittiwakes, razorbills, and puffins. On Spitsbergen you'll be watching for reindeer, Arctic Fox, Walrus, and Polar Bear. Zodiacs are used for landing in remote areas. Maximum of 30 participants; 1 leader in addition to the ship's naturalists.

TravelWild. 17 days / $$$$ (from Copenhagen) / July. Aboard the 96-passenger icebreaker *Sovetskiy Soyuz,* this is a trip to the North Pole! You leave from Kirkenes, Norway, and cruise the Barents Sea en route to Franz Josef Land, where you land at Cape Flora, then continue on Calm Bay, the site of a large seabird nesting colony. As you leave Franz Josef Land, the Polar Bear search begins, and you'll look for these magnificent creatures all the way up to the North Polar Ice Cap. The return route depends on ice conditions, but you should pass through the Severnaya Zemlya island group, where you may see Walrus, Polar Bear, and arctic birds. You then recross the Barents Sea and land in Kirkenes, Norway. Various scientists, including geologists and ornithologists, accompany the trip.

Wilderness Travel. 12 days / $$$$ (from Oslo) / June–August. A cruise aboard the M.S. *Polarstar* to Svalbard, just 800 miles from the North Pole. This is the realm of the Polar Bear. Birds, other mammals, and numerous plants can also be seen on daily excursions (and landings) via Zodiacs.

World Wildlife Fund. 16 days / $$$$ (from Bergen) / July–August. "Beyond the North Cape" is a general natural history cruise aboard the M.S. *Polaris* (see "Massachusetts Audubon Society," above, for details). A WWF naturalist accompanies the trip.

Sweden

The third largest nation in Western Europe, Sweden is a popular naturalist destination for Europeans. Its 100,000 lakes and long coastline provide good nesting sites as well as resting places for vast numbers of migratory birds. Its varied habitats—alpine regions; birch, conifer, and beech forests; and glacial plains—are home to Elk, Badger, Fox, Otter, and large herds of reindeer. And the far northern regions boast a wide variety of wildflowers.

NOTE: Sweden has an enlightened attitude toward the environment; the government expects to have phased out the country's nuclear power plants by 1996.

TOUR OPERATORS

Birds and Birders/Motmot. 9 days / $$ (from Amsterdam) / September, October. Fall migration at Falsterbo. This peninsula, which juts out into the Baltic Sea, is the scene of a spectacular fall migration of southbound birds. In addition to a broad cross section of typical European species, Falsterbo attracts an impressive number of raptors, including Common Buzzard, Rough-legged Buzzard, Sparrowhawk, Red Kite, Black Kite, Peregrine Falcon, Merlin, Hobby, Goshawk, Hen Harrier, Osprey, and several species of eagle. At night, one can expect waves of warblers, pipits, thrushes, wagtails, and larks. Each autumn may have special attractions, such as Nutcracker, Waxwing, Pallas's Warbler, Red-backed Shrike, or Red-breasted Flycatcher.

Branta Holidays

6 days / $ (from London) / April. For a week each April, flocks of up to 6,000 cranes assemble at Lake Hornborga before dispersing to their breeding grounds. Tour participants will witness their courtship dance, an incredible display. In addition, a local birder will take you to see forest and wetland birds and owls. Recent tours have provided participants excellent views of Eagle, Tengmalm's, and Pygmy Owls. Other birds seen include Black Woodpecker; Red-necked, Slavonian, and Black-necked Grebes; Bean Goose; Capercaillie; and Red Crossbill.

8 days / $$ (from London) / June. A birdwatching trip to Öland Island, off the Baltic coast. Wet meadows, marsh, steppe, woodland, and shore habitats hold many nesting species, including Caspian Tern, Crane, Osprey, Long-tailed Duck, Red-backed Shrike, Icterine Warbler, Barred Warbler, and Red-breasted Fly-catcher, among others.

8 days / $ (from London) / September. A birdwatching trip to witness the fab-ulous fall migration at Falsterbo. Of particular interest are the many raptors that migrate at this time. Occasionally rare Asian species also appear.

Cox & Kings. 10 days / $$$ (from London) / June. A botany tour to Öland and Gotland, two islands off the southeast coast of Sweden. Some of the flowers par-ticipants may see include Alpine Butterwort, Marsh Helleborine, Dragon's Tooth, Baltic Wormwood, Labrador Tea, and Öland Roch-rose. Also *Orchis spitzelii* and *Dactylorhiza sambucina,* the Elder-flowered Orchid in both the pale yellow and ruby-red flower forms, which are known in Sweden as "Adam and Eve." Interest-ing birds are possible as well; perhaps you'll even hear Corncrake. Maximum 20 participants. Mary Briggs, well-known botanist, leads the tour.

Field Studies Council. 14 days / $$ (from London) / June. "Flowers and Photography in Swedish Lapland." You will be based at a scientific research sta-tion of the Royal Swedish Academy of Sciences, near Abisko National Park, 125 miles north of the Arctic Circle. The varied geology affords an excellent cross section of northern Scandinavian flora. Heathlands are covered with flowers at this time of year, and birdlife is also abundant during the long days of the brief summer.

The Netherlands

With one of the highest population densities in Europe, the Netherlands needs every inch of land it has—or can reclaim from the sea. In fact, 3,000 square miles of land have been wrested from Neptune's grasp, creating the *polderland,* a vast area surrounded by dikes and drainage canals. Thus, the landscape is relentlessly flat, rising slightly only in the south.

All this manipulation of the land has had its effect; some species—Badger, River Lobster, and Marsh Turtle, for example—have disappeared. On the other hand, with its mosaic of lakes, ponds, rivers, lagoons, and ditches, the Nether-lands is a paradise for waterbirds. Add to that the North Sea and Wadden Zee, in the west and north, and you have the full complement of waders, ducks, marsh birds, and raptors. Large areas of heathland and woodlands also support many species of songbird.

Birds and Birders/Motmot

4 days / $ (from Amsterdam) / November–March. Weekend birding trips to the Flevopolders, where there is a chance of seeing White-tailed Eagle. Other reserves are also visited.

7–9 days / $$ (from Amsterdam) / May, June, August. Birdwatching tours. A full program of excursions includes visits to the wetlands and marshes of the Oost-vaardersplassen in the province of Flevoland, the Wadden Zee, the islands of Schiermonnikoog and Ameland, the Lauwersmeer, the marshes of the Oude Venen, and the woodlands of Drente. Red-backed Shrike, Black Woodpecker, Tree Lark, Marsh Harrier, Garden Warbler, Sedge Warbler, and Wren, as well as a wide variety of waterfowl and waders are all likely to be seen.

Branta Holidays. 3 days / $$ (from London) / February. A birdwatching weekend to look for wintering geese, ducks, and waders around Zeeland. These include White-fronted, Pink-footed, Bean, Greylag, and Barnacle Geese. There's always a chance of the rarer Red-breasted and Lesser White-fronted Geese. Smew, Scaup, Eider, and Long-tailed Ducks are regulars.

Field Studies Council

5 days / $ (from Harwich, England) / March. "Early Spring in the Netherlands" is an exploration of the Flevopolders to see waterfowl and waders. You'll also visit the large tract of heathland and pine woodlands east of Harderwijk for forest birds, such as Short-toed Treecreeper, Crested Tit, and Black Woodpecker, among many others.

7 days / $ (from Harwich) / August. "Wildlife and Flowers of Texel—for the Family." A general natural history trip to the largest of the Frisian Islands, with its woodlands, sand dunes, and salt marshes. With fall migration getting under way, participants have the opportunity to see many waders, ducks, and seabirds in addition to more familiar garden species. There is a discount for children under 14.

THE BRITISH ISLES

Great Britain

Great Britain—England, Scotland, and Wales—is a stronghold in Europe for nature study. Many British tour companies specialize in nature tours focusing mostly on either birds or botany. Add to this Great Britain's general interest in and care for things natural (what other country posts a Frog Crossing sign on its roads?) and you have some excellent programs with top-notch leaders.

Of special note are two organizations—Learn at Leisure and the Field Studies Council—that offer, in addition to nature travel programs, three- to seven-day field study courses in a variety of natural history subjects ranging from "Life in Ponds and Streams" to "Ferns" to "Butterflies and Moths." These weekend and short courses are usually given at one of the organizations' learning centers scattered throughout England, making for "light" educational getaways. Programs vary from season to season, so contact them directly for their current or future offerings (see the section on Tour Operators, page 279, for addresses).

TOUR OPERATORS

HF Holidays
7 days / $ (from various locations within Britain) / May–October. Week-long bird-watching holidays are offered at eight residential centers throughout England and Scotland. Each is led by an experienced naturalist, and each location has its specialty: Scottish Crossbill at Dalwhinnie; Cetti's Warbler at Swanage; seabirds at Scarborough; Dipper and Goosander at Brecon; Bearded Tit at How Hill; alcids at Alnmouth; and Golden Eagle on Arran. Days typically are spent in the field, and programs are presented in the evenings.

7 days / $ (from various locations within Britain) / May–September. "Natural History Walking Tours." Based in comfortable houses, these programs offer general natural history tours of various areas in Britain—from Arran Island, Scotland, in spring to Dorset in the fall. Walks are four to seven miles in length, and each day you go to a different area (buses take participants to points from which walks begin). Some specialty programs are offered: "Wildlife Photography" in Derbyshire, "Wildflowers" on Arran, and "Fossil Hunting" at Lyme Regis.

Wings. 23 days / $$$ (from London) / June. "The Great British Experience" is a birdwatching tour beginning at Windsor Great Park and ending at New Forest, with just about everything in between, including the fens of East Anglia, seabirds and alcids among the Farne Islands, historic castles, Roman baths, wild moors, Scottish mountains, and a Shakespearean play in Stratford-on-Avon. As for the birds, about 200 species can usually be seen, including such specialties as Stone Curlew, Bearded Tit, Black Grouse, Crested Tit, and Scottish Crossbill (Britain's only endemic bird). In addition there are Corncrake, Red Kite, Chough, Pied Flycatcher, Hobby, and Dartford Warbler, as well as the commoner species: Great Crested Grebe, Kestrel, Common Cuckoo, House Martin, Song Thrush, Greenfinch, and Jackdaw.

England and Wales (including the Isles of Scilly and the Channel Islands)

The English landscape is primarily a green one, with fields, hedgerows, marshes, and wooded areas. However, since the bulk of the land has been under cultivation for centuries, the diversity of fauna species is limited except for migrating birds and winter visitors. Wildflowers, on the other hand, bloom in profusion, especially in the moorlands of the northeast.

The preservation of remaining green areas has been a high priority for decades; the National Trust, a private organization established in part to save natural areas, is the single largest landowner in England. In addition there are hundreds of volunteer organizations that work to protect the environment. Government and local groups maintain public footpaths and parks, while educational programs run by such nature organizations as the Royal Society for the Protection of Birds (RSPB) help educate the public to the plight of endangered species.

TOUR OPERATORS

Earthwatch. 13 days / $ (from Guernsey) / July, August. "The Cliffs of Guernsey" is a research trip to study the ecology of the cliffs. Volunteers measure plant cover and soil depth, collect insects, and identify plants and birds.

Field Studies Council

7 days / $$ (from Southampton) / April. A natural history trip with an emphasis on botany. Guernsey's 25 square miles are abloom with gorse, bluebell, and campion in spring, but a closer look reveals many more species—both British and continental. The islands of Herm and Sark are also visited (weather permitting).

3–7 days. $$ (from various locations in Britain) / January–December. The Field Studies Council offers a variety of programs at eleven residential centers throughout England and Wales. Recent offerings have included: "Winter Birds Weekend," "Bird Songs and Calls," "Life on and Around the Seashore," "Butterflies and Moths," "The Badger," "The Otter," "Bat Ecology," "A Weekend with Orchids," "Wildflowers of Shropshire and the Borderland," "Lichens near London," "Fern Weekend," "Geology and Landscapes in Southeast England," and "Upland Ecology Surveys."

7 days / $$ (from Penzance) / May, September. A general natural history tour of the Isles of Scilly, the "fortunate isles." The Scillies are home to a wide variety of seabirds, and the mild climate fosters a flora more typical of southwestern Europe than Britain.

Learn at Leisure

3 days / $ (from various locations in Britain) / May–November. Learn at Leisure offers a variety of weekend programs. A sampling of these include: "Coastal

Dunes," "Ancient Woodlands," "Geology and Scenery in North Norfolk," "Birds of Minsmere and Flatford," "Peak District Wildflowers," and "Fungi in the Forest of Dean." All these are study programs and are based either at Horncastle Residential College or at various field study centers; the "tutors" are experienced naturalists. In addition there is a series of programs at the Gibraltar Point Field Station, an 1,100-acre nature reserve located near Skegness, on England's east coast in Lincolnshire.

7 days / $ (from Guernsey) / September. "Guernsey: An Inside View" is a general natural history trip for birds, plants, geology, and marine science. A marine biologist leads the trip.

Scotland

Occupying about one third of the island of Great Britain, Scotland is a cool, wet country bounded on three sides by the sea. Just off its northern coast are the Orkney and Shetland islands; the Hebrides are off the western coast, in the North Atlantic.

Scotland divides naturally into three regions: highlands, lowlands, and southern uplands. Most natural history trips visit the highlands and often the islands, the latter for their nesting seabirds. The highlands are rich in animal life, including Fox, Badger, Pine Marten, Otter, Hare, and herds of Red and Roe Deer. There are also nesting Osprey, Golden Eagles, Common Buzzards, and Kestrels. The Capercaillie, Scottish Crossbill, and the many seabirds—such as Northern Gannet, Northern Fulmar, and Guillemot—attract birdwatchers each year. Among the marine mammals found in Scottish waters are Atlantic Gray Seal and Common Seal.

Most of Scotland's ancient forests were cleared in the course of the centuries, and some areas, especially in the north, subsequently were replanted for timber production. The remaining landscape comprises grassy areas and heaths or bogs, the latter covered with bearberry, crowberry, blueberry, and bog cotton. At higher elevations are alpine and Arctic species of wildflowers.

TOUR OPERATORS

Borrobol Birding. 7 days / $$$ (from Kinbrace) / April–July. A week-long birdwatching and natural history program based in a sporting lodge built in 1900 by the Duke of Sutherland. Conservationists call the region "Britain's Serengeti," and for a week birdwatchers and wildlife enthusiasts have a chance to explore this remote area, one of the world's rarest ecosystems. The 23,000-acre estate is replete with moors, heather-covered heathlands, lochs, a long section of the River Helmsdale, woodlands, Stone Age ruins (neolithic brochs), and pastureland. Over 150 species of birds can be seen on the estate, as well as many mammals, including

Red and Roe Deer. On the first day, participants explore the estate, where they can easily see Short-eared Owl, three species of divers (loons), Red Grouse, Northern Lapwing, Greylag Goose, Grey Heron, Blue Tit, and Common Cuckoo. A Tawny Owl roosts in the woods right by the house and can be seen (and heard) regularly. (We saw it from our rooms.) The program includes excursions to nearby localities of interest, such as Handa Reserve—an island with millions of nesting Atlantic Puffins, Razorbills, Black Guillemots, Parasitic Jaegers, and Black-legged Kittiwakes. Trips to Ben Hope and the northernmost tip of Scotland (John O' Groats) yield Golden Eagle, Peregrine Falcon, and a great view of the Orkney Islands. Attention is paid to plants as well, and throughout the season (May to July) many species can be found. Some time is also devoted to the historical and cultural aspects of northern Scotland: There are tours of Dornoch Cathedral and Dunrobin Castle as well as of the Camster Cairns, believed to be many hundreds of years old. Maximum of 6 participants (each week). A RSPB ornithologist is the guide on all trips.

Earthwatch. 9 days / $$ (from Islay) / April–June. "Birds of the Hebrides" is a research trip to study the Yellow-billed Chough, a large black bird related to magpies.

Field Studies Council

7 days / $ (from Glasgow) / March. "Geese, Peat and Malt Whiskey: Winter Birdwatching on Islay." To some, Islay is one of the foremost ornithological sites in Europe. Hundreds of geese winter on this small island. Other species to be expected include divers (loons), ducks, and raptors. In addition you'll see Common and Gray Seals and Otter.

10 days / $$ (from Aberdeen) / June. A general natural history trip to the major islands of Shetland and Orkney, on which the North Sea oil industry has fallen with an intrusive presence.

Oceanic Society Expeditions/California Academy of Sciences. 14 days / $$ (from Edinburgh) / May. A combination birding and archaeology trip to northern Scotland, the Shetlands, and the Orkneys. Hiking in the moors you should see Merlin and Hen Harriers, while Golden Eagles and Ptarmigan are at higher elevations. A special visit to the Aigas Estate provides access to diverse habitats used by waders, ducks, and passerines such as the Scottish Crossbill, Crested Tit, and Siskin. There's even a chance of finding the Capercaillie. Historic sites visited include the Clava Cairns and Cawdor Castle. On the Shetlands, more exceptional birding opportunities are offered, such as the bird cliffs of Sumburgh Head, home to thousands of seabirds, including puffins, razorbills, and kittiwakes, and at the Isle of Noss, one of Europe's greatest seabird colonies—a refuge for Great Skua,

Northern Gannet, and Black Guillemot. A scientist from the California Academy of Sciences accompanies the trip.

Questers. 21 days / $$ (from Glasgow) / June, July. A combination cultural and natural history trip to the northern highlands and the outer islands (the Hebrides, Orkneys, and Shetlands). A trip to the bird sanctuary on Handa—site of some amazing bird cliffs—is also included. Walks in woodlands and birdwatching give participants a general understanding of the natural forces of this unique area. In the highlands, mountains, and moors you can see Red Deer, Golden Eagle, and Mountain Hare.

Wilderness Travel. 16 days / $$ (from Glasgow) / June–August. Combination cultural and natural history trips to the Scottish highlands and isles. The sight-seeing is vehicle-based; natural history hikes are from one to three miles. On the Isle of Skye you'll look for alpine plants and Golden Eagles, then return to the mainland and continue up the west coast to Scourie before going on to the Orkneys.

World Wildlife Fund. 11 days / $$$$ (from Scotland) / May. A general natural history cruise aboard the 140-passenger *Illiria.* A WWF representative accompanies the trip.

Ireland

The republic of Ireland is an island of natural beauty across the Irish Sea from Great Britain. It comprises a broad central plain ringed by coastal highlands. The plain is broken by low hills, boggy areas, and lakes. Most of the country is rural, primarily agricultural areas and peat bogs. The peat bogs are Ireland's unique resource, but at present they remain unprotected from commercial exploitation.

Animal species in Ireland are similar to those in Great Britain but fewer in number, so it is primarily plants—some of which have migrated to Ireland from the Mediterranean— that are the focus of most nature tours. The islands off the southwest coast, however, are noted for their bird populations.

TOUR OPERATORS

Branta Holidays. 7 days / $$ (from London) / June. A birding trip to the Skelligs, Puffin Island, and the southwest coast, where you are based. Some time is spent land birding around the Shannon estuary and at the cliffs of Moher. Birds are primarily seabirds: Northern Gannets, Atlantic Puffins, Manx Shearwaters, and storm-petrels. In the wet meadows are nesting waders and Corncrakes, while

Peregrine Falcons and Yellow-billed Choughs are found around the cliffs. At this season there is also a profusion of wildflowers.

Field Studies Council

7 days / $ (from Holyhead) / April. "Trees of Ireland." The high humidity and temperate climate of Ireland are conducive to the rapid and healthy growth of trees. Irish gardens are particularly rich in specimens from the Southern Hemisphere. The tour visits several fine collections, including Birr Castle and Mount Usher. Evening discussions cover general subjects in basic tree botany.

7 days / $$ (from London) / July. "Flowers of the Burren" is a botanical exploration of County Clare, long famed for its rich flora. Here there is a mysterious mixture of plants—Arctic subalpines growing side-by-side with Mediterranean species. Flowers that can be seen include Mountain Avens, Bloody Cranesbill, Shrubby Cinquefoil, and several species of orchid.

Learn at Leisure. 7 days / $$ (from London) / May. "Wildflowers of the Burren." The burren is an area of limestone country located on the west coast of Ireland, near Galway Bay, where many species of wildflowers can be found. A botanist accompanies the trip.

WESTERN EUROPE

France

In a country with so many other fine attractions—good food, great wine, wonderful art—it could be difficult to pack your bag and head for the hills. But France's countryside is every bit as inviting as its cities, with a diversity of habitat unmatched in the rest of Western Europe. About 25 percent of the land is still covered by forests, and about 8 percent is set aside in preserves and parks. The country is especially rich in flora, with about 40 percent of all European species.

France is bordered on the north by Belgium, Luxembourg, and the English Channel; on the west by the Atlantic Ocean and the Bay of Biscay; on the south by Spain and the Mediterranean Sea; and on the east by Germany, Switzerland, and Italy. It has two major mountain chains: the Alps in the east and the Pyrenees in the southwest. As the following trips show, the Alps and Pyrenees are major attractions for botanists and birders. In addition, the Camargue—a vast wetland in southern France—is a strong draw for birders eager to see the Greater Flamingo, while several areas in the south and center of the country are excellent for butterflies.

TOUR OPERATORS

Birding. 7 days / $$ (from London) / May. A birdwatching trip to Corsica, a French island in the Mediterranean, home to the endemic Corsican Nuthatch.

Other birds that can be seen on this trip include Lammergeier, Goshawk, Peregrine Falcon, Alpine Accentor, Citril Finch, and several breeding warblers, including Marmora's, Dartford, Subalpine, and Sardinian. Maximum of 16 participants, 2 leaders.

Field Studies Council

7 days / $$ (from London) / May. "The Wildlife of Western Brittany." Although this is a general natural history trip, there is a special emphasis on butterflies and other insects. A wide variety of habitats are visited, including moorland, heathland, oak forest, and coastal dunes and cliffs.

14 days / $$ (from London) / May. "Flowers of the Eastern Pyrenees" is a botanical trip based in the valley of Vernet-les-Bains. Habitats vary from limestone gorges to high meadows (possibly white with *Narcissus*) to woodlands. One of the gorges explored is home to a number of *Ramonda* plants; *Ramonda* is one of the many species endemic to the Pyrenean mountains. Two botanists accompany the trip.

12 days / $$ (from London) / June. "The High Pyrenees: Flowers." A botanical trip to the lower meadows, the forests of the middle slopes, and the high pastures of this mountain range. Endemics—such as *Saxifraga longifolia* and *Ramonda myconi*—are searched for.

14 days / $$ (from London) / June. "The High Pyrenees: Flowers, Birds, and Butterflies." This is one of Europe's best places for flowers and butterflies, of which many endemics can be found here. Participants will also look for raptors and the many species of montane birds that inhabit the Pyrenees. This trip goes to higher elevations, and is in general more strenuous, than the "Flowers" trip (see above). Two leaders accompany the trip.

7 days / $$ (from London) / July. "Birds and Dragonflies of the Camargue." Among the Greater Flamingos, Short-toed Eagles, and Squacco Herons can be found an amazing array of dragonflies. Participants study and enjoy both, as well as the mammals and amphibians of this rich delta region. There are also good opportunities for wildlife photography. Two leaders accompany the trip.

HF Holidays. 14 days / $ (from London) / July. A "Natural History Ramble" that centers around Bareges in the Haute Pyrenees.

Naturetrek. 9 days / $$ (from London) / June. A birdwatching and botanical trip exploring the Parc National des Pyrenees. Among the many species you may encounter are: Citril Finch, Lammergeier, Griffon Vulture, Golden Eagle, Yellow-billed and Red-billed Choughs, Bonelli's Warbler, and Black Woodpecker. Two leaders—an ornithologist and a botanist—accompany the trip.

Questers. 14 days / $$$$ (from New York) / May. A combination natural history and cultural trip to Provence and the Côte d'Azur in the south of France. You'll visit the Camargue and La Crau, both premier birding sites. Maximum 20 participants, 1 leader.

Sunbird

3 days / $$ (from Dover, England) / February. A birding trip to northern France for wintering White-tailed Eagle and Common Crane. Other birds that can be seen on this trip include Bean Goose, Smew, Red Kite, Peregrine Falcon, Black Woodpecker, Short-toed Treecreeper, and Crested Tit.

10 days / $$ (from London) / June. A birding trip to southern France—the Camargue and the Pyrenees. Participants can expect to see upwards of 100 species of birds, including Greater Flamingo, Collared Pratincole, Bittern, and Moustached Warbler in the Camargue. On the stony plain of La Crau you'll look for Little Bustard, Stone Curlew, Calandra Lark, and Tawny Pipit. While in the Pyrenees, Capercaillie, Lammergeier, Golden Eagle, Black Woodpecker, Wallcreeper, Red-billed Chough, and Snow Finch are among the target birds.

Spain, Gibraltar, and Portugal

The second largest country in Western Europe, Spain has an abundance of wild and serene areas for the visiting naturalist. Indeed, according to Frederic Grunfeld, author of *Wild Spain: A Traveler's and Naturalist's Guide,* Spain is still the "wildest country in Europe; not far from any of the big cities you can always find areas that are light-years removed from modernity." Although the amenities exist here, many parts of the country remain rugged and remote, perfect habitat for some of Europe's more elusive species.

Most of the country is on the Meseta, a vast plateau about 2,000 feet high with mountains on almost all sides: the Cantabrians and Pyrenees in the north, the Iberians in the east, the Sierra Nevada in the south, and the lower mountains on the border with Portugal. Northern Spain is covered with deciduous forests and meadows. The mountains are premier spots for endemic wildflowers—fritillarias, gentians, jonquils, violets, toadflax, buttercups, crocuses, and columbine. Although most large mammals are gone from the wild, the national parks support populations of bear, deer, wild pig, Spanish Ibex (threatened), and Chamois, as well as partridges and grouse, songbirds, vultures, owls, and eagles.

On the plains, where much of the land has been turned over to agriculture, the lakes and ponds attract waterbirds, while the steppe habitat is the only Western European home for the Great and Little Bustards; this half-cultivated land is also habitat for the Pin-tailed Sandgrouse, Red-necked Nightjar, Andalusian Hemipode, and Stone Curlew. The *dehesa* (mixed grassland and trees) supports populations of Montagu's Harrier, Azure-winged Magpie, Golden Oriole, Roller, and Bee-eater. Some areas of the coast, especially in the south, have marshes, dunes, and coastal forests with numbers of egrets, herons, and Spoonbills. One of Europe's three breeding sites for Greater Flamingo is here, too, as are large flocks of migrating waders in springtime. Lakes and ponds in Andalusia remain the only Western European refuge for the widely threatened White-headed Duck.

Off the eastern coast are the Balearic Islands, whose beaches are popular tourist destinations, but Majorca in particular also is a major naturalist getaway, primarily because of its wet, high mountains—good for migrating birds as well as wild orchids and a host of other wildflowers.

Spain has been protecting its natural areas since 1918, when the first parks were established in the north. At present there are nine national parks, five of which are on the mainland. In addition, a group of locally managed natural parks has been established—especially in Catalonia, Galicia, and Andalusia—to set aside areas of exceptional value. Hunting in reserves operated especially for that purpose has been curtailed to protect threatened species. Although Spain's economy is growing by leaps and bounds—and that usually means habitat destruction— if tourists give more attention to the country's "natural" resources, there's a good chance this corner of Europe will retain much of its primary growth and rugged character.

In sharp contrast, the minuscule southern tip of the Iberian Peninsula that is Gibraltar is mostly solid rock honeycombed with tunnels and roads. Although there is very little vegetation here, nevertheless this bastion of British life attracts birdwatchers, botanists, and butterfly lovers. Owing to its geographical position, migrating birds literally drop from the skies each spring and fall. And there are the famous Barbary Apes, the only wild apes remaining in Europe.

Portugal occupies the other 15 percent of the Iberian Peninsula. Despite its small area, the country has a variety of habitats—lowlands, plains, river basins, and gentle undulating hills rising to mountains that reach 3,200 feet. Not many nature trips go exclusively to Portugal, although it is sometimes included on tours to Spain.

TOUR OPERATORS

Birding

7 days / $$ (from London) / March. "The Straits of Gibraltar and Spain" is a birdwatching trip based in the Gib with daily excursions into Spain. Special birds that you'll look for include Barbary Partridge, Audouin's Gull, Lesser Crested Tern, and Little Bustard. A feature of the trip—providing the winds are right—is sighting the many migrating raptors.

7 days / $$ (from London) / March. Based at Coto Doñana, one of Europe's best and most famous birding spots. Doñana is a wilderness of marshes, dunes, and forests at the mouth of the Guadalquivir River. Waders and raptors are specialties of the area, and many passerines can be seen as well. A series of blinds (hides) overlooks a fine marsh, offering opportunities to see Water Rail, Purple Swampher, and Savi's Warbler.

7 days / $$ (from London) / May. A birdwatching holiday to Spain and Portugal, concentrating on the dehesa habitat of the border and Monfragüe Natural Park (Spain). Participants may expect to see upwards of 110 species of birds, including raptors (at Monfragüe's spectacular Peña Falcon cliffs), storks, both Great and Little Bustards, Azure-winged Magpie, and a variety of passerines.

7 days / $$ (from London) / April. A birding trip to Coto Doñana and Andalusia. A special feature of this trip is a visit to Laguna Medina, where you'll see the rare and endangered White-headed Duck and possibly Red-crested Pochard, Marbled Teal, and Crested Coot as well. Blue Rock Thrush and Rock Bunting are likely in Grazalema, while Yellow-billed Chough and Lesser Kestrel can be seen in the Ronda gorge.

Branta Holidays

8 days / $$ (from London) / April. The rich birdlife of the sierras, plains, and lagunas of the Extremadura are explored on this week-long trip. At least 20 of the more than 40 sites listed (by the International Council for Bird Preservation) as "Important Bird Areas of Europe" are visited, including Monfragüe, the lagoons of La Mancha, the plains of the Rio Salor, and the Tablas de Montiel. Nearly 200 species of birds can be seen, including both Black and White Stork, Montagu's Harrier, both Great and Little Bustard, Collared Pratincole, Black-bellied Sandgrouse, Bee-eater, Roller, Hoopoe, Wryneck, Green Woodpecker, Calandra Lark, Nightingale, Blue Rock Thrush, Dartford Warbler, Golden Oriole, and Hawfinch. Ibex and Hedgehog are among the mammals to be seen.

7 days / $$ (from London) / May. A trip that combines birdwatching and wildflower finding in the magnificent scenery of the Pyrenean foothills. Based in Berdún, a flexible program takes you from the sheer gorge at the Hoz de Arbayun into the Haute Pyrenees. There are daily field excursions, and birds in the Berdún area include Golden Eagle, Bonelli's Eagle, Lammergeier, Blue Rock Thrush, Melodious Warbler, Citril Finch, Golden Oriole, and Red-billed Chough.

5 days / $$ (from London) / June. "The Eagles of Guadarrama." This short birding trip concentrates on birds of prey in the Sierra de Guadarrama and the area to the southwest of El Escorial. Four species of eagle breed there (Golden, Bonelli's, Imperial, and Booted). Eagle Owl, Black Stork, Ortolan Bunting, and

Crested Tit can be seen as well. The area is also widely known for its splendid wildflowers; one tour group found a meadow full of orchids.

Cox & Kings

14 days / $$ (from London) / May. A natural history tour to Berdún, a village in the Aragon foothills of the Pyrenees. Participants observe and learn about birds, butterflies, flowers, and freshwater amphibians. The flora is varied, and in the high pastures late spring alpines that are blooming include gentians, orchids, wild daffodils, and the Pyrenean Fritillary. Among the many species of birds to be seen is a wide variety of raptors, Rock Thrush, Rock Sparrow, Black-eared Wheatear, Ortolan Bunting, and Alpine Accentor. Butterfly life is exceptionally rich. Over 50 species are commonplace, among them Camberwell Beauty, Apollo, Clouded Yellow, Spanish Festoon, blues, and skippers. In the many wet areas, frogs, newts, and salamanders can be found.

14 days / $$ (from London) / June, July. A natural history tour to Coto Doñana and the sierras of southwest Andalusia. You'll look for birds, dragonflies, plants, and animals—possibly finding the endemic Spanish Ibex. Maximum of 8 participants, 1 leader.

Earthwatch. 14 days / $ (from Palma, Majorca) / April, May, October. "Albufera Wildlife" is a research trip studying global environmental change and how such change is reflected in this unspoiled Mediterranean wetland. Volunteers and scientists are working on a comprehensive study over several years—everything from "ground truthing" satellite images to taking core samples to establishing the marsh's prehistoric natural history. The directors of the project hope to make the site part of the United Nations' Geosphere-Biosphere Program's network of monitoring stations. Volunteers walk transects to record plants, butterflies, mollusks, birds, and mammals, and to collect water samples. They measure water flow and depth, analyze soil nutrients, and survey the marsh's topography.

Field Studies Council

7 days / $$ (from London) / April. "Another Brush with Birds: Painting and Watching Birds in Andalusia" offers you the opportunity to engage in either one or both of these activities. The rugged Serrania de Ronda mountains provide a stronghold for birds of prey. A bonus is the many flowering plants at this time of year.

14 days / $$ (from London) / April. "Flowers and Birds in Andalusia." Birdwatchers will enjoy the migration across the Strait of Gibraltar, while botanists will be pleased with the unique flora of Spain's most southerly region.

Focus on Nature. 10 days / $$ (from Madrid) / June. A birdwatching trip to the Extremadura, including Monfragüe—famous for its raptors—the Sierra de

Gredos, the Pyrenees, and the Ebro Delta. Participants may expect to see about 130 species of birds, including many raptors. Special birds that will be looked for include Eurasian Black Vulture, Lammergeier, Spanish Imperial Eagle, Eagle Owl, Audouin's Gull, Wallcreeper, Black-bellied Sandgrouse, Dupont's Lark, and Savi's and Marmora's Warblers.

Learn at Leisure. 7 days / $$ (from London) / May. "Flowers of the Serrania de Ronda." Spain's most southerly mountains, the Serrania de Ronda, are in one of the prettiest areas in Europe—with a wonderful landscape of jagged peaks and narrow gorges. Flowers are everywhere. On walks, participants explore the blend of montane and Mediterranean vegetation of these mountains. Some time is spent at Grazalema National Park. Walks also take you through the aromatic garrigue, heavy with the scent of thyme, lavender, and rosemary. Of course, the birdlife is not ignored: Many species breed here, including Blue Rock Thrush, Nightingale, Firecrest, Green Woodpecker, Wren, Northern Wheatear, and Black Redstart.

Wings/Sunbird

10 days / $ (from Palma, Majorca) / April. A birdwatching trip to Majorca. Varied habitats—mountains, marsh, and coast—make for a wide variety of birds, and each location has its special attractions. Gargany, Water Rail, Moustached Warbler, and Slender-billed Gull can be found at Albufera marsh. Eurasian Black Vulture, Eleonora's Falcon, Booted Eagle, and Blue Rock Thrush are in the Arta Mountains. While at Porto Colóm, seawatching should bring views of the rarest gull in the world, Audouin's. The nearby salt pans of the Salinas de Levante can be crowded with waders of many species. For many birdwatchers, Majorca's main appeal is the impressive spectacle of migrants, and this trip is timed to coincide with the height of spring migration.

8 days / $$ (from Madrid or Barcelona) / May, June. Hard-core birdwatching tours to either central Spain and Andalusia (May) or to the Pyrenees and Ebro Delta (June). You'll travel with Tom Gullick, who has lived in central Spain for many years. He has thus gained access to estates that would otherwise be closed to the public, and, as a result, his groups regularly observe many of Europe's rarest birds. Maximum of 4 participants.

Switzerland

Although a tiny country—about half the size of Maine—Switzerland claims as its primary naturalist feature the Alps, which run east-west across the southern part of the country, occupying about one third of its land mass. The remainder consists of the Jura Mountains to the west and a broad plateau called the Mittelland.

All of the following tours go to the Alps, for their wildflowers, butterflies, birds, and glacial features. Animals that might be seen are the Marmot, Chamois, and Ibex.

TOUR OPERATORS

Cox & Kings. 14 days / $$ (from London) / June, July. A botany tour to Wengen in the central Alps. Among the many alpine flowers are the lovely Trumpet Gentians. The June trip will see such species as Crocus, Narcissus-flowered Anemones, Yellow Auricula, and other primulas and campanulas. In July, Glacier Buttercups, Martagon Lily, and Alpine Sowthistle are in bloom, among many other plants. Orchids can be seen on both tours, as well as birds, including Black Woodpecker, Snow Finch, Nutcracker, and, perhaps with luck, a Wall-creeper. Maximum of 20 participants. Noted botanist Mary Briggs leads both tours.

Field Studies Council. 14 days / $$ (from London) / June, July. "Butterflies, Flowers, and Nature Photography" in the Swiss Alps. The Valais region is partic-ularly rich in butterflies and flowers. This is a general natural history tour with ample opportunity to photograph the flowers and insects and to explore natural habitats. The July trip is the more strenuous. In the evenings the leaders present illustrated talks.

HF Holidays

7 days / $$ (from London) / June. Based in Wengen, in the Swiss Alps, this is a "Nature Ramble" exploring all aspects of natural history—flowers, birds, butter-flies, and glaciers.

7 days / $$ (from London) / July. Based at Les Marecottes in the Valais, south of Lake Geneva, this is a general "Nature Ramble."

Swan Hellenic

8 days / $$$ (from London) / June. A botanical tour of the Bernese Oberland, based in Wengen. A botanist and tour manager accompany the trip.

8 days / $$$ (from London) / July. A botanical tour of the Valais. Among the many alpine flowers you may see are orchids, primulas, campanulas, saxifragas, and gentians. A botanist and tour manager accompany the trip.

Austria

Austria is a scenic, wooded, and largely mountainous country about the size of Maine. In fact, Austria is one of the mostly densely forested countries in central Europe, with stands of larch, beech, and oak, and conifers in alpine regions. The eastern edge of the Alps extends far into Austria, while the lowland area down-stream from Vienna is a western extension of the Great Hungarian Plain. There are many lakes, some of which are alpine, but others—like the Neusiedlersee near the eastern border—are marshy.

Austria values its natural riches and takes care of them. There are over 125 nature reserves or protected areas. The country protects over 300 plant species and over 100 animal species, the latter including Brown Bear, Golden Eagle, Common Buzzard, cranes, swans, and storks. The country also has the strictest standards for auto emissions in Europe and operates an extensive recycling program.

TOUR OPERATORS

Birds and Birders/Motmot

10 days / $$ (from Vienna) / August. A birding tour visiting the Neusiedlersee, the alpine forests and meadows of the Schneeberg, and the WWF Reserve at Marchegg. About 100 species of birds can be seen on this trip, including Saker Falcon; Purple, Grey, and Squacco Herons; Spoonbill; Little Ringed Plover; both Black and White Storks; Ring Ouzel; Alpine Accentor; Black Woodpecker; and Moustached, Reed, Savi's, and Sedge Warblers.

14 days / $$ (from Vienna) / July. A birdwatching tour to Austria, Hungary, and the Czech Republic. Hills, lowlands, forests, steppe, and alpine habitat guarantee a wide range of species. Birds don't recognize international boundaries! From Lake Neusiedl, Europe's largest saltwater lake, to the World Wildlife Fund's reserve at Marchegg (Austria), you can expect to see several species of woodpeckers, Bee-eater, Bluethroat, and a host of warblers and waders. The Czech counterpart of the Marchegg Reserve lies on the juncture of two rivers near Mikulov. Saker Falcon, Water Rail, and Bearded Tit can be found here. The third base is the Hungarian side of Lake Neusiedl, called Lake Ferto. Here the vast reedbeds shelter herons, warblers, and crakes. On the steppe, you can see Kentish Plover and Crested Lark, while the meadows of the Hansag Reserve are ablaze with flowers. Lesser Grey Shrikes often can be seen perched on the phone wires. A trip to the Eszterhazy Palace and its grounds rounds out the tour.

HF Holidays. 14 days / $ (from London) / June. "Nature Rambles" are general interest natural history walks. Participants are based in one of two centers: Mayrhofen in the Tyrol or Telfes in the Stubai, south of Innsbruck. Animals, birds, and wildflowers abound in this region in June, and you can walk as much (or as little) as you like.

Sunbird. 10 days / $$ (from London) / May. A birdwatching trip to the varied habitats of eastern Austria. Around the Neusiedlersee you can expect local specialties such as Black-necked Grebe, Purple Heron, and Spoonbill, as well as ducks and other waders. The reedbeds in the area provide shelter for Savi's Marsh, Moustached, and Great Reed Warblers. Bluethroat, Nightingale, and Golden Oriole will be singing and so easier to find. The flat plains around Tadten provide a good chance for finding displaying Great Bustard. In the mountain areas you'll look for Red-billed Chough, Crested Tit, and Nutcracker, while the formal gardens of Schönbrunn Palace (in Vienna) provide a chance to see Grey-headed Woodpecker and Hawfinch.

Wings/Sunbird. 12 days / $$ (from London) / September. "Birds and Music" is a birdwatching trip timed to coincide with the Eisenstadt International Haydn Festival. Birding in the daytime, concerts in the evening. Cost includes good tickets for all concerts. Maximum of 16 participants, 2 leaders.

Italy and Malta

A boot-shaped peninsula extending into the Mediterranean Sea, with the islands of Sicily and Sardinia alongside, Italy is characterized by alpine peaks in its far north; the less lofty Apennine Mountains down its spine and extending to Sicily; and areas of lowland plains, rivers, and lakes. Italy is a major attraction geologically, with the recent (1992) activity of Mount Etna of special note.

On the plains, especially in the Po Valley, there is almost no original forest; it has been replaced by agriculture. At higher altitudes in the south there are traces of native woods, and more extensive beechwoods in Calabria and Puglia and silver fir and pine in Abruzzi. In the Alps, however, the situation is better, with native species of wildflowers, mosses, and other plants that are the focus of several of the tours listed in the following pages.

Animal life in Italy has been reduced severely over the centuries, primarily from hunting and habitat destruction. In the Alps one can see high-altitude species such as Marmot, Ermine, Ibex, and Chamois, while farther south, in Abruzzo National Park, are Bear and Wolf. But at lower elevations and in more inhabited regions the situation is poor. Interest in protecting the environment is growing, and the existing national parks and preserves protect about 4 percent of the country's land resources, but hunting—of birds as well as animals—remains very popular and there is but weak enforcement of the existing environmental legislation.

Malta comprises a small group of islands in the central Mediterranean, south of Sicily, that have occupied a central position in Mediterranean geography and history up to the present day. The islands are thought to be the remnants of a land bridge between Sicily and North Africa. Despite their small size, they offer a rich and diverse flora as well as an interesting avifauna, especially migrating birds in spring. The few native mammals include the Hedgehog, Least Weasel, Water and White-toothed Shrew, and Pipistrel and other bats. There are also several species of butterflies.

Hunting is a problem in Malta. Recently there has been a dispute between hunting tour operators and the Malta Ornithological Society, as a result of the latter's attempts to discourage the hunting of birds. Since tourism is a growing part of Malta's economy, we urge you to watch this issue closely, with the hope that the resolution is in favor of sustaining wildlife.

TOUR OPERATORS

Birding. 7 days / $$ (from London) / March. A birdwatching trip to Italy concentrating on the area just south of Rome. Most of the time is spent in Circeo National Park. Maximum of 16 participants, 1 leader.

Cox & Kings

12 days / $$ (from London) / April. "The Orchids of Gargano." Gargano is a mountainous promontory off the Adriatic coast of Italy, about 100 miles northeast of Naples. In spring and early summer, flowers abound in this area, including many rare species of orchids, while the shady woodlands of the Foresta Umbra, coastal dunes, and cliffs provide a number of alternative habitats. Over 35 species of orchids are possible, as well as many other plants. Two botanists lead the tour.

14 days/ $$ (from London) / June. A botany trip to the Dolomites. Participants are centered in Selva, in the upper reaches of the Val Gardena (4,500 feet elevation), near Val Lunga National Park. Daily excursions to the park, nearby passes, the Gardena Valley, and the alpine meadows of the Alpe di Suisi enable you to observe the rich and interesting flora. Special attention is paid to the alpine rock plants of this area, including Edelweiss. Up to 45 species of butterflies and 60 species of birds can also be seen here. Two botanists lead the tour.

Field Studies Council. 14 days / $$ (from London) / June. "Flowers of the Central Apennines." This botany tour visits two mountain ranges, the Sibilline Alps and the Abruzzi, each having a distinctly different character. High grassy limestone plateaus predominate in the central Apennines.

Swan Hellenic. 9 days / $$$ (from London) / June. A botanical tour of the Dolomites. During the daily excursions participants may expect to see orchids, gentians, saxifrage, and anemones among many other species. You'll be based in Corvara and visit Vallelunga National Park, Ortisei in the Gardena Valley, and the Pordoi Pass (over 6,500 feet), the highest pass in the Dolomites. A botanist and a tour manager accompany the trip.

Greece

Stretching across the tip of the Balkan Peninsula from the Ionian to the Aegean seas, and including islands in both seas, Greece is bordered by Albania, Macedonia, Bulgaria, and Turkey. The Greek landscape is varied, with the sea always a major factor. Much of the land is rocky and mountainous, and the vegetation is classic Mediterranean scrub, with evergreen trees and herbaceous plants in the lowlands and pine forests at higher levels. Botanists find Greece, especially Crete, rich in endemic species.

Athens is renowned for its air pollution, but the trappings of urban life can quickly be left behind with a natural history tour to the Pindos Mountains in the north, a walk through fields of thyme on the Peloponnese, or a hike down the rugged Samaria Gorge on Crete.

TOUR OPERATORS

Birding. 7 days / $$ (from London) / April. A birdwatching tour to Crete, largest of the Greek islands. Special species to look out for include Lammergeier, often found on the Lassithi and Omalos plateaus; Eleonora's Falcon, seen near the Minoan ruins at Knossos; and Ruppell's Warbler, seen near Sfakion, on the Libyan Sea.

Cox & Kings. 14 days / $$ (from London) / March. A botanical tour of Crete covering the entire island—from the Minoan harbor at Falasarna (in the west) to the palms at Vai (in the east). Participants visit the Minoan ruins at Knossos, Malia, Gournia, and Phaestos; the Lassithi and Omalos plateaus; and walk the Imbros Gorge. It is not unusual to see fields of anemones, and over a dozen species of orchids may be seen in a single day. In addition you may see peonies; Asian Buttercups in white, yellow, and pink; several varieties of iris; *Tulipa cretica* and *Tulipa saxatilis;* and Cyclamen. Maximum of 20 participants. Noted botanist Mary Briggs leads the tour.

Earthwatch. 14 days / $$ (from Litochoro) / July, August. "Mount Olympus" is a research trip based on Olympus. Armed with topographical maps, volunteers map, measure, and record glacial deposits and features as part of an ongoing study of this famous mountain.

Field Studies Council. 14 days / $ (from London) / June. "Flowers and Landscapes of the Pindos Mountains." This is a different Greece from the islands and fishing villages; it's a chance to explore the flora of the mainland. The Pindos Mountains, dry and rugged, punctuated by dry valleys, gorges, and ravines, are the backbone of central Greece. The varied relief provides ample opportunities for botanizing. Even though there are vast rock-covered areas, forests still blanket much of the northern Pindos. While above the treeline, high meadows harbor many alpine plants. Daily walks are at a moderate pace; naturalists never walk very fast!

Naturetrek

14 days / $ (from London) / June. A combination birdwatching and botanical trip to the Pindos Mountains. Close to the Albanian border, the Pindos still provide a sanctuary for Brown Bear, Lynx, Wolf, Chamois, and many species of birds. Two leaders accompany the trip.

14 days / $$ (from London) / March. A holiday in search of spring flowers and migrating birds on the island of Crete. Participants are based at two locations on the island from which daily excursions are made—to the Lassithi Plateau, the salt pans at Malia, and the Dhikti Mountains. One day is spent walking the Imbros Gorge—a spectacular hike—to its end at Hora Sfakion, on the Libyan Sea.

Questers. 16 days / $$$ (from New York) / April, September. Although there are 1,500 or so Greek islands, this tour visits only a few: Mykonos, Delos, Santorini, Crete, and Rhodes. But these five are representative, and excellent places to study wildlife and historical sites. This is a combination natural history–cultural trip. You sail the wine-dark sea from Piraeus to Mykonos, on the lookout for Manx and Cory's Shearwaters. Nearby Delos is covered (in spring) with poppies. And on Mykonos, 6 species of falcon are possible, including the rare Eleonora's. On to Santorini to study its volcanos, and thence to Crete, the highest and largest of the islands. Here you will look for warblers and other perching birds as well as Griffon Vulture and Lammergeier; a day will be spent hiking the spectacular Samaria Gorge. On Rhodes you might see the rare Audouin's Gull, which is endemic to a few Mediterranean locations; an afternoon excursion inland will take you to the Valley of Butterflies, named for the thousands of Jersey Tiger Moths found here from June to September.

Sunbird. 7 days / $$ (from London) / August. A birdwatching trip to northern Greece in search of waterfowl and waders. An exploration of the Nestos Delta should produce Little Egret, Purple Heron, Collared Pratincole, and Spur-winged Plover. In the surrounding reeds and bushes you might find Cetti's Warbler and Penduline Tit. Other birdwatching sites to be visited are the Evros Delta (where you might sight an Isabelline Wheatear) and Avas Gorge—raptors and small birds such as Sombre Tit. Evening excursions may turn up Eagle and Scops Owls. A final stop at Lake Mitrikou can sometimes yield crakes. Previous trips have seen Spotted, Little, and the rare Baillon's.

Swan Hellenic. 11 days / $$$ (from London) / April. A botanical tour to the Peloponnese. The vegetation ranges from typical Mediterranean maquis and garrigue to forested slopes. Flowers at this time of year include Campanula, Corydalis, Dianthus, orchids, fritillarias, anemones, Euphorbia, and Viola. The hillsides of Mount Parnassus will be covered with thyme. Historical sites are visited as well. A botanist and a tour manager accompany the trip.

CENTRAL AND EASTERN EUROPE

When Europe's ideological boundaries crumbled in 1989, more than just potential new markets opened up for the West. It has become a great deal easier to visit nature reserves and national parks in former Eastern bloc countries, to enjoy the diversity of species and the often almost pristine natural conditions.

Yes, we said "pristine." There has been a lot of bad press about environmental damage in this part of the world, and we're certainly not denying that it exists. There are severe acid rain problems, areas with shockingly bad air quality, rivers and lakes that are heavily polluted, and toxic waste reserves that make your skin crawl. But remember that these are Western problems as well; we've just gotten used to hearing about them.

The good news is that some areas that were once off-limits, such as border regions, have been opened up to the public. And wise governments, like that of the Czech Republic, have made them into national parks or nature reserves. These areas have abundant wildflowers, butterflies, birds, insects, and mammals.

Also, because commercial development in the Eastern bloc countries was a great deal slower than in the West, some parts of these countries retain the rural character of Western Europe fifty years ago. In short, they are not as paved over. Indeed, there are parts of Poland, for example, that are as rugged and wild as Alaska.

Curiously, however, many visitors to Eastern Europe don't want to see wildlife. According to Jerry Balek, an environmental consultant for the United Nations who also runs a nature tour company in the Czech Republic, "To my surprise, an interest in unspoiled environment in Eastern Europe is rather marginal."

We'd like to think that ecotourism can play a big role in the future development of Eastern Europe. Rather than gloat about the failure of central control, responsible travelers to these parts can show the economic benefits to be derived from preserving what's wild and free.

Hungary

Located in the heart of Europe, Hungary is bordered by Slovakia on the north, Romania and Ukraine on the east, Austria on the west, and Slovenia, Croatia, and Yugoslavia on the south. Of all the Soviet bloc countries, Hungary had the strongest links with the West, and so today it is the furthest along on the road to a market economy. To the visitor, it seems the most Western in its amenities and services.

For the most part, Hungary is ringed by mountains with lowland in the center. Its most prominent natural features are the Great Hungarian Plain and Hortobagy

National Park, an area of grassland, marshes, and wetlands in central and north-eastern Hungary. All told, about 14 percent of Hungary is covered by meadows and pastures, with an additional 16 percent as forests. About 6 percent of the land is in nature preserves.

TOUR OPERATORS

Birding. 7 days / $$ (from London) / October. A birding tour through the Hortobagy and Zemplen Hills. Timed to coincide with the migration of raptors and waders, this trip also offers participants the opportunity to see eight species of woodpecker and possibly also the elusive Hazelhen. There are good chances for Eagle Owl as well.

Birdquest. 8 days / $$ (from London) / May, October. These are birdwatching trips. Although many of the same areas—the Hortobagy, Tokaj, and the Zemplen Hills—are visited on both trips, some of the birds will be different. On the spring trip you might see Stone Curlew, Golden Oriole, Great Bustard, Collared Pratincole, Red-footed Falcon, Savi's Warbler, Spotted Crake, Barred Warbler, and White-backed Woodpecker. Participants on the fall trip may see Saker Falcon, Lesser White-fronted Goose, Ural Owl, Eagle Owl, and White-tailed Eagle.

Birds and Birders/Motmot. 10 days / $$ (from Budapest) / September, October. Birdwatching tours timed to coincide with the migration peaks: waders and raptors in September; cranes and geese in October. The first part of the trip is based in Tokaj and visits the hills and forests of the Zemplen Hills as well as the marshes between the Tisza and Bodrog rivers. The second half is spent on the great plains of the Hortobagy National Park. In addition, Birds and Birders offers a combination trip to Austria, Hungary, and the Czech Republic (see the section on Austria, page 168).

Branta Holidays. 8 days / $$ (from London) / October. A birding trip to the Great Hungarian Plain. Fall migration in Hortobagy National Park is the scene of large movements of birds. Up to 10,000 Common Cranes, countless geese (White-fronted, Red-breasted, and Bean), and many species of raptor (including White-tailed Eagle, Long-legged Buzzard, Pallid Harrier, and Osprey) all pass through on their way to their wintering grounds. Great Bustard gather in flocks, and among the waders you may spot Broad-billed Sandpiper and Temminck's Stint. Both Eagle and Ural Owl can be seen, as well as lots of woodpeckers—notably Black, Grey-headed, and White-backed.

Earthwatch. 14 days / $ (from Budapest) / April, September. A research trip to study Lake Balaton. Runoff from vacation homes and farms is filling the lake with nutrients and sediment. Four teams of volunteers assess soil types, erosion rates, stream flow, and rainfall, and map land use.

Field Studies Council. 14 days / $$ (from London) / April. A birding trip to Hortobagy National Park and the Zemplen Hills. Participants can expect to see about 125 species of birds, including several woodpeckers, raptors, Eagle Owl, and a wide variety of passerines.

The Czech Republic and Slovakia

Two inland countries in the heart of Europe, the Czech Republic and Slovakia are bounded by Poland on the north, Ukraine on the east, Hungary and Austria on the south, and Germany on the west.

The hills and mountains of the western half of the Czech Republic constitutes Bohemia, while Slovakia is dominated by the Carpathians, including the scenic Tatra Mountains, some of which reach over 8,000 feet. In general, this is the area where Western and Eastern European species of flora and fauna meet, so the birding and botanizing are especially exciting.

Over half the region is still forested, mostly in Slovakia, less so in South Moravia (Czech), where fish farming and agriculture predominate. About 16 percent of the land has been set aside as reserves. Acid rain has been a major problem, although mostly in the north, and industrial pollution is heavy in Slovakia. The extensive borderlands with Germany and Austria, however, have recently been opened to the public, creating species-rich preserves and parks.

TOUR OPERATORS

Birding. 7 days / $$ (from London) / April. A spring birdwatching trip to the forests of Sumava and the Trebon Protected Landscape Area. You'll have the chance to see all ten of Europe's woodpeckers in addition to a host of other species.

Birds and Birders/Motmot. 10 days / $$ (from Prague) / April. A birding tour of southern Bohemia and Moravia, including a visit to the new Sumava National Park. Sumava is a mountainous area with forests, peat bogs, and wetlands—a unique European habitat. Special birds include Hazelhen, Black Grouse, Capercaillie, Black Woodpecker, and White-backed Woodpecker. It's also excellent for Pygmy, Eagle, and Tengmalm's (Boreal) Owls. The second part of the trip is spent exploring the fish ponds of southern Bohemia (Trebon Protected Landscape Area), where waterfowl abound, and there's a chance of seeing White-tailed Eagle. In the lowland area of Moravia, around Mikoluv, you might expect to see Lesser, Middle, and Great Spotted Woodpeckers; Grey-headed Woodpecker; Collared

Flycatcher; Saker Falcon; Bearded and Penduline Tits; and Black Stork. In addition, Birds and Birders offers a combination Hungary, Austria, and Czech birding tour (see the section on Austria, page 168).

Enex/Cal Nature Tours. 12 days / $ (from Prague) / May–September. Join the director of an environmental engineering consulting firm for a week-long program of environmental walks. The tour focuses on the environment of western and southern Bohemia—from acid-rain-destroyed forest to thermal springs to regions of tectonic activity. Since the fifteenth century a system of ponds has been built for freshwater fish production, and in the course of five centuries a unique ecosystem of water and riparian forest has been formed.

Sierra Club. 13 days / $$$ (from Prague) / July. This is a general natural history–cultural trip in the Tatra Mountains. Visits with concerned citizens will give you insight into local environmental problems.

Romania

Bounded by Hungary to the west; Ukraine to the north; Moldavia and the Black Sea to the east; and Bulgaria and Yugoslavia to the south, Romania is dominated by the soaring, forest-clad peaks of the Carpathian Mountains—high peaks with alpine and subalpine habitats for such rare European mammals as the Chamois, Brown Bear, Carpathian Stag, Wolf, Wild Boar, Lynx, Fox, and Pine Marten. Plains cover one third of the country, particularly in the south and west. The swampy Danube Delta in the east is known for its fish production, especially sturgeon and caviar, but it is also a stopping place for migratory birds, including pelicans, swans, ibis, flamingos, and the beautiful but endangered Red-breasted Geese.

Having recently experienced a severe break with its dictatorial past, Romania is only just beginning to host nature tours. Accommodations are basic, but we expect that conditions will improve as more groups head in this direction for some exceptional naturalist opportunities.

TOUR OPERATORS

Naturetrek. 14 days / $$ (from London) / June. A general natural history trip to the Black Sea coast, the Danube Delta, and the Carpathian Mountains. You'll be on the lookout for birds, plants, and mammals. The Danube Delta is an area larger than the Camargue and Coto Doñana combined! Many thousands of birds nest there, including Pygmy Cormorants; Squacco, Purple, and Night Herons; and both Dalmation and White Pelicans. While visiting the delta, you'll stay aboard a motor boat. This enables the group to travel through the delta's numerous channels and to some of the remote islands. These are explored on foot, enabling you to look for Rose-colored Starling and Red-footed Falcon that often are seen here.

Poland

Poland is bordered by Germany on the west; the Czech Republic and Slovakia on the south; and Ukraine, Belarus (formerly Byelorussia), and Lithuania on the east and northeast. To the north is the Baltic Sea. The country is largely plains, with mountains primarily in the south.

As a naturalist destination, Poland is just beginning to be discovered by the West. Although there are critically serious pollution problems in some places, particularly in the southwest, there are also remarkably unspoiled areas, including vast primeval forests, acres of marshes, and hundreds of untouched lakes. Over the years, Western Europe has largely drained its marshes and cut its timber, but Poland's traditional agricultural practices have kept such places within its borders intact.

TOUR OPERATORS

Birding. 7 days / \$\$ (from London) / June. A birdwatching trip to the Bialowieza Forest and the marshes of Biebrza. These wilderness areas lie in eastern Poland, near the border with Belarus. Bialoweiza is the largest remnant of the forest that once covered vast areas of Europe and today is home to over 200 species of birds. The Biebrza Marshes extend along the Biebrza River and many birds that are rare elsewhere in Europe can be found here, among them Great Snipe and Aquatic Warbler. Participants can expect to see about 140 species of birds on the trip. Maximum of 16 participants, 1 leader.

Birdquest. 10 days / \$\$ (from London) / May. A birdwatching trip to Poland— to both the Biebrza Marshes and Bialowieza Forest in the northeast. The marshes, among the most extensive in Europe, are the site of a Great Snipe lek, or mating ground. A highlight of this trip is an evening visit to this lek, where you can see the birds hurl themselves into the air, all the while making strange grunts, clicks, whistles, and whooshing sounds. During daylight hours, the marshes are good for birds of prey; several pair of Spotted Eagles nest here. The second half of the tour concentrates on the Bialowieza Forest, where you can see both White and Black Storks, Short-toed and Lesser Spotted Eagles, Golden Oriole, Wood Warbler, Red-backed Shrike, and Thrush Nightingale. Nine species of woodpecker can be found here. In addition to the rich avifauna, the forest is home to the European Bison (or Wisent). Maximum of 16 participants, 2 leaders.

Earthwatch

14 days / $ (from Kraków) / March, May–July, September. "Carpathian Wolves" is a research trip to the Bieszczady Mountains of southeastern Poland. Six teams of volunteers study the impact that wolves and hunters have on Poland's Red Deer population in an effort to help the wolves survive.

13 days / $$ (from Warsaw) / January, June, July. "Poland's Primeval Forest" is a research trip to study the ancient woodlands of Bialowieza National Park—a small patch of primeval forest in central Europe. How best to preserve it? That's what the Earthwatch teams will be studying. Fifty years or more of disastrous environmental policy have polluted much of the land all around the park. Though Bialowieza's 42 square kilometers are unpolluted, they may not be enough to maintain sufficient populations of Lynx, Moose, Wolf, European Bison, Deer, and Wild Boar, not to mention dozens of rodent species. By studying the relationships between prey and predator, scientists are hoping to devise a wildlife management plan for Bialowieza that can also be used as a model for other areas.

Field Studies Council. 12 days / $$ (from London) / May. This is a general natural history tour concentrating on the plants and birds of three contrasting habitats: the Tatra Mountains in the south, with their rich alpine flora; and two locations in the northeast—Bialowieza Forest and the Biebzra Marshes. An astonishing variety of birds is also likely to be observed. A botanist and an ornithologist accompany the trip.

Tatra Mountain Recreation. 12 days / $ (from Warsaw) / June–September. "Nature and Ecology in Poland" is a general natural history trip that visits Bialowieza Forest (home to 62 species of mammals and over 200 species of birds), the Biebrza Marshes, and Luknajno Lake Natural Reserve.

Wilderness Travel. 9 days / $$ (from Warsaw) / February. "The Last Wolves of Europe" is wildlife tracking by vehicle, horse-drawn sleigh, and on foot in cold, snowy conditions. But the reward is great: Wolves. Here in the dark forest of northern Poland it is still possible to find the large mammals that have been extirpated from most of Europe. Birdlife includes White-tailed Eagle, Black Woodpecker, and Nutcracker. Trips are limited to 6 participants.

Albania

Located on the eastern shore of the Adriatic Sea, Albania is a mountainous country only slightly bigger than Maryland. Largely agricultural, it is one of the poorest countries in Europe; indeed, in recent years there have been grave food shortages, and many people have fled to neighboring countries.

Albania's Mediterranean climate attracts migratory birds for wintering, while in the north the alpine meadows are rich in central European and Mediterranean species of wildflowers. There aren't many tours going to Albania at present, although if conditions improve it may well become a key central European nature destination.

TOUR OPERATOR

Field Studies Council. 14 days / $$ (from London) / May. A botanical tour of Albania, the heart of the Balkans. This is an opportunity to visit the least-known country in Europe. Special features are areas of limestone and soils that yield unique flora, including several species of *Alyssum,* coloring the spring landscape. A visit is made to the Botanic Garden in Tirana. In addition to the flowers, there is much of interest in the bird and insect life.

Russia and Ukraine

At present, there are only a few trips to Ukraine and European Russia; more go to Siberia (see the section on Siberia, Central Asian Republics, and Mongolia, page 242). Southern Ukraine is usually associated with open steppes and the Black Sea coast, and its avian life is just being discovered. Russia is the largest of the newly independent former Soviet republics, and since the Russians are not blind to the economic benefits of ecotourism, they are likely to begin attracting more nature tourists before long.

Stretching halfway around the northern portion of the globe, Russia occupies a large part of eastern and northeastern Europe as well as all of northern Asia. European Russia has a vast range of habitat: both Arctic and subtropical deserts, tundra, forests, mountains, steppe, and wetlands. It follows, therefore, that the country offers innumerable possibilities for birding, botanizing, and the like.

TOUR OPERATORS

Earthwatch

13 days / $ (from St. Petersburg) / June, July. "Endangered Russian Lakes" is a research trip to study the effects of pollution and agricultural runoff on lakes. Volunteers map lake shores, collect animals and plants, and carry out hydrochemical analyses.

8 days / $$ (from Kirkenes, Norway) / May, June, August. "Soviet Arctic Haze" is a research project that studies industrial pollution in the far north. Volunteers hike around the Kola Peninsula to find out what chemicals taint the air and water, where they come from, and what effect they may have on the finely balanced Arctic ecosystem.

Russian Nature Tours

10 days / $$$ (from London) / May. A trip for keen birdwatchers to the Teberda Nature Reserve in the Caucasus Mountains. The main goal is to see displaying Caucasus Snowcock and Caucasus Black Grouse. Other birds include Kruper's Nuthatch and Great Rosefinch. The reserve covers over 200,000 acres, and accommodations are modest. Maximum of 3 participants.

17 days / $$ (from London) / May. A birding trip to South Ukraine, Crimea, and the Caucasus Mountains. On the steppes you can see Demoiselle Cranes and Red-footed Falcons, reedbeds produce Savi's and Reed Warblers, and Rose-colored Starling and Great Bustard are also possible. The Caucasus Mountains—the zoogeographical border between Europe and Asia—are home to the Caucasus Snowcock and Caucasus Black Grouse. Maximum of 16 participants, 2 leaders.

THE DESERT AS A RESERVOIR OF LIFE: NORTH AFRICA AND THE MIDDLE EAST

Though largely desert, this area of the world is far from a wasteland. From the fertile Tigris and Euphrates rivers to the Atlas Mountains of Morocco, from the rich Mediterranean to the Dead Sea, wildlife flourishes—even in the desert. Ibex, Hyrax, and Camels populate Israel; rare birds such as the Slender-billed Curlew can be found in Morocco; and the Bosporos in Turkey is renowned for its huge flights of raptors every fall. Rare plants thrive on war-torn Cyprus, while the Canaries are host to a variety of endemic plants.

The needs of an ever-growing population in this part of the world have resulted in environmental problems that center on land degradation such as erosion, over-grazing, and depletion of vegetation. Increasing urbanization has meant a corre-sponding loss in habitat for wildlife. The deserts are spreading outward. With water in short supply in much of the region, there are also problems with silting of reservoirs, intrusion of salt water into underground aquifers, contamination of water supplies, and inadequate wastewater treatment. For countries on the Mediterranean, untreated sewage is contributing to overfertilization of the sea.

Strategically important in a petroleum-dependent world, the Middle East in particular has suffered the consequences, with pollution from heavy oil tanker traffic and oil spills threatening the existence of sea turtles, whales and dolphins, shellfish, and waterbirds. It is testimony to the resiliency of life, then, that North Africa and the Middle East continue to support large populations of birds, plants, insects, and mammals. Some of the countries in the region recognize the value of preserving habitat and correcting past environmental mistakes, while also improv-ing the lot of their people. By visiting this part of the world, ecotourists help sup-port those efforts.

MOROCCO, TUNISIA, THE CANARY ISLANDS, AND THE AZORES

Morocco

Morocco is one of the most exciting and rewarding countries for the birdwatcher to visit: It is the place where Europe meets Africa, and so plays host to many species from both continents.

The Atlas Mountains in Morocco are the highest in northern Africa, and Morocco is in a unique position—having both a Mediterranean and an Atlantic coastline. The High Atlas are as high as the Alps and stretch for nearly 500 miles across the country. A vast blanket of spring flowers provides the perfect element for botanists, while fields of wheat cover ancient terraces and green walnut groves nestle in the valleys. Local bird specialties include Moussier's Redstart, Tristram's Warbler, Booted and Golden Eagles, Lammergeier, Blue Rock Thrush, Cream-colored Courser, Barbary Partridge, Crimson-winged Finch, and Rock Bunting. Various lizards are also common, as are ground squirrels. Even the endangered Barbary Sheep can still be seen in this region. On the coast, south of Agadir, is the wide, sandy tidal estuary of the Sous River, an area frequented by flocks of waders, gulls, and terns. Here one can see Greater Flamingos, and there is always the chance of Slender-billed Gull and the scarce Audouin's Gull. The increasingly rare Bald Ibis is sometimes seen here, and would be a real thrill, a highlight of any trip.

TOUR OPERATORS

Birdquest

16 days / $$ (from London) / April. A birdwatching trip that visits a full range of habitats—from the coastal lowlands to the Atlas Mountains to the edge of the Sahara. Participants can expect to see about 150 species of birds, and rarities are energetically sought.

12 days / $$$ (from London) / time of year varies. "Morocco with a Difference" is a birdwatching trip designed to find the exceedingly rare Slender-billed Curlew. Participants will see other birds as well, but the curlew is the focus.

Branta Holidays. 9 days / $$ (from London) / March. This birdwatching trip covers the desert, mountain, and coastal habitats. Desert specialties include Desert Lark, Blue-cheeked Bee-eater, Kittlitz's Plover, Spotted Sandgrouse, Crowned Sandgrouse, Houbara Bustard, and Arabian Bustard. In the mountains: Red- and Yellow-billed Choughs, Lammergeier, Crimson-winged Finch, and Alpine Accentor. On the coast: Baillon's Crake, Little Crake, Marbled Teal, Audouin's Gull, Brown-throated Sand Martin, and Bald Ibis.

Field Studies Council. 14 days / $$ (from London) / April. A botany trip.

Naturetrek. 16 days / $ (from London) / May. A combination birding and botany tour centering on the High Atlas and including an 8-day trek to Mount Toubkal National Park. Moussier's Redstart, Tristram's Warbler, Seebohm's Wheatear, Barbary Partridge, and Levaillant's Green Woodpecker can be found here, while, later in the trip, in Essaouira, seabirds and Eleonora's Falcon can be seen.

Wings/Sunbird
    14 days / $$ (from London) / April. A birdwatching tour starting in the forests southwest of Rabat where you'll see Calandra Lark, Double-spurred Francolin, and African Marsh Owl. A variety of habitats are visited and participants can anticipate such specialties as Dupont's Lark, Moussier's Redstart, Levaillant's Green Woodpecker, Tristram's Warbler, Cream-colored Courser, Fulvous Babbler, Desert Sparrow, and various wheatears. While on the Atlantic coast you'll look for Audouin's and Slender-billed Gulls, Spoonbill, and waders. Maximum of 16 participants, 2 leaders.
    7 days / $$ (from London) / November. A shorter birding trip based in Agadir, on the Atlantic coast. A few miles south is the estuary of the Massa River, one of the richest ornithological sites in Morocco. Vagrants have been found here over the years and you might see almost anything, but the more regularly seen species include Bald Ibis, Marbled Teal, Spotless Starling, House Bunting, and Spanish Sparrow.

Tunisia

A country only a little larger than Florida, Tunisia has a favorable mix of life zones. The country is characterized by a 750-mile-long coastline bathed by the Mediterranean Sea, its northeast tip of land almost directly across from Sicily. In the north, the countryside is relatively fertile and moist, while the central region is semiarid, the east coast has an olive-growing Mediterranean climate, and the south is largely Saharan desert, devoid of vegetation. Within this range of habitat are species that inhabit Kroumirie cork forests and ferns, esparto grasslands, marsh and wetlands, and Saharan desert.

TOUR OPERATORS

Branta Holidays. 8 days / $$ (from London) / January. "Wetland and Desert in Tunisia." This is a birdwatching trip—from the plains and desert in the southwest to Lake Ichkeul and Cape Bon in the northeast. Birds seen in the wetlands include Black-necked Grebe, Spoonbill, Greater Flamingo, White-headed Duck, Common Crane, Kentish Plover, Slender-billed Gull, Whiskered Tern, and Cetti's

Warbler. In the steppe and desert areas: Long-legged Buzzard, Barbary Partridge, Stone Curlew, Cream-colored Courser, Black-bellied Sandgrouse, and a feast of larks—Temminck's, Desert, Calandra, Thick-billed, and Crested may be expected—along with a variety of wheatears, Fulvous Babbler, Trumpeter Finch, and Serin.

Canary Islands

For small islands, the Canaries have a surprising range of scenery: from deserts and lava fields to pine forests and alpine slopes. As with many islands, endemic plants have evolved, so the native flora is of special interest to botanists. Timanfaya National Park, where major volcanic eruptions have left a lunarlike landscape, is a good place to see the progression from bare rock to colonization by plants.

TOUR OPERATORS

Earthwatch. 14 days / $ (from Grand Canary) / June–August. A research trip, the purpose of which is to study the marine ecosystem of the Canary Islands in an effort to help the government devise strategies for developing tourism without destroying coastal waters. Team members record algae growth, fish numbers, and other basic habitat conditions. Nondiving team members document life in tide pools and preserve fish specimens.

Field Studies Council. 10 days / $$ (from London) / January. A geology trip exploring Tenerife and Lanzarote, two oceanic volcanic islands. You'll explore the natural history and scenery of these two quite different islands. Tenerife offers lush semitropical vegetation on the coast; you then pass through pine and ever-green forests on your way to alpine areas atop the 9,000-foot El Tiede. In con-trast, Lanzarote gives you the chance to see desert plants, fresh volcanic landscapes, and the progress of plant colonization.

Sunbird. 7 days / $$ (from London) / August. A birding trip to Tenerife, home of 6 endemics, and to Fuerteventura, home of another. The avifauna of the islands is Palearctic in origin, and the endemics show affinities to species found in Europe. Laurel and Bolle's Laurel Pigeons can be found in the steep-sided, misty valleys of the remaining patches of native laurel forest; Berthelot's Pipit occurs in drier, rocky habitats; while Plain Swifts are common enough that you should see them every day. The other endemics are Blue Chaffinch, the Canary Islands Chat (the one on Fuerteventura), and, of course, the bird that made the islands famous—the Canary, really a finch that probably evolved from a group of Serins. Other North African birds can also be seen on the islands, and on boat trips out between the islands you'll look for seabirds. Maximum of 14 participants, 2 leaders.

The Azores

Located 800 nautical miles from Lisbon and 2,300 nautical miles from New York, the Azores are a long way from anywhere. They are volcanic in origin, and each island has its own microclimate. The flora is European in origin, but despite the invasive nature of imported plants (exotics), many endemics remain.

TOUR OPERATOR

Field Studies Council. 14 days / $$ (from London) / May. A general natural history trip to six of these Atlantic islands to study their ecology while enjoying the scenery. The study of human impact on an island environment is a special feature of this trip.

ISRAEL AND EGYPT

Israel

Although Israel is a tiny country (somewhat larger than the state of New Hampshire), its varied habitats, from the Mediterranean to the Dead Sea, from the marshes in the north to the desert in the south, provide for a wealth of flora and fauna. Year-round there is a remarkable diversity of animal and bird life: Hyrax near the Dead Sea, rare tropical fish at Elat, Water Buffalo in the northern marshes, and huge raptor flights each spring and fall along the African Great Rift Valley. Israel is also a leader in conservation, and native flora and fauna are protected. An active environmental organization, the Society for the Protection of Nature in Israel (SPNI, ASPNI in the United States), guides several natural history tours throughout the country.

TOUR OPERATORS

Anglo-Israel Association. 15 days / $$ (from London) / February, April, September. Working with SPNI, the association runs three trips: "Flora and Fauna of Israel," in February; "Spring Migration Birdwatching Tour," in April; and "Autumn Migration Birdwatching Tour," in September.

ASPNI. ASPNI runs trips throughout the year ranging from a 1-day nature walk in the Judean hills to an 8-day trip through the desert environs of Jerusalem to a 2-week tour of Israel and Egypt. Costs range from $41 to $460, depending on the trip chosen. All trips begin in either Jerusalem or Tel Aviv.

Birding. 7 days / $$ (from London) / March. A birdwatching holiday to Elat, at the southern tip of Israel. Among the many local specialties are Little Green Bee-eater, Desert and Bar-tailed Desert Larks, Mourning and Desert Wheatear, Sinai Rosefinch, and extraordinary raptor flights. Maximum of 8 participants, 1 leader.

Birdquest. 16 days / $$$ (from London) / March. A birding trip. Species seen include White-breasted Kingfisher, Lesser Spotted and Imperial Eagles, Barbary Falcon, Eagle Owl, Hume's Tawny Owl, Egyptian Nightjar, Houbara Bustard, Cream-colored Courser, Black-bellied Sandgrouse, Black Francolin, Sand Partridge, Spotted Crake, Sociable Plover, Pallid Swift, Blue-cheeked Bee-eater, Bimaculated Lark, Long-billed Pipit, Sombre Tit, Rock Nuthatch, Cetti's and Moustached Warblers, Tristram's Serin, Cinereous Bunting, and Sinai Rosefinch.

Sunbird

7 days / $$ (from London) / March, April. A bird photography trip based in Elat, at Israel's southern tip. Blinds (hides) are set up, and participants have excellent chances to photograph birds at close range. In the evenings there are informal tutoring sessions on photographic techniques. Maximum of 6 participants, 1 leader.

14 days / $$ (from London) / September. A birding trip concentrating on raptors and seabirds. At this time the autumn-breeding Sooty Falcons are present. The highlight of the tour is a 5-day pelagic trip in search of seabirds around the northern end of the Red Sea. There is ample time for snorkeling in these tropical waters. Maximum of 14 participants, 2 leaders.

Wings/Sunbird. 25 days / $$ (from London) / March. A birding tour of Israel and Egypt, though either section may be taken separately. The Israeli part of the tour (15 days) covers the country from Elat, on the Red Sea, north to Kefar Blum and Mount Hermon. About 250 species of birds are likely to be seen, including Sand Partridge; Calandra, Desert, and Hoopoe Larks; Steppe Eagle; Pallid Harrier; Lanner Falcon; Hume's Tawny Owl; Marbled Teal; Western Reef Heron; Little Stint; Little Green Bee-eater, Arabian Brown Babbler; Stone Curlew; Houbara Bustard; Cream-colored Courser; Arabian and Clamorous Reed Warblers; Syrian Woodpecker; and Sombre Tit. Maximum of 14 participants, 2 leaders.

Egypt

Who says natural history and sight-seeing don't mix? Here, in the Nile Valley, they do so splendidly. In the spring, thousands of birds follow the broad green ribbon of the Nile as they migrate from their wintering grounds in Africa to their nesting grounds in Europe. It would not be possible to ignore the wonderful archaeological sites along the river, and, indeed, ancient Egyptians felt keenly the relationship between themselves and the natural world around them. This is portrayed in many of the temple paintings, carvings, reliefs, and statues. Most trips to Egypt, though concentrating on natural history, also visit the famous temples and tombs of Luxor/Thebes and Aswan; some visit more historical sites than others.

TOUR OPERATORS

Birdquest. 16 days / $$$ (from London) / October. A fall birdwatching trip to Suez, the Sinai, the Fayoum (an oasis south of Cairo and west of the Nile), Luxor, Aswan, and Abu Simbel. Not much time is spent at historical sites, although visits to the Coptic monastery of St. Katherine (at the foot of Mount Sinai), the Valley of the Kings (at Luxor), and the temple of Ramses at Abu Simbel are included. Bird specialties that will be looked for include Painted Snipe, Senegal Coucal, Scrub Warbler, Hooded Wheatear, Orange-tufted and Nile Valley Sunbirds, Greater Sandplover, Lanner Falcon, Sand Partridge, Bar-tailed Desert Lark, Little Green Bee-eater, Pied Kingfisher, Egyptian Goose, and Trumpeter Finch. Rarities that might be seen at Abu Simbel include Goliath Heron, Pink-backed Pelican, and Yellow-billed Stork.

Naturetrek. 16 days / $$ (from London) / March. This is a combination natural history–cultural trip along the Nile Valley from Cairo to Abu Simbel. Many species of birds can be seen along the Nile, including Painted Snipe, Egyptian Vulture, Senegal Thick-knee, various wheatears, numerous herons and egrets, and Trumpeter Finch. A 4-day felucca journey is included. An optional 7-day extension to the Red Sea coast and the Sinai is offered.

See & Sea. 7 days / $$$ (from Sharm-el-Sheikh) / January-December. Based in Sharm-el-Sheikh, on the tip of the Sinai Peninsula, the 60-foot *Colona II* and the 75-foot *Colona IV* offer live-aboard diving trips to the Red Sea's most famous reefs: Ras Muhammad, Jackson, and the Temple, among others. Trips are also made to the more remote Shadwan, where you can enjoy the coral gardens. The boats are small enough to anchor directly over the dive site, but provide Zodiac inflatables for diver pickups as well, thereby giving you the opportunity to dive some of the more out-of-the-way reefs. Many of the marine species you will see are unique to the Red Sea. Spectacular Lemon Butterflyfish dart by in pairs, while huge schools of Orange Fairy Basslets shimmer in the sunlight.

Swan Hellenic. 18 days / $$$$ (from New York) / May, September, November. A luxury cruise on the Nile aboard the *Nile Monarch*. Although primarily a cultural trip, these three departures run in connection with the Royal Society for the Protection of Birds, and an RSPB representative accompanies the trips.

Wings/Sunbird. 10 days / \$\$\$ (from London) / April. A birding trip, also available as part of the Wings/Sunbird trip to Israel (see the section on Israel, page 186). Participants will watch raptors at Suez, then fly to Aswan on the Nile. Specialties there include Nile Valley Sunbird, Pied Kingfisher, and Egyptian Goose, while at Luxor you can see Senegal Thick-knee, the green-mantled race of the Purple Gallinule, Rock Martin, and Trumpeter Finch. At Hurgada, on the Red Sea coast, there will be a pelagic trip. A day trip to Abu Simbel is also included. Maximum of 16 participants, 2 leaders.

CYPRUS AND TURKEY

Cyprus

Cyprus is a rugged, sunny island that lies off the southern coast of Turkey in the Mediterranean Sea. Its geographical position has made it a major stopover for migratory birds, while at the same time it's a veritable botanical crossroads, with contributions to its flora coming from Asia, North Africa, and Europe. In an area slightly smaller than Connecticut grow some 1,500 species of flowering plants, 75 of which are endemic to Cyprus, including Scarlet Broomrape, 3 species of Crocus, and the Cyprus Bee Orchid.

There are endemic birds as well, such as the Cyprus Warbler (*Sylvia melanothorax*)—a small bird with a rounded black head, blue back, barred black-and-white underparts, and red legs. Over 200 species of birds are regularly seen on migration, including Lammergeier, Roller, Blue-cheeked Bee-eater, Caspian Plover, White-breasted Kingfisher, Hoopoe, and Cretzschmar's Bunting. Although the disgusting habit of "liming" birds (to kill them) is still carried out in some places on the island, the Cypriot government is determined to stamp out the practice, as more and more birdwatchers are making their presence felt. This is a good example of the way ecotourism can help to preserve and protect species.

An inlet of clear water off the north coast of the Akamas Peninsula provides ideal snorkeling. This is also where Loggerhead and Green Turtles breed; they have been the subject of an active conservation program for over a decade.

TOUR OPERATORS

Birding. 7 days / \$\$ (from London) / April. A birdwatching trip based in Paphos, on southern (Greek) Cyprus. Among the many species to be found here during spring migration are Greater Flamingo, Griffon Vulture (breeding), Black Francolin, Great Spotted Cuckoo, Bimaculated Lark, Ruppell's and Orphean Warblers, and both the Cyprus Warbler and the Cyprus Pied Wheatear.

Cox & Kings. 9 days / $$ (from London) / March. A botanical tour based in Paphos, on Greek Cyprus. Though it concentrates on the vegetation of the southwest, cultural sites are not overlooked. Purple Rockcress, Asian Buttercup (in a variety of colors), *Gladiolus tryphyllus,* and several orchid species, including the Sulphur Yellow Marsh Orchid, are among the many flowers to be seen. An optional trip to the Troodos Mountains is offered. Maximum of 22 participants. Noted botanist Mary Briggs leads the tour.

Naturetrek. 10 days / $$ (from London) / April. Birdwatching and botanizing in southern Cyprus. Among the flowers: Asphodel, Anemone, and a variety of orchids. Among the birds: Caspian Plover, Cretzschmar's Bunting, Cyprus Pied Wheatear, and Cyprus Warbler. The rich cultural heritage of the island is not ignored either—you'll visit the Baths of Aphrodite and see the mosaics in ancient Kourion.

Turkey

Turkey is a land of contrasts—from the warm waters of the Aegean in the west to the snowbound Pontic Alps in the east; from the Black Sea coast in the north to the Mediterranean in the south; from wetlands to forests, and from lakes to steppes. The spectacle of the fall migration of raptors across the Bosporus is world-famous. Equally famous are Turkey's endemic plants, spectacular scenery, and cultural and archaeological sites.

TOUR OPERATORS

Birdquest. 18 days / $$ (from London) / May. A birdwatching trip, with the possibility of seeing about 250 species; extra effort is made to see some of the rarer species, such as Caucasian Snowcock, Caucasian Blackcock, Radde's Accentor, and Wallcreeper. Maximum of 16 participants, 2 leaders.

Cox & Kings. 15 days / $$ (from London) / April. This is a botany tour to southwest Turkey, an area rich in flowering plants and ancient ruins. Visits are made to Ephesus, Marmaris, Dalyan, Fethiye, and the archaeological site of Xanthus, among others. Species to be expected include scarlet Asian Buttercups, *Ranunculus asiaticus, Anemone blanda,* and *Cyclamen trochopteranthum,* as well as such bulbous plants as *Fritillaria, Scilla,* and Crocus. Additionally, there may well be up to 20 species of orchid. Birds—about 70 species—can also be seen, including Greater Flamingo, Montagu's Harrier, Roller, and Hoopoe. There are many butterflies, too, such as the scarce Swallowtail, Southern Festoon, and Comma.

Earthwatch. 14 days / $ (from Mugla) / July, August. A research trip to study and work with Loggerhead Sea Turtles. Tasks include tagging nesting mother turtles, measuring nest sizes, and chaperoning the tiny hatchlings down to the Aegean Sea.

Field Studies Council

14 days/ $$ (from London) / May. A general natural history trip exploring the many facets of the Turkish landscape. Based in Antalya, you'll visit Termessos National Park as well as the ruins of the Hellenic cities of Phaselis and Chimera. The flora and fauna (birds in particular) are worthy of any naturalist.

7 days / $$ (from London) / May. "Spring in the Aegean: Landscapes, Natural History, and Painting for the Family." Based on the island of Kos, just a mile from the Turkish coast, you'll also visit the islands of Kalimnos (famous for its sponges) and Nisyros (a dormant volcano).

Naturetrek. 17 days / $$ (from London) / June. This is a birdwatching and botany tour to eastern Turkey. Although concentrating on natural history, cultural sites are not overlooked. Among the birds to be seen are Marbled Teal, White-headed Duck, Great Bustard, Saker Falcon, Demoiselle Crane, Lammergeier, Wallcreeper, and Caspian Snowcock. Mammals, including Wild Goat, Chamois, Brown Bear, and even Wolf, can be found in the Pontic Alps. You'll also spend a day in Istanbul for sight-seeing. An ornithologist and a botanist accompany the tour.

YEMEN

Yemen is rapidly becoming a destination for birdwatchers. Situated on the Gulf of Aden, south of Saudia Arabia and across the Red Sea from Ethiopia, Yemen is ideally located and is currently the most accessible country for finding Arabian endemics. Many Palearctic birds also winter in Yemen. There is a surprising range of habitat, from mountains and woodlands to beaches; trips will, of course, spend quite some time at the wadis and on the fringes of the great Rub' al Kahali, the vast sand sea that covers much of Arabia. Among the many species to be seen are Red-eyed Dove, Arabian Serin, Barbary Falcon, Red-capped Lark, African Rock Martin, Long-billed Wheatear, Little Rock Thrush, Yemen Warbler, Orange-tufted Sunbird, Golden-winged Grosbeak, Bald Ibis (extremely rare), Black Bush Chat, and Arabian Bustard.

TOUR OPERATORS

Birdquest. 18 days / $$ (from London) / October. A birding trip covering the entire country—from the capital of San'a to the ancient seaport of Al Mukalla on the shores of the Indian Ocean (in former South Yemen). Many species of birds can be expected, including Socotra Cormorant, Dunn's Lark, and such Arabian endemics as Yemen Serin, Yemen Linnet, and Philby's Rock Partridge. Arabia's only primate—the Hamadryas Baboon—can be seen in the Tihamah area. Maximum of 16 participants, 2 leaders.

Wings/Sunbird. 18 days / $$$ (from London) / November. This is a birdwatching trip to North Yemen. Special effort will be made to find rarities and endemics, including Arabian and Philby's Partridges, Arabian and Yemen Serins, Arabian Woodpecker, and Yemen Thrush. There's also a chance of seeing the extremely rare Bald Ibis. Other species to be watched for are Golden-winged Grosbeak, Ruppell's Weaver, Singing Bushlark, Abyssinian Roller, Black-crowned Finch Lark, and various raptors, wheatears, and sandgrouse. Maximum of 12 participants, 2 leaders.

TRIPS INTO THE HEART OF DARKNESS: AFRICA

In the 1950s and 1960s, when we were growing up, the map of Africa was undergoing radical changes. Headlines about newly independent countries were as exciting then as they were in 1989 and 1990, when the Berlin Wall crumbled along with the Communist party in Eastern Europe and the former Soviet Union. In Africa, new countries were forming and borders were changing as the colonialists began relinquishing power. The Belgian Congo became Rwanda and Burundi; French Equatorial Africa is now the Central African Republic, Chad, the Congo Republic, and Gabon.

We still occasionally check the atlas to locate places in Africa. It just isn't as well-known to us as are South America and Europe. And though a great deal of the political turmoil of those earlier times has subsided, there are still some trouble spots. Remember, however, that tour companies rarely offer a trip if there is any real danger involved.

African countries have a bundle of social, political, and economic problems, and these are often reflected in the health and care of their natural resources. Countries like Burundi and Rwanda have such high population densities that the preservation of wildlife is almost a luxury. In Uganda, the destructive policies of Idi Amin's regime, and the political confusion that followed, decimated much of that country's parks and wildlife; the parks are only now beginning to be rebuilt. In Kenya, wildlife can be seen both inside and outside of the parks, largely because poaching has been outlawed for many years. But in some other countries, such as Tanzania, poaching limits wildlife sightings to within the parks. Even so, in some African national parks, especially those that border populated areas, poaching is still a major problem, primarily because of limited resources and training.

Africa is a part of the world where ecotourism really can help change the course of events. Tourist dollars spent in viewing (not shooting) game, watching birds, or hiking mountain trails can demonstrate the economic importance of preserving all endemic wildlife. Kenya has made nature tourism a major source of income; Tanzania and others are continuing to develop along that line. Even tiny Rwanda, with the highest population density in Africa, has set aside sizable portions of land to preserve its Mountain Gorillas, and has established ecosensitive rules and guidelines for viewing those groups of the gorillas that were habituated to tourists. Many of these countries charge high fees for visiting the parks and preserves—much higher than we Westerners are used to. But the governments do not otherwise have the money to finance preservation. These fees help pay for maintaining the parks and paying local people to discourage poaching, so it is only right that ecotourists do their part.

Africa is the largest continent (if you count Europe and Asia as separate entities), with approximately 11.7 million square miles of land area—20 percent of the total land mass on earth. Several countries on the continent—Namibia, Botswana, Tanzania, and Zambia—are at least the size of Texas, while Zaire and South Africa both are at least three and four times that size, respectively. Nature tours, however, concentrate in certain areas, which we've divided into East Africa, West and Central Africa, southern Africa, and the islands of the Indian Ocean.

EAST AFRICA

The countries of Kenya, Tanzania, and Rwanda are key wildlife safari destinations. Kenya and Tanzania in particular present the quintessential African scene: large game moving through grassy savannahs or clustered at waterholes beneath a cloudless sky. And indeed, this is glorious country, rich with wildlife and landscapes of singular beauty.

Extending southward from southern Turkey, through Israel and the Red Sea, the Great Rift Valley curves through Kenya and Tanzania into Mozambique. A series of lakes on the valley floor, plus the valley's steep sides dotted with active or recently extinct volcanos, marks this tear in the earth's crust where two major tectonic plates are slowly pulling apart. Most of the region is open grassland or grassland marked by widely scattered acacia trees.

Here is the Africa of Ernest Hemingway and Isak Dinesen—as all the glossy tour brochures will remind you. And they will lure you with beautiful color photos of spacious tents set up in isolated spots overlooking an active waterhole or migration path. Indeed, this is the deluxe way to go—a classic tented safari, complete with waiters in white jackets serving elegant multicourse meals, and hot showers every night. These trips are usually individually designed, with your choice of destination and trip length. Abercrombie & Kent and Special Expeditions offer such luxurious accommodations. In this same deluxe vein, air safaris offered by A & K and Bruce Safaris allow the traveler with limited time to locate big game from up above. For the slightly less rushed, there are balloon trips. Equally exotic are the camel tours offered by a few companies.

For most of us who are seeking looks at elephants, lions, and the like, however, the choice is simpler: the more moderate safaris "under canvas" and those that return each evening to a comfortable, usually well-appointed, lodge. Day trips are via minibus or four-wheel-drive vehicle. Obviously the tour options vary depending on the number of people, the level of accommodation, and the type of viewing vehicle. If you take a camping trip, you can get a little farther away from habitation. And as always, the smaller the group the easier it is for the tour operator to accommodate individual interests. Night viewing (or a night drive) is an important feature, since many animals are nocturnal. There are safaris in a wide price range, as well as walking or hiking trips, which usually are cheaper but demand the ability to hike in hot, sunny conditions. If you have a special interest—such as bird-watching or photography—look for trips that concentrate on those interests; you'll see other things too, but the guide will be more informed about your subject.

Generally, the best time to go to East Africa is either during the dry season, when game concentrates around the waterholes and the vegetation is less dense (enabling you to see the animals more easily), or during migration, when movements of large game make them easier to track. In Kenya, the dry seasons are January to April and July to October. In Tanzania, there is heavy rain from February to May, with light rain in October and November. The Serengeti is active from November to June, while other parts of the country are best June through October or November. Migration in the Serengeti is December through February; in Kenya's Masai Mara—the northern extension of the Serengeti—it is June through September. In Rwanda, gorilla-viewing time is mostly April to September. For more detailed information on dry and wet seasons, see *African Safari: The Complete Travel Guide to Ten Top Game Viewing Countries* by Mark Nolting.

Since Kenya's tourism program is the most developed of those of East African countries, it is usually suggested that people start with a visit to Kenya and follow with a trip to Tanzania or Rwanda. Many tour operators also offer combination Kenya-Tanzania trips.

Kenya

Big game is the primary target for most nature tours to Kenya. Typical tours include trips to the Masai Mara Reserve, known for the best game viewing in Africa. Amboseli National Park, with 19,340-foot-high Mount Kilimanjaro in the background, is known for its rhinos and elephants, but also has cheetahs. Tsavo National Park comprises two parts—East and West—with an underwater glass tank at Mzima Springs (West) for watching hippos and fish. Meru National Park was where Joy Adamson cared for her lioness Elsa and her cheetah Pippa. Nairobi National Park, so very near the capital, boasts a remarkable number of migratory Wildebeest, Zebra, and Coke's Hartebeest. Samburu and Buffalo Springs have Grevy Zebra, Oryx, Impala, Reticulated Giraffe, Gerenuk, and Dik-dik. In the higher elevations, Aberdare National Park is a good place to see Elephant, Bongo,

Giant Forest Hog, Bushbuck, and Red Duiker, as well as Black Leopard and Serval. Mount Kenya National Park is best for Black-and-white Colobus Monkey, Sykes Monkey, Giant Forest Hog, and Bongo.

Kenya is superb for birds, too. The diversity of habitat supports over 1,100 species—more than any other comparable part of Africa. A large number of animals supports a varied population of predatory birds, and over 150 species of Palearctic migrants winter here. The landscape makes seeing the birds fairly easy, so it's no wonder that Kenya holds the world's record for the most bird species seen in a twenty-four-hour period. The lakes along the rift valley are prime birding spots, especially Lake Nakuru, with its huge flocks of Lesser Flamingo and shorebirds, and Lake Baringo, where one can see Verreaux's Eagle, Hemprich's Hornbill, and Bristle-crowned Starling.

There is fishing in the higher elevations and along the coast. Crocodiles, snakes, lizards, turtles, and tortoises inhabit coastal creeks and river mouths, dry bush, and forestland. The tropical marshlands and semideserts sport a large variety of wildflowers. And for scuba divers, there are marine parks along the coast.

About 10 percent of Kenya is protected land, and the country has an aggressive antipoaching program, so the prospects of seeing wildlife here are high. Indeed, Kenya is a prime example of how nature tourism can pay off: Tourism is a major element in Kenya's economic structure, with 650,000 people coming each year and spending about $350 million. According to Perex Olindo (in *Nature Tourism: Managing for the Environment*), this means, for example, that one elephant in Kenya is worth about $14,375 a year (or $900,000 in its lifetime) in tourist dollars. Since tourism is now the country's biggest source of foreign currency, Kenya has set as its 1996 goal hosting as many as 1 million tourists annually. Unfortunately, this is already the place for Africa's highest concentration of tourists. In fact, ecologists are concerned that excessive tourist traffic is damaging the parks, and wildlife has become so disturbed by the many minibuses that they have altered their hunting patterns. The government has changed some of its administration of the parks, and is making attempts to deal with the problems excessive tourism is causing. It is also trying to funnel more tourist dollars to local communities. Only time will tell if responsible ecotourism will work for Kenya's natural wonders.

TOUR OPERATORS

Abercrombie & Kent. 12–17 days / $$–$$$ (from Nairobi) / January–December. "Kenya Highlights," 12 days, with stays at park lodges; participants visit Aberdare, Samburu, Mount Kenya, Lake Nakuru, Masai Mara. An optional trip to the coast is available. "Adventurer Safari," 15 days, with deluxe park accommodations, visits Aberdare, Samburu, Mount Kenya, Amboseli, Lake

Naivasha, and Masai Mara. There's an optional additional tent-camp extended visit to Masai Mara. "Livingstone Safari" is a combined Kenya and Tanzania 17-day tour, with part of your stay in a luxury tented camp. In addition, A & K offers traditional luxury tented safaris; these cost from $465 to $785 per person, per day, depending on the number of persons.

Birding. 15 days / $$$ (from London) / August. A birdwatching safari. You'll visit Nairobi National Park, Samburu, Lake Baringo, Lake Nakuru, Lake Naivasha, and Masai Mara. Well over 500 species of birds can be expected, in addition to many animals. Two leaders and local bird guides accompany the trip.

Birdquest. 22 days / $$ (from Nairobi) / October, November. Two birding trips that visit Mount Kenya, Samburu, Lakes Baringo and Nakuru, Kakamega Forest, Lake Victoria, Masai Mara, Lake Naivasha, and Tsavo. The November trip forgoes most mammal sightings and heads into areas most other tours do not reach, including the Shimba Hills and the Dida Galgalla Desert. Participants may expect to see over 700 species of birds! Maximum of 14 participants, 2 leaders.

Breakaway Adventure Travel. 15 days / $ (from Nairobi) / June–December. Camping safari with opportunities for hiking as well as game drives. Visits Samburu; Lakes Baringo, Naivasha, and Nakuru; and Masai Mara.

Bruce Safaris. 5–21 days (or more) / $$ (from Nairobi) / January–December. A wide variety of tours, including photo safaris, flying safaris, mountain climbing (Mount Kenya), camel safaris, balloon trips, and overland trips in four-wheel-drive vehicles. All manner of custom itineraries can be arranged, including stays at private ranches, such as Elsamere Conservation Centre, former home of Joy and George Adamson (and Elsa). Situated on the shore of Lake Naivasha in the Rift Valley, the center covers 60 acres of woods and grassland, and is ideal for birdwatchers and serious conservationists. Accommodation on the tours is in park lodges or permanent tent camps; some tours involve camping.

Cheesemans' Ecology Safaris. (See the listing in the section on Tanzania, page 202.)

Earthwatch. 15 days / $$ (from Nairobi) / March, April, July, August. A research trip to Lake Naivasha. Based at the Elsamere Conservation Centre, volunteers identify and observe birds and aquatic plants, analyze water and root systems, and trace the lake's food chains. All this in an effort to help save the lake from drought, introduced species, and human pressure.

Field Guides. 23–28 days / $$ (from Nairobi) / June, September, November. Birding tours with prospects of seeing over 650 species of birds and more than 50 species of mammals. Participants stay in lodges and permanent tent camps; day trips are in nine-passenger, pop-top minibuses. The summer trip is during the peak breeding period, and is the prime time to observe the bishops, whydahs, weavers, and widowbirds in their fancy breeding plumages. The September trip is the standard introductory tour, sampling each of Kenya's major inland habitats. Though this is the end of the dry-season breeding period, on the plains many birds will still be in breeding plumage. You'll visit Mount Kenya, Samburu, the Baringo area, Kakamega, and Lake Victoria. The November trip is at the beginning of the short rains—a prime time to see Palearctic migrants—and goes to some locations not covered by most tours: the Kongelai Escarpment, Saiwa Swamp, Mengatsi, Tsavo West and the Taita Hills, Lake Jipe, and the coast at Malindi, where you can see Crab Plover. Maximum of 6 participants; Terry Stevenson, noted authority on the birds of Kenya, leads. The June trip is limited to 12 and 2 leaders.

Geo Expeditions. 12–20 days / $$ (from Nairobi) / January, July, August–October, December. Tented safaris to Aberdare, Samburu, Lake Nakuru, Masai Mara (12 days). The Kenya-Tanzania combo tour is 20 days.

Holbrook Travel. 10–14 days / $$$ (from New York or Miami) / January–March, June–December. General natural history trips and photographic safaris. You'll visit the major parks and reserves, including Lake Baringo, Samburu, and Masai Mara, and stay at the Ark. Daily excursions are made in small safari vehicles with open roofs. A combination Kenya and Tanzania trip is also offered.

International Expeditions. 20 days / $$$ (from New York) / February, June–December. This trip visits Amboseli, Masai Mara, Tsavo West, and Lake Nakuru, with stays in lodges and tented camps. A Kenya-Tanzania combo trip is 20 days in October and November.

Mountain Travel/Sobek. 15–20 days / $$ (from Nairobi) / December–March, June–October. Hiking and camping trips. "Kenya Walking Safari" (20 days) involves moderate hiking and some road travel, with overnight camps. Visits Samburu, Lakes Baringo and Nakuru, Loita Hills, and Masai Mara. "Kenya Camping Safari" (15 days) is an all-camping trip with some easy walking and road travel. Visits Aberdare, Samburu, Masai Mara, and Hell's Gate Gorge. "Kenya Bush Trails" (18 days) entails moderate to strenuous hiking in Tsavo National Park, traversing mountain, forest, moorland, and alpine zones. "Great Parks of East Africa" is a Kenya-Tanzania combo trip.

Nature Expeditions International. 16–23 days / \$\$\$ (from Nairobi) / December–February, June–October. A variety of wildlife safaris. "Kenya Adventure Safari" includes a camel safari and a hike up Mount Kenya. "East Africa Wildlife Safari" goes to Kenya, Tanzania, and to see the Mountain Gorillas of Rwanda (or Zaire).

Naturetrek. 17 days / \$\$\$ (from London) / January, August, December. A general natural history trip to Masai Mara, the lakes of the Rift Valley, and Samburu, plus a climb up Mount Kenya. Strong, but not exclusive, focus on birds. An optional 7-day extension to Amboseli, Tsavo, and to the coast for snorkeling and shorebirds.

Oceanic Society Expeditions. 14 days / \$\$ (from New York) / February, September. Stays in park lodges and tent camps, with travel by safari bus and plane. Visits Aberdare, Samburu, Lake Nakuru, Masai Mara. A combination Kenya-Tanzania camping safari (17 days) is also offered. Maximum of 16 participants.

Perry Mason Safaris. Individualized safaris planned according to client interest. Cost: about \$420 per person, per day, from Nairobi, based on three or four persons. Operator uses four-wheel-drive vehicles with large photographic pop-up hatches. Horseback and camel safaris may also be arranged.

Special Expeditions. 17 days / \$\$\$\$ (from Nairobi) / December–March. Luxury tented safari to Kenya's Lake Nakuru, Lake Naivasha, and Masai Mara; then 4 days in Serengeti National Park, just across the border in Tanzania. Trip continues to Ngorongoro Crater and Lake Manyara National Park before return to Kenya.

Special Interest Tours and Travel. 14–17 days / \$\$\$ (from New York) / January–December. "Kenya Wildlife Safari" stays at park lodges and tent camps. Visits Amboseli, Mountain Lodge, Samburu, Mount Kenya Safari Club, Lake Nakuru, Masai Mara, and the Kenya coast, using 6-person minibuses. "Authentic Camping Safari" features private camps and visits Samburu, Lake Nakuru, Masai Mara, and Mombasa Beach or Amboseli. "In the Land of Kilimanjaro" is a combo Kenya-Tanzania trip.

Sue's Safaris. 12–17 days / \$\$ (from Nairobi) / January–December. "Monkey Safari" (17 days) stays in lodges and visits Tsavo West, Amboseli, Samburu, Mount Kenya Safari Club, Ark or Mountain Lodge, Lake Nakuru, and Masai Mara. Uses 9-passenger minibus with pop-up roof. "Luxury Winged Safari" (16 days) flies to parks to save travel time. Stays are in lodges and safari camps. Visits Amboseli, Samburu, Mount Kenya Safari Club, Masai Mara, using 9-passenger minibus with pop-up roof. "Exclusive Tented Safari" (12 days) stays in safari camps; travel is by four-wheel-drive vehicle. Visits Samburu, Lake Baringo, Lake Naivasha, Masai Mara. Balloon safaris and custom safaris can be arranged.

Sunbird

16 days / $$$ (from London) / June, November. Birding trips to Tsavo and Amboseli National Parks; Lakes Nakuru, Naivasha, and Baringo; and Masai Mara Reserve. About 500 species of birds can be expected, along with a wide variety of mammals.

23 days / $$$ (from London) / January. A tour for keen birders, involving dawn-to-dusk birdwatching on most days. Great rewards: 700 or so species to be seen! In addition to the sites visited on the standard Kenya tour (see above), you'll visit Mountain Lodge on the wooded slopes of Mount Kenya, Kakamega Forest in the far west, and the coast and nearby Sokoke Forest.

Swan Hellenic. 16 days / $$$$ (from London) / February, September. A "Big Game and Bird Safari" to Kenya and Mauritius. Major reserves visited include Samburu and Masai Mara, and travel is by 9-passenger minibus. Five days are then spent on Mauritius, an island off Madagascar (see the section on Madagascar and Other Islands of the Indian Ocean, page 225). There you may see some rare birds, including the Mauritius Parakeet and Pink Pigeon. A visit is made to the station where the Mauritius Kestrel captive breeding program is enjoying some success. Two leaders accompany the trip.

TraveLearn. 15 days / $$$ (from New York) / June, July. Seminar-lecture trip with visits to Samburu, Masai Mara, and Amboseli. Includes stay at a deluxe tented camp and nature hikes on the lower slopes of Mount Kenya. Also visits the Louis Leakey Institute for Prehistory and Olorgesalie Prehistoric Site. With an optional 4-day extension to Mombasa for snorkeling. Also offered is a balloon safari in Masai Mara (extra cost).

TravelWild. 11–15 days / $$$$ (from Nairobi) / July, August. Kenya photo tours. Flying to some of the more distant parks assures more time at each location to photograph the wildlife. Visits Lake Nakuru, Samburu, Masai Mara. The Masai Mara photo tour (11 days) concentrates on this most fruitful and diverse photo location. Maximum of 15 participants.

University Research Expeditions Program. 15 days / $ (from Kisumu) / July, August. "Monkeys of the Kenyan Rain Forest" studies the Black-and-white Colobus Monkey (*Colobus guereza*) in the Kakamega Reserve. Volunteers track groups of monkeys through the forest, observing and noting their activities. Although not strenuous, the field work requires concentration and patience.

VENT. 24–29 days / $$ (from Nairobi) / July, October. Birding tours that also include game watching. Both trips visit Samburu and Masai Mara, as well as Lake Nakuru, Maralal, and Kakamega Forest, and stays at the Ark Lodge to observe nocturnal animals. Optional extension available to Kenyan coast for shorebirds, including the unusual Crab Plover. Participants can expect to see well over 500 species of birds.

Voyagers International. 17 days / $$ (from Nairobi) / January–March, June–December. Stays in tented camps and lodges. Visits Nairobi National Park, Mount Kenya, Aberdare, Samburu, Lake Nakuru, and Masai Mara. Optional extensions to Kenya coast and Amboseli are offered. Balloon and flying safaris also available. A combo Kenya-Tanzania trip is another option. Private safaris can be arranged.

Wilderness Travel. 14 days / $$ (from Nairobi) / December–February, June–September. Emphasis on walking, with stays at lodges and safari camps. Visits Samburu, Lake Nakuru, Nguruman, Naivasha, Masai Mara. An "East African Wildlife Safari" (19 days) combo Kenya-Tanzania trip is offered.

Wings. 25 days / $$ (from Nairobi) / October, November, February. Birding tours that visit Nairobi National Park, Samburu, Mount Kenya, Lake Baringo, Lake Nakuru, Kakamega Forest, and Masai Mara. Optional extension to Tsavo and coastal forests near Sokoke. Participants can expect to see 600 to 750 species of birds in addition to an extraordinary range of mammals.

Woodstar Tours. 20 days / $ (from Nairobi) / March. A birding tour that visits Samburu, Mountain Lodge, Lake Baringo, Kakamega Forest, Lake Nakuru, Masai Mara, Tsavo, and coastal Kenya. In addition, 16-day "Birdventures" are offered year-round.

Tanzania

Although most wildlife safaris head for Kenya, a goodly number also visit Tanzania, either in combination with a trip to Kenya or as a separate trip offered under slightly more rugged conditions. As Kenya's parks become more and more crowded, it's only natural that ecotourists will opt for Tanzania. The Serengeti, Mount Kilimanjaro, Lake Tanganyika, Ngorongoro Crater—the country has plenty to attract visitors. All of this plus the Selous Game Reserve—the largest such reserve in the world—adds up to a country with about 13 percent of its land set aside for nature.

Serengeti National Park is famous for its herds of wildebeest. You'll also see hippos, giraffes, zebras, gazelles, elands, topi, hartebeest, buffalos, and lions. Rarer are hyenas, jackals, cheetahs, and wild dogs. There are also over 350 species of birds. The Ngorongoro Crater and its surrounding Conservation Area is rich in grassland animals and is also one of the most reliable places in the world for seeing the endangered Black Rhinoceros. (In a conservation measure, the government has banned camping in the crater.) The nearby forest and swamps are the home of elephants, waterbuck, and bushbuck, while around the marshes are reedbuck and waterbirds.

TOUR OPERATORS

Abercrombie & Kent. 12 days / $$ (from Nairobi) /January–December. Stays in hotels and lodges. Visits Arusha, Lake Manyara, Serengeti, Ngorongoro Crater.

Birdquest. 23 days / $$$ (from London) / January. Birding tour to find some of the least known species in East Africa. Visits Pugu Hills, Selous, Kilombero River, Mikumi, Usambara Mountains, Arusha, Ngorongoro Crater, Serengeti and Lake Ndutu, and Tarangire. Some long, hot drives and simple accommodations, but with great rewards. A special effort is made to see the Black Rhinoceros at Ngorongoro, in addition to the amazing herds of animals in the Serengeti. Tanzania is home to some of the least known birds of East Africa, including 15 endemics, 4 of which have been discovered since 1981. All of these will be looked for, of course; participants can expect to see about 500 species of birds. Maximum of 16 participants, 2 leaders.

Breakaway Adventure Travel. 8 days / $ (from Arusha) / December–March, June, July, September. Camping safari to Ngorongoro Crater region, Serengeti, and Olduvai Gorge.

Bruce Safaris. 5–21 days (or more) / $$ (from Nairobi) / January–December. A variety of private tours visiting Ngorongoro, Lake Manyara, Serengeti, Mikumi, the Selous Game Reserve, and Ruaha National Park. A Mount Kilimanjaro climb is also offered.

Cheesemans' Ecology Safaris. 25 days / $$$ (from Nairobi) / June. "The Ecology of Tanzania and Kenya" is a general natural history trip. All the traditional sites are visited, including Lake Manyara National Park, the Serengeti, Ngorongoro, the Aberdares Mountains, Samburu, Nakuru National Park, and the Masai Mara. Many species of birds and animals can be seen on both day and night (extra cost) game drives. An optional extension to Rwanda is offered. Maximum of 16 participants; 2 leaders accompany the trip.

Cox & Kings. 12 days / $$$$ (from London) / December–March, June–October. You stay at first-class tented camps in the Serengeti, Ngorongoro, and Tarangire.

Game drives are offered twice a day and are escorted by professional guides. Maximum of 20 participants.

Field Guides. 23 days / $$$ (from Nairobi) / April. A birdwatching tour to the vast plains of the Serengeti, the Ngorongoro Crater, and some lesser known areas, including the Suambara Mountains (home to a number of endemics), Mikumi National Park, Tarangire, and the huge Kibasira Swamp, where three new species of birds have been found since 1988. Birds of interest include Dappled Mountain Robin, Long-billed Apalis, Violet-crested Turaco, Swallow-tailed Bee-eater, Trumpeter Hornbill, Ashy Starling, and Yellow-collared Lovebird. Participants can expect to see about 500 species of birds, plus many mammals. Maximum of 12 participants; noted African naturalist Terry Stevenson leads the tour.

Geo Expeditions. 16 days / $$ (from Nairobi) / January, June, August, October, December. Stays in safari camps. Visits Arusha, Lake Manyara, Lake Natron, Engare Sero Gorge, Serengeti, Ngorongoro Crater.

International Expeditions. 18 days / $$$$ (from New York) / January, February, July, October. Visits Tarangire, Ngorongoro Crater, Serengeti, Lake Manyara, Olduvai Gorge.

International Research Expeditions. 14 days / $ (from Dar es Salaam) / January–July. A research trip studying birds in the forests of the remote mountains. Volunteers are trained in mist-netting procedures and morphology measurement skills. Trips involve hiking and camping.

Mountain Travel/Sobek. 15–18 days / $$$ (from Nairobi, Arusha, or Dar es Salaam) / December–March, May–October. A variety of safaris, with both camping and lodge stays, to Ngorongoro, Tarangire, Lake Manyara, and the Serengeti. Easy day hikes. A "Tanzania Walking Safari" (18 days) visits less-touristed parts of the country, including south Masailand and Ol Ololosokwon Game Area on the edge of the Serengeti, and also visits Mount Meru, Ngorongoro Crater, and Lake Manyara. Moderate hiking. The "Kilimanjaro Climb" (16 days) involves strenuous hiking at high elevation.

Nature Expeditions International. 16 days / $$$ (from Nairobi) / February, July, October. On the "Tanzania and Kilimanjaro Walking Safari" participants track herds across the Serengeti, explore Lakes Natron and Manyara, and visit the Masai people around their sacred mountain, Oldonyo Lengai. Optional 7-day trek to the top of Kilimanjaro, Africa's highest peak.

Naturetrek. 17 days / $$$ (from London) / December, January. A wildlife trip to Arusha, Tarangire, Ngorongoro Crater, Olduvai Gorge, the Serengeti, Lake Manyara, and Kilimanjaro Park. The strenuous climb to the summit is optional.

Oceanic Society Expeditions. 12 days / $$$$ (from Kilimanjaro) / July. Luxury tented wildlife safari to Tarangire, Lake Manyara, Ngorongoro Crater, and the Serengeti. Maximum of 8 participants; a naturalist accompanies the trip.

Overseas Adventure Travel. 12–14 days / $$$ (from Arusha) / December–March, June–October. Visits Arusha, Oldeani, Saguna and Masailand, Serengeti, Olduvai Gorge, Ngorongoro Crater, Tarangire, and Lake Manyara. Also offered is a strenuous climb up Mount Kilimanjaro. Various combination trips—Tanzania-Rwanda and Tanzania-Rwanda-Burundi—are available as well.

Sue's Safaris. 6 days / $$ (from Nairobi) / January–December. Individualized tours to the major parks in Tanzania.

Swan Hellenic

14 days / $$$$ (from London) / February, October. A safari to the parks and reserves of the north, including Ngorongoro Crater, Lake Manyara, Olduvai Gorge, and the Serengeti. Travel and game viewing is via 9-passenger minibus. Two leaders accompany the trip.

17 days / $$$$ (from London) / July. A safari to the parks and reserves of the south, including Lake Tanganyika, Mikumi and Ruaha National Parks, Selous Game Reserve, the Gombe Stream Chimpanzee Reserve, and the island of Zanzibar. Two leaders accompany the trip.

Tamu Safaris. 17 days / $$ (from Nairobi) / June. A wildlife tour that visits the dry savannah of the Terengire–Lokisale ecosystem, the western escarpment of the Great Rift Valley, the forested highlands of Ngorongoro, the alpine meadows of Mount Meru, and the Serengeti Plain, with an emphasis on natural history and environmental diversity. Travel is to national parks via four-wheel-drive Land Rovers and 7-seater minibuses with roof hatches for wildlife viewing. Also includes nature walks. Maximum of 16 participants.

VENT. 20 days / $$$ (from Nairobi) / February. A birding and wildlife tour with visits to the Serengeti, Ngorongoro Crater, Olduvai Gorge, Lake Manyara, Tarangire, and Arusha. Excellent opportunity for photography. Among the many birds to be seen are Ostrich, Secretary Bird, and other species typical of Africa such as coursers, sandgrouse, honeyguides, and larks. Endemics include Gray-breasted Spurfowl, Fischer's Lovebird, Rufous-tailed Weaver, Jackson's Widowbird, and Ashy Starling. Maximum of 7 participants, 1 leader.

Wilderness Travel. 17–19 days / $$$ (from Arusha) / January, March, July, September, December. Camping and lodge stays. Visits Arusha, Lake Manyara, Olduvai Gorge, Gol Mountains, Serengeti, Tarangire, and Ngorongoro Crater. A Kilimanjaro climb is also offered.

Wildlife Conservation Society. 15 days / $$$$ (from New York) / February. Tented camps in the Serengeti, Tarangire, and Ngorongoro National Parks, plus overnights at Gibbs Farm and Ngare Sero Lodge. Maximum of 16 participants; a NYZS naturalist will accompany the trip.

Rwanda, Eastern Zaire, and Burundi

Mountainous Rwanda is spectacularly beautiful, with steep valleys, shimmering lakes, and rolling grassy hills. It borders Tanzania on the east, Uganda in the north, eastern Zaire to the west, and has Burundi as its southern neighbor. Alas, for all its richness in wildlife and scenery, it is among the most densely populated countries in Africa and thus its forests—and consequently its wildlife—are threatened. Most famous in this regard, of course, is the work of naturalists George Schaller and Dian Fossey, both of whom brought the plight of the Mountain Gorilla to world-wide attention. Until the recent political unrest, the gorilla populations had begun to recover from earlier poaching. Only particular family groups, habituated to humans, were visited, and these only by small tour groups led by experienced trackers and guides. Here was another testimony to the effectiveness of ecotourism—there had been no poaching of the gorilla groups visited by tourists. Additionally, the high fee that the country charged for the permit to see the gorillas helped finance conservation efforts.

Tour operators had been offering a Mountain Gorilla–viewing extension to their wildlife safaris to Kenya or Tanzania. We haven't listed or discussed these, so check with the individual outfitters. Full tours to Rwanda usually head for the Parc National des Volcans, the Virunga Mountains. These volcanic peaks straddle Rwanda and Zaire; their equivalent in Zaire is the Parc National des Virunga. Besides the Mountain Gorillas there are elephants, hogs, duikers, buffalos, and several species of monkey. The park is especially rich in birdlife—Rwenzori and Great Blue Turacos, Western Green Tinkerbird, Purple-breasted and Regal Sun-birds, and Black Partridge, for example. Among the prime birding spots are the Nyungwe Forest and the larger Akagera National Park, on the border with Tanzania. In addition, there is the chance to see Impala, Topi, Waterbuck, Hippo, Eland, Tapir, Oribi, Roan Antelope, and Buffalo, as well as Aardvark, Civet, and Genet. Problems in Rwanda may interrupt trips to see the Mountain Gorilla; check with tour operators.

Zaire is a huge country—about the size of the eastern half of the United States. As a consequence, the habitat is diverse: from tropical rain forest to alpine mountains, from grassy savannah to forested slopes. The Zaire (Congo) River, which cuts across the country, drains an area so huge it is second only to the Amazon Basin. Zaire also has the second largest remaining area of tropical forest in the world. Alas, poaching is a large problem here, and it is estimated that within a few decades, there will be no large mammals left.

Most tour operators go to eastern Zaire, and primarily for the Mountain Gorillas. In addition, the Parc National de Kahuzi-Biega in the south is a good spot for looks at the eastern Lowland Gorilla, though the trip is demanding. The Ruwenzori Mountains, the "Mountains of the Moon," are popular for hiking.

Like Rwanda, Burundi is a tiny, poor country, and densely populated, thus putting great pressure on its resources. Less than 1 percent of the country's virgin forests remain, and those may soon be gone. Poaching has virtually wiped out most of the wildlife. Nevertheless, the country has recently created three national parks and a nature reserve. There aren't many trips to Burundi, but the ones that are offered usually look for Chimpanzee, Red Colobus Monkey, and Crested Mangabey in the Parc National de la Kibira. Birders head for the Lake Rwihinda Nature Reserve and other lakes in the north. The Rububu basin is also a destination for looks at hippos, crocodiles, and antelope.

Bear in mind that getting up the mountains and tracking the Mountain Gorilla can be strenuous and often involve climbing over rough, wet, matted vegetation and mud. Also, if you have a cold or stomach problems, you will not be allowed to proceed, lest you infect the animals.

Tour Operators

Birdquest. 20 days / $$$ (from London) / July. A birding trip to all the major regions of Rwanda and Zaire, including Akagera, where a boat trip into the papyrus swamps in search of the Shoebill is sure to be a highlight of the tour. Vying for the top spot, though, is a trip into Kahuzi-Biega National Park to see the Mountain Gorilla. Participants can expect to see about 450 species of birds along with the mammals that abound in this region.

Field Guides. 21 days / $$$ (from Nairobi) / March. A birdwatching tour that visits Nyungwe Forest Reserve in southwestern Rwanda, then travels into eastern Zaire to the Kahuzi-Biega National Park to see Mountain Gorilla as well as birds, and finally into the cultivated and second-growth forest of the eastern Congo Basin for lowland birds. Participants may expect to see about 450 species of birds, including Spot-breasted Ibis, Hartlaub's Duck, White-spotted Flufftail, Akun Eagle Owl, Cassin's Spinetail, Chocolate-backed Kingfisher, Black-casqued Wattled Hornbill, Speckled Tinkerbird, African Piculet, and 12 species of sunbird.

This trip may be combined with Field Guides' Tanzania trip (see the section on Tanzania, page 203). Maximum of 12 participants, 2 leaders.

Geo Expeditions. 17 days / $$$ (from Nairobi) / July, December. Combination Tanzania, Rwanda, and Zaire wildlife safari. Stays in safari camps. Visits traditional sites in Tanzania; Rwanda's Nyungwe Forest and Parc National des Volcans, from where participants can track Mountain Gorilla (rugged trip); and Kahuzi-Biega in Zaire.

Natural Habitat Wildlife Adventures. 12 days / $$$$ (from New York) / August, September. A trip concentrating on primates. Participants visit Kahuzi-Biega National Park and the Tongo Chimpanzee Reserve in Zaire, as well as Nyungwe Forest (home to 13 species of primates) and the Virunga Mountains in Rwanda. You'll see Lowland and Mountain Gorillas and Chimpanzee. Optional safari extensions to Kenya and Tanzania.

Naturetrek. 23 days / July / $$$ (from London). A mammal and birdwatching trip to Rwanda and Zaire. You'll visit the Akagera and Volcanoes National Parks and Nyungwe Forest in search of Mountain Gorilla, L'Hoest's Monkey, and Chimpanzee. In Kahuzi-Biega you'll search for Lowland Gorilla. Among the birds are Shoebill, Black-billed Turaco, Hartlaub's Duck, Congo Serpent Eagle, Wattled Cuckoo-shrike, and Red-fronted Antpecker.

Oceanic Society Expeditions. 14 days / $$$$ (from New York) / February, August. Combined tour to the Virunga Mountains in Zaire and safari to Kenya's Masai Mara Reserve. Maximum of 8 participants, 1 leader.

Overseas Adventure Travel. 19–25 days / $$ (from Nairobi, Arusha, or Kigali) / December–March, June–October. Combination wildlife trips to Rwanda-Uganda, Rwanda-Burundi-Tanzania, and Rwanda-Tanzania. Visits Gombe Stream Park for Chimpanzee and Parc des Volcans for Mountain Gorilla. Also visits Akagera, Nyungwe Forest, and traditional sites in Tanzania.

Sunbird

16 days / $$$ (from London) / June, September. Two birding trips to Burundi, Zaire, and Rwanda (including 3 days in Kenya). In Burundi the group spends 3 days in Ruvubu National Park, where the shy African Finfoot can be seen. Then on to Rwanda, where 2 days are spent in the Nyungwe Forest, Africa's largest montane forest. Specialties there include Rwenzori Turaco, Red-collared Babbler, Archer's Robin Chat, Grauer's Rush Warbler, Rwenzori Batis, White-tailed Blue Flycatcher, and Strange Weaver. In Zaire you'll visit Kahuzi-Biega National Park, home to Lowland Gorilla, and you'll have a morning visit with a group of these magnificent primates. While birding at the park you may see such specialties as

Handsome Francolin, Green Broadbill, Albert's Helmet Shrike, and Dusky Crimson-wing. This trip may be combined with a trip to the Seychelles (see the section on Madagascar and Other Islands of the Indian Ocean, page 225). Maximum of 12 participants, 3 leaders.

Wilderness Travel. 16 days / $$$$ (from Nairobi) / July, August. Visits Virunga, Tonga, and Kahuzi-Biega for broad variety of primate sightings.

Ethiopia

According to the World Resources Institute (*Environmental Almanac*), as recently as fifty years ago as much as 30 percent of the Ethiopian plateau was forested; only 3 percent is today. This country—one of the oldest in the world—has come on hard times. Economic collapse, political turmoil, and drought have combined to sap the strength of a once magnificent country.

More than twice the size of Texas, Ethiopia is largely a plateau split in half, with several peaks and valleys. This topological arrangement encouraged plant and animal species to develop independently from the rest of Africa. Thus, you find endemic species specially adapted to the unique conditions here. There are several national parks, although, given the current circumstances, their maintenance is not a high priority. Nevertheless, there are a few trips to Ethiopia and travel is relatively safe.

TOUR OPERATORS

Birdquest. 17 days / $$ (from London) / November. A birding tour to the "Roof of Africa." Special effort is made to find as many of the 29 endemic species as possible. Participants visit Awash National Park, Debre Libanos, Lake Tana (source of the Blue Nile), the Bale Mountains, and Wondoguenet Forest, where hot springs bubble up through the vegetation. You can expect to see upwards of 400 species of birds, plus several species of mammals.

Naturetrek
22 days / $$$ (from London) / December. A camping wildlife adventure through the remote parks of the lower Omo Valley in search of animals and birds. Visits Nechisar for Burchell's Zebra, Grant's Gazelle, Swayne's Hartebeest, Kori Bustard, and Abyssinian Ground Hornbill. In the savannah and bush are the Guenther's Dik-dik and Greater Kudu, as well as Red-billed and Gray Hornbills. Forest species include Bushbuck, Bushpig, Anubis Baboon, and both Colobus and Vervet Monkeys. The trip continues to Mago and Mui National Parks for Lion, Cheetah, Leopard, Elephant, Buffalo, Hippo, Giraffe, Zebra, Oryx, Waterbuck, Gerenuk, and smaller mammals.

20 days / $$ (from London) / November. A birdwatching and animal safari to the lakes of the Rift Valley, Blue Nile Falls, Lake Tana, Awash National Park, and a 4-day trek into the Bale Mountains. Participants may expect to see about half of Ethiopia's 830 bird species. The trek is through unspoiled wilderness, the last refuge of the endemic Mountain Nyala, the Simien Jackal, and Menelik's Bushbuck. Here you also may see Klipspringer, Duiker, Bohor Reedbuck, Warthog, Rock Hyrax, and baboons. Fourteen endemic species of birds inhabit this area, and it is also of great interest to the botanist.

WEST AND CENTRAL AFRICA

Most nature tourism is concentrated in the eastern and southern parts of the continent, but there is reason to visit western and central Africa as well. This is the heart of black African culture. Stretching southward from the Sahara, the land is arid or semiarid, gradually becoming savannah or forest until it turns marshy or into mangrove swamps along the coastal belt. The rain forests of Central Africa are extensive, second only to those of the Amazon Basin. These diverse habitats are home to a rich variety of wildlife, including many endemic birds, elephants, lions, giant eland, buffalo, warthogs, baboons, monkeys, and giraffes. Unfortunately, the Central African Republic is a major area for hunting. The more peaceful tours go primarily to Gambia, Senegal, Cameroon, Mali, and Ivory Coast.

Gambia is an English-speaking country that was developed as a winter holiday destination for Europeans. Therefore, there are many good-quality hotels along the coast, from which you can explore the country's varied habitats, including Abuko Nature Reserve. It's an ideal introduction to sub-Saharan Africa.

Traveling in Senegal, which does not have as highly developed a tourist trade as Gambia, is nonetheless relatively easy, with modest but comfortable hotels. The variety of habitat always means there is plenty to see, whether in savannah, mangrove swamp, or woodlands. Though the country has some problems with deforestation and wildlife poaching, the government recently allocated over 10 percent of the land to parks and reserves.

Cameroon straddles the border between West and Central Africa. It is the inspiration for some of Gerald Durrell's nature writings, in part because it is graced with a large number of endemic species. Unfortunately, the country's forestlands are being destroyed at a rapid rate, especially along the coast. National parks and preserves cover about 5 percent of the land.

Mali is a generally flat country in central West Africa, in recent years suffering severe drought, which, together with habitat loss, is decimating the large mammals such as Oryx, Elephant, Lion, Cheetah, Eland, Giraffe, and Ostrich. Only 1 percent of the country is protected as parks and preserves.

Liberia was settled by black American slaves in a project organized by the American Colonization Society in 1817. Because of internal strife, the country is virtually at a standstill, and all plans for development of national parks have been put on hold.

TOUR OPERATORS

Bird Bonanzas. 21 days / $$ (from New York) / October. A birding tour of Cameroon, Ivory Coast, and Guinea. Participants have the prospect of seeing 73 endemic and 159 near-endemic species. The trip includes visits to agricultural and research stations, Tai National Park, and montane forest habitat at the foot of Mount Cameroon. Maximum of 7 participants, 1 leader.

Birding. 7 days / $$ (from London) / November. A birdwatching trip to Gambia. You'll visit sandy beaches, a tidal estuary, mangrove swamps, riverine forest, and marshes—a wealth of habitat producing many species of birds. At the Abuko Reserve there are Green-crested and Violet Turacos, Paradise Flycatcher, Blue-billed Weaver, Giant Kingfisher, and White-faced Scops Owl (among the 250 species that have been recorded here). Along the Senegal border you may see Hammerkop, Allied Hornbill, Fine-spotted Woodpecker, and Black Heron.

Birdquest. 22 days / $$$ (from London) / February. A birding trip to Cameroon. Nearly 900 species of birds have been recorded here, of which 26 are endemic. Participants visit Waza and Benoue National Parks, the Adamawa Plateau, the Bamenda Highlands, and Mount Cameroon; you may expect to see upwards of 500 species of birds. Special effort is made to find rarities and endemics. Maximum of 16 participants, 2 leaders.

Field Studies Council. 14 days / $$$ (from London) / February. "The National Parks of Senegal in Search of Birds and Mammals" is an educational trip that visits the varied habitats of three of Senegal's national parks: the grassland habitat of Parc National des Oiseaux du Djoudj, in the northwest; the woodlands of Parc National du Niokolo-Koba, in the south; and the mangrove swamps of Parc National du Delta du Saloum, near the Atlantic coast. In addition, there is a visit to Parc National des Isles du Madeline in search of the Red-billed Tropicbird. Prospects are good for seeing wintering European birds, African species of waders and raptors, and mammals such as Hippo, Duiker, Warthog, and Honey Badger.

Foundation for Field Research
12 days / $ (from Bamako) / February–May. "Mammals of Mali" is a research expedition in the Bafing-Makana Faunal Reserve. Volunteers census animals and follow herds when necessary.

12 days / $ (from Bamako) / March, April. "Raptors of Mali" is a research trip. Volunteers band birds and collect data concerning the demographics, growth, molt, and general conditions of raptors. This research will be a valuable contribution to the preliminary work involved in establishing a new national park in Mali. The trip may be combined with "Mammals of Mali" (see above).

12 days / $ (from Bamako) / February. "Mali Nightlife" is a research trip studying nocturnal animals such as Giant Pangolin, Civet, Aardvark, and Elephant-shrew. Volunteers trap the animals and take relevant data regarding their size, appearance, and weight before setting them free. The trip may be combined with "Mammals of Mali" (see above).

12 days / $ (from Bamako) / July–August. "Hannibal's Elephants" is a research trip studying—and helping—the last biologically viable population of North African Elephant.

14 days / $ (from Monrovia) / January–April. "Primate Census in Liberia" is a research trip into the Cape Mount area. Volunteers walk transects to find, identify, and count primates. Several species are expected, among them Red Colobus, Black-and-white Colobus, Diana Monkey, Bushbaby, and Chimpanzee. The trip may be combined with either the moth or leatherback trip described below.

14 days / $ (from Monrovia) / January. "Stalking Liberia's Moths" is a research trip. Liberia—with its huge population of butterflies and moths—is an entomologist's dream.

14 days / $ (from Monrovia) / January–February. "Leatherbacks of Liberia" is a research trip studying Leatherback Turtles on the beaches of Cape Mount. Participants camp on the beach and assist scientists in locating nest sites.

Sunbird. 14 days / $$ (from London) / November. A birding trip to Gambia. Participants visit the Abuko Reserve and West Kiang National Park, and take a boat trip around MacCarthy Island. Highlights at Abuko include Palm-nut Vulture, Black Crake, Allied Hornbill, and Snowy-crowned Robin Chat. But there are many animals there as well, including Western Red Colobus, Green Vervet, and Red Patas Monkeys. While based at Georgetown, near the end of the trip, you'll make an expedition to see the Egyptian Plover, Gambia's most famous bird, and one that is difficult to see elsewhere in Africa.

SOUTHERN AFRICA

Moving southward to the Tropic of Capricorn and beyond, we enter the region of the vast African continent that we've termed southern Africa. This includes—in addition to South Africa—Botswana, Namibia, Mozambique, Zimbabwe, Malawi, Zambia, Angola, and the tiny kingdom of Swaziland.

Botswana

The delightful movie *The Gods Must Be Crazy* brought wide attention to the bush people of the Kalahari several years ago. At about the same time, Public Television's "Nature" series on the Okavango Delta helped catapult this area into a prime ecotourist destination. Since most of the population is congregated near the water sources in the east, opportunities for seeing wildlife in the north especially are very good. Approximately 18 percent of the country's land has been protected, a high percentage, indeed. Several areas—Chobe National Park and Moremi Wildlife Reserve, the Okavango Delta in particular, and the lesser visited Nxai Pan National Park and Makgadikgadi Pans Game Preserve—are excellent for seeing game and birdwatching.

Botswana has a primarily subtropical semiarid and arid environment, with a lot of desert and savannah, though there are some wetlands and forests in the north. Except for a problem with ranch fencing inhibiting the natural migration of animals, and some overgrazing, the country's environment is pretty stable. For visitors, the desirable dry season is from May to September for the primary destinations; Nxai and Makgadikgadi Pans are best during the wet season, from December to April.

TOUR OPERATORS

Abercrombie & Kent. 12 days / $$$ (from Gaborone) / January–December. Air safari, dugout canoe, and riverboat exploration of the Okavango Delta, then by plane to Moremi and Chobe; optional trip to Victoria Falls, Zimbabwe.

Birdquest. (See the section on Zimbabwe, page 214.)

Cox & Kings. 13 days / $$$$ (from London) / May–October. Fly in to safari camps in the Okavango Delta, with day trips to see Giraffe, Zebra, Leopard, Baboon, plus many species of birds, including African Jacana and African Fish Eagle. Trips to otherwise inaccessable areas are made by canoe. The last 2 days are spent at Victoria Falls in Zimbabwe. Two optional extensions are offered: an "Elephant Back Safari" through the grasslands of the delta; and a trip to Namibia's Skeleton Coast (5 days).

Earthwatch. 14 days / $$ (from Maun) / June, August. "Okavango Elephants" is a research trip. The problem in southern Africa is that elephant populations have grown so much that they now threaten to overwhelm their resources and destroy their habitat. Volunteers survey vegetation and analyze soils to help determine what elephants are eating and how much damage they are doing.

Fish Eagle Safaris. 7–12 days / $$ (from Maun) / March–December. Various birdwatching trips are offered, including a week-long exploration of the Okavango Delta, and a 12-day northern Botswana camping safari. You'll travel in four-wheel-drive vehicles and dugout canoes. Some trips also visit Victoria Falls. Among the many species of birds to be seen are Pel's Fishing Owl, Lesser Gallinule, African Crake, Painted Snipe, Black Coucal, Brown Firefinch, Dwarf Bittern, Broadbilled Roller, Arnot's Chat, and Long-tailed Shrike. Birding trips are led by noted author Ken Newman.

Geo Expeditions. 18 days / $$ (from Maun) / March–October. Visits Okavango, Chobe, and Nxai Pan via four-wheel-drive viewing vehicles to see Lion, Leopard, Elephant, and African Buffalo, along with many water birds. Includes a trip to Victoria Falls.

Nature Expeditions International. 16 days / $$$ (from Maun) / June–July, August. An exploration of the Okavango Delta and the Kalahari—habitat of Wildebeest, Springbok, and Oryx.

Naturetrek. 17–24 days / $$$ (from London) / August, November. A combination birdwatching and animal trip to Chobe National Park, Moremi Wildlife Reserve, the Kalahari's Nxai Pan National Park, and Makgadikgadi Pan Game Reserve (November trip only), Victoria Falls, and the Okavango Delta. Among the many birds to be seen are Taita Falcon, Heuglin's Robin, Arnot's Chat, Slaty Egret, and a host of waders, woodpeckers, barbets, and weavers. In the Okavango exploration is by *mokoros,* the traditional canoes of the delta.

Sue's Safaris. 10 days / $$$ (from Maun) / January–December. Wildlife safari via four-wheel-drive vehicle to Okavango Delta, staying at three different camps. Individualized tours to Okavango, Chobe, Victoria Falls, Makgadikgadi and Kudikam Pans, Moremi, and the Savuti Channel can be arranged.

Swan Hellenic. (See the listing in the section on Zimbabwe, page 216.)

TravelWild. 12 days / $$$$ (from Maun) / September. Photo safari to the Okavango Delta and Chobe National Park. Participants fly from camp to camp, staying in first-class lodges and camps. A number of different ungulates can be seen and photographed, such as Red Lechwe, Roan and Sable Antelopes, Black Rhinoceros, and Cheetah. Also a wide variety of birds. Maximum of 14 participants; a professional photographer accompanies the trip.

VENT. (See the listing in the section on Namibia, page 221.)

Wilderness Travel. 22 days / $$$ (from Maun) / March–December. Camping safari and travel via four-wheel-drive vehicle, boat, dugout canoe, and small plane. Visits Nxai Pan, Okavango, Moremi, Chobe, Victoria Falls; some trips also visit Mkgadikgadi Pan and the central Kalahari.

Wildlife Conservation Society. (See the listing in the section on Namibia page 221.)

Zegrahm Expeditions. 14 days / $$$$ (from Maun) / August, September. Luxury camp safari with strong emphasis on birds but also seeking game. Visits different spots in Chobe, Moremi, and Okavango.

Zimbabwe

Roughly the size of California, Zimbabwe is bordered on the north by Zambia, with the Zambezi River in between. To the west is Botswana and the Kalahari Desert. To the east, mountains up to 7,000 feet high mark the border with Mozambique. In the south is South Africa. The climate as been described as "agreeable."

Formerly Rhodesia, Zimbabwe is today a prosperous country with outstanding game preserves. Approximately 7 percent of the land has been set aside, protecting over 50,000 elephants and Africa's largest remaining Black Rhino population. Unfortunately, as in many other places in the world, a growing human population is putting severe pressure on the country's forested land, as wood is cut for fuel and land is cleared for agriculture.

Tourist facilities in Zimbabwe are good and the parks are well maintained. Most trips visit Hwange National Park for its Elephant herds, African Buffalo, Zebra, Wildebeest, Giraffe, and both Black and White Rhinoceros. Matusadona and Mana Pools National Parks in the north are also good game-watching spots. Other popular destinations are the Great Zimbabwe Ruins and Victoria Falls, which is on the border with Zambia. The dry season, when animals come to scarce waterholes, is from August to October.

TOUR OPERATORS

Birdquest. 22 days / $$$ (from London) / October. A birding trip to Zimbabwe and the Okavango Delta. Birding is especially rich here because Zimbabwe stands at the habitat crossroads of southern Africa: To the east are the moist montane forests of the eastern highlands, while to the west is the edge of the Kalahari Desert. Although this is primarily a birding trip, participants will see many mammals as well, including White Rhinoceros, whose last stronghold is here. You'll visit the Vumba Mountains, Lake McIlwaine National Park, Lake Kariba, Hwange National Park, and Victoria Falls; then fly to the Okavango—a vast delta amid the sands of the Kalahari. Participants can expect to see some 450 species of birds, including Saddle-billed Stork, Lappet-faced Vulture, Red-billed Quelea, Steel-blue Widowfinch, Bearded Robin, and Red-winged Starling. Maximum of 15 participants, 2 leaders. In Botswana, local naturalists assist the leaders.

Breakaway Adventure Travel. 5 days / $ (from Kariba) / January–December. Canoe safaris on the Zambezi River. Game viewing from the canoe, with excellent birdlife also.

Cox & Kings. 12 days / $$$$ (from London) / January–December. Steam train safaris through the plains. Visits Matobo Hills, the teak forests of Matabeland, Hwange National Park, and Victoria Falls; also includes game drives and optional whitewater rafting, canoeing, and a Zambezi River cruise.

Earthwatch. 11 days / $$ (from Harare) / July–September. "Black Rhino" is a research trip. In 1970 there were 65,000 Black Rhinos, by 1987 there were only 4,000, and numbers are still falling at an alarming rate. In an effort to protect and manage the remaining population, Earthwatch volunteers will photograph rhinos for an identification bank.

Field Guides. 20 days / $$ (from Harare) / January. A birding trip. Travel is via plane, minibus, and four-wheel-drive vehicle. Among the many birds to be seen are Wattled Crane, Dickinson's Kestrel, Double-banded Sandgrouse, Green Turaco, Racket-tailed Roller, Bradfield's Hornbill, Boulder Chat, Crimson-breasted Shrike, Marico Flycatcher, and Shaft-tailed Whydah. Nighttime owling should produce African Scops-Owl, African Barred Owlet, and Spotted Eagle Owl. At Victoria Falls one hopes to see Taita Falcon, one of the world's rarest raptors.

Field Studies Council. 21 days / $$ (from London) / October. A trip for botanizing and game viewing in Zimbabwe and the Okavango. Two leaders accompany the trip.

Fish Eagle Safaris
   6 days / $$$$ (from Johannesburg) / October. A mammals trip to Chizarira National Park. Participants stay at a tented camp and look for Lion, Black Rhino, Cape Buffalo, Eland, Kudu, Sharpe's Grysbok, Klipspringer, and Warthog. Many birds can also be seen, including Augur Buzzard, Black Eagle, Taita Falcon, and Collared Palm Thrush.
   14 days / $$$ (from Johannesburg) / February. A birdwatching trip from Victoria Falls to the Haroni-Rusitu valley. Specialties include Taita Falcon, Vanga Flycatcher, Coppery Sunbird, Brown Firefinch, African Finfoot, and Chestnut-fronted Helmetshrike. Ian Sinclair, of the South African Ornithological Society, leads the trip.

12 days / $$ (from Kariba) / April–December. "Rhino Camping Safari" begins at Victoria Falls and visits Hwange, Chizarira, Matusadona, and Mana Pools National Parks, where you can see big game and plenty of birds.

Garth Thompson Safaris. 4–21 days (or more) / $–$$$$ (from Harare or Kariba) / January–December. Individualized special-interest tours, safaris, camps, and stays at park lodges are arranged. Included are trips to Victoria Falls, walking safaris, photographic tours, and canoe trips.

Goliath Safaris. 4–7 days / $–$$$ (from Harare) / January–December. Canoe safaris along the Zambezi River, from either Chirundu or Kanyemba to Mana Pools. You'll pass through the Mupata Gorge and its forests of Tamarind, Ebony, Sausage, and Fig trees. Abundant birdlife along the river includes waders, raptors, Malachite Kingfisher, and Long-toed Plover. Maximum of 8 participants.

International Expeditions. 16 days / $$$$ (from New York) / August, September. Game drives, walking safaris, and animal viewing from boats along the Zambezi River make this a varied wildlife and birdwatching trip.

Learn at Leisure. 16 days / $$$$ (from London) / August. A learning vacation that examines the different habitats of this remarkable country. You'll visit national parks, go on both day and night game drives, and explore some of the more remote areas both on foot and by boat or canoe. The trip begins at Victoria Falls, then goes on to Hwange, Lake Kariba, and Mana Pools. A wide variety of birds and animals are to be expected. A zoologist accompanies the trip.

Mountain Travel/Sobek. 18 days / $$ (from Harare) / January–December. Wildlife adventure trip that visits Hwange, Chizarira and the Zambezi Escarpment, Lake Kariba and Matusadona Park, Mana Pools, and Victoria Falls. Hiking, camping.

Nature Expeditions International. (See the section on Zambia, page 217.)

Shearwater Adventures. 3–9 days / $$ (from Harare) / March–January. Trips of varying lengths and types, from camps to rafting or whitewater canoeing, to walking or horse safaris. Canoeing safaris are along the lower Zambezi; whitewater rafting at Victoria Falls gorges. All trips are accompanied by licensed river guides.

Swan Hellenic. 19 days / $$$$ (from London) / May, August. Beginning at Mana Pools National Park, one of the most prolific game areas in Zimbabwe, you'll travel to Lake Kariba and Hwange National Park, before going on to the Okavango and

Victoria Falls. Many species of animals and birds can be seen. Two leaders accompany the trip.

TravelWild. 18 days / $$$ (from Harare) / August. Photo safari concentrating on wildlife along the Zambezi River. You'll visit Mana Pools and Hwange National Parks, Lake Kariba at Fothergill Island, the mysterious ruins at Great Zimbabwe, and Victoria Falls. Maximum of 10 participants; a professional photographer accompanies the trip.

University Research Expeditions Program. 13 days / $$ (from Harare) / August. "Good Grooming: Impala of Southeastern Africa" is a trip to study the Impala and its unique mutual grooming behavior. Volunteers are based at the Sengwa Research Reserve in a tented camp.

Zambia

Though the country is the size of Texas, it has only half the population—about 8 million people, most of whom live in towns and cities. About 9 percent of the land has been set aside as parks, with additional preserves not open to the public. South Luangwa National Park in the north is a huge area with a high concentration of elephants, in addition to Kudu, Giraffe, Leopard, Wildebeest, Lion, Hyena, African Buffalo, Waterbuck, Impala, Puku, Zebra, and Hippo. Birdlife, too, is well represented. Sumbu and Kafue National Parks are other good wildlife-viewing spots. Victoria Falls is, of course, also a primary destination.

Zambia is primarily a savannah plateau between 3,280 and 5,249 feet high. Thus the climate is subtropical and much of the region is wooded. Unfortunately, the trees near towns and cities are being cut down for fuel and land is being cleared for agriculture, disrupting habitat for many species. Also, poaching of Elephant (for their tusks) and Rhino (for their horns) has been a problem.

TOUR OPERATORS

Cox & Kings. 13 days / $$$ (from London) / July–September. Walking safari in Luangwa Valley, at the southern tip of the Great Rift Valley. Participants stay in tented camps.

International Research Expeditions. 7–14 days / $ (from Ngoma) / May–September. Research trips to study animal diets in national parks, including those of Elephant, Buffalo, Lion, Leopard, Kudu, and Wildebeest.

Nature Expeditions International. 16 days / $$ (from Lusaka) / July, August. A walking safari to Zambia and Zimbabwe that includes a visit to Victoria Falls.

Naturetrek. 17 days / $$$ (from London) / September. A walking safari in search of game and birdlife in the national parks—exploring the Luangwa Valley, the Kafue River, and Victoria Falls. Night game drives are a feature of the tour, as are visits to islands in the Zambezi River (via canoe). Birds to be looked for include Ross's Lourie, Crowned Eagle, Bearded Woodpecker, and Carmine Bee-eater, among many others. Participants can expect to see over 200 species in Luangwa National Park alone.

Special Interest Tours. 8 days / $$ (from Lusaka) / January–December. Walking safari in Luangwa National Park and a visit to Victoria Falls.

Malawi

Lake Malawi takes up one fifth of the total area of this tiny, very poor country, and the land that remains is terribly overpopulated. Consequently, although 11 percent of this subtropical land has been set aside for preserves, there are severe problems of deforestation and poaching. Particularly hard hit are the elephants and rhinos.

Lake Malawi, the third largest lake in Africa, has more species of freshwater fish than any other lake in the world. The national park here, in fact, has been established to protect these colorful fish species. Dr. Livingstone, who "discovered" Lake Malawi in 1859, called it "the lake of stars."

The national parks most often visited by the few operators that come here are Liwonde, on the Shire River, for Hippo, Elephant, Waterbuck, Sable Antelope, and Greater Kudu; Lengwe National Park, for the Nyala Antelope, Suni, and Bushbuck, as well as such birds as Green Coucal, Rudd's Apalis (a warbler), and Woodward's Batis (a small, leaf-gleaning flycatcher); and Nyika National Park, for Eland, Roan Antelope, Zebra, Blue and Red Duikers, and Leopard, and Wattled Crane, Denham's Bustard, Bar-tailed Trogon, White-breasted Alethe, Sharpe's Akalat, and Olive-flanked Robin.

TOUR OPERATORS

Fish Eagle Safaris

12 days / $$ (from Johannesburg) / November. A birding trip to the Viphya Highlands, Vwasa Marsh, Nyika National Park, Chintheche, and Dzalanyama. High-altitude birds on Nyika include Yellow Malachite Sunbird, Churring Cisticola, Baglafecht Weaver, Yellow Mountain Warbler, and Blue Starling.

16 days / $$ (from Johannesburg) / November. A birding trip that visits Liwonde National Park and Cape Maclear on Lake Malawi, in addition to the sites above. Birds to be looked for at Liwonde include Pel's Fishing Owl, Lilian's

Lovebird, Western Banded Snake Eagle, Bearded Robin, and Lesser Black-winged Plover. There is also ample time to snorkel in Lake Malawi and observe the many cichlid fish for which the lake is renowned.

15 days / $$ (from Liwonde) / March–December. General safaris visiting a variety of habitats.

Journeys. 18 days / $$ (from Liwonde) / March–December. Overland or flying safari to the Mulanje Mountains, Shire River, and Liwonde National Park, then on to Lake Malawa and the Nyika Plateau.

Naturetrek. 24 days / $$ (from London) / August, October. General natural history trips with time for birding, viewing game, and snorkeling. You'll visit Nyika, Liwonde, and Lengwe National Parks; the Zomba and Mulanje mountains; and, of course, Lake Malawi, where you'll see many species of colorful tropical fish.

Wilderness Travel. 17 days / $$ (from Liwonde) / May–October. Walking safari for wildlife and birds. Visits Tuma Forest Reserve, Liwonde National Park, Mount Mulanje, Lengwe National Park, and Lake Malawi.

Namibia

Situated along Africa's southwest coast, between Angola and South Africa, is a sparsely populated country of singular beauty. Namibia is a fairly new tourist destination, having only gained total independence from South Africa in 1990. Prior to South African control, it had been a German colony. Today, democratic Namibia is developing its resources, especially diamonds and uranium, and its parks are well maintained. In fact, it is one of the last great wildernesses in Africa, yet, we're told, "you don't have to be 'off the beaten track'" to enjoy it. Namibia ranks with the East African highlands as an area of greatest endemicity on the continent. However, all the news isn't good: There is some poaching here, especially of rhinos.

The country is mainly a high plateau, with a pleasant subtropical climate. The rainy season is in the summer, largely in the north. A chief destination is Etosha ("Big White Place") National Park, with a huge Elephant population (migration in October through November and March), plus Zebra, Wildebeest, Gemsbok, Springbok, Lion, White and Black Rhinos, Red Hartebeest, Giraffe, Black-faced Impala, Honey Badger, Warthog, Mongoose, Hyena, Aardwolf, Eland, Roan Antelope, and Gray Duiker. Birds are plentiful, too, including Ostrich, Clapper Lark, Red-necked Falcon, Double-banded Sandgrouse, Martial Eagle, Black-faced Babbler, Blacksmith Plover, Yellow-billed Hornbill, White Helmetshrike, and Long-billed Crombec (a buff-and-gray warbler). The striking thing about Etosha is the Namib Desert's close proximity to the coast, making for enormous dry dunes at the water's edge.

Many trips also visit the foggy Skeleton Coast National Park, with its beach, rock formations, and ships' remains being the strong attractions. Here is where the cold Benguela Current moves northward, bringing with it plankton-rich Antarctic waters, making this a prime spot for fish, seals, and seabirds. Lion, Desert Elephant, and Baboon are also found here. In the south, Namib-Naukluft National Park offers a variety of habitat supporting Mountain Zebra, Gemsbok, Springbok, and Ostrich. Fish River Canyon is good for Baboon and Klipspringer.

The Caprivi Strip is in northeastern Namibia, on the border between Angola and Botswana. Apparently it is virtually unexplored territory with regard to its biological attributes. It had been closed owing to skirmishes, but is now open.

TOUR OPERATORS

Birdquest. 27 days / $$ (from London) / October. A birdwatching trip that combines a visit to the Skeleton Coast and Etosha with South Africa's Cape of Good Hope and Natal. Participants can expect to see a good many mammals in addition to the profusion of birdlife. Special effort is made to locate endemic species. Maximum of 14 participants, 2 leaders.

Field Studies Council. 14 days / $$$ (from London) / March. "Deserts and Elephants: A Journey Through Namibia." You'll begin by exploring the Namib, the world's oldest desert, with its dwarf but massive endemic tree, the *Welsitschia mirabilis,* then move on to greener country—the Erongo Mountains, Brantberg Mountains, and Twyfelfontein—and finally to Etosha National Park. Mammals, birds, and plants will all be observed. Two leaders accompany the trip.

Fish Eagle Safaris

8 days / $$$$ (from Johannesburg) / May. "Kaokoveld Desert Ramble" takes you to see the endangered Desert Elephant and Black Rhino. This is a remote and beautiful area. Among the bird species to be seen are Hartlaub's Francolin, Ruppell's Parrot, Dusky Sunbird, and Cinderella Waxbill.

16–18 days /$$ (from Windhoek) / August, October. Birding trips to the Namib Desert, Etosha Game Reserve, and Caprivi Strip. Most of Namibia's endemics will be seen, as well as other African birds and mammals.

10 days / $$$ (from Windhoek) / March–April. A birding trip to the Caprivi Strip and Victoria Falls. Look for Slaty Egret, Carmine Bee-eater, Swamp Boubou, Pel's Fishing Owl, Yellow-billed Oxpecker, and as many as 25 species of raptor, including Western Banded Snake Eagle.

12–16 days / $$ (from Windhoek) / March–December. Wildlife safaris to the Namib and Etosha.

18 days / $$$ (from Johannesburg) / August. A birding trip to the Namib Desert, Etosha Pan, and western Caprivi. Noted field-guide author Ian Sinclair leads the trip.

Journeys. 12–21 days / $–$$ (from Windhoek) / March–December. Wildlife safaris to Etosha, Chobe, the Linyanti Delta in the Caprivi Strip, Damaraland, and Victoria Falls. Some camping.

Mountain Travel/Sobek. 20 days / $ (from Windhoek) / January–December. "Participatory" camping and lodge safaris to the Namib Desert, Skeleton Coast, and Etosha National Park.

Naturetrek. 19 days / $$$ (from London) / November. A birdwatching and game-viewing wildlife safari. You'll visit the Etosha Pan, Namib Desert, Water-berg Mountains, Damaraland and the petrified forest at Twyfelfontein, and the Skeleton Coast. Among the animals to be seen are Black Rhinoceros, Cheetah, and Damara Dik-dik. Birds include Monteiro's Hornbill, White-tailed Shrike, and Rockrunner. On the coast you'll see thousands of Greater and Lesser Flamingos. A pelagic trip offers opportunities to observe marine mammals and seabirds.

Oceanic Society Expeditions. 14 days / $$$$ (from Windhoek) / August. Wildlife safari to Etosha, the Namib Desert, and the Skeleton Coast. Maximum of 16 participants, 1 leader.

Swan Hellenic. 18 days / $$$$ (from London) / May, August. A general natural history trip. You'll visit the Cape Fur Seal colony at Cape Cross on the Skeleton Coast, watch birds at the lagoon in Walvis Bay, see the petrified forest in Damara-land, and view game in Hobatere and Etosha. Two leaders accompany the trip.

TravelWild. 18 days / $$$$ (from Windhoek) / July. Photo tour to Etosha National Park, the Namib Desert, and the Skeleton Coast. You have a good chance for some great shots here! Maximum of 10 participants; a professional photographer accompanies the trip.

VENT. 33 days / $$$ (from Johannesburg) / August. A birding tour to Namibia and Botswana, including a trip to Victoria Falls in Zimbabwe. All the major habitats are visited. You'll have the opportunity to see a lot of big game in addition to the many birds. Participants can expect to see upwards of 400 species, includ-ing Black Egret, Wattled Crane, Pel's Fishing Owl, Giant Eagle-Owl, Ground

Hornbill, Arnot's Chat, Boulder Chat, Swynnerton's Robin, and Forest Prinia. Special effort is made to find endemics. Maximum of 14 participants, 1 leader.

Wildlife Conservation Society. 16 days / $$$$ (from New York) / June. "Wild Africa Safari" visits Namibia's Skeleton Coast and Etosha National Park, Botswana's Okavango Delta, and Zimbabwe's Victoria Falls. Maximum of 15 participants; a NYZS curator accompanies the trip.

Wilderness Travel. 22 days / $$ (from Windhoek) / May–September. Wildlife safaris to Namib Desert, Skeleton Coast, Damaraland, Kaokoveld, Etosha, and Waterberg National Park.

South Africa

Now that the South African government has eased its apartheid policies, it is acceptable to visit this country. At present there are only a handful of operators who go to South Africa, but we expect that situation will soon change.

Unfortunately, with the curtain of racial inequity pulled aside, the view of South Africa's natural world is becoming obscured by smog and other evidence of industrial and economic development. Acid rain, for example, is a big problem; soil erosion and overgrazing are two others. Nevertheless, there are approximately 22,400 square miles, or 5 percent of the country, set aside as protected land. Owing to its excellent parks, reserves, and sanctuaries; good roads; and comfortable accommodations, South Africa is an easy and rewarding destination for viewing wildlife. Its climate has been described as similar to that of southern California. Perhaps with the growing influx of ecotourists, South Africa's administrators will become more aware of the environmental improvements to be made.

Major destinations in South Africa include Kruger National Park and its neighboring private reserves. At Kruger—on the border with Mozambique—Elephant, African Buffalo, Burchell's Zebra, Giraffe, Impala, Rhinoceros, Hippo, Leopard, Cheetah, Hyena, and over 465 species of birds can be found. The park is huge, but unfortunately, it is entirely fenced in, preventing migrants from passing through. There are fewer fences in the private reserves nearby, allowing for some natural passage of animals.

Kalahari Gemsbok National Park in the northwest is best for desert mammals like Blue Wildebeest, Eland, Springbok, Gemsbok, Red Hartebeest, Duiker, Steinbok, Cheetah, Hyena, and Lion. The Garden Route is a scenic highway that runs along the southern coast from Swellendam to Humansdorp, with views of mountains and sea. Tsitsikamma Coastal National Park is rich in marine life, while Tsitsikamma Forest National Park has indigenous trees such as Yellowwood, Cape Chestnut, Stinkwood, Ironwood, and Assegaai.

TOUR OPERATORS

Birdquest. (See the section on Namibia, page 220.)

Earthwatch. 14 days / $$ (from Durban) / June–August. "Whales of the Indian Ocean" is a research trip studying whale populations. In 1980, the International Whaling Commission declared much of the Indian Ocean a whale sanctuary. Have whale populations increased since then? Volunteers will survey Humpback and Right Whales as they migrate past the Cape Vidal Nature Reserve. Some teams will launch through the surf to intercept and photograph individual whales and record their songs.

Fish Eagle Safaris

14 days / $ (from Johannesburg) / March, September. Trips to the Transvaal and Kruger Park. Participants are likely to see big game at the waterholes. There are also many species of birds, including Cape Vulture and Klaas's Cuckoo.

15 days / $$ (from Johannesburg) / October. A "birding bash" to the Zululand Rhino Reserves and the St. Lucia Estuary, a wetland of international importance. You'll also visit Ngoye Forest, home to the rare Woodward's Barbet.

9 days / $$$ (from Johannesburg) / March. A bird and botany trip to the Southwestern Cape and Langebaan Lagoon. Several species of *Protea, Erica,* and other delicate plants combine to form the distinctive "fynbos" vegetation, providing suitable habitat for various endemic birds such as the Cape Sugarbird, Orange-breasted Sunbird, Cape Rockjumper, Cape Bulbul, Cape Francolin, and Victorin's Warbler.

20 days / $$ (from Johannesburg) / March. A birdwatching and game-viewing trip to Kruger Park, Swaziland, Natal, and the Cape. Participants can expect to see some 400 species of birds, including many endemics.

15 days / $$$ (from Johannesburg) / August. A birding trip to Natal's birding hot spots, including the Drakensberg, St. Lucia Estuary, Ngoye Forest, and Mkuze Game Reserve. One day will be spent on a pelagic trip into the Indian Ocean off Durban, where albatrosses, petrels, shearwaters, and gannets may be seen. In the Drakensberg, you'll search for such montane species as Bearded Vulture, Sentinel Rock Thrush, Bush Blackcap, and Gurney's Sugarbird. Noted ornithologist Ian Sinclair leads the trip.

Geostar Travel. 21 days / $$$ (from New York) / August. A botany trip to Namaqualand, called "the rarest garden on earth." It will be springtime here, the peak time for wildflowers. You'll visit various botanic gardens and nature reserves that are devoted to the cultivation of indigenous plants; Knysna Forest, one of the few remaining examples of Afro-montane forest, where Yellowwood and

Stinkwood trees are protected; and Fernkloof Nature Reserve, rich in fynbos. Among the Cape flora the tour hopes to find are several species of *Protea;* pebble-like succulents such as *Dinteranthus wilmotianus;* and various heaths, *Babianas,* and *Ixias.* There will be a number of birds as well, including Cape Gannets at Bird Island Sanctuary and sunbirds (similar to hummingbirds) sipping nectar from the flowers in the Ramskop Reserve. Well-known botanist Anne Bean leads the trip.

Sue's Safaris. 16 days / $$ (from Johannesburg) / April–October. General tours visiting Kruger, Sabi Sabi Private Reserve, Hluhluwe Game Reserve, and Eastern Transvaal, plus city tours. Some trips include the Garden Route.

Woodstar Tours. 23 days/ $$ (from Johannesburg) / October. A birding tour to South Africa and Swaziland. You'll visit Kruger Park, St. Lucia and Mkuze (in Swaziland), Drakensberg, Royal Natal National Park, Tsitsikama Coastal and Forest Parks, Fernkloof Nature Reserve, and the Rondelvlei Bird Sanctuary. Participants can expect to see about 400 species of birds plus some big game. Local ornithologists accompany the trip.

Swaziland and Lesotho

Examples of a vanishing breed, Swaziland and Lesotho are two of the three remaining kingdoms in Africa (Morocco is the third). They are tiny.

Swaziland is only 6,703 square miles, but it has five national parks; 5 percent of its land is protected. There's a variety of habitat, from mountains to plateau to lowland. As in many other places in Africa, overgrazing and erosion have degraded the land. In addition, grass fires have wiped out much of the high veld forest. There's not much wildlife left outside the preserves.

Visitors to Swaziland usually head for Malolotja National Park and Mlilwane Wildlife Sanctuary for Oribi, Rhebok, Klipspringer, Reedbuck, Rhino, Black Wildebeest, Aardwolf, Serval, Zebra, Giraffe, Buffalo, Jackal, Civet, Nyala Antelope, Eland, Kudu, Duiker, and Bushbuck.

Lesotho is an independent entity entirely surrounded by South Africa—an odd situation that resulted when Queen Victoria granted it protection from invading neighbors. On today's map, it looks stranded in the midst of the South African veld.

Pony trekking is a very popular tourist activity, and there is a national park with opportunities to view Oribi, Eland, Wildebeest, Baboon, and much birdlife. The 26 square miles that make up Sehlabathebe National Park constitute the total acreage set aside for preservation. Deforestation and overgrazing are the major environmental problems, with much land steadily lost to erosion each year and virtually no forests remaining. To add to the problem, according to the *Environ-*

mental Almanac, water pollution from human and industrial waste is another exacerbating factor. Unless something positive is done soon, there won't be anything left to this very small country.

TOUR OPERATORS

Field Studies Council. 24 days / $$ (from London) / January. A combination birding, botany, and mammals trip. You'll visit Malolotja National Park for its wildflowers and birds, including the rare and endangered Blue Swallow. Then on to the Mlilwane Wildlife Sanctuary for views of Hippo, Nyala, Giraffe, and Eland; and finally to the Mkhaya Nature Reserve, where wildlife has been relocated from Zimbabwe. You'll also go to Mlawula to observe the behavior of Lappet-faced and White-backed Vultures. Short hikes will take you through the ironwood forests, where you can see *Encephalarlos umbuluziensis,* an endemic cycad (a tropical plant that resembles a palm). Two leaders accompany the trip.

Journeys International. 10 days / $$ (from Johannesburg) / January–December. Walking safaris with an optional pony trek to out-of-the-way places in Swaziland and Lesotho.

MADAGASCAR AND OTHER ISLANDS OF THE INDIAN OCEAN

Madagascar

At one time attached to the African mainland, when it was part of the vast supercontinent Gondwana, the land that is now Madagascar spun off from Africa about 100 million years ago, just after the great continent broke up. Therefore, the forms of life on Madagascar (as on most islands) evolved in isolation; and now three fourths of its species are endemic—they exist nowhere else on earth. Doug Adams, in his book *Last Chance to See,* describes it as a "life raft from a different time."

This island, the fourth largest in the world (after Greenland, New Guinea, and Borneo), is marked by three zones: a central plateau, the eastern coastal strip, and western low plateaus and vast plains. Its mountains, some of which are of volcanic origin, reach 9,400 feet. They bisect the country and slope to the coasts, offering a variety of habitat: desert, savannah, rain forest, and upland forest. The moist trade winds from the Indian Ocean make for high rainfall in the east, while the south is semidesert.

Madagascar is home to 1,000 species of orchids—in fact, 80 percent of all Malagasy plants are endemic, as are half the world's chameleon species, all the world's true lemurs (29 species), and more than 120 species of birds, including five endemic families—mesites, ground rollers, cuckoo-rollers (courols), asities (false sunbirds), and vanga shrikes—as well as the subfamily of couas.

Madagascar has set aside only 2 percent of its land (there are two national parks and thirty-four nature reserves). Deforestation is a critical problem, and 75 percent of the island's forest land is already gone. The situation is exacerbated by religious beliefs that discourage efficient use of the land. The World Wildlife Fund has put Madagascar at the top of its list of the most threatened ecosystems in the world. However, recent debt-for-nature swaps are helping relieve some of the pressure.

Many people go to Madagascar for the sheer idea of being somewhere so exotic. Nature-lovers, birdwatchers, and ecotourists go to see the lemurs—those mouse-to-cat-size monkeylike animals. Some are red, black, brown, gray; all have long tails, big soulful eyes, and tiny ears. They are primates, usually nocturnal, mainly vegetarian, and most often arboreal; they're sociable, too, living in families or tribes.

Popular stops on nature-tour itineraries are the Berenty Reserve in the southeast, where the rare fauna includes Fruit Bats and some fifty-six species of birds, and the Perinet Rainforest Station (on the east coast), noted for its accessible tropical rain forest. Perinet has nine species of lemur, as well as tenrecs (small insectivorious mammals), insects, and reptiles. There are several small islands nearby, some of which are uninhabited, that are rich in birdlife as well as good for snorkeling.

TOUR OPERATORS

Birdquest. 24 days / $$$ (from London) / November. A birding tour that visits the rain forest at Perinet, then goes southward through the heart of the island to the rain forests at Ranofamana, and southwest to the coast at Tulear to explore the Didierea. You'll also visit the lemur reserve at Berenty and forests and lakes of Ankarafantsika in the northwest. Special effort is made to find endemic birds, and participants also see several species of lemur. Maximum of 16 participants, 2 leaders.

Earthwatch. 14 days / $ (from Antananarivo) / January. "Madagascar Wildlife Survey" is a research trip to help assess the needs of some of Madagascar's unique wildlife. Volunteers capture animals, weigh and measure them, and observe animal behavior.

Field Guides. 30 days / $$$ (from Antananarivo) / November. A birding trip to Madagascar, Mauritius, and Réunion, including a 7-day pretour extension to the Seychelles. All the major zoogeographic regions of the island are visited on this tour—from riverine gallery forests at Berenty to deciduous tall forest near Majunga and rain forest at Perinet. Participants have an excellent chance of seeing most of the endemic birds. Many species of lemur will also be encountered. On Réunion and Mauritius—islands whose names are synonymous with rare birds—the tour hopes to find all the surviving endemics. Maximum of 14 participants, 2 leaders. Local bird guides on Réunion and Mauritius assist the leaders.

Geostar. 19 days / $$$ (from Antananarivo) / September. A trip to explore the natural history of Madagascar. You visit Perinet (rain forest and lemurs), Mahajanga (geology), Ampijoroa, (Malagasy Turtle), Nosy Tanikely (great for snorkeling), and the Berenty Reserve (endemic plants and lemurs). You then continue on to Mauritius, where you visit Black River Gorge, the last home of the Mauritius Kestrel. An optional extension to Réunion is offered. Maximum of 16 participants; a botanist accompanies the trip.

International Expeditions. 18 days / $$$ (from New York) / April, September, October. General nature trip to a variety of habitats on the island.

Journeys International
27 days / $$ (from Nairobi) / June–October. General nature tours visiting some remote parts of the island, including Montagne D'Amber National Park, Perinet, Tulear, Berenty, Isalo National Park, Bezaha Mahafaly, Ranomafana; some night hikes to see nocturnal animals. Maximum of 10 participants.

11 days / $$ (from Nairobi) / January–December. General nature tours that visit Nosy Be, Lokobe, Fort Dauphine, and Berenty Reserve; they also go to Perinet Reserve for day and night hikes.

Lemur Tours. 7–11 days / $$ (from Antananarivo) / January–December. General trips that include culture along with nature. You'll visit Perinet and Berenty as well as the islands of Nosy Be, Nosy Komba, and Nosy Tanikely, where you can see Black Lemurs and go snorkeling.

Nature Expeditions International. 16 days / $$ (from Antananarivo) / July, November. Wildlife tours that include visits to Berenty, Perinet, Ampijoroa, and Nosy Be.

Oceanic Society Expeditions. 17 days / $$$ (from New York) / July. Sampling of the country's resouces, with focus on wildlife and environments. Maximum of 16 participants.

Questers. 26 days / $$$$ (from New York) / October. General nature tour of Madagascar, Mauritius, and the Seychelles. Visits Perinet, Fort Dauphine, Berenty,

Tulear, Nosy Be, Nosy Komba, and Nosy Tanikely on Madagascar; then Macabe-Mare Longue Reserve and Black River Gorge on Mauritius; and Praslin, Cousin, La Digue, and Bird Islands in Seychelles.

Sea Quest. 14 days / $$$$ (from Mombasa) / January. A luxury cruise to the Comoros, Madagascar, and south to Durban, South Africa. In Madagascar you'll visit Ambre Nature Reserve, where lemurs can be seen. There will be time for birdwatching and snorkeling as well.

Sue's Safaris. 18 days / $$$ (from New York) / January–December. Visits Fort Dauphine, where you can see carnivorous plants and Baobab trees; a private reserve to see Ring-tailed Lemur; the Macaco Lemur Reserve on Nosy Kamba; and Perinet for Indris (another endemic primate), orchids and primeval forest.

VENT. 28 days / $$ (from New York) / September. A birding trip to Madagascar, Mauritius, and Réunion. You'll visit all the major habitats and see lemurs and endemic reptiles—including an array of weird and colorful chameleons—as well as plenty of birds. Indeed, participants have a good chance of seeing nearly all the endemics.

Mauritius, Réunion, the Seychelles, and Comoros

Though once part of a land bridge between Africa and Asia, the island-nation of Mauritius is now a vacation crossroads. It's actually a small collection of islands totaling a land mass the size of Rhode Island, but most travelers visit the main island for its beaches. There are many endemic plants and animals, but they are rapidly disappearing because of development—deforestation, overuse of pesticides and fertilizers, overfishing, and introduction of invasive shrubs. Some of rarest birds on earth are here: the Mauritius Kestrel, Mauritius Parakeet, and Pink Pigeon. Remember, Mauritius was the home of the Dodo, whose name is synonomous with extinction. This large, gentle, fearless bird was clubbed to death by Dutch colonists for sport, not even for food, and was extinct by 1681.

Réunion, a French Overseas Department, is situated in the Indian Ocean between Mauritius and Madagascar. With its volcanic landscape and tropical climate, it too is a popular vacation spot. Like Mauritius, its ecosystem is fragile and existing species are losing ground, literally and figuratively.

Of the 155 islands making up the Seychelles, 49 are granite—the only mid-oceanic group of granite islands in the world. But that's not all that's unique about this archipelago. Here are some of the world's rarest birds, such as the Black Parrot and the Black Paradise Flycatcher. Bird Island is home to 1.5 million Sooty Terns;

Aride Island has nesting Lesser Noddy and Roseate Terns; Cousin Island, another seabird nesting spot, is owned and administered by the International Council for Bird Preservation (ICBP). Hawksbill and Green Turtles lay their eggs on shore. Up high, the granite peaks of the islands have primary forest shrouded in mist. Lower down, cinnamon, coco-plum, and vanilla flourish. The coastal plateau is peppered with Coconut Palms and Casuarina Trees. In short, the Seychelles are prime destination for the "twigs and twitchers," as botany and birding enthusiasts are sometimes called. Many ecotourists feel that "doing Africa" must include the Seychelles.

Formerly French, the Comoros Islands declared its independence in 1975, and it was several shaky years before things settled down. It is a poor country, with only a very small tourist industry. Nevertheless, it is an occasional stop on Indian Ocean cruises, mainly for its lush forests of Ebony, Mahagany, and Palisander, and its beaches of black lava and white coral.

TOUR OPERATORS

Birding. 14 days / $$$$ (from London) / July. A birding trip to "Paradise." You'll visit Mahe, Praslin, and Bird Island looking for endemics and seabirds. A special day trip to Fregate Island (accompanied by an ICBP ornithologist) in search of the Seychelles Magpie-Robin is a feature of the trip. Other birds you'll be looking for include Bare-legged Scops-Owl, Seychelles Brush-Warbler (on the tiny island of Cousin, an ICBP reserve since 1968), Seychelles Turtle Dove, and Fairy Tern. Maximum of 16 participants, 2 leaders.

Birdquest. 20 days / $$$$ (from London) / September. A birding trip to the Seychelles, Mauritius, and Réunion. Special effort is made to find all the endemics.

Cox & Kings. 17 days / $$$$ (from London) / September. A botanical tour to the Seychelles for the many endemic trees and plants—over 300 species. You'll visit Praslin for the Coco-de-mer Palms, Aride for Wright's Gardenia, and Bird for the Tournefortia tree. There will also be time for wildlife spotting and snorkeling. On Praslin, Black Parrot can be seen, while on La Digue you look for the Black Paradise Flycatcher. A botanist accompanies the trip.

Field Guides. (See the section on Madagascar, page 226.)

Field Studies Council. 14 days / $$$$ (from London) / February. Botany and bird learning vacation to Seychelles. One week is spent on Mahe, exploring high forests, coastal plateaus, and plantations in hopes of seeing exotic plants, giant tortoises, and birds. A day trip is made to Fregate Island in search of the Seychelles Magpie-Robin. The other week you'll be based on Praslin, where you'll visit the Vallee de Mai Nature Reserve for endemic palms, including the Coco-de-mer, and see Black Parrot and Blue Pigeon. Day trips (by boat) will be made to La Digue for Black Paradise Flycatcher, to Aride for Wright's Gardenia, and to Cousin for Seychelles Brush-Warbler.

Questers. (See the section on Madagascar, page 227.)

Sea Quest. 12 days / $$$$ (from Mombasa, Kenya) / January. "Island Treasures of East Africa" is a luxury cruise to the Comoros, Madagascar, and Zanzibar. There's an active volcano on Grande Comore, as well as forests of precious woods and clear waters ideal for snorkeling.

Sunbird. 14 days / $$$$ (from London) / July. A birding tour to several of the islands in the Seychelles. You'll look for endemics such as Seychelles Bulbul and Seychelles Sunbird in and around the island's capital on Mahe. Crab Plover can sometimes be seen here as well. Other islands visited include Aride and Cousin, both nature reserves and home to seabird colonies (Aride) and the endemic Seychelles Brush-Warbler (Cousin) in addition to other species. This trip can be taken in a shortened version as an extension to the Kenya trip (see the section on Kenya, page 200). Maximum of 16 participants, 2 leaders.

Swan Hellenic. (See the section on Kenya, page 200.)

VENT. (See the section on Madagascar, page 228.)

THE EXOTIC FLORA AND FAUNA OF THE EAST: ASIA

 We call it the Far East, although with jet planes and fiber-optics, China, India, Indonesia, and other Oriental nations are not so very far away anymore. Within hours, we can leave our familiar North American woodlands and step into the tropics of Malaysia or onto the sands of China's Gobi Desert. Just how distant and exotic will (or can?) the Sloth Bears of Nepal's Himalayan slopes remain?

But let's not be too blasé about it. For almost all of us, the prospect of spotting a Tiger in India is still pretty exciting. And so would be seeing the Black-necked Crane in China or watching an Orangutan in Borneo. After all, this really is the other side of the world, and the wildlife and habitats—not to mention the culture—are quite different from what we are used to.

If a continent is a large unbroken land mass completely surrounded by water, then Europe must be viewed as part of the same continent as Asia—the Eurasian Continent—which would make it the largest continent on earth. However, in this book, Europe is covered in Chapter 4, while Turkey, Cyprus, Israel, and Yemen are discussed in Chapter 5, as part of the Middle East. Here we cover tours to China and Japan, Siberia and the eastern part of the former Soviet Union, Southeast Asia, Indonesia (including Irian Jaya), the Philippines, and the Indian subcontinent.

THE INDIAN SUBCONTINENT

With the Himalayas to the north, the Indo-Iranian borderlands on the west, the Indo-Burmese borderlands on the east, and the Indian Ocean to the south, the large Indian subcontinent is in a biological world of its own. Though within the earth's tropical zone, India does not have a tropical climate, owing largely to its annual monsoon and subsequent drought. Instead, there is a great diversity of habitat, ranging from evergreen forests and mountain meadows to deciduous woodlands, scrubby plains, and coastal mangroves. The region is rich in plants and wildlife. Much of the land is set aside in preserves, with many established for the express purpose of saving endangered species.

We've grouped the trips in this section into three parts: (1) the bulk of India, from the Himalayan foothills southward; (2) Sri Lanka and the Maldives; and (3) Himalayan countries (Nepal and Bhutan) and northern India (including the states of Sikkim and Ladakh).

India, South of the Himalayas

Though India is twice the size of Alaska, it has one sixth of the world's total population. Happily, it is also home to 15,000 species of plants and 75,000 species of animals, many of which are indigenous. There are 55 national parks and 247 wildlife sanctuaries—some 4 percent of the country's total land mass, which is respectable considering the pressures of overpopulation. As would be expected, the major environmental problems are severe air and water pollution, and soil degradation through overcultivation. The list of threatened species—now up to 70 mammals, 16 reptiles, and 36 birds—continues to grow. Especially endangered are the Snow Leopard, Musk Deer, Desert Fox, Golden Langur, Himalayan Ibex, Sloth Bear, and Black-necked Crane.

The Tiger is one of the primary reasons most nature tourists go to India. Its prospects for survival were not promising as recently as the early 1970s, but a ban on hunting and the establishment of seven reserves have helped to ease that situation. As well as possibly seeing a Tiger, you might catch a look at monkeys, pythons, crocodiles, or some of the 1,200 species of birds, frequently from an elephant's back, on a camel safari, or when traveling by boat or on foot. There are comfortable lodges for overnights, some as luxurious as a maharajah's hunting lodge overlooking faraway hills.

Corbett National Park, in the foothills of the Himalayas, is a well-known haven for Tiger, but it also boasts more than 50 other mammal species, including Elephant, Leopard, Leopard Cat, Jungle Cat, Fishing Cat, Sloth Bear, Jackal, Otter, Chital, Wild Boar, and four species of deer. Birding is good here, too, with the chance to view nearly 600 species, mostly migrating waterbirds.

Kaziranga National Park, in northeastern India, is at the foot of the Bhutan hills, and is noted for its plentiful wildlife and beautiful scenery. This was once a stronghold of the Indian Single-horned Rhinoceros, until the animal was nearly hunted to extinction in the early 1920s. In 1926, the area became a forest reserve and an intensive effort was made to halt the decline. Indeed, the populations increased, making this a naturalist's success story, although there is still poaching when the Rhino crosses the park boundaries. But in addition to Rhino here, Kaziranga has Tiger, Wild Buffalo, Elephant, Barasingha, Wild Boar, Gaur, and sometimes Leopard. Birdlife is also plentiful.

Other popular nature tour stops are Bharatpur Bird Sanctuary (now Keoladeo Ghana National Park) for its heronry; Sariska Tiger Reserve for Tiger as well as

Leopard, Wild Dog, Nilgai, Chital, Panther, Jackal, and Hyena; Gir National Park and Lion Sanctuary for the Asiatic Lion and Indian Wild Ass; Ranthambore National Park for its wide range of mammals, including Tiger and the many excellent birds such as Crested Serpent Eagle; Bandhavgarh National Park for Tiger, Leopard, Chital, Wild Dog, and Sloth Bear; and Kanha National Park for a wide variety of species, including the formerly endangered Barasingha.

In southern India, the nature tour groups usually visit Ranganathittu Bird Sanctuary for its nesting bird species as well as crocodiles and fruit bats; Nagarhole National Park for excellent game viewing, especially of Gaur, Elephant, Sambar Deer, and many bird species; Bandipur National Park and Tiger Reserve for Elephant; Anamalai Wildlife Sanctuary for the Lion-tailed Macaque and Nilgiri Langur, Elephant, Chital, Sambar, Mouse Deer, Barking Deer, and extensive birdlife; and Periyar Tiger Reserve and National Park for woodland birds.

The Andaman Islands are in the Bay of Bengal, near Myanmar. Most nature tours going there are intent on seeing its birdlife or reptiles, since most of the animals are introduced species. In the adjacent waters are dolphins and dugongs, sea turtles and crocodiles.

One of the fascinating things about visiting India is, of course, that you not only see a great deal of wildlife in the flesh, so to speak, but you also see animal imagery through the Hinduism that predominates. Animals are vehicles for the gods here.

TOUR OPERATORS

Birdquest

23 days / $$ (from Madras) / January. "Southern India and the Andaman Islands." Concentrating on birds of the Western Ghats, this birdwatching tour begins in Madras and covers all the major habitats of the south: the eastern coastal lowlands, the evergreen forests of Periyar in the Cardamom Hills, and the dry deciduous forests of Mudumalai and Nagarhole. You'll also visit the waterbird sanctuary at Ranganthittu, near Mysore. Special attention is paid to finding rarities and endemics, such as White-breasted Laughing Thrush, Nilgiri Flycatcher, and Rufous-bellied Shortwing, in addition to various barbets, parakeets, babblers, trogons, hornbills, and woodpeckers. On the Andaman Islands, off the coast of Myanmar, you'll be looking for Andaman Dark Serpent-Eagle, Alexandrine Parakeet, Andaman Coucal, White-headed Myna, and possibly Andaman Scops Owl. Maximum of 16 participants, 2 leaders.

22 days / $$ (from Delhi) / November. A birding trip to northern India. that visits a cross section of environments, from the fertile plains of the Ganges to the Himalayas and the arid region around Rajasthan. You'll also visit the Ranthambore Tiger Reserve, Corbett National Park, the hill station of Naini Tal, and the great

wetland reserve at Bharatpur. Specialties include the Ibisbill, which winters along the rivers near Naini Tal; the Pheasant-tailed and Bronze-winged Jacanas at Bharatpur; and Jungle Wren-Warbler at Ranthambore. Maximum of 16 participants, 2 leaders.

Cheesemans' Ecology Safaris. 29 days / $$ (from Delhi) / November. Visits Kaziranga and Bandavgarh National Parks to spot Elephant and search for Single-horned Rhino. You also may see Bengal Tiger, various deer, and other mammals and birds. At Bharatpur, you'll be looking for Siberian Crane. You'll also visit Little Rann of Kutch, a desert reserve with Wild Ass and other mammals.

Cox & Kings. 20 days / $$ (from Delhi) / January, November. A "Jungle Odyssey" beginning in the Vindhya Mountains of central India, where, via elephant safari, you'll search for Tiger. You also visit Ranthambore Tiger Reserve, then travel by Jeep to Bharatpur Bird Sanctuary for wintering rare Siberian Crane. The tour also goes to Gujarat for a variety of birdlife and game, including Black Ibis and Wild Ass.

Geo Expeditions. 17 days / $$ (from Delhi) / December–February. Natural history trips via Jeep and elephant, with stays in hotels and modest lodges at wildlife reserves. There are visits to the Kaziranga and Ranthambore Tiger Reserves, plus birding at Bharatpur, where more than 300 species of birds can be seen.

Geostar Travel. 28 days / $$ (from Delhi) / February, October. A general nature trip with an emphasis on botany. You'll visit evergreen rain forests, dry deciduous forests, estuaries, and lagoons.

International Expeditions. 16 days / $$$ (from Delhi) / October–April. General nature tours visiting Ranthambore Tiger Reserve, Kanha National Park, Keoladeo Ghana National Park (Bharatpur), Kaziranga National Park, and Sariska Tiger Reserve. Optional extension to Chitwan National Park in Nepal.

King Bird Tours. 23 days / $$ (from Delhi) / January. South India birding trip visiting a broad and diverse cross section of habitat from the desertlike scrub of the Madras to the lush tropical rain forests of the Andaman Islands and Kerala, to the montane forests of Western Ghats. Also visits Periyar National Park for the best birding in southern India. Participants can expect close encounters with Tigers as well as a list of about 350 birds. Special attention is paid to finding rarities and endemics. An ornithologist leads the trip, assisted by local guides.

Mountain Travel/Sobek. 21 days / $$ (from Delhi) / November–March. Wildlife trips to Ranthambore, Bharatpur, Kanha, and Kaziranga parks for views of Rhino, Elephant, and more.

Nature Expeditions International. 16 days / $$ (from Delhi) / November–March. Wildlife expeditions that visit Ranthambore and Kanha National Parks for Bengal Tiger via elephant safari. Also goes to Bharatpur Bird Sanctuary for Siberian Crane and other birds.

Naturetrek

19 days / $$ (from London) / January. Wildlife trip, with an emphasis on birding, to the national parks of southern India. You'll visit the Nilgiri and Cardamom Hills, and the sanctuaries and national parks of Nagarhole, Anaimalai, and Periyar. Animals you may see include Sloth Bear, Gaur, and Leopard. In the Nilgiri Hills you may see the endemic Nilgiri Tahr (a species of wild goat) as well as specialty birds such as the Malabar Pied Hornbill, Nilgiri Pipit, and White-bellied Treepie. An optional extension to Andaman Islands (5 days) is available.

20 days / $$ (from London) / March. Wildlife trip to Rajasthan's Great Thar Desert and the Ranthambore Tiger Reserve. You'll also visit Gajner Wildlife Sanctuary. The desert region contains some of India's most threatened wildlife. Travel is via camel safari during the coolest times of the day, in search of such birds as the Indian and Houbara Bustards, Chestnut-bellied and Spotted Sandgrouse, Cream-colored Courser, and Stoliczka's Bushchat. Mammals include Indian Gazelle, Indian Fox, Striped Hyena, and Wolf.

Questers. 19 days / $$ (from Delhi) / November. Wildlife trip that concentrates on the center of the Indo-Gangetic plain, with visits to the foothills of the Himalayas and the Great Indian Desert in the west. Visits Desert National Park, Bharatpur, Corbett, and Ranthambore.

VENT. 21 days / $$ (from Delhi) / January. An elephant safari that is a general wildlife and birding trip. Prior to the actual safari, you'll spend several days birding around Naini Tal, in the Himalayan foothills. An optional extension to Bandhavgarth is offered. Maximum of 14 participants, 2 leaders.

Voyagers International. 21 days / $$$ (from New York) / March. General wildlife trip.

Wings/Sunbird. 16 days / $$ (from Delhi) / January, February, November. Three birding trips visiting Bharatpur Bird Sanctuary, Corbett National Park, and the hill town of Naini Tal. Special attention is paid to rarities and endemics. At Bharatpur there is a possibility of over 200 species, including Siberian Crane, Painted Stork, Coppersmith Barbet, and Small Minivet. At Corbett you have the chance to see Blue Whistling Thrush, Orange-fronted Leafbird, Jungle Owlet, Himalayan Rubythroat, and Great Stone Plover. Mammals include Tiger, Indian

Elephant, Chital, Barking Deer, and Common Langur. Maximum of 13 participants, 1 leader.

Woodstar Tours. 19 days / $$ (from Delhi) / February. A general nature trip with an emphasis on birds. Visits Sultanpur Jheel waterfowl sanctuary, Sariska Tiger Reserve, Ranthambore Tiger Reserve, Bharatpur, and Kanha National Park. You'll also make stops to view game, take an elephant safari, and visit cultural sites.

World Wildlife Fund. 17 days / $$$$ (from New York) / February. Luxury wildlife trip to India's national parks in search of elephants, deer and antelope, buffalos, leopards, tigers, and birds. Visits wetlands of Keoladeo Ghana (Bharatpur), Kanha National Park, and Kaziranga grasslands and forest.

Sri Lanka and the Maldives

Sri Lanka (formerly Ceylon) is a small island in the Indian Ocean off the southeast tip of India. In recent years there has been political upheaval, but thankfully this seems to be ending. A good thing, since Sri Lanka is endowed with over seventy indigenous species. The country has officially preserved about 11 percent of its land, including tropical forests and its coastal lowlands. Conservation efforts to save the country's giant marsh elephants are under way, with an extensive system of national parks and jungle corridors. We think that with a few more years of political quiet and stability this country is going to become an excellent ecotourism destination.

The Maldive Islands are about 500 miles to the west of Sri Lanka, off the southwestern coast of the Indian subcontinent. This is an atoll-nation, a cluster of 1,196 tiny coral islands noted for tame fish and shallow reefs.

TOUR OPERATORS

Earthwatch. 14 days / $$ (from Colombo) / January–March, June. "Monkey Politics" is a research trip to study the social behavior of Toque Macaques by looking for activities that determine their use of territory and relations with neighbors.

King Bird Tours. 18 days / $$ (from Colombo) / January. A birding trip to lowland and montane rain forest, coastal lowlands, highland tea plantations, acacia scrub, marshes, mudflats, and sandflats. You have an excellent chance of seeing 20 of Sri Lanka's 23 endemic species, plus Palearctic migrants. You'll also observe Spotted Deer, Mongoose, Water Buffalo, Wild Boar, and maybe a Leopard. Noted Asian specialist Ben King leads the trip, assisted by local field naturalists.

Mountain Travel/Sobek. 13 days / $$ (from Colombo) / March, November. Varied adventure trips that include cycling to Bundala Bird Sanctuary, a visit to Yala National Park for Elephant, and snorkeling along Indian Ocean coral reefs.

See & Sea. 10 days / $$$$ (from Colombo) / September, October, March, April. Dive trips to the Maldives aboard the 12-passenger *Keema.* Live-aboard diving and underwater photography. A photographer accompanies the trip.

Countries of the Himalayas
—Nepal and Bhutan and Northern India,
Including Sikkim and Ladakh

The Great Himalayan Range extends in a wide arc from the Tibetan Plateau in the north to India's alluvial plains in the south. Here are some of the highest mountains in the world—30 of them exceeding 24,000 feet. Mount Everest tops them all at 29,028 feet. Within their range lie the countries of Nepal and Bhutan, and the states of Sikkim and Ladakh.

The Himalayas are home to about one third of the world's mammal species. Its birds include broadbills, honeyguides, finfoots, and parrotbills. Many birds that winter in more southern parts of India nest in the Himalayas between May and October. Though much of the Himalayan range is above the treeline, the slopes at lower altitudes are covered with conifer forests and rhododendrons.

For fans of George Schaller or Peter Matthiessen, the elusive Snow Leopard is the symbol of this region's fragility. Though the mountains seem rugged and impenetrable, the rarified world here is in danger, with the outlook rather bleak. Growing human populations are putting pressure on the natural resources, especially trees cut for firewood. In addition, road development and poor agricultural methods are further degrading the land. It often comes as a shock to hear that Nepal has the most unhealthy drinking water in the world.

Tourism is a major source of income for these countries, but it has also contributed to land degradation. Most recently, however, more responsible tourism has entered the picture, as some trekking companies substitute liquid fuel for cooking fires. There are also tree-planting programs and other environmental projects. Should you travel to the Himalayas, keep the principles of responsible travel in mind.

Nepal is a small country, about the size of Florida, but it has a great variety of terrain, from subtropical lowlands to the summit of Mount Everest. Here is the famous Royal Chitwan National Park, one of Asia's premier wildlife reserves. Generally, a visit to the park includes an elephant safari to see the Bengal Tiger, Asian Rhino, Sloth Bear, Leopard, Sambar, Barking Deer, Chital, Gaur, and Gharial and

Marsh Mugger Crocodiles. The park is also a birder's paradise, with over 440 species. Also notable is Royal Bardia National Park in western Nepal, with its dry deciduous tropical forests. Groups come here to see the river bird species as well as Otter and perhaps Gangetic Dolphin. Sagarmatta (Everest) National Park is a UNESCO World Heritage Site, with funding to help protect its remaining woodlands and rhododendrons.

Most trips to this high part of the world head for Nepal, although there are treks in Bhutan, Sikkim, and Ladakh. Even the trips indicated as "moderate" are physically demanding.

Bhutan, a tiny nation, was reluctant to accept tourism until recently, and so the country is relatively unchanged. Its Manas Wildlife Sanctuary is a Tiger reserve with some of the richest fauna of any Asian national park—Water Buffalo, Gaur, Elephant, Indian Rhino, Tiger, and Leopard, as well as Hispid Hare, Pygmy Hog, and Golden Langur.

Sikkim is a tiny state walled in by the Himalayas. Until recently it was difficult to visit because of severe travel restrictions. It has one national park and three sanctuaries, including an orchid sanctuary with 250 species. Kangchendzonga National Park is home to Snow Leopard, Tahr, Musk Deer, Serow, Red Panda, and Binturong.

Ladakh is a remote and rugged area with one of the lowest population densities in the world. It is noted for its dramatic extremes, with spectacular scenery and a fine selection of birds, flowers, and mammals. Ladakh is also the home of Wild Yak, Snow Leopard, Marmot, and Blue Sheep.

TOUR OPERATORS

Betchart Expeditions. 18 days / $$ (from Delhi) /January. Natural history expedition to India and Nepal. Visits Bharatpur and Bandhavgarh National Park in India and Chitwan National Park in Nepal.

Birding. 15 days / $$$ (from London) / February. A birding holiday to Nepal, concentrating on the Terai region. You'll visit Gokarna Ban, Royal Bardia National Park, and Chitwan. As well as 300 or so species of birds, you may see Gharial Crocodile, Indian Rhino, Chital, and Sloth Bear. Maximum of 16 participants, 2 leaders.

Birdquest
22 days / $$ (from London) / March. A birding trip to Sikkim, Darjeeling, and Assam. You'll visit Kaziranga for lowland birds, areas in Sikkim for high-altitude birds, and a hill station in Darjeeling for montane birds. Includes a visit to Sandakphu, a high ridge on the border between India and Nepal famous for its oak

forests and rhododendrons. A special effort is made to find endemic species, and participants can expect a wide variety of birds, including drongos, spiderhunters, kingfishers, hornbills, doves, cuckoos, owls, tits, parrotbills, and flycatchers. Maximum of 16 participants, 2 leaders.

20 days / $$ (from London) / March. A birding trip to Nepal. Maximum of 16 participants, 2 leaders.

Cox & Kings. 17 days / $$ (from London) / July. "Alpine Flowers of the Western Himalayas" is a botany tour timed to avoid the rigors of trekking during the monsoon. The alpine flora includes 350 species—in the Kulu Valley and the area around Rhotang Pass. Manali (and its surroundings) is of special botanical interest because it combines elements of both eastern and western Himalayan flora. A botanist leads the trip.

Earthwatch. 18 days / $$ (from Katmandu) / January–March. A research trip to study the Sloth Bears of Nepal. Volunteers help capture, examine, and radio-collar the animals to determine if they will survive an increasingly crowded world.

Escapes Unlimited. 14–17 days / $$$ (from Los Angeles) / October, April. Easy-to-moderate hiking and adventure trips to Nepal, with an environmental focus.

Field Studies Council. 21 days / $$ (from London) / October. "Nepal Namaste: Beyond the Valley" is a learning vacation involving a rigorous trek through the Katmandu Valley to study flora and fauna. Two leaders accompany the trip.

Geo Expeditions. 18 days / $$ (from Katmandu) / February, October. Natural history treks in Nepal's Annapurna Range, with an elephant safari in Chitwan National Park. Operator also offers a 14-day trek staying at Sherpa lodges in the Everest region.

Himalaya Trekking and Wilderness Expeditions. 21 days / $$ (from Katmandu) /August. A trip in search of the rare Snow Leopard. In addition, a variety of other moderate-to-strenuous low-impact treks are offered.

International Oceanographic Foundation. 16 days / $$$$ (from Katmandu) / April. Wildlife and conservation safari to Nepal, including Chitwan National Park, Royal Bardia Wildife Reserve, Annapurna Conservational Area Project, Ghandruk trek.

King Bird Tours

24 days / $$ (from Delhi) / January. A birding trip to northwest India. With 1,300 species of birds, including nearly 150 endemics, India offers some of the

most exciting birdwatching in the world. Past participants on this trip have seen as many as 44 species of raptors, 11 owls, 5 hornbills, 8 storks, and 4 cranes. There is a very good chance of finding an Ibisbill as well. And a variety of animals can be seen—including Indian Rhino, Indian Elephant, Tiger, and various deer and monkeys. Noted Asian specialist Ben King leads the tour.

22 days / $$ (from Delhi) / January. A birding trip to Nepal and northeast India. Special attention is paid to finding endemics. Ben King leads the tour.

Mountain Travel/Sobek. 13 days / $ (from Katmandu) / March–May, August–December. Easy treks in Chitwan National Park and the Annapurna foothills looking for Tiger. Operator also offers more strenuous treks in Annapurna Sanctuary, Everest and Sherpa lodge trips, a trek to the relatively unexplored Lake Rara National Park, a rafting trip in western Nepal, and a tented camp in Royal Bardia National Park.

Nature Expeditions International. 16 days / $$ (from Katmandu) / March, October. General nature trips to Nepal, including a 4-day trek in the Annapurna Range and an elephant safari in Royal Chitwan National Park.

Naturetrek

23 days / $$ (from London) / January. "Manas and the Jungles of Bhutan" is a mammal and birding trip to southern Bhutan for a trek in the Manas Wildlife Sanctuary. Some long, hot days ahead! But the rewards are great: Himalayan Honeyguide, Blyth's and Blue-eared Kingfishers, Black-necked Crane, plus a wide variety of mammals and possibly even the endangered Gharial Crocodile.

16–23 days / $$ (from London) / April, May. Treks through the forests and alpine meadows of Nepal's Langtang Valley, with an emphasis on birdwatching. You'll also visit Chitwan, where you have a chance to see Sloth Bear and Tiger. Participants may see some 300 species of birds on this trip, plus about 20 species of mammals—15 in Chitwan alone!

22 days / $$ (from London) / April. A botanical trip to the Bumthang Valley of Bhutan. Emphasis will be on the rhododendrons, magnolias, and other spring flowers and shrubs. The trip includes an 8-day trek through the forests of central Bhutan. A botanist accompanies the trip.

15 days / $$ (from London) / May. A botanical trip to the remote and little-known Black Mountains of central Bhutan, including a 6-day trek. Near the Taktsang monastery you'll see *Rhododendron arboreum, Euphorbia griffithii, Clematis montana,* and *Buddleja crispa,* among many other species. In the oak woodlands on the trek you may expect to encounter *Skimmia laureola, Hydrangea heteromalla,* and *Viburnum mullaha.* A botanist accompanies the trip.

22 days / $$ (from London) / May. A holiday to see the spring flowers and breeding birds of Everest National Park in Nepal. A 15-day trek is included, much

of it at high elevations. Animals and birds you may encounter include Himalayan Tahr, Snow Partridge, and Blood Pheasant. Some time will also be spent at Chitwan, where you can see larger mammals.

30 days / $$ (from London) / May. A rigorous, 23-day trek to the forests and alpine valleys of Kanchenjunga in the northeastern corner of Nepal. You'll find some 15 or more species of rhododendron, numerous orchids, and forests of fir, hemlock, juniper, magnolia, and bamboo. Among the many birds you'll be looking for are Coral-billed Scimitar-Babbler, Purple Cochoa, Blue-fronted Robin, and Sapphire Flycatcher.

22 days / $$ (from London) / August. "The Indus Valley and Vale of Kashmir" is a general natural history and cultural trip to these two contrasting regions. The trip includes a 6-day trek in Kashmir and a 4-day trek in Ladakh. Animals and birds should be plentiful, with chances to see the Himalayan Black Bear, Kashmir Stag, and the beautiful Orange Bullfinch.

30 days / $$ (from London) / July. A 25-day trek in the Marsyandi Valley of central Nepal in search of Himalayan alpine plants.

22 days / $$ (from London) / November. A wildlife trip combining trekking (9 days), rafting, and jungle exploration—in search of plants, birds, and animals. You'll visit a variety of habitats, including Chitwan National Park, home to 450 species of birds. You'll look for animals on foot, in canoe, and on elephant back.

Questers. 19 days / $$$ (from Katmandu) / March. Combination wildlife-cultural trip to Nepal and Bhutan, visiting Royal Chitwan National Park for the Bengal Tiger and Indian Rhino.

VENT. 23 days / $$$$ (from Seattle) / February. A birding trip to India, Nepal, and Bhutan, visiting Bharatpur, the Little Rann of Kutch, Sultanpur Bird Sanctuary, Chitwan, and various sites in Bhutan. Included is an excursion to the wintering area of the rare Black-necked Crane. Maximum of 16 participants; 2 leaders, including Robert Fleming, noted bird-guide author.

Voyagers International. 18 days / $$$ (from Los Angeles) / October. Wildlife photo trip to Nepal. Visits Royal Chitwan park for views of wildlife.

Wilderness Travel. 18 days / $$ (from Katmandu) / January–December. General wildlife, rafting, and moderate trekking trips to Nepal; includes a visit to Royal Chitwan.

Wings/Sunbird. 15 days / $$$ (from London) / December. A birding trip to the moist forests of the Katmandu Valley and Royal Chitwan National Park. Participants may expect to see some 300 species of birds, including Kaleej Pheasant,

Barred Owlet, Blue Magpie, Orange-bellied Leafbird, and even the Nepal Cutia, if you're lucky. Tigers and Rhinos can also be seen at Chitwan. Maximum of 16 participants, 2 leaders.

Woodstar. 8 days / $$ (from Katmandu) / February. Birding trip to Royal Chitwan National Park, Bhulikhel, and Gokarna.

World Wildlife Fund. 19 days / $$$$ (from Bangkok) / November–December. Combo trip to Thailand and Nepal. In Nepal, you'll visit Royal Chitwan via elephant safari.

SIBERIA, CENTRAL ASIAN REPUBLICS, AND MONGOLIA

For most Westerners this part of the world connotes isolation—from other people, from life as we know it. So cold, so far away. It is hard, therefore, to believe that there is much life here worth studying. Yet this vast area stretching from the Ural Mountains to the Pacific Ocean, and from the Arctic Ocean to Mongolia and China, has a varied and diverse habitat with mountains, plateaus, and river valleys. In the north are permafrost, bogs, and taiga (boreal forest); swampy forest, desert, and steppe in the central region; and tundra and mountains in the south. Among the ice floes of the far north are the Chukot and Kamchatka peninsulas, Komandorskiye Islands, and Wrangel Island.

In the southern part of Siberia, east of the Ural Mountains, are the Altai-Sayan Mountains, with their deep valleys carved by dramatic glacial action. Lake Baikal, to the east, is the world's deepest—5,712 feet. Along the coast, and on the Komandor and Kuril islands, are mountainous tablelands that show volcanic activity. The tours to Siberia that we've listed here concentrate on eastern Siberia, with a majority visiting Lake Baikal.

In all the hubbub about the destruction of the world's tropical forests, it is unfortunate that the plight of temperate, especially evergreen, forests has gotten short shrift. The stands of fir, larch, spruce, and pine that stretch across Siberia represent the largest forest in the world—an area that could cover the entire continental United States. The financially strapped countries of the former Soviet Union doubtless will be tempted to log these forests for cash. In an article in *Nature,* Dr. Armin Rosencranz and Antony Scott of the Pacific Energy and Resources Center in California have noted that a new Siberian railway helps make expanding the timber industry possible, and that contracts are being issued to drastically increase the cutting. They insist that "the allure of hard currency and modern technology does not outweigh the long-term health of the forests."

The number of nature tours to this part of the world is growing, and we expect that even more groups will be making the trip to enjoy this very special, still largely unspoiled part of Asia.

TOUR OPERATORS

Abercrombie & Kent. 15 days / $$$$ (from Tokyo) / July. A luxury cruise aboard the 96-passenger M.V. *Explorer* to Kamchatka and the Komandor and Kuril islands. Day excursions are made in small boats.

Birdquest

22 days / $$ (from London) / May. "Siberia with a Difference" is a birdwatching trip. The boreal forest (taiga) of this Eurasian region harbors some of the most sought-after species. On this trip you'll explore Sakhalin Island in the Sea of Okhotsk (off the coast of eastern Siberia), the forests and marshy islands of Amurland, the dry steppe of Transbaicalia, the Selenga Delta on Lake Baikal, and the Baikal Range in central Siberia. Species to be seen include Aleutian Tern, Ancient Murrelet, Steller's Sea Eagle, Schrenck's Little Bittern, Oriental White Stork, Asiatic Dowitcher, Japanese and Siberian Accentors, Middendorff's Grasshopper Warbler, Daurian Starling, Pallas's Rosefinch, and Pallas's Reed Bunting. Maximum of 16 participants, 2 leaders.

20 days / $$$ (from London) / May. A birding trip to Mongolia in search of rare birds. Maximum of 16 participants, 2 leaders.

23 days / $$$ (from London) / June. A birding trip to Arctic Siberia. You'll see not only a wide variety of birds but many marine mammals as well. Although the climate is chilly, daylight lasts nearly 24 hours and the birds will be singing and very approachable. Maximum of 11 participants, 1 leader.

Earthwatch

12 days / $$ (from Barnaul, Russia) / July, August. A research expedition to southern Siberia to study the potential ecological harm of a proposed hydroelectric plant below the Altai Mountains. Volunteers work among the glaciers and camp in coniferous forests and subalpine meadows.

13 days / $$ (from Khabarovsk, Russia) / July, August. "Kamchatka!" is a research trip to study the role of volcanic gases in the destruction of the ozone layer. Volunteers collect rock samples, identify sources of volcanic fluids, and record data.

Field Studies Council. 22 days / $$$ (from London) / May. A botany trip to the mountains of Central Asia, which are rich in species of bulbous, herbaceous, and alpine plants. Besides the wonderful range of colorful plants, the region is also noted for its splendid diversity of birds and butterflies, and there will be ample time to observe these as well. Maximum of 20 participants; a botanist leads the tour.

King Bird Tours. 20 days / $$$ (from London) / May. A birding trip to Siberia. You'll explore the area around the Ussuri River, on the Manchurian (China) border.

Oceanic Society Expeditions. 21 days / $$$$ (from San Francisco) / August. A learning vacation to Siberia and Mongolia visiting Yol Eagle in the Gobi Altai Mountains and the Cemetery of the Dragon; also some cultural stops. Emphasis is on evolution and dinosaurs.

Quark Expeditions. 22 days / $$$$ (from Anchorage, Alaska) / July. Luxury natural history cruise aboard the Soviet icebreaker *Sovetskiy Soyuz* through the Northeast Passage. You'll travel from Murmansk to Novaya Zemlya, through the Wilkitsky Strait to the New Siberian Islands, Wrangel Island, and on through the Bering Strait. Participants can see Polar Bear, Lemming, Arctic Fox, and many nesting birds, in addition to mammoth tusks and skulls imbedded in the ice.

Russian Nature Tours. 21 days / $$–$$$ (from London) / May–September. Seven birdwatching tours to Siberia. In May there's a trip to Kazakhstan in search of the Relict Gull. June finds you in Ussuriland (north of China). In July one can travel to Taimyr—the highest Arctic latitude where the lovely Red-breasted Geese breed—or to the Kolyma Delta for Siberian White Crane and Ross's Gull. August is devoted to Kamchatka, a huge peninsula in the Far East, the land of Steller's Sea Eagle. There are more than 100 volcanos here, with several of them active at any time. In September, Russian Nature Tours teams up with Sunbird to offer a trip to the Volga Delta and the Tien Shan Mountains (see below). Maximum of 12 to 16 participants, 2 leaders.

Sunbird. 14 days / $$$ (from London) / August. A birding tour to the Tien Shan Mountains and the Volga Delta. The Volga Delta was established as a nature reserve in 1919. The trip is timed to coincide with fall wader migration through the delta. The second half of the trip visits the Aksu-Dzabagly Nature Reserve, where migrating birds concentrate at the famous Chokpak Pass. Participants can expect to see about 200 species of birds. Maximum of 14 participants, 2 leaders. Trip is run jointly with Russian Nature Tours (see above).

TransSiberian Tours/Arctic Edge

13 days / $$$ (from Anchorage, Alaska) / June–August. Several different trips to Lake Baikal for scuba diving, natural history, and ornithology. The trips are aboard a 62-foot diesel expedition vessel. Maximum of 10 participants. Scientists from the Limnological Institute accompany the trips.

10 days / $$$ (from Anchorage, Alaska) / September. A boat trip down the Bukyn River, the wilderness border country of the Khabarovsk and Primorye provinces. You'll have opportunities to see Ussuri Tigers, Wild Boar, Himalayan Black Bear, Red Deer, and Sable. Maximum of 10 participants.

Wings/Sunbird. 21 days / $$ (from London) / May. A birding tour to Central Asia and Siberia. You'll visit a selection of the region's best bird habitats, including the Tien Shan Mountains on the Chinese border, the Kazakhstan Steppe, the dense taiga forest of Siberia, and Lake Baikal. Specialty birds include Himalayan Griffon Vulture, Demoiselle Crane, Black-winged Pratincole, Citrine Wagtail, Red-flanked Bluetail, Pander's Ground Jay, Upcher's Warbler, and Rose-colored Starling. Maximum of 16 participants, 2 leaders.

Zegrahm Expeditions. (For this Northeast Passage trip see the listing under "Quark Expeditions," above.)

CHINA (INCLUDING TIBET), HONG KONG, AND JAPAN

China

About as big as the continental United States, China has as diverse a landscape—with high mountains, coastal areas, plains, and desert. Although environmental protection doesn't have a high priority right now, nevertheless there are some 30,500 square miles of land set aside—1 percent of the country's total acreage. Deforestation is a major problem because China burns large amounts of wood for both heat and cooking. According to the *Environmental Almanac,* China began planting a belt of trees—the Great Green Wall of China—to eventually cover 5.3 million acres. It is also trying to decrease its dependence on wood (and hoping to improve the air quality at the same time).

China is still largely uncharted territory as far as nature tours are concerned, in part because accommodations away from the usual cultural destinations are basic, and getting around is difficult. Nevertheless, there is growing interest in visiting China's Giant Panda reserves as well as the vast wilderness areas of western China.

TOUR OPERATORS

Birdquest
23 days / $$ (from Hong Kong) / May. A birding trip to western China and Hong Kong. Western China has enormous wilderness areas, offering some of the

finest birding in Asia. Participants can expect to see well over 300 species without a lot of traveling around. The trip begins in Hong Kong, visiting the New Territories for migrant waders, then travels westward to Chengdu, in Sichuan Province, for birds found at the western edge of the Tibetan Plateau. This area of China has the richest concentration of endemics. From Chengdu it's on to the World Wildlife Fund's Wolong Panda Reserve to look for pheasants. Maximum of 16 participants, 2 leaders.

29 days / $$ (from Beijing) July. "The Roof of the World" is a birding trip to the Tibetan Plateau. You'll have a chance to finding all of the endemic birds of this region, the highest area of land on earth. Specialties include the Tibetan Eared-Pheasant, Prince Henri's Laughingthrush, Kozlov's Bunting, Black-necked Crane, Roborovski's Rosefinch, White-browed Tit, Red-necked and Blanford's Snow Finches, and Tibetan Sandgrouse. Maximum of 16 participants, 2 leaders.

Earthwatch

12 days / $ (from Beidaihe, Hebei Province) / September. "Wings over China" is a research expedition studying migrating birds along one of China's three great flyways. Volunteers record migrants from watchpoints; on lower migration days, teams census bird populations at nearby sites.

14 days / $$ (from Guangzhou) / June–August. A research trip to study how much methane tropical rice paddies produce, contributing to the greenhouse effect.

International Expeditions.

20 days / $$ (from San Francisco) / May, July, September. Combination culture and nature trips, with visits to Wolong Panda Reserve.

King Bird Tours

24 days / $$ (from Hong Kong) / May. A birding tour to western China and Tibet where participants can expect to see well over half of the 45 endemic species, including 8 species of pheasant and 5 species of partridge. You'll visit two panda reserves on the eastern slopes of the Tibetan Plateau. Noted Asian specialist Ben King leads the trip.

30 days / $$ (from Beijing) / May. Birding trip to Manchuria and Inner Mongolia. You'll visit a wide variety of habitat, including grassy steppes, boreal forests, and marshlands, in search of rarities and endemics. Ben King leads the trip.

Naturetrek.

22 days / $$$ (from London) / May. This is a birding and botany trip to Mount Emei and Mount Gongga Shan in China's Sichuan Province. Here, among the rhododendron forests and bamboo thickets, are orchids and numerous other flowers, as well as such elusive birds as Temminck's Tragopan and Lady Amherst's Pheasant. Some time will also be spent sight-seeing. A botanist and an ornithologist lead the trip.

Hong Kong

In 1997, Hong Kong will become part of China, but for now we list it separately. As a U.K. dependency, this crown colony comprises the island of Hong Kong, Stonecutters' Island, Kowloon Peninsula, and the New Territories on the adjoining mainland.

There aren't many trips to Hong Kong, since it is usually offered as a stop on trips to China, Thailand, or Japan.

TOUR OPERATORS

King Bird Tours. 20 days / $$ (from Hong Kong) / April. This birding trip is timed to coincide with both Hong Kong's peak migration and courtship season on Taiwan. Nearly 50 species of migrating shorebirds can be seen, including Asiatic Dowitcher, Spoon-billed Sandpiper, and Nordmann's Greenshank. On Taiwan you have a good chance of seeing all 14 endemics, including the Mikado and Swinhoe's Pheasants. Other specialties are Taiwan Magpie, Chinese Bamboo-Partridge, Formosan Barwing, Flamecrest, and White-tailed Robin. Three leaders, including local ornithologists, accompany the trip.

Japan

An archipelago extending more than 1,700 miles, Japan is separated from the east coast of the Asian continent by the Sea of Japan. Its four major islands are mountainous, with numerous active volcanos, and they extend from the subtropics in the Ryukyus to the temperate climate of Hokkaido. Japan's scenery is among the most spectacular in eastern Asia, home to a rich and diverse avifauna. The country remains heavily forested, largely because the terrain is so mountainous. This makes Japan dependent on imported wood, much of which comes from tropical rain forests and U.S. forestland.

By far the majority of tours to Japan are cultural, even though the potential for nature tours is exceedingly high.

TOUR OPERATORS

Focus on Nature Tours

8 days / $$$ (from Tokyo) / January. A birding trip to three islands—Honshu, Hokkaido, and Kyushu—to see sea eagles, cranes, and pelagic birds. Winter, surprisingly, is one of the birdiest times in Japan. The trip includes a bird walk in the garden of a Japanese temple and a quest for the rare Blakiston's Fish Owl. Surely the most spectacular sight will be the huge flocks of Japanese Cranes in the fields

of southeast Hokkaido. An optional 4-day pelagic trip (by ferry) in and out of Tokyo is offered.

10 days / $$$$ (from Tokyo) / June. A birding trip to Honshu and Hokkaido. You'll search for cuckoos (4 species), thrushes (4 species), ptarmigan, and Japanese Crane. Four days are spent in the Japanese Alps before heading north to Hokkaido. The ferry trip from Tokyo (Honshu) to Kushiro (Hokkaido) enables you to see many pelagic birds, including huge flocks of Streaked Shearwaters. On Hokkaido your time is divided between the marshes and wetlands of the southeast and the forests of Akan National Park—home to owls, nightjars, and woodpeckers.

King Bird Tours. 6 days / $$$$ (from Tokyo) / March. A 3-day pelagic trip from Yokohama to Torishima Island, the main breeding island of the endangered Short-tailed Albatross. Landing is not permitted, but the nesting site is visible from a distance. A full morning is planned to be spent with the albatrosses near the island. Participants have the chance to see several other pelagic species as well, including Japanese Auklet, Tristram's Storm-petrel, and Temminck's Cormorant.

Questers. 21 days / $$$$ (from Tokyo) / June. A natural history trip to the national parks of Hokkaido, the temperate forests of Karuizawa in central Honshu, Miyake-jima in the Izu Islands, and some cultural stops as well. An optional extension to the southern islands, including Kirishima-Yaku National Park and Amami-Oshima (Ryukyu Islands), and northern Okinawa is offered. Noted author Mark Brazil leads the tour.

SOUTHEAST ASIA

Indochinese Peninsula

The extension of land that is Thailand, Laos, Vietnam, and Cambodia juts south from the Asian continent like a smaller parallel of the Indian subcontinent. On one side is the Bay of Bengal, on the other the South China Sea. Extending southward in a narrow finger of land pointing to Indonesia is the Malay Peninsula, with Singapore at its very tip.

At one time, vast forests covered this part of the world, and there was abundant wildlife. What remains today is but a remnant, yet the biological diversity is still mind-boggling. A region of the world with the potential for conservation as it develops, Southeast Asia richly deserves the attention of ecotourists.

Vietnam

A long strip of land running down the western coast of the Indochinese Peninsula, Vietnam is where the avifauna of China, Malaysia, and the Himalayas meet.

Though ravaged by thirty years of conflict, the country still has a very rich birdlife. In fact, Vietnam has the most diverse avifauna in Indochina, and its birds are among the most sought-after species in the Orient.

TOUR OPERATORS

Birdquest. 19 days / $$ (from London) / December. A birding trip to rice paddies, forested hills, pine forests, and wetlands. It includes visits to Nam Bai Cat Tien National Park in the south, Lang Bian plateau farther north, and Bach Ma National Park in the central mountains. Special effort is made to find rarities and endemics; participants can expect to see some 300 species of birds, including Red-collared Woodpecker, Short-tailed Scimitar-Babbler, and Ratchet-tailed Treepie. Maximum of 16 participants, 2 leaders.

Earthwatch. 14 days / $$ (from Ho Chi Minh City) / February. "Saving Cranes in Vietnam" is a research project run by George Archibald of the International Crane Foundation in an effort to help establish a preserve to protect the Saurus Crane. Teams observe crane behavior and give lectures in local schools to increase awareness of cranes.

Thailand

Many of the Southeast Asia nature trips go to Thailand, most likely because it is probably the easiest country to visit in this region. (Accommodations are good and the people are used to tourists.) Extending southward from the high mountains of the eastern edge of the Himalayas, Thailand has a diverse environment that includes alpine valleys, alluvial plains with rice paddies, tropical forests, and sandy beaches. Some 9 percent of its land has been set aside in preserves, in a network that protects representative habitats and their occupants.

Almost all of the tours visit Khao Yai National Park—about 100 miles from Bangkok—in the central north of the country. Its primarily mountainous terrain boasts one of the largest remaining intact tropical forests on mainland Asia. With good trails, this is an excellent place to see some of the 300 species of birds in the region, as well as a wealth of ferns and other plants, and such animals as Elephant, Gaur, Tiger, Deer, and Wild Pig. The other major destination is Doi Inthanon National Park, near Chiang Mai in the mountainous far north. Though mammal populations have been reduced here because of hunting, Asiatic Black Bear can still be found along with several primates, including Slow Loris, Pig-tailed Macaque, and Phayre's Leaf Monkey. As they do in many other countries, the tours usually move from one national park to another in their search for wildlife to view.

Thailand has experienced steady growth, to the point where deforestation has become a major problem—and along with it, wildlife destruction. To complicate matters, Thailand has been accused of being a transfer point for trade in endangered species. Its markets sell the meat of wild animals, some of which clearly is from critically threatened species. And it is most disheartening to see so many caged birds and animals for sale here, offered as pets to an increasingly affluent population. It is our hope that ecotourism to this country will encourage the government to be more aggressive in its enforcement of protective laws; that Thailand will live up to its CITES (Convention on International Trade in Endangered Species) obligations; and that the ways in which the Thai people enjoy the beauty of their native birds and animals will change.

TOUR OPERATORS

Betchart. 16 days / $$$ (from Bangkok) / November. Led by an anthropologist, this is a combo nature and culture trip that includes visits to Khao Yai, Phang Nga, and Phi Phi Island National Parks as well as Bang Sai Bird Park. A visit to Hong Kong is included.

Bird Bonanzas. 22 days / $$ (from Bangkok) / February. A birding trip to find some of the rare birds of Southeast Asia, with a visit to Thailand's Khao Soi Dhao Reserve in the southeast, and some time in the north near Doi Inthanon for montane species. You then visit Taman Negara National Park in Malaysia, where some 300 species of birds can be found.

Birdquest

22 days / $$ (from Bangkok) / December. A birding tour visiting a variety of habitats, including mangroves, mudflats, salt pans, and rice paddies. You'll visit Khao Yai, Khao Sam Roi Yot, and Doi Inthanon National Parks. Participants can expect to see upwards of 300 species of birds, including trogons, malkohas, hornbills, drongos, babblers, bulbuls, and warblers. You may also encounter Sambar, Barking Deer, Gibbon, and Pig-tailed Macaque.

19 days / $$ (from Bangkok) / March. A tour concentrating on the rare and endemic birds of western and peninsular Thailand. The prize of this trip is the enormously rare Gurney's Pitta—a small bird with an iridescent blue crown, black face, golden chest, and golden-brown back and wings. You'll visit Umphang Wildlife Sanctuary, Khao Pra Bang Khram Preserve, and small islands in the Andaman Sea.

International Expeditions. (See the section on Malaysia, page 254.)

King Bird Tours. 22 days / $$ (from Bangkok) / January. A birding trip that surveys the country's various habitats. Participants can expect to see about 350 species, including hornbills, broadbills, sunbirds, babblers, bee-eaters, kingfishers, minivets, barbets, and laughingthrushes. Noted ornithologist Phil Round (who rediscovered Gurney's Pitta) leads the trip.

Oceanic Society Expeditions. 18 days / $$$ (from Los Angeles) / November. General nature trip that visits a variety of habitats, from the northern hills to the national parks in the south. You'll also go snorkeling off Krabi.

Questers. 23 days / $$$ (from Bangkok) / January, August. A nature tour to Southeast Asia. Half the time is spent in Thailand, visiting Khao Yai, Doi Suthep-Pui, and Doi Inthanon National Parks. You then continue on to Singapore and Malaysia, where you visit the lowland rain forest of Taman Negara National Park.

Sunbird. 7–21 days / $$ (from London) / February. A birding trip. The tour is divided into 3 parts, which can be taken for 1-week or 2-week periods, or for a maximum of 3 weeks. You'll visit a range of habitats in search of endemics. Specialties include Olive-backed Sunbird, Scarlet-backed Flowerpecker, Red-headed Trogon, and a wealth of bulbuls, babblers, hornbills, minivets, laughingthrushes, niltavas, tailorbirds, and warblers. There is a chance (during the third week) to see Gurney's Pitta, as well as the equally colorful Banded Pitta. Maximum of 10 participants, 2 leaders; noted ornithologist Phil Round leads the third week.

VENT. 20–25 days / $$ (from Bangkok) / November, December. Two birding trips for both resident and migrant species. You'll visit Khao Yai and Doi Inthanon National Parks, the shores of the Isthmus of Kra, and the coastal marshes of the Gulf of Thailand. A wide variety of birds is to be expected, including Coral-billed Ground-Cuckoo, Gould's Sunbird, Striated Bulbul, Rufous-naped Pitta, and Pygmy Wren-Babbler. Maximum of 10 participants, 2 leaders.

Wings. 16 days / $$ (from Bangkok) / February. A birding trip that visits Khao Yai and Doi Inthanon National Parks. Participants can expect to see some 300 or more species of birds, including wintering Palearctic birds such as Grey-headed Lapwing, Red-flanked Bluetail, Grey-sided Thrush, and Common Rosefinch. This trip can be taken in conjunction with the Malaysia trip (see page 255). Two leaders, including noted ornithologist Phil Round.

Woodstar Tours. 16–24 days / $$ (from Seattle) / February. Short and long versions of a birding tour that includes visits to Bung Boraphet Wildlife Reserve and

Doi Inthanon, Thung Salaeng Luang, Khao Yai, and Khao Sam Roi Yat National Parks. The longer trip also visits Thale Noi Wildlife Preserve in the south.

Malaysia

Follow the narrow strip of land that is southern Thailand and you will cross the border into Malaysia. Somewhat of a mystery to many Americans, Malaysia—"So you're going there, but where exactly is that?"—sounds tropical, remote, and exotic. Indeed, it is tropical, lying only a few degrees above the Equator and bathed in heat and humidity all year. There is no question that parts of the country are also remote—getting to Taman Negara National Park means taking a thirty-seven-mile ride in a motorized dugout. And Malaysia is very much the exotic East, even though Kuala Lumpur is a modern, bustling city.

Malaysia is divided into two parts: Western, or Peninsular Malaysia, on the southern portion of the Malay Peninsula, and Eastern Malaysia on the island of Borneo. The two parts are now separated by the South China Sea, but geological evidence shows that at one time they were connected by a land bridge.

Malaysia is a country with sufficient wealth and the political will to protect its natural heritage. There is strong local interest in birds and plants, which is unusual outside of most Western countries, and about 3 percent of the country's land is set aside in preserves. Unfortunately, although about 60 percent of Malaysia is still covered by forests, logging of tropical woods is a serious problem, particularly in Sabah and Sarawak, the two states on Borneo. Much attention has been paid to this matter worldwide, especially in regard to the plight of the Penan and other forest peoples, whose way of life and only source of food are quickly being chopped down. This is in exchange for the great income derived from exporting these tropical woods to such voracious consumers as the Japanese to supply frivolous needs like throwaway wooden chopsticks. Sadly, it appears at present that the practice will continue until there is no forest left to harvest.

Nevertheless, the visitor to Malaysia rarely sees this destruction. The parks are magnificent, the birds spectacular, and the wildlife, although vanishing quickly, still possible to see if you are quiet, wear dark clothing, and move slowly, if at all.

Taman Negara is Malaysia's first national park, located within the heart of Peninsular Malaysia. Its vast, virgin, lowland rain forest is estimated to be 130 million years old, the oldest in the world. Cool streams, dense undergrowth, and huge trees provide habitat for Elephant, Tiger, Sumatran Rhino (very rare), Tapir, Sambar, Barking and Mouse Deer, Wild Pig, Gibbon, macaques, leaf monkeys, treeshrews, Slow Loris, and Giant Flying Squirrel. There are also more than 250 bird species, resident and migratory, including Great Argus, Malay Peacock Pheasant, Crested Fireback, and raptors, kingfishers, and pittas.

The Cameron Highlands and Fraser's Hill are where Malaysians traditionally have gone to escape the stifling heat and humidity of the peninsular lowlands. This cool, foggy setting is rich in moss- and fern-covered hills where a broad variety of colorful epiphytic orchids and tall fishtail palms can be found. Here also are Tapir, Wild Pig, and many smaller animals such as fruit bats and monkeys. The montane ecology is also prime for birds.

Endau-Rompin is a state park, recently part of a forest reserve that suffered from heavy logging until the country's Wildlife and National Parks Department helped bring about a change in status. The area is important for its rare and endemic plants, including various types of African violets, Fan Palm, Sealingwax Palm, orchids, and heath.

Mount Kinabalu Park, in Sabah, offers a panorama of North Bornean flora and fauna and has the highest mountain in Southeast Asia. This park and its mountain is a favorite haunt of zoologists, botanists, and ornithologists, and a challenge to mountaineers. The plant life includes the largest flower in the world—the rare Rafflesia, a parasite whose bloom measures almost three feet across. Fern trees, rhododendrons, orchids, and pitcher plants, however, are the more customary sights. Animals likely to be seen include monkeys, squirrels, and treeshrews, and over 280 species of birds have been recorded, including three endemics: the Friendly Bush-Warbler, Mountain Black-eye, and Flavescent Bulbul.

Danum Valley Conservation Area in Sabah is a field station for scientific research. The area is lowland forest, home to Elephant, Banteng, Sumatran Rhino, Clouded Leopard, Honey Bear, and Orangutan and other primates. Birding trips come here to see Great Argus, Bulwer's Pheasant, Bornean Bristlehead, and the usual assortment of kingfishers, owls, frogmouths, pittas, wren-babblers, and over 215 other species.

Sepilok, a lowland forest reserve in the northeast of Borneo, is where tours go to see Orangutans, both in the wild and at the rehabilitation center. But also to be seen here are the Bornean Gibbon and over 85 other mammal species. The world can thank Barbara Harrisson for Sepilok's existence. In the 1950s, she began rescuing young Orangutans that were being kept as pets. Then, with the backing of the newly formed World Wildlife Fund, she worked with Malaysia's forest department to help set up the center to deal with Orangutans displaced by logging. The center is financed by the Sabah government, and over 200 orphaned Orangutans have been trained to live in the wild and subsequently released.

Mulu National Park is situated along the Melinau River in Sarawak. Though it contains around 20,000 animal species (mostly insects) and over 3,500 plant species, not including 8,000 types of fungi, it is best known for the Pinnacles—gigantic limesone rocks with arrowhead-sharp tips. It's not easy to get here.

Asian Pacific Adventures. 16 days / $$ (from Kuala Lumpur) / June–September. Adventure trip with whitewater boating, hiking, caving, swimming, and camping. General nature focus, with attention to giant tropical trees, bird-watching, insects. Visits Mt. Kinabalu and Taman Negara.

Bird Bonanzas. (See the section on Thailand, page 250.)

Birdquest. 22 days / $$ (from Kuala Lumpur) / June. A birding trip to Borneo and peninsular Malaysia. Visits Sabah (including Danum Valley and Mount Kinabalu), Taman Negara, and Fraser's Hill. Participants can expect to see upwards of 300 species of birds. Endemics and rarities are searched for. Maximum of 16 participants, 2 leaders.

Geo Expeditions. 17 days / $$ (from Kuala Lumpur) / April, August. Natural history trips that include rain forest expeditions by road and longboat, and a moderate trek. Stays in native longhouses, forest cabins, and mountain huts. Visits Sarawak, Sabah (Mount Kinabalu), Taman Negara, and Fraser's Hill.

International Expeditions. 17–22 days / $$–$$$ (from Los Angeles) / February, March, July, October. A general nature trip to peninsular Malaysia and Sarawak and Sabah on Borneo. You'll visit Taman Negara, the Sepilok Orangutan Sanctuary, and the Turtle Islands. The longer itinerary visits Thailand and Singapore as well. Features of the trips include a search for the Proboscis Monkey (by boat), a night in a blind (hide) to observe nocturnal animals, and a visit to the jungle canopy walkway.

King Bird Tours. 25 days / $$ (from Kuala Lumpur) / July, August. Intense birding trips to peninsular Malaysia and Sabah. You'll visit a variety of habitat from lowland rain forest at Taman Negara and Danum Valley to the delightfully cool Fraser's Hill and the high elevations of Mount Kinabalu. Participants can expect to see about 350 species of birds, along with many mammals. Specialties include Malaysian Honeyguide, Orange-tailed Shama, Red-crowned Barbet, Barred Eagle Owl, Garnet Pitta—a bird that appears to glow from inside—Pin-tailed Parrotfinch, Malayan Whistlingthrush, Marbled Wren-Babbler, Large Frogmouth, Bornean Bristlehead, and Finsch's Bulbul. Noted field naturalist Dennis Yong leads the tour.

Mountain Travel. 15 days / $$ (from Kota Kinabalu) / January–December. Adventure trips to Borneo, with moderate day hikes (optional strenuous hiking) in the rain forest to look for jungle wildlife. You'll also explore caverns and take a longboat ride up a jungle river to visit the Penan, who are struggling against deforestation. Includes a climb up Mount Kinabalu.

Naturetrek. 23 days / $$ (from London) / August. A general trip in search of the tropical birds and mammals of lowland rain forests, coral reefs, and the alpine ecosystem of Mount Kinabalu. You visit Fraser's Hill, Endau-Rompin Park in East Malaysia; Bako Park in Sarawak; and, in Sabah, Mount Kinabalu, the Tenom Orchid Research Center, Sepilok Orangutan Center, and the beach at Selingan, where you can watch sea turtles lay their eggs. In Kinabalu, many Bornean endemics can be seen, including Bornean Mountain Whistler, Golden-naped Barbet, and Mountain Black-eye. There is an optional climb up the mountain, on whose hillsides thousands of endemic plants thrive. An ornithologist accompanies the trip.

Overseas Adventure Travel. 14 days / $$ (from Sandakan) / April–October. Demanding trekking and natural history trips to Borneo, including a river trek and rain forest trek, and a hike through caves and rock climbing. Visits Mount Kinabalu and the Pinnacles of Mulu National Park.

VENT. 23 days / $$$ (from Kuala Lumpur) / March. A birding trip to Borneo and the Malay Peninsula. Visits Taman Negara, Fraser's Hill, and Mount Kinabalu. Participants can expect to see some 350 species of birds, including pheasants, pittas, broadbills, bulbuls, babblers, trogons, and spiderhunters. Maximum of 16 participants; 2 leaders, including noted naturalist Dennis Yong.

Voyagers International. (See the section on Indonesia, page 260.)

Wilderness Travel. 22 days / $$ (from Sandakan) / March, June, October. A cultural and natural history adventure trip to Borneo featuring a longboat trip into the rain forest of Sarawak, a visit to an Orangutan refuge, and an exploration of the limestone caves of Mulu National Park. You'll climb up Mount Mulu with Penan guides to the cloud forest, and swim with sea turtles off Sipadan, a coral island in the South China Sea.

Wings. 22 days / $$ (from Kuala Lumpur) / February. A birding trip to Taman Negara and Fraser's Hill on the peninsula, then on to north Borneo to Sandakan and Kinabalu Park. Participants can expect to see about 350 species of birds as well as many mammals, especially primates. Birds include Orange-breasted Flowerpecker, Tiger Shrike, Mangrove Blue Flycatcher, Black-and-crimson Oriole, Straw-headed Bulbul, and various kingfishers, babblers, pheasants, and hornbills. Maximum of 16 participants; 2 leaders, including noted field naturalist Dennis Yong.

Indonesia

Once called the Dutch East Indies, Indonesia is an archipelago of 13,667 islands lying between the Indian and Pacific oceans, and extending for more than 3,000 miles from the mainland of Southeast Asia to Australia. It is the world's sixth largest nation (land area of 736,000 square miles) and the fifth most populous (173 million people).

The diverse habitat of Indonesia is home to the greatest concentration of wildlife in Asia, with 10 percent of all the plants and trees in the world, some of the world's rarest birds, and more mammals than in any other country in the world—over 515 species. Underwater, the Indo-Philippine area is also the richest in species diversity in the world. Tours to Indonesia usually concentrate on one or another part of the country rather than spending time in transit from island to island. Sumatra, Java, Bali, and Komodo are common destinations; cultural tours also visit Kalamantan (Borneo), Sulawesi, and more remote islands.

Indonesia stretches along the Equator, and you know what that means: steady heat and humidity all year long. But it also means extensive tropical rain forests, coral reefs, and sandy beaches. Here too are several active volcanos—after all, Indonesia is a big chunk of the Pacific "ring of fire." From both a cultural and an environmental standpoint, Indonesia is truly a fascinating destination.

With the good comes the bad. Although more than half the country is covered by tropical rain forest, it is being harvested at an alarming rate. In the last thirty years, the country has lost no less than 40 percent of its trees. According to Richard Bangs and Christian Kallen, in their book *Islands of Fire, Islands of Spice,* "in less time than it takes to read a chapter in [their] book, enough trees in Indonesia will fall to reforest [New York's] Central Park." And attempts to solve the country's overpopulation problem by resettling people on less crowded islands have only aggravated the situation.

But ecotourism has recently been recognized as a potential source of income for Indonesia. There have long been tourist facilities for viewing the Komodo Dragon and the Orangutans, but now there is talk of developing butterfly ranches; a law passed in 1991 prohibits hunting of certain sea turtles; there is hope for protecting the country's reefs; and there is the possibility of making the trails into the rain forest more unobtrusive. Let's hope that these measures—combined with decreased poaching, controlled harvest of the forest, and education in more ecologically sound agricultural methods—will help develop this country while retaining its natural wonders.

Sumatra is in the western part of Indonesia, the second largest island in this nation of islands. Its Mount Leuser and Kerinci National Parks protect the highly endangered Sumatran Rhino, but they are also home to over 320 species of birds, 175 mammals, 195 reptiles, and 52 amphibians. The famous Orangutan rehabilitation center, supported by the World Wildlife Fund, is also found in Mount Leuser.

The island of Java, where Jakarta is located, is densely populated, but perched on its virtually inaccessible westernmost tip is Ujung Kulon National Park, best known as the home of the Javan Rhino. Also here, among the mangrove swamps and rattan forests, are Long-tailed Macaque, Monitor Lizard (smaller relations of the Komodo Dragon), Rhinocerous Hornbill, and White-bellied Sea-Eagle. The remains of Krakatau volcano—*west*, not east, of Java—include Anak Krakatau ("Child of Krakatau"), which is active but climbable. Mount Gede-Pangrango National Park, which includes the Cibodas Botanical Gardens, is home to 260 species of birds, including 20 Javan endemics. Bromo-Tengger National Park, in southeastern Java, displays this region's volcanic activity, with the still-active Mount Semeru erupting every eight minutes. Baluran National Park, in easternmost Java, is a good place to see the Black Leaf Monkey and Long-tailed Macaque.

Bali is Indonesia's other densely populated island, so very different from the rest of the country because of its Hindu culture (most of Indonesia is Moslem), which, along with its beaches, is Bali's main attraction for visitors. Although the island has severe ecological problems, Bali Barat National Park exists to protect and captive-breed one of the world's rarest and most endangered birds, the Bali Starling. This elegant white beauty has been favored as a cage bird and is still sold at high profit on the black market. (In truth, it is disheartening to see so many birds robbed of their freedom in a Hindu land where all life is considered holy, and to walk beneath trees now silent because the heavy use of pesticides in the rice paddies has virtually wiped out the songbirds.)

Komodo Island is home to the world's largest reptile, the Komodo Dragon—actually a large Monitor Lizard. (The Komodo Dragon was featured in the movie *The Freshman*.) Unfortunately, overfeeding has made these big guys a little too lazy and easy to spot, but the island also has bird species that belong to both the Asian and Australian biospheres.

TOUR OPERATORS

Abercrombie & Kent. 7 days / $$$ (from Jakarta) / November–March. "Volcanos and Rainforests" cruise in the Sunda Strait between Java and Sumatra. You'll climb Anak Krakatau (with champagne at the top!) and visit Ujung Kulon National Park, where you hike in the rain forest and go snorkeling. A morning is also spent birdwatching in Pulau Dua Bird Sanctuary, where you can see Rhinoceros Hornbill, Javan Turtle Dove, and Scarlet-backed Flowerpecker. Cultural stops are made as well. Day excursions are complemented by evening lectures and slide presentations. Maximum of 20 passengers.

American Museum of Natural History. (See the section on Australia, page 265.)

Bird Bonanzas. 20 days / $$$ (from Kuala Lumpur) / May. A birding tour concentrating on Sumatra. You'll visit Kerinchi, one of the prime birding areas, where all 14 mainland Sumatran endemics are to be found. Participants can expect to see about 300 species of birds, including raptors, pheasants, coucals, swifts, kingfishers, barbets, babblers, flycatchers, sunbirds, and white-eyes. Maximum of 6 participants; noted field naturalist Dennis Yong leads the trip.

Birdquest
30 days / $$ (from Jakarta) / September. A birding trip to both sides of the Wallace Line—the clear division between two very different faunal and floral regions. You'll see both Asian and Australian species as you visit Ternate, Halmahera, Sulawesi (Dumoga-Bone and Lore Lindu forest reserves), Bali, and Java (Cibodas and Ujung Kulon). Participants can expect to see a good cross section of species, including Wallace's Standardwing, one of the most exotic of the birds of paradise. Maximum of 16 participants, 2 leaders.

30 days / $$ (from Biak) / July. "Irian Jaya: Unknown New Guinea" is a birding trip to the Indonesian (western) side of this island. Irian Jaya is still covered by some of the largest tracts of undisturbed forest on earth. You'll visit a variety of habitats in search of birds of paradise, bowerbirds, Pale-billed Sicklebill, Salvadori's Fig-Parrot, and Northern Cassowary. Maximum of 14 participants, 2 leaders.

Cox & Kings. 11–20 days / $$$$ (from London) / May–July. Six different luxury cruises in the Indonesian archipelago: Asmat, Timor, and Lesser Sundas; Bali to Borneo; Borneo to Bangkok; Gulf of Siam and Java Sea; Ikat Islands; and Micronesia. You'll go snorkeling and visit various national parks, with day excursions made by Zodiac. Cultural sites are visited as well.

Earthwatch
14 days / $$ (from Kalimantan) / January–March, September. A research project helping to rehabituate ex-captive Orangutans to life in the rain forest. Volunteers track Orangutans and observe and record behavior.

14 days / $$ (from Jakarta) / July, August. "Krakatau!" is a research project studying how an ecosystem rebuilds itself after a volcanic eruption. Volunteers sample ash to see how vegetation responds to the islands' ongoing volcanism.

14 days / $ (from Ubud, Bali) / June–August. "Bali's Temple Monkeys" is a research project that studies the effects of tourism on the local Crab-eating Macaques. Volunteers document foraging behavior and social interactions.

Field Studies Council. 22 days / $$ (from London) / August. A learning vacation to Java to study the connection between environment and culture. Visits coastline, mangrove swamps, rain forest, and volcanic areas, attempting to show links to Indonesian culture.

Geo Expeditions. 19 days / $ (from Jakarta) / June, August. Visits Ujung Kulon National Park on Java; goes to Borneo to see Orangutan; to Komodo for the Komodo Dragon; and to Bali.

International Research Expeditions. 10 days / $$ (from Jakarta) / July, August. Research expedition. Based on remote tropical islands, volunteers collect sponges and other invertebrates that may have potential for use in the manufacture of medicines.

King Bird Tours. 15–21 days / $$ (from Jakarta) / July, August. Two birding trips, each to different islands. The first trip goes to Halmahera and Sulawesi; the second visits the Lesser Sundas (Flores, Timor, and Sumba). In 1994, the trip will go to Java, Bali, Sumatra, and Kalimantan. Special effort is made to find rarities and endemics. There is a variety of mammals, too, including Proboscis Monkey and Orangutan. Noted author Ben King leads the trips.

Mountain Travel. 7–12 days / $$ (from Jakarta) / January–December. Adventure trips with moderate hiking and rafting. Some trips visit Bali, and raft the Ayung River; trek in the highlands of Sulawesi, and raft the remote Salo Sadan river; or float down the Alas River through northern Sumatra's Gunung Leuser National Park, home of the Orangutan.

Naturetrek. 24 days / $$ (from London) / April. "The National Parks of Indonesia" is a birding and wildlife trip. In Gunung Leuser National Park there's a 3-day float trip down the Alas River. In Meru Betiri National Park, you'll see the sea turtles coming up on the beach to lay their eggs. While in Bali Barat, there's a chance to see the rare Bali Starling. You'll also visit Komodo to see the dragons.

Questers. 22 days / $$$ (from Jakarta) / April, July, September. Natural history trips to Java, Sumatra, and Bali. Visits Ujung Kulon and Baluran National Parks, Bogor and Cibodas Botanical Gardens, Krakatau, the coastal mangroves of Bali, and some of the wilder parts of Sumatra.

See & Sea. 7–10 days / $$$ (from Biak) / January–December. Dive trips aboard the 17-passenger *Tropical Princess.* You'll dive 60 miles north of Biak (Irian Jaya), where you can see various species of fish as they migrate along open-water routes. Sponges and corals, reef fish, octopus, nudibranchs, lionfish, and soft corals will provide new subjects for photographers.

VENT. 29 days / $$$ (from Jakarta) / June. A birding trip to Java, Bali, and Sulawesi. Indonesia is home to 350 endemic species of birds, at least 120 of which are considered threatened. You'll visit both sides of the Wallace Line, crossing it to visit Sulawesi, considered to be in the oceanic realm of Wallacea. Characteristic birds of this area include Sulawesi Serpent-Eagle, Maleo (a megapode), Barred Rail, Ochre-breasted Hawk-Owl, Red-knobbed Hornbill, Piping Crow, and a good assortment of honeyeaters, flowerpeckers, and munias. Maximum of 10 participants, 1 leader.

Voyagers International. 17 days / $$$ (from Los Angeles) / April, August. A combination natural history and cultural trip to Borneo, Bali, and Komodo (August) and a photographic trip (April). Optional extension to Sarawak. Photographer Boyd Norton accompanies the April trip.

Christmas Island and the Cocos Islands

The Indian Ocean's version of the Galápagos Islands, Christmas Island has a unique ecological history and is home to several endemic species. The surrounding waters have rich coral reefs, and the shorelines are home to eighteen species of land crabs, plus Green and Hawksbill Turtles.

The Cocos Islands are a group of twenty-seven small coral islands with a variety of nesting seabirds. As far as we can determine, only one operator runs nature trips to these remote islands, perhaps because there are no hotels.

TOUR OPERATORS

Cox & Kings. 18 days / $$$ (from London) / March, April, June, October, November. A natural history trip to Christmas Island and the Cocos Islands. The trip begins with a boat trip to look for dolphins and seabirds. You then visit the Christmas Island Frigatebird colonies and the Daniel Roux Caves, which harbor a large colony of the endemic Glossy Cave Swiftlets. Next you fly to the Cocos Islands, where you'll be based on West Island (in private apartments). Day trips to Home and North Keeling islands.

King Bird Tours. 7 days / $$$ (from Jakarta) / August. A birding tour to Christmas Island in search of endemic birds: Abbott's Booby, Christmas Island Frigatebird, Christmas Island Imperial Pigeon, and Glossy Cave Swiftlet. Other birds, especially seabirds, will be encountered as well.

The Philippines

Stretching in a 1,500-mile line of over 7,000 islands, the Philippines is the world's second largest archipelago nation. Despite the fact that some of its islands are close to the Asian mainland, the country has enjoyed vast periods of isolation—resulting in an evolutionary explosion of species special to this area, and with considerable variation among the islands. Some 4,000 species of trees, 160 mammals, 270 reptiles, and 550 birds are here—many endemic to the Philippines or to individual Philippine islands.

Yet a growing population and a weak economy are contributing to a major environmental disaster here, as deforestation and land destruction proceed at alarming rates. According to Ben King, author of *A Field Guide to the Birds of Southeast Asia* and noted authority on birds of this region, "the Philippine Islands are the worst ecological disaster in the South East Asia region. . . . If you want to go to the Philippines, do it soon while there are still some birds left."

TOUR OPERATORS

Birdquest. 22 days / $$ (from Manila) / February. A birdwatching trip to four of the major islands: Luzon, Mindanao, Cebu, and Palawan. Special effort is made to find as many of the 170 endemics as possible. Among the rarities are Palawan Peacock-Pheasant, Philippine (Monkey-eating) Eagle, Tabon Scrubfowl, Black Shama, Philippine Water Redstart, and a variety of flycatchers, kingfishers, and warblers.

Earthwatch. 10 days / $$ (from Dumaguete) / April, May. A research trip to Tubbataha Reef. Legendary among scuba divers, Tubbataha was declared a National Marine Park in 1988. Volunteers live aboard the research vessel *Melaena.* Teams map reef areas by habitat community, census marine life, and monitor indicator species, such as Giant Clams and Butterfly Fish.

International Research Expeditions. 10 days / $ (from Manila) / January–December. Research trip to study the wildlife, peoples, and archaeology of Mindoro Island.

King Bird Tours. 28 days / $$ (from Manila) / February. A birding trip to several islands in search of endemics and rarities. Participants can expect to see about 300 species of birds, including Philippine (Monkey-eating) Eagle, Philippine Trogon, Philippine Fairy-bluebird, Philippine Falconet, plus a good assortment of kingfishers, flycatchers, and flowerpeckers. With luck, you may see a Luzon Bleedingheart. Noted Asian specialist Ben King leads the trip.

Sea & See. 10 days / $$ (from Manila) / January–December. Dive trips to the rich and prolific reefs of the Philippines. You'll live aboard the 120-foot yacht *Tristar,* and travel to remote Tubbataha and Jesse Beasley reefs, as well as to various islets such as Cagayancillo, Basterra, and Arena. This trip can be combined with a week in Palau or Truk Lagoon (see the section on the South Pacific Islands, page 277). Maximum of 20 passengers.

NATURE TRIPS DOWN UNDER: AUSTRALASIA

 With jet planes to take us from country to country, it is easy to forget that the earth is almost 25,000 miles around. Indeed, we can accumulate that many frequent-flyer miles in short order. But travel to Australia or the South Pacific, especially from the United States or Europe, gives you an appreciation for the size of the earth. This part of the world is far away; it's almost halfway around the world, in terms of both latitude and longitude.

Distance from home is probably one of the reasons Australasia is so appealing. There's very little of the familiar and a lot that's exotic. Islands of exceptional beauty, unusual plants and animals, the rugged Outback, steaming jungle—all can be had on the other side of the International Date Line and south of the Equator.

There's an abundance of nature tours to the islands of Oceania, with the largest number to Australia.

AUSTRALIA

Spinning off from the supercontinent Gondwana about 100 million years ago, the island that is now Australia was isolated from the rest of the world for more than 60 million years. And as is the case with many islands, its animals and plants developed in a world totally their own, modifying and increasing their ability to thrive under unique conditions. This, together with its size (almost 3 million square miles), accounts for Australia's record numbers of endemic species.

Australia is especially known for its marsupials, which continued to flourish here while they largely disappeared elsewhere: Kangaroos, Cuscus and Flying Phalangers (flying squirrels), Koala, Wombat, Marsupial Mice, Numbat (Banded Anteater), Tasmanian Wolf, and Marsupial Mole. Monotremes (egg-laying mammals)—the Duck-billed Platypus and the Echidna (Spiny Anteater)—also remain here.

About 750 species of birds have been recorded in Australia; best known are the flightless Emu, Southern Cassowary, and Laughing Kookaburra, but there are also cockatoos, lyrebirds, fairy-wrens, honeyeaters, birds of paradise, and bowerbirds. In addition, there are 380 species of reptiles, 122 frogs, 180 freshwater fish,

54,000 insects, and 750 mollusks. Eucalyptus trees, of which there are over 500 species, are native to Australia and are the sole food source for the Koala.

Only in the far eastern region of Australia are there some hills and mountains, covered with rain forest, and markedly different from the generally dry, brushy woodlands and arid plains that characterize a large part of the country. The interior—the Outback—is among the world's largest deserts. But there are woodlands and heaths in the southwest, eucalyptus forests in the southeast, and swamps and forests in the north.

Tasmania, an island that is part of Australia, lies about 150 miles south of Victoria, and has a climate similar to that of northern California. The island is essentially mountainous, with some peaks reaching over 5,000 feet. But its primary feature is its central plateau, dissected by rivers and lakes. Extensive eucalpyt forests abound with wildlife, including Wallaby, possums, native cats, and the famed Tasmanian Devil—a marsupial, vaguely bearlike in appearance.

The world's premier dive spot—the Great Barrier Reef—lies off the northeastern coast of Australia. Extending 1,250 miles, it supports 350 species of coral and is the largest living structure on earth. Two thousand species of fish depend on the reef for food and shelter, as do anemones, worms, gastropods, lobsters, crayfish, shrimp, and crabs. The giant clams are famous—they're 4 feet wide and weigh 200 pounds. The coral islands within the reef serve as beachheads for nesting Green Turtles. Indeed, only tropical rain forests compare with the Great Barrier Reef in terms of species diversity and complexity.

Australia is about the size of the continental United States but has far fewer people. About 5 percent of the land is protected in parks and preserves. Agriculture is important here, and, consequently, habitat destruction is a problem for some species. Unfortunately there is a history of attempts to manipulate nature; people have introduced species that prey upon native species.

On the whole, most people journeying Down Under are struck by the wild, unspoiled nature of the country and its strikingly unusual wildlife. As songwriter Alix Dobkin sings, "Dingoes and koala bears/Land of kangaroos/Emus, wallabies and kookaburras in/The old gum trees . . ." ("Yahoo Australia").

NOTE: Trips to the Australian subantarctic islands and the Ross Ice Shelf can be found in the section on South America, page 105.

TOUR OPERATORS

Abercrombie & Kent. 17 days / $$$$ (from Melbourne) / June, July. "Natural Wonders" visits various sites in eastern and central Australia including Kakadu National Park, Ayers Rock, and Heron Island National Park on the Great Barrier Reef.

American Museum of Natural History. 16 days / $$$$ (from Cairns) / February. A visit to the Great Barrier Reef is part of a Discovery Cruise "Bali to the Barrier Reef." A geologist and a marine biologist accompany the trip, aboard the 50-cabin *Renaissance.*

Betchart Expeditions. 10 days / $$$ (from Melbourne) / October. A general trip to Australia that includes some time on the Great Barrier Reef. Optional extension to New Zealand (8 days) is possible. Australian (and New Zealand) naturalists accompany the trip. Betchart also runs this trip for the Zoological Society of San Diego.

Biological Journeys. 21 days / $$$ (from Cairns) / October. A snorkeling trip to the Great Barrier Reef, where you can see hundreds of fish and corals. You'll then go ashore to explore the rain forest of Queensland, where you can see parrots, possums, kangaroos, koalas, and possibly a rare Duck-billed Platypus. Maximum of 16 participants, 3 leaders.

Birding. 19 days / $$$$ (from London) / October. A birding trip from the Barrier Reef to Mallee Desert to the rain forest. You'll visit such birding hot spots as the Atherton Tablelands and the Grampions. A trip to see the Fairy Penguins on Phillip Island will cap off this extraordinary adventure. Participants can expect to see a wide variety of birds. Maximum of 16 participants, 2 leaders.

Birdquest. 29 days / $$$ (from Perth) / August. "Australia with a Difference" is a serious birdwatching trip that visits Western Australia, the Kimberley Plateau, the Outback, and Tasmania in search of such rarities as Noisy Scrub-bird, Black Grasswren, Letter-winged Kite, and Scarlet-chested Parrot. Some of the time will be spent camping. Maximum of 16 participants, 2 leaders. A more traditional bird-watching tour of Australia, concentrating on the eastern half of the continent, is also offered. October departure; costs are comparable.

Cheesemans' Ecology Safaris. 20 days / $$ (from Cairns) / October. "Incredible Australia," a trip to eastern Australia, visits the Great Barrier Reef, Atherton Tablelands, Lamington National Park, and Little Desert National Park to look for birds and animals. Maximum of 14 participants; local naturalist guides assist the trip leaders.

Cox & Kings. 20 days / $$ (from London) / September. A botany tour to Western Australia. The wildflowers here are amazing, and there are entire families of flowering trees and shrubs that are completely unknown in the Northern Hemisphere. Noted botanist Mary Briggs leads the trip, accompanied by a local botanist.

Earthwatch. A variety of research trips includes: "Australia's Island Lizards," a study of skink lizards on the limestone Jurien Bay Islands of Western Australia; "Honey Possum," a study of this important nonflying pollinator of Western Australia's heathlands; "Echidnas on Kangaroo Island," research into monotremes (egg-laying mammals) on Kangaroo Island; "Sex and Parenting in Tasmania," an exploration of cooperative polyandry among Tasmanian native hens; "Eucalyptus Forest Life," a study of marsupials, including the Koala and the extremely rare Hastings River Mouse, in three state forests of the southeast; "Kangaroo," observing and tracking these popular marsupials; "Queensland River Survey," to determine the impact of pollution from modern farming on the fragile coral reef environment; and "Australia's Rain Forest Canopy," a study of the species that live in this rich habitat. Most teams go for a 2-week period; there are frequent departures. Costs: $1,000 to $2,000, depending on project chosen.

Field Guides

15 days / $$ (from Cairns) / July. A birdwatching tour to Kakadu National Park, the Atherton Tablelands, and the Kimberley Plateau. Participants may observe bowerbirds and birds of paradise as well as such specialties as Banded Fruit-Dove, White-throated Grasswren, and White-lined Honeyeater. Maximum of 16 participants, 2 leaders.

33 days / $$ (from Sydney) / October. "Australia" is an exploration of the island continent and its birds. You'll visit all the important geographic regions from the Great Barrier Reef to Perth. A pelagic pretour (3 days) and an extension to Tasmania (4 days) are also offered at extra cost. Special effort is made to find endemics; participants can expect to see upwards of 450 species of birds. Maximum of 16 participants, 2 leaders.

Field Studies Council. 28 days / $$$ (from London) / October. A general natural history trip to South Australia. You'll botanize, birdwatch, and study the plants and geology of this fascinating region.

Geo Expeditions. 17 days / $$ (from Sydney) / April, July, November. Combination cultural and natural history trips. You'll visit Heron Island on the Great Barrier Reef, Lamington National Park on the east coast, and Ayers Rock. Maximum of 15 participants.

Geostar Travel. 14 days / $$$$ (from Los Angeles or San Francisco) / September, October. "Botanizing Down Under." Two botanical trips: the first from Perth to Kalbarri; the second from Perth to Albany (the two trips can be taken consecutively). Western Australia offers the plant lover one of the greatest displays of native wildflowers of any region on earth. A botanist leads the tours, accompanied by local experts on flora and fauna.

Inland Bird Tours. An Australian birdwatching tour company led by Philip Maher, who specializes in finding the hard-to-find and rarer species. Trips range from 7 days visiting wetlands in New South Wales, where about 180 species can be seen, to 30 days in Gulf Country/Kakadu, where over 300 species are possible. The wetlands trip is run in November; the Kakadu trip in June. Other trips go in August and September, including day trips out of Deniliquin, Mr. Maher's home. Costs: $650 to $2,500, depending on trip chosen. Some trips require camping.

International Expeditions. 17–21 days / $$$ (from Los Angeles) / April–November. Three trips are offered, including an exploration of Queensland and the Northern Territory; a trip to Queensland and the "Top End"; and a trip to South Australia. Natural history sites, national parks, and some cultural/historical sites are visited; the first two trips go to the Great Barrier Reef.

International Research Expeditions. 7 days / $ (from Cape Tribulation) / January–December. A zoology/botany research project at the Cape Tribulation Field Centre in Queensland surveys plants and animals in an effort to protect the area from development and logging. Volunteers trap and radio-collar animals and collect plant specimens.

Journeys. 16 days / $$ (from Sydney) / February, July, October. "Ocean and Outback Odyssey" is a general natural history trip accompanied by local naturalist guides. Add-ons to Kakadu National Park, Kangaroo Island, and Tasmania are available, and custom itineraries can be arranged.

Monarch

14 days / $$$ (from Brisbane) / March, April, September, November, December. "Birding and Wildlife Bonanza" begins in Brisbane and visits Lamington National Park, the Atherton Tableland, the Great Barrier Reef, Kakadu National Park, and Alice Springs, ending with a cruise of Sydney Harbor. Over 300 species of birds can be expected.

28 days / $ (from Sydney) / March–May, July, August. "Back of Beyond" is a 28-day exploration of the Outback, Great Barrier Reef, Queensland coast, and Lamington National Park. Some camping is involved.

Mountain Travel/Sobek

14 days / $$$ (from Sydney) / December–July. "Reefs, Rain Forests, and Islands" describes this trip to the Great Barrier Reef, Lamington National Park, and Fraser Island.

11 days / $$ (from Hobart) / December–March. The more adventurous may wish to raft the Franklin River in Tasmania, located in Wild Rivers National Park and featuring Class IV rapids with names like Churn and Thunderush. This is a moderate-to-strenuous trip and includes camping.

Nature Expeditions International. 22 days / $$ (from Sydney) / February–April, July, October. General natural history trips to the Great Barrier Reef, Kakadu, Lamington, the Grampians, and the Outback. A combination trip to Australia and New Zealand (30 days) is also offered.

Naturetrek

21 days / $$$ (from London) / August. A camping safari through the wilderness regions of northeastern Australia, including the rain forests of Queensland, the Great Barrier Reef, Katherine Gorge, and Kakadu National Park. Special attention is paid to birds and animals; you can also snorkel on the reef. An optional extension (7 days) to Alice Springs, Ayers Rock, and the Olgas is available. Maximum of 16 participants.

22 days / $$$ (from London) / October. "Wildlife of Western Australia" begins in Perth and spends time at Kalbarri National Park, Shark Bay, Fitzgerald River National Park, and Stirling Range National Park. This is a combination botany, birding, and animal-watching trip. Maximum of 16 participants.

New York Zoological Society. 16 days / $$$$ (from New York) / August. "Ocean to Outback" is a deluxe safari. You'll visit Cape Tribulation National Park, the Great Barrier Reef, Kakadu National Park, and Lamington National Park, where you're likely to see 90 species of birds in a single day plus many animals, including Duck-billed Platypus, Ring-tailed Possum, and Red-shouldered Pademelon. Maximum of 16 participants; a zoologist accompanies the trip. Cost includes a tax-deductible contribution to the NYZS.

Osprey Wildlife Expeditions. 8 days / $$ (from Adelaide) / January–December. This operator is an Australian natural history tour company that offers a variety of trips. Among them are "Wintering with Whales," a research trip to study Southern Right Whales with Dr. John Ling; and "South Australian Highlights," which visits Kangaroo Island, Flinders Chase National Park, Mount Remarkable National Park, Chambers Gorge, and the Warrawong Sanctuary.

Outer Edge Expeditions

15 days / $$$ (from Cairns) / August. "Australian Humpback Whales" is a dive-and-sail odyssey visiting the Great Barrier Reef and Fraser Island. Maximum of 10 participants.

11 days / $ (from Alice Springs) / March, August, October. "Camel Safari in the Red Centre" is just that—camel riding and hiking in the Macdonnell Ranges among birds and animals such as kangaroos, brumbies, dingos, and wild camels. Camping throughout. Maximum of 8 participants.

14 days / $$$ (from Cairns) / January–December. "Eastern Australian Odyssey" is a general natural history trip to Lamington, the Great Barrier Reef, Fraser Island, and the Clarke Range. Maximum of 10 participants.

Pacific Exploration Company. 10–14 days / $$ (from various locations in Australia) / January–December. Walkabouts in Australia: hiking and camping safaris to the Central Australian Desert, Kakadu National Park, Tasmania, and Cape York. Mostly run for independent travelers and small groups.

Questers. 22 days / $$$ (from Sydney) / November. A general natural history trip from the Blue Mountains to Alice Springs, from Uluru National Park (Ayers Rock) to the Great Barrier Reef, and to Tasmania as well. You'll observe and learn about geology, plants, animal life, and birds. A combination Australia–New Zealand trip (17 days) is also offered.

See & Sea. 8–10 days / $$$ (from Cairns) / January–December. A variety of dive trips and live-aboards in the Coral Sea and on the Great Barrier Reef. The Coral Sea Islands Territory is located between New Caledonia and Australia, 300 miles from land, and these trips give divers the opportunity to see sharks, rays, turtles, and giant groupers in abundance. Three to 7-day cruises are offered to the reef.

VENT. 33 days / $$ (from Cairns) / October. "Grand Australia" is a birding trip. Participants visit all the major habitats from the Kimberleys to Kakadu to Queensland and can expect to see upwards of 450 species, with special attention paid to finding endemics. The trip is offered in two sections (west and north, 17 days; southeast, 16 days), which may be taken separately. Maximum of 14 participants; noted local bird guide Len Robinson leads the trip.

Wilderness Travel. 19 days / $$$ (from Cairns) / May, August, December. "Wild Australia" is a general natural history adventure visiting the Great Barrier Reef, Kakadu National Park, and Cape York. Some camping. Maximum of 15 participants.

Wings/Sunbird. 27 days / $$ (from Melbourne) / October. A birdwatching trip beginning on Phillip Island, where you'll watch the "Penguin Parade"—Little Penguins returning from the sea to their nesting burrows. Various national parks—including Lamington, Wyperfeld, and Simpson's Gap—and the Great Barrier

Reef are among the places visited. In addition, there is a pelagic trip out of Wool-longong, during which albatrosses, storm-petrels, *Pterodroma* petrels, and shearwaters can be seen. Participants may expect to see about 400 species of birds. Maximum of 14 participants, 1 leader plus 5 local guides.

World Wildlife Fund. 14 days / $$$$ (from Cairns) / October. A general natural history trip visiting the rain forests of Queensland, the Great Barrier Reef, and Kakadu National Park. An optional extension to New Zealand (8 days) is offered. A representative of the WWF accompanies the trip.

Zegrahm Expeditions. 4 days / $$$$ (from Darwin) / September. A trip to the Outback, visiting Ayers Rock, the Olgas, Kakadu National Park, Katherine Gorge, and Seven Spirit Bay on the Cobourg Peninsula. Maximum of 25 participants.

NEW ZEALAND

Known to the Maoris as Aotearoa ("The Land of the Long White Cloud"), New Zealand encompasses two major islands and several smaller ones. Its stunning landscapes are legendary—where else could a camera capture fern trees, palms, flowering lupines, a glacial lake, a snow-capped mountain, and a blue sky all in a single frame? The country is both down under and upside down; north is warm, south cold. Of special interest in New Zealand are the thermal activity at Rotorua, the volcanos on the North Island, the glaciers on the South Island, and Milford Sound—a vast fjord on the South Island's western coast. In addition, there are caves filled with Glow-worms (a particular type of insect that glows in the dark), and the Tuatara, the sole survivor of an ancient order of reptiles (Rhynchocephalia) that included the dinosaurs.

Like many other island nations, New Zealand evolved in isolation. As a result, there are no native mammals (apart from two species of bat), but there are several endemic and unique birds, not the strangest of which is the New Zealand national emblem—the Brown Kiwi, a large, flightless, brown ball on legs. Other endemics include the huge, flightless Takahe (quite rare) and its more successful compatriot, the cheeky Weka (also flightless). The Weka can be found on both the main islands, while the Takahe makes its home only on small, outlying, predator-free islands (where it is being reintroduced).

A large number of flightless birds evolved in New Zealand because there were no native predators (either mammalian or reptilian). Sadly, many of these birds are now extinct. One, the Kakapo, an owl-parrot, is holding on by a thread. This gentle, fearless, and flightless bird has been removed to predator-free islands in the north (Little Barrier) and the south (Codfish), and may be staging something of a comeback. That is to say, a chick has been born; whether or not it survives is another matter.

Most trips to New Zealand are birding trips, since the country's high number of endemics makes it a popular destination. New Zealand has a vast network of hiking trails, called tracks. Tramping (or hiking) the tracks is a good way to experience the natural history of the country, and some trips include a few days on one of the tracks. General-interest natural history tours often combine Australia with New Zealand (see the section on Australia, page 263).

NOTE: Trips that go to the subantarctic islands of New Zealand are described in the section on South America, pages 145–47.

TOUR OPERATORS

Birdquest. 21 days / $$$ (from Auckland) / November. A birding trip to the major habitats of New Zealand in search of all the endemics. Participants may expect to see about 125 species of birds, including the delightful Wrybill, the elusive Blue Duck, the strange and musical Kokako, and several species of seabirds. Maximum of 16 participants; Mark Hanger, one of New Zealand's most respected field naturalists, accompanies the trip, along with another leader.

Branta Holidays. 14 days / $$$$ (from London) / November. "Fiords, Shores, and Islands of New Zealand" is a birding trip—from the Firth of Thames to Stewart Island. Participants can expect to see a wide variety of endemics and seabirds. Maximum of 15 participants; local guides join the trip at various stages.

Earthwatch
9 days / $$ (from New Plymouth) / January, February. "Pacific Basin Volcanoes" is a research trip based at Mount Taranaki, in Egmont National Park, on the North Island. Volunteers study the volcanic history of the region, collect rock samples, and conduct topographic and magnetic surveys.

13 days / $$ (from Kaikoura) / January. A research trip to study the seabirds of the Kaikoura Peninsula, on the South Island. Volunteers help capture and band chicks and record gull behavior.

Field Guides. 14 days / $$$ (from Auckland) / November. A birding trip to all the major habitats from the thermal geysers of Rotorua to Milford Sound to the Royal Albatross nesting colony at Taiaroa Head. Pelagic trips off both the North and South Islands allow you to observe many seabirds—half of all New Zealand's birds are seabirds. Maximum of 16 participants, 2 leaders.

Field Studies Council. 28 days / $$$ (from London) / November. "Land of the Kiwi: A Tour of New Zealand" is a natural history study tour. You'll visit Little

Barrier Island, the giant Kauri forests of the north, Rotorua and its thermals, and several of New Zealand's twenty national parks, including Urewera, Tongariro, Fiordland, and Mount Cook. There is also a trip on Milford Sound, where it's possible to spot the jaunty Fiordland Crested Penguin. A day is spent on the Hollyford Track, and there is a visit to the Royal Albatross and Yellow-eyed Penguin colonies near Dunedin. Two leaders accompany the trip.

Geo Expeditions. 14 days / $$ (from Auckland) / February, October. A general natural history trip. Participants walk the Milford Track in Fiordland National Park, visit Stewart Island, and walk on glaciers at Mount Cook National Park. Maximum of 15 participants; Mark Hanger, well-known New Zealand naturalist, leads the trip.

International Research Expeditions. 14 days / $ (from Auckland) / November–May. A research trip exploring the role that mountain streams play in the diverse ecology of southern New Zealand.

Journeys. 14 days / $$ (from Auckland) / February, May, July, September–December. "Natural Heritage Odyssey" is an exploration of the birds, plants, and geology of the North and South Islands. You'll visit glaciers, mountains, hot springs, forests, and the coast. The trip is led by Mark Hanger, a well-known local naturalist and founder of Nature Quest New Zealand. The July and November departures are family trips.

Mountain Travel/Sobek. 14 days / $$–$$$ (from Auckland) / December–March. "New Zealand Explorer" and "Walking Wild New Zealand" are both trips to the South Island. You'll hike the Routeburn and Greystone tracks across the Southern Alps, explore Franz Josef Glacier in Westland National Park, and visit Mount Cook National Park as well.

Nature Expeditions International. 21 days / $$ (from Auckland) / February, March, November, December. "New Zealand Walking Expedition" hikes the Milford Track and visits Mount Cook National Park, the fern forests of Urewera National Park, and the thermal wonders of Rotorua.

Naturetrek

17 days / $$$ (from London) / November. A botanical journey to both the North and South Islands, focusing on the ancient plant families: Lichens, Bryophytes, Psilophytes, and Steridophytes. All the major regions are visited, including the podocarp and kauri forests of the north, the high herb fields of the Hollyford Valley, the Red Beech forest in Fiordland National Park, the rain forest of Milford Sound, and Mount Cook—home of the endemic Mount Cook Lily (which is not a lily at all, but rather a giant buttercup, *Ranunculus lyalli*).

32 days / $$ (from London) / November. "National Parks of New Zealand" explores the North, South, and Stewart Islands, and includes two short treks as well—one to Martin's Bay in Fiordland National Park and the other to Mason's Bay on Stewart Island. This trip is designed to provide a comprehensive overview of the wildlife of the country. Two leaders accompany the trip; one is Rodney Russ, well-known New Zealand naturalist.

Overseas Adventure Travel. 14 days / $$ (from Auckland) / November, December. On the South Island, this trip includes the Routeburn Track—4 days through Mount Aspiring and Fiordland National Parks.

Pacific Exploration Company. 7–14 days / $$ (from Auckland) / October–April. Hiking in New Zealand, including the Milford, Routeburn, and Greenstone Valley tracks, among others. Mostly run for independent travelers and small groups.

Questers. 21 days / $$$$ (from Los Angeles) / October. A general natural history trip with visits to Stewart Island, Fiordland National Park, Milford Sound and the Eglinton Valley, Martin's Bay (where the Fiordland Crested Penguin nests), Mount Cook National Park, Cape Kidnappers Gannet Sanctuary, Rotorua, the Bay of Islands, and Cape Reinga (New Zealand's northernmost point). You'll study birds, plants, trees, geysers, and glaciers as you explore the country from south to north. A combination New Zealand–Australia trip is also offered (see the section on Australia, page 269).

Southern Heritage Tours. A variety of natural history tours including: "The Nature of New Zealand, Bird Trail"; "Geology Trail"; "Forest Trail"; and "Marine Trail." These four trips are each 15 days in length, and each is accompanied by a specialist in the field. Other trips concentrate on particular areas of the country: Fiordland, Stewart Island, Marlborough Sound, the Chatham Islands, the subantarctic islands, and the "Bird Islands of the Hauraki Gulf." A more general program, "In Search of the Southern Ark," spends 15 days exploring the country from Auckland to Dunedin. Frequent departures; costs vary, depending on trip chosen. Stewart Island, aboard the research vessel *Acheron,* is $1,700 for 7 days; the Southern Ark trip is $2,400 for 15 days.

VENT. 14 days / $$$ (from Auckland) / November. A birding trip with special emphasis on finding endemics. Maximum of 14 participants; Mark Hanger, noted New Zealand naturalist, leads the trip.

Voyagers International. 14 days / $$$ (from Los Angeles) / April, November. Two wildlife and plant photography trips: the April trip is led by Mary Ellen

Schultz and Charley Krebs, and offers an optional extension to Fiji; the November trip is led by Ron Rosenstock and offers an optional extension to Australia. Maximum of 12 participants.

Wings/Sunbird. 17 days / $$ (from Auckland) / November. A birdwatching trip visiting the Firth of Thames, Little Barrier Island, Kapiti Island, Taiaroa Head, and Stewart Island in search of seabirds and endemic landbirds. Participants can expect to see nearly all of New Zealand's 40 endemics, including Brown Kiwi, Weka, Wrybill, Black Stilt, Kaka, Kea, Rifleman, Stitchbird, and Saddleback. Maximum of 12 participants, 2 leaders. This trip can be taken as an extension of the Australian tour (see the section on Australia, page 269).

Zegrahm Expeditions. 17 days / $$ (from Auckland) / November. A birding expedition led by Arnold Small and Rodney Russ, noted birders.

NEW GUINEA

The largest of the South Pacific islands, and the second largest island in the world, New Guinea is divided in half politically. The western half of the island is the province of Irian Jaya, part of the huge archipelago nation of Indonesia; the eastern half is the nation of Papua New Guinea.

This is the land of birds of paradise and bowerbirds, of tree kangaroos and crocodiles. Animal life here is closely related to that of Australia. Because the dominant vegetation cover is lowland rain forest, there are hundreds of species of orchids and rhododendrons, and, adding to this abundance, over 11,000 species of plants, including 2,000 ferns.

Owing to PNG's location at the intersection of two biogeographic regions, there are over 750 species of birds here, including 33 birds of paradise. Also here are the giant Bird-wing Butterfly and the Ulysses Swallowtail, possibly the most beautiful butterfly in the world.

Popular destinations include the Sepik River, the central highlands, and Ambua and Bensbach lodges, the latter having comfortable first-class accommodations. PNG still has some of the least disturbed tropical forestland in the world (although that, sadly, is changing as a result of poor logging practices), making this culturally fascinating country also a prime ecotourist destination.

TOUR OPERATORS

Birdquest. A birdwatching tour to Irian Jaya. (See the section on Indonesia, page 258).

Field Guides. 20 days / $$$ (from Port Moresby) / July. This birdwatching trip concentrates on finding as many birds of paradise (and other birds, of course) as possible. Past trips have seen 24 different birds of paradise! Maximum of 14 participants, 2 leaders. A 6-day extension to Bensbach Lodge and a 4-day Fiji stopover are available at additional cost.

Geo Expeditions. 14 days / $$ (from Port Moresby) / March, June, October. Combination natural history and cultural trips to the Sepik River and the central highlands. You'll trek through the territory of the Huli Wigmen and raft the Tagari River. Maximum of 15 participants.

International Expeditions. 13 days / $$$$ (from Port Moresby) / July, September. A general natural history tour, including a 3-day boat trip on the Sepik River.

Journeys. 17 days / $$ (from Port Moresby) / January–December. A combination natural history, trekking, and cultural trip to the Sepik River and the central highlands.

Nature Expeditions International. 16 days / $$$ (from Port Moresby) / June, August, September. A combination natural history and cultural trip to the highlands, rivers, and coast.

See & Sea. 11 days / $$ (from Port Moresby) / January–December. Diving and live-aboards. Some of the world's most unusual reef creatures are found on the oceanic reefs in the waters of the Bismarck Sea. You may see Calico Scorpionfish, the hot-pink and deadly Stonefish, and the red-and-yellow Leaf-Fish, in addition to rays, sharks, and sometimes Whale Shark. Cruises up the Sepik River are also available.

Special Expeditions. 17 days / $$$$ (from Port Moresby) / August, October. "Three Faces of Papua New Guinea" is a combination natural history and cultural trip, and includes an 11-night cruise aboard the *Melanesian Discoverer*. You'll visit the southern highlands and Ambua Lodge, then spend 4 days on the Sepik River, before continuing to several outer islands, including the Trobriands and the D'Entrecasteaux Islands. On Fergusson Island, you can see the many extinct volcanos, geysers, fumaroles, and hot springs.

Swan Hellenic. 18 days / $$$$ (from London) / June, September. A combination natural history and cultural trip including a 3-day cruise on the Sepik River and 2 nights at Ambua Lodge, a birdwatching hot spot. In the Tari Basin you'll have a chance to see some birds of paradise. Two leaders accompany the trip.

Trans Niugini Tours. 9 days / $$ (from Port Moresby) / January–December. A natural history trip that includes stays at the Ambua and Karawari lodges—good for birding—and a trip on the Sepik River. Other natural history and cultural tours are offered.

Wings. 22 days / $$$ (from Port Moresby) / August. A birdwatching trip visiting all the major habitats in search of endemics, especially birds of paradise—participants may expect to see about 20 of the possible 33. Then on to New Britain Island for 5 additional days of hunting up more endemics (about 30 are possible). Nighttime owling could produce the New Britain Boobook. Other endemics include Dahl's Fantail, New Britain Paradise Kingfisher, New Britain Friarbird, and Grey Myzomela. You'll visit Pokili, famous for its thermal nesting megapodes, which deposit their eggs in the loose soil heated by active volcanism.

VENT. 21 days / $$$ (from Cairns) / August. A birdwatching trip in search of birds of paradise—about 20 are usually seen, sometimes more—and other endemic species. The trip is timed to maximize the chance of seeing these spectacular birds displaying at their traditional leks in full plumage. All the major regions are visited, including both Ambua and Bensbach lodges. Maximum 10 participants, 1 leader.

SOUTH PACIFIC ISLANDS

There are hundreds of islands scattered like buckshot all across the vast South Pacific, straddling the International Date Line and lying roughly between the Tropics of Cancer and Capricorn. Though largely coral reefs and atolls, some are volcanic in origin. Most of these islands have (or had) endemic species of birds, animals, and plants. Sadly, however, many are now extinct (or extirpated). Some of the islands still have their own families of birds, such as the Kagu, on New Caledonia.

One of the countries frequently visited on nature tours is Fiji, comprising the two major islands of Viti Levu and Vanua Levu and 800 smaller islands. The range of habitat—rain forest, savannah, marsh, river valleys and lakes, and reefs—has made for a corresponding diversity of species. Despite logging, soil erosion, and over-fishing, which are environmental threats here as elsewhere in the region, Fiji and other small islands of the South Pacific still retain their "island paradise" character.

TOUR OPERATORS

Betchart Expeditions. 14 days / $$$ (from Majuro, Marshall Islands) / July. A combination natural history and cultural trip to Micronesia: the Marshall Islands,

Pohnpei, Nan Madol, Chuuk, Guam, Yap, and Palau. You'll go birdwatching, snorkeling, and visit archaeological sites in addition to traditional villages and markets. The trip is run by Betchart for the Natural History Museum of Los Angeles County.

Cousteau Society. 14 days / $$$ (from Los Angeles) / July, August. "Project Ocean Search" is an educational project offered in different South Pacific locations each summer. In 1991 it was in Fiji. Marine biologists, photographers (Nikonos V underwater equipment is available on board), and Cousteau Society representatives accompany the trip. There are daily dives and evening slide presentations and lectures. Participants must be certified divers; there is no instruction. Maximum of 30 participants.

Earthwatch. 9 days / $$ (from Malololailai Island, Fiji) / July, August. "Micro-Atolls of Fiji" is a research expedition. Volunteers map the micro-atolls and collect a few as specimens for lab analysis in an effort to discover how reefs recover from cyclones and other natural disasters.

Field Guides. A 4-day stopover to Fiji is offered as part of their birding tour to Papua New Guinea (see the section on PNG, page 275).

Oceanic Society Expeditions. 14 days / $$$ (from Los Angeles) / May, June. A combination snorkeling and cultural trip to Micronesia. You visit Pohnpei, Nan Madol, Guam, Yap, and Palau, and have the opportunity to snorkel some of the best sites in the South Pacific. Maximum of 16 participants.

Scripps Aquarium. 14 days / $$$$ (from Los Angeles) / May, June. A diving and specimen-collecting trip to the Astrolabe Reef, off Kadavu, Fiji. One week is spent on a live-aboard. Seminars and discussions are an important part of the daily routine. Only certified divers may join the expedition. Maximum of 14 participants.

See & Sea. 7 days (or more) / $$$ (from various South Pacific locations) / January–December. Dive trips and live-aboards in Fiji, the Solomon Islands, Vanuatu, Palau, Yap, and Chuuk Lagoon, all of which offer exciting diving—from the great wreck of the S.S. *Coolidge* off Vanuatu to Palau's legendary Quadruple Blue Hole. Most trips take 16 to 20 participants.

VENT. 27 days / $$$ (from Apia, Western Samoa) / September. A birdwatching trip to the southwest Pacific—Samoa, Fiji, New Caledonia, Vanuatu, Solomon Islands, and New Britain—in search of endemics and rarities, including the Kagu, a rare denizen of New Caledonian forests. A final stop is made at Varirata National Park in Papua New Guinea to see Raggiana Birds of Paradise displaying. Maximum of 12 participants, 1 leader.

Voyagers International. 17 days / $$$ (from Honolulu, Hawaii) / February–March. A birding trip to the islands of Micronesia. Participants fly among the islands searching out endemics. Maximum of 12 participants; well-known field-guide author Doug Pratt leads the trip.

Wilderness Travel. 14 days / $$$ (from Nadi, Fiji) / June, September. A combination natural history and cultural trip to Fiji. Participants snorkel, hike, and river raft; diving is available to certified divers. Islands visited include Mana, Viti Levu, and Taveuni. Maximum of 15 participants.

Wings. A 5-day stopover in New Britain is offered as part of their birding trip to Papua New Guinea (see the section on PNG, page 276).

THE TOUR OPERATORS

This chapter presents an annotated list of the tour operators whose trips are described in the previous chapters. To the right of the company name, we list the types of tours offered. The vast majority are "general," meaning either that the tours have an overall focus on nature or that the company's offerings are so broad that they cover nearly all fields of interest. The next most popular are those for specific interests—birding, whale watching, botany, photography, diving, and so on. We've also indicated whether the company has service trips, research expeditions, or educational programs, and whether they offer trips that are designed for senior citizens, children, or families.

The introduction to this book includes suggestions on choosing a tour. Be aware that the companies listed here are almost exclusively tour operators, not tour packagers. With rare exception, they research, plan, organize, and operate the tours described. Packagers are really just agents. Often you can buy a nature tour through a packager, although in most cases it is preferable to deal directly with the operator.

All foreign tour operators that we discuss offer tours with English-speaking guides. Prices for their trips have been given in dollars, but some companies prefer that you pay in their local currency (Dutch guilders, British pounds, and so on). Also, many British companies include airfare from London in their tour price. If you prefer to join a British tour at the destination, you can make that arrangement, and it is likely to result in a lower tour price.

For the most part, a tour with a foreign company can offer some striking differences—accommodations are sometimes modest, and participants are likely to be more knowledgeable about natural history in general. Foreign operators also go where U.S. companies do not. British companies frequently visit continental European destinations, and they have pioneered travel to Eastern Europe.

In choosing a tour operator, the primary considerations are leadership and experience in regard to both the company and the guides it chooses to use. Nearly all the trips listed in this book are accompanied by naturalist guides. Some companies have only a U.S. guide, some a U.S. guide plus local guides, and some use only local guides. Many also feature specialty guides—botanists, ornithologists, geologists, and the like. We feel the best combination is a U.S. guide to see that everything goes smoothly and a local guide or two who really know the terrain. As mentioned in the introduction, look for trips with a small ratio of participants to guides—1:6 or 1:7 is about perfect for a birding trip or animal safari; botany or geology trips can have a higher ratio. There's less noise or distraction in a small group, but a larger group has more eyes with which to spot things.

Just about all these companies link up with a local operator to handle meals and accommodations or local travel. Most have clearly defined ecotourism objectives, which we've highlighted in our descriptions. Although the degree to which these companies are "green" varies, they all consider preservation of the environment a major objective. Many of the operators contribute financially to local or worldwide environmental and conservation organizations, such as the Programme for Belize, Conservation International, or the East African Wild Life Society.

Abercrombie & Kent
1520 Kensington Road, Suite 212
Oak Brook, IL 60521-2141
800-323-7308

General
Animal Safari Cruises

A large and well-established travel company, A & K offers luxury trips to exotic places. They do all the usual trips: tented safaris in Africa, Galápagos cruises, and Antarctic cruises. But they also go to some out-of-the-way corners of the world. A trip we particularly enjoyed was their "Volcanoes and Wildlife" cruise in the Sunda Strait, that bit of water between Java and Sumatra, Indonesia. Rhinocerous Hornbills whooshed overhead nearly every morning! And every day we made a different shore excursion. Our guide was knowledgeable about many aspects of natural history and culture. One evening he performed Balinese dances in the lounge. If you want creature comforts in the wilderness, A & K is the way to go.

Adirondack Mountain Club
Box 867
Lake Placid, NY 12946
518-523-3441

Hiking
Service trips

The club maintains lodges and camps in the Adirondack Park. Facilities and trips are open to the public, though members are entitled to a discount. There is a varied program of one-day and weekend outdoor activities. The service trips are one, three, or five days, and mostly involve trail maintenance.

Adventure Network International
(see Quark Expeditions)

Alaska Wildland Adventures
P.O. Box 389
Girdwood, AK 99587
800-334-8730

General
Seniors

Alaska Wildland has been guiding trips since 1977. They feel that their trips can be both an alternative and an addition to conventional bus tours and cruises. They use experienced guides and take you to places where the crowds don't go. You go to fewer places but spend more time in each, enabling you to have a fuller, richer experience. Their trips are occasionally booked by other tour companies.

Amazon Explorers   General
499 Ernston Road
Parlin, NJ 08859
800-631-5650; fax: 201-721-2344
In business since 1956, the company has never cancelled a confirmed departure, so bookings may be made with confidence. River trips on the Amazon are their specialty.

Amazon Outreach   General
1500 S.E. 3rd Court
Deerfield Beach, FL 33441
305-698-6302
A truly "green" company, run by a Peruvian Indian, Ney Piñero, who specializes in rafting trips down the Amazon. Mr. Piñero builds a raft for each trip and then donates the rafts (at the end of each trip) to local Indians to be used as floating hospitals in the jungle. He is deeply concerned about the rain forest and its delicate ecosystem—as well as the native peoples who live there.

Amazon Tours and Cruises   General
1013 South Central Avenue
Glendale, CA 91204
800-423-2791, 800-477-4470; fax: 818-246-9909
Headquartered in Iquitos, Peru, Amazon Camp and Cruises was established in 1970. Continuously under U.S. management, they handle passengers of major tour companies from many countries. They operate three riverboats and a jungle lodge. Expeditions are escorted by native (local) guides.

American Museum of Natural History   General
Central Park West at 79 Street   Cultural
New York, NY 10024-5192
800-462-8687, 212-769-5700
The museum runs a variety of luxurious natural history trips—tours and cruises. The cruises are aboard ships such as the *Illiria,* M.V. *Sea Bird,* or M.S. *Polaris.* All are accompanied by museum naturalists in addition to the shipboard guides. The program changes from year to year, but standard destinations include the Galápagos, Central America, and Alaska. Cultural trips are offered as well, and sometimes are combined with natural history.

Anglo-Israel Association
9 Bentinck Street
London W1M 5RP
United Kingdom
01-486-2300; fax: 01-224-3908

Birding
Botany

AIA has been running tours since 1987, and they only go to Israel. Their nature tours are guided by ornithologists, botanists, and naturalists from the Society for the Protection of Nature in Israel.

Appalachian Mountain Club
5 Joy Street
Boston, MA 02108
617-523-0636

Hiking
Service trips

The AMC maintains huts and lodges in the White Mountains of New Hampshire. These are open to the public; members are entitled to a discount. Hut-to-hut hiking is but one of many options. A full range of educational workshops and guided hikes are offered each year. The trail service projects operate in New Hampshire, Maine, Alaska, and the Virgin Islands.

Arctic Edge/TransSiberian Tours
P.O. Box 4850
Whitehorse, Yukon Territory
Canada Y1A 4N6
403-633-5470; fax: 403-633-3820

General
Canoeing
Diving
Birding

These two companies operate together. Arctic Edge offers rafting, canoeing, trekking, and dogsledding in the Yukon and Northwest Territories. As conservationists, their trips have always been "ecotours."

TransSiberian Tours, their Russian partners, offers natural history and cultural trips, including scuba diving in Lake Baikal and birdwatching. Trips are accompanied by local naturalist guides.

Arctic Odysseys
3430 Evergreen Point Road
Medina, WA 98039
206-455-1960

General
Polar Bears

Natural history trips to the High Arctic. Custom itineraries can be arranged.

Asian Pacific Adventures
826 South Sierra Bonita Avenue
Los Angeles, CA 90036
800-825-1680; fax: 213-935-3156

General
Cultural

The company offers adventure tours of Asia and the Pacific, mostly in combination with cultural tours. Some of their treks have a natural history emphasis. Guides are Americans, some of whom live in Asia.

ASPNI   General
330 Seventh Avenue
New York, NY 10001
212-947-2820; fax: 212-629-0508
This is the U.S. office of the Society for the Protection of Nature in Israel. SPNI is known as "Israel's Sierra Club," and they are a membership organization—the only mass-participation environmental movement in the Middle East. They run a variety of tours ranging from one day to two weeks; all trips are accompanied by experienced field naturalists.

Attour   Birding
2027 Partridge Lane
Highland Park, IL 60035
708-831-0207; fax: 708-831-0309
Attour does one thing only and does it well: birding tours to Attu, the westernmost island in the Aleutian chain. The trip is like a summer camp—you stay in one place and bike, hike, or drive around the island looking for birds, mostly Asian vagrants. Leaders take you out in small groups made up of keen birdwatchers—beginners and experts alike.

Baja Expeditions   General
2625 Garnet Avenue   Whale watching
San Diego, CA 92109   Diving
619-581-3311; fax: 619-581-6542
This company was begun in 1974, and, as the name implies, it specializes in trips to Baja California and the surrounding waters. It offers sea kayaking, natural history cruises, scuba diving, and whale watching. Guides and crews are both Mexican and American, and there is an office in La Paz. Baja Expeditions acts as an outfitter for several organizations such as the Sierra Club and the American Cetacean Society.

Betchart Expeditions   General
21601 Stevens Creek Boulevard
Cupertino, CA 95014
800-252-4910
A natural history travel company that specializes in developing programs for non-profit organizations—museums, zoos, and so forth. U.S. guides are naturalists.

Biological Journeys   Whale watching
1696 Ocean Drive   Birding
McKinleyville, CA 95521   Photography
800-548-7555; fax: 707-839-4656

We have nothing but good things to say about BJ! Formed in 1981, they are a
small company whose objective is to provide direct involvement with the earth's
great marine wilderness areas. The trips we've been on (a whale-watching trip in
the Sea of Cortez and a Galápagos cruise) were superb—both in quality of leadership and the expertise and enthusiasm of the (U.S.) guides.

Bird Bonanzas   Birding
P.O. Box 611563
North Miami, FL 33161
305-895-0607

A small company offering birding tours at a low price. Destinations vary from year
to year, and there are many repeat clients. Check itineraries and trip conditions
carefully, since we've heard reports that meals, for instance, are sometimes not
included in the published cost. Leaders are experienced ornithologists, often residents of the destination country.

Birding   Birding
Periteau House
Winchelsea, East Sussex TN36 4EA
United Kingdom
0797-223223

John Gooders, author of popular "where to go birding" guides for Britain and
Europe, and his wife, Robbie, run the company. Most of their trips are week-long,
single-center holidays; groups are limited to sixteen members, usually with one or
two leaders. Many trips are guided by the Gooders, others by in-country leaders.

Birdquest   Birding
Two Jays, Kemple End, Birdy Brow
Stonyhurst, Lancashire BB6 9QY
United Kingdom
0254-826317; fax: 0254-826780

"Birdquest is strongly committed to bird protection and to conservation in general. We have raised funds for bird-oriented conservation projects in such countries as Poland, Madagascar, Mauritius, Thailand, and China. . . . Operators of
birding or wildlife holidays are particularly well placed to influence governments
when decisions are to be made concerning the future of important areas for birds
and wildlife in general, since the potential local income from developing special

interest tourism can . . . offset the potential short-term gain from destroying an area. We keep a close watch on environmental issues in the countries we visit and frequently do whatever we can to support local or international conservation initiatives."

Most trips run with a maximum of sixteen participants and two leaders. Birdquest travels the globe—from Tibet to Tanzania. People we've talked to swear by Birdquest; clearly they have a good reputation, since many (about 70 percent) of their clients are repeat customers.

Birds and Birders   **Birding**
P.O. Box 737
9700 AS Groningen
The Netherlands
050-145925; fax: 050-144717
"Birds and Birders, we care for both" is the motto of this nature tour company founded in 1988. Trips are mainly to northern, central, and eastern Europe. Small groups (ten participants, one leader), good accommodations. On our trip to the Czech Republic we visited new national parks and learned about wildlife conservation. Cultural stops were included. Tours can be booked directly or through Motmot Nature Tours.

BirdWatch Costa Rica   **Birding**
Apartado 7911
1000 San Jose
Costa Rica
fax: 506-281-573
This is a small, specialist company offering personalized, flexible trips to many nature lodges in mostly "off the beaten track" birding locations in each of the major habitats, from the southwestern Pacific lowlands to the northern Caribbean coast. Among the lodges booked are Tiskita, Selva Verde, Rara Avis, and Solimar. Details are well looked after and trips run smoothly, owing to the thoughtfulness of owner Simon Ellis.

Borrobol Birding   **Birding**
c/o Josephine Barr
519 Park Avenue
Kenilworth, IL 60043
800-323-5463
One-week birding programs based at Borrobol Lodge in the flow country of northern Scotland. First-class accommodations. Small groups (six participants) and knowledgeable guides. Some cultural stops as well. Our experience at Borrobol was superior in every regard.

Bottom Time Adventures   Diving
P.O. Box 11919
Fort Lauderdale, FL 33339-1919
800-234-8464; fax: 305-563-0584

Specializing in dive trips in the Bahamas. You live aboard the *Bottom Time II,* an owner-built and -operated catamaran.

Branta Holidays   Birding
7 Wingfield Street
London SE15 4LN
United Kingdom
071-639-1257; fax: 071-277-7720

This company's aim "is to offer good quality birding in a relaxed and enjoyable atmosphere. Experienced birdwatchers have the chance to see the specialties around but we do not forget the wishes of less experienced or less mobile members of our group." Good accommodations, wine with picnic lunches, and small groups (up to fifteen, with one leader). Trips are to northern and western Europe and North Africa and the Middle East.

Brazil Nuts   General
1150 Post Road   Cultural
Fairfield, CT 06430
800-553-9959

The company only handles travel to Brazil. Natural history destinations include the Amazon and the Pantanal. There are lodges and river trips. Guides are Brazilian.

Breakaway Adventure Travel Hiking   General
93 Cherry Street
New Canaan, CT 06840
800-955-5635; fax: 203-972-6557

Mostly an adventure tour company, but some of their hiking and sailing trips include natural history activities.

Bruce Safaris   Birding
P.O. Box 40662   Animal safaris
Nairobi   Botany
Kenya   Geology
254-2-227311; fax: 254-2-223647

In business since 1962, Bruce Safaris offers special-interest and unusual safaris. They operate mainly in Kenya and Tanzania, but can also make arrangements with companies in other African countries.

Cal Nature Tours   General
S.V.L. 7310   Cultural
Victorville, CA 92392
619-241-2322

Cal's trip to northern Europe and Scandinavia is a combination cultural and natural history trip, accompanied by U.S. guides. They also book tours for ENEX.

Caligo Ventures   General
156 Bedford Road   Birding
Armonk, NY 10504
800-426-7781

A travel agency that runs trips to Trinidad and Tobago, Venezuela, Panama, and Belize. Caligo Ventures works with local operators and tour guides, "ensuring that the economic benefits of our travel programs have a significant impact on the local economy. . . ." Some profits are donated to local conservation organizations in the countries visited. We can't speak for all their tours, but we experienced difficulties with the arrangements they made for us.

Canadian Nature Tours/Federation of   Birding
   Ontario Naturalists   Botany
355 Lesmill Road   General
Don Mills, Ontario M3B 2W8   Children
Canada
416-444-8419; fax: 416-444-9866

Small groups, varied program, specialist guides. All proceeds are used for environmental conservation in Canada.

CanoAndes
(see Sunny Land Expeditions)

Cheesemans' Ecology Safaris   General
20800 Kittredge Road
Saratoga, CA 95070
408-867-1371

All tours are nonsmoking. Most trips are accompanied by Doug (a zoology professor) and Gail Cheeseman, and a resident naturalist in the country where they tour. Small groups, one leader for six people. Read the tour conditions carefully, as we have heard there are extras (such as night drives in Kenya) that might be at additional cost.

Churchill Wilderness Encounter
P.O. Box 9
Churchill, Manitoba R0B 0E0
Canada
204-675-2248

Polar Bears
Birding
Whale watching

A local company offering a variety of natural history vacations in Churchill. All trips are led by local guides.

Clipper Adventure Cruises
7711 Bonhomme Avenue
St. Louis, MO 63105-1956
314-727-2929

General

Luxury natural history cruises aboard medium-sized vessels such as the *Yorktown Clipper* and larger ships such as the 138-passenger *World Discoverer.* Often the ships (or blocks of cabins on them) are used by other nature tour companies; they run some of the trips themselves. U.S. naturalist guides accompany all cruises.

Colorado River and Trail Expeditions
P.O. Box 57575
5058 South 300 West
Salt Lake City, UT 84157-0575
800-253-7328; fax 801-268-1193

General
Photography

These folks have been rafting rivers since 1971. Most trips are down the Green and Colorado rivers in Utah, and the Colorado River through the Grand Canyon in Arizona. Discounts for children under sixteen.

Cornell's Adult University
626 Thurston Avenue
Ithaca, NY 14850-2490
607-255-6260

General
Educational

Learning vacations in Maine, out West, and in Hawaii.

The Cousteau Society/Project
  Ocean Search
930 West 21 Street
Norfolk, VA 23517
804-627-1144

Educational

Marine biology projects aboard the *Calypso* with the Costeau Society. Minimum age is sixteen.

Cox & Kings   **General**
511 Lexington Avenue   **Botany**
New York, NY 10017
800-999-1758

A British natural history touring company. Some of their North and South American trips are run through U.S. companies, such as Biological Journeys. Their
botany tours of Europe are wonderful! We particularly enjoyed our botanical tour
of Crete. One of the keys to a good trip, such as that one was, is excellent leadership, which we had in the form of Mary Briggs. Cox & Kings and the Field Studies Council are the only companies that offer a range of botany tours. This is a
pity, since botany is readily enjoyable by nearly everyone, even inveterate birdwatchers like ourselves.

Cox & Kings is dedicated to responsible and constructive tour operating. "Our
philosophy is quite simple: conservation and long-term environmental tourism
must be developed as a powerful force to preserve some of the world's most threatened and beautiful areas. . . . Cox & Kings will buy one acre of rain forest in Belize
for every client booking a wildlife holiday." They donate to other environmental
protection and research projects as well: "In this way all our clients will actively
participate in the conservation of fragile species and their habitat."

Denver Museum of Natural History   **General**
2001 Colorado Boulevard   **Educational**
Denver, CO 80205-5798
303-370-6387; fax: 303-331-6492

Like many natural history museums and zoos around the country, the Denver
Museum offers a variety of domestic and foreign travel study courses. Museum
staff accompany the trips. Some courses are available for teacher credit.

Dire Wolf Natural History Tours   **General**
97 Genung Road
Ithaca, NY 14850
607-273-9316

General natural history tours to New York State concentrating on geology and
botany, as well as history, and led by Dr. Ronald Schassburger, founder of Dire Wolf,
who says you will "see the land of the Iroquois through the eyes of a naturalist."

Discovery Charters   **General**
P.O. Box 1182
Dunedin
New Zealand
03-453-6986

Discovery Charters operates the S.V. *Tradewind,* a tall ship that sails to Fiji, the subantarctic islands of New Zealand, and to the Falkland Islands and Antarctica. The *Tradewind* is a two-masted auxiliary topsail schooner, 123 feet long, with twelve sails—it's a beauty! Nineteen passengers can be accommodated. Discovery Charters has been at the forefront of subantarctic tourism since 1987. Naturalist guides have detailed knowledge of endemic plants, birds, and animals. Sailing time is minimal, so you have "days rather than hours in these areas and superb photographic and firsthand wildlife experiences."

The Dream Team   Diving
P.O. Box 033271
Indialantic, FL 32903-0271
407-723-9312
Live-aboard dive trips on the M.V. *Dream Too.* Since 1980, the Dream Team has swum with dolphins. Friendly atmosphere; all safety standards met; "good diving without frills."

Earth Tours   General
93 Bedford Street, Box 3C   Seniors
New York, NY 10014
212-675-6515
Earth Tours is an adventure tour company with an environmental focus. Their main program is hiking and natural history on the island of Dominica, in the Caribbean. "We always incorporate the use of local tour guides in addition to Earth Tours personnel. . . . We are currently working out details to support the preservation of this ecosystem [rain forest] on Dominica with both not-for-profit conservation groups and the Forestry Department."

Earthwatch   Research
680 Mt. Auburn Street
Watertown, MA 02272
617-926-8200
The leader in research vacations, Earthwatch has well over 100 "Missions to Earth" every year. Most projects are ongoing over a period of three, five, or even fifteen years. You can study and help everything from Echidnas (primitive monotremes) in Australia to Coyotes in Yellowstone, from rain forests in Mexico to lakes in Hungary. No previous experience is required, and everyone is welcome on these trips. As you work together, a feeling of camaraderie quickly develops. But choose your expedition carefully; for example, some trips involve tracking, but not seeing, the animals you're helping. Remember, first and foremost these are research expeditions—you're assisting scientists. (Of course there's free time to

explore related interests.) Everyone we've spoken to who's been part of an Earth-watch team has loved it.

Eco Expeditions
(see Zegrahm Expeditions)

Ecotour Expeditions   **General**
P.O. Box 1066   **Families**
Cambridge, MA 02238-1066
800-688-1822; fax: 617-576-0552
Ecotour specializes in trips to the Brazilian Amazon, and their trips are real in-depth natural history studies of this rich ecosystem. Guides are all scientists. The aim of their trips is to expose participants to the tremendous diversity of life that exists in tropical forests. "Our expeditions are thorough, but please keep in mind, scientific does not mean boring! . . . In the course of every expedition we see something we've never seen before." The devastating pace of deforestation, and the accompanying extinction of species, is a vast tragedy. With their touring program, Ecotour Expeditions hopes to awaken everyone to the gravity of this crisis.

Elderhostel   **Seniors**
75 Federal Street   **General**
Boston, MA 02110   **Educational**
617-426-8056
Hundreds of courses in the United States, Canada, and abroad to suit any interest, including natural history. These programs are for over-sixties only, although a younger person (at least fifty) may accompany a participant. Accommodations are modest, and you often stay in college dormitories or biology field stations, but this helps to keep the costs down. Elderhostel trips are never very expensive—U.S. trips cost about $50 a day; foreign trips include international airfare and are somewhat more, largely depending on the country visited (Costa Rica is about $125 a day, Australia runs $185 a day). U.S. and Canadian programs are one week long, foreign programs two to four weeks. (Because the programs vary so much, and so many are offered, we haven't included Elderhostel courses in the trip descriptions. But their natural history courses are well worth taking—everyone seems to enjoy them.)

Enex   **General**
Mateje Kopeckeho 8
16900 Prague 6
Czech Republic
Environmental excursions in western and southern Bohemia. The walking tours are led by an experienced environmentalist, a former hydraulic engineer with the

United National Environmental Programme in Nairobi. Historical and cultural sites are also visited. Trips can be booked directly or through Cal Nature Tours.

Escapes Unlimited   General
269 N. Glassell
Orange, CA 92666
800-243-7227; fax: 714-771-8549
A combination adventure–cultural–natural history travel company. Small groups, some trekking.

Eye of the Whale   Whale watching
P.O. Box 1269   Hiking
Kapa'au, HI 96755   General
800-657-7730
Run by Mark and Beth Goodoni, Eye of the Whale offers people a different Hawaii. "Through firsthand experience, Eye of the Whale strives to develop awareness, appreciation, and understanding of Hawaii's delicate ecosystem." The Goodonis lead all their trips, taking small groups only. They developed the "Earth, Fire, and Sea" seven-day holiday that is now used by several large tour operators.

Far Flung Adventures   River rafting
P.O. Box 377
Terlingua, TX 79852
800-359-4138; fax: 915-371-2325
Far Flung runs several of the major rivers in the Southwest, most notably the Rio Grande in Big Bend National Park. "Rivers are the roots of the oceans and the arteries of the continents. They bind and nourish the lands through which they flow." Some of the trips have a natural history emphasis. Experienced guides accompany all trips. Far Flung is licensed by the National Park Service and other federal and state agencies.

Federation of Ontario Naturalists   General
428 Falconer Street
Port Elgin, Ontario NOH 2C2
Canada
519-832-5928
The federation, founded in 1931, is committed to protecting and increasing awareness of Ontario's natural areas and wildlife. They do run some trips, and all profits are used for conservation programs. The majority of their offerings are one to three days, and each covers a single aspect of natural history: botany, butterflies,

geology, birds, and so forth. Programs are for members only, and all are limited to fifteen participants.

Field Guides   **Birding**
P.O. Box 160723
Austin, TX 78716-0723
512-327-4953; fax: 512-327-9231
A company that cares about birds, ecology, and environmental conservation, Field Guides "funds and otherwise supports a variety of carefully selected conservation foundations, projects, and special appeals. Is it not only natural that worldwide birding and worldwide conservation travel hand in hand? . . . Birds preceded humans on this planet. . . . Their intensity brightens our existence." Among the projects that Field Guides contributes to is Conservation International's El Triunfo Project (El Triunfo is a preserve in southern Mexico). Field Guides is also a corporate sponsor of the Nature Conservancy, Conservation International, and the International Council for Bird Preservation.

This is a professional outfit with extraordinarily well-informed guides; all are excellent field naturalists as well as fine birders. Many have done important research and authored books and articles. The office staff sees to it that all runs smoothly in the field. Groups are small, usually ten to fourteen people, with one or two leaders. We have been very happy with the trips we've taken with Field Guides, and other people we know travel exclusively with them.

Field Studies Council   **Educational**
Preston Montford, Montford Bridge   **General**
Shrewsbury, Shropshire SY4 1HW   **Botany**
United Kingdom
0743-850674; fax: 0743-850178
FSC's motto is "Environmental understanding for all," and having been around for over fifty years, they are truly pioneers in the field. They maintain thirteen centers in Britain and Wales and run an ambitious overseas program as well. Courses are given continuously at the centers; foreign destinations change occasionally, but frequently include Africa and the Middle East, as well as many countries in Europe. Many courses focus on botany and birding, but there are also geology, photography, and ecology courses—both at the centers and abroad. Some courses are suitable for families. A weekend birding workshop we participated in at the Flatford Mill Field Centre was very informative and well run. Each day we went to a different birding locale and habitat; in the evenings there were discussions and informal talks. A small group (twelve) and an experienced field naturalist made all the difference.

Fish Eagle Safaris   **Birding**
102 Stoney Creek   **Animal safaris**
Houston, TX 77024
713-467-5222; fax: 713-464-0103
Fish Eagle Safaris specializes in trips to southern Africa. Many of their birding trips employ local specialists, including authors Ken Newman, Gordon McLean, and Ian Sinclair; these trips appear to be for keen birdwatchers. Bert du Plessis, founder of Fish Eagle Safaris, leads animal safaris to Kruger Park and Mkuzi Game Reserve, among other destinations.

Flora and Fauna Fieldtours   **Birding**
232 Bellair Drive
Bolton, Ontario L7E 1Z7
Canada
416-857-2235
A small Canadian company. Birding workshops are offered as well as tours.

Focus on Nature Tours   **Birding**
P.O. Box 9021
Wilmington, DE 19809
302-529-1876; fax: 302-529-1085
A small, personal company, with an ever-expanding tour program of birder-friendly trips: small groups and a relaxed pace. They go to some unusual destinations, such as Japan (in winter and spring), southern Costa Rica, and Spain. FONT uses local operators in addition to U.S. guides. There's plenty of informative pre-trip information. Our experience with this operator, as well as that of other people we've heard from, has been excellent.

Foundation for Field Research   **Research**
P.O. Box 2010
Alpine, CA 91903-2010
619-445-9264; fax: 619-445-1893
Research expeditions in Mexico, Grenada, West Africa, and the western United States. Many projects have been going on for a number of years. A staff member accompanies every expedition; teams average about ten people. Volunteers pay their share of food and lodging costs; the second week is less expensive than the first. It is frequently possible to combine work on two or more trips.

Four Corners School of Outdoor Education　　　　　　　　　　**Education**
East Route
Monticello, UT 84535
800-525-4456
A nonprofit corporation offering educational and research trips.

Galápagos Holidays　　　　　　　　　　**General**
745 Gerrard Street East
Toronto M4M 1Y5
Canada
416-469-8212; fax: 416-463-5131
As the name implies, they specialize in trips to the Galápagos. Packaged or individual tours are available. A donation of $25 per passenger is made to the Charles Darwin Research Station; contributions are currently being used to eradicate feral pigs from Santiago Island—a very important project.

Galápagos Travel　　　　　　　　　　**General**
2674 North First Street, Suite 112
San Jose, CA 95134
800-223-3767; fax: 408-434-5917
A specialist in natural history cruises to the Galápagos. The owner of the company (Barry Boyce) is the author of *A Traveler's Guide to the Galápagos Islands.*

Garth Thompson Safari Consultants　　　　　　　　　　**Animal safaris**
P.O. Box 5826
Harare
Zimbabwe
795202; fax: 795-287
Specialists in travel througout Zimbabwe. Operating since 1980.

Geo Expeditions　　　　　　　　　　**General**
P.O. Box 3656
Sonora, CA 95370
800-351-5041; FAX: 209-532-1979
In business since 1982, Geo is "dedicated to the ethic of responsible ecotourism: traveling lightly, thus leaving the land and its peoples undisturbed; and contributing safely to local economies and conservation." Geo visits Africa, India and Nepal, Indonesia, South America, and Australia. Trips are limited to ten to fifteen participants. Overseas trips are coordinated by local outfitters.

Geostar Travel   **Botany**
1240 Berglund Court   **General**
Santa Rosa, CA 95403
800-624-6633; fax: 707-579-2704

Established in 1977. Some Geostar trips are run for organizations such as the Nature Conservancy, Pacific Horticultural Foundation, and the Natural History Museum of Los Angeles. Small groups (ten to fifteen participants); some trips have specialist guides.

Goldeneye Nature Tours   **Birding**
P.O. Box 30416
Flagstaff, AZ 86003
800-624-6606

A small company, Goldeneye has been operating since 1986. Tours are confined to the United States and Canada; all are led by owner John Shipley. No smoking, small groups (usually nine or ten). We've heard good reports from past participants.

Goliath Safaris   **Canoeing**
P.O. Box CH 294   **Animal safaris**
Chisipite, Harare
Zimbabwe
708843; fax: 707994

Safaris in Zimbabwe and river trips on the Zambezi River. The company began operations in 1986. "We are a small family concern with a dedication to animals and their habitat." All trips are led by professional river guides, licensed by National Parks.

Grand Canyon Dories   **River running**
P.O. Box 216
Altaville, CA 95221
209-736-0805; fax: 209-736-2902

Running the Colorado River the way John Wesley Powell did it in 1869—in a wooden boat. The company was created in 1971. All trips are guided and take six to twenty passengers.

Grand Canyon Expeditions   **River rafting**
P.O. Box O
Kanab, UT 84741
800-544-2691

Raft trips down the Colorado River. The company has been in business since 1964. Some special-interest expeditions are offered, including astronomy, geology, and photography. Children eight to sixteen years of age must be accompanied by an adult.

The Great Auk   Birding
105 Admiral Road
Toronto, Ontario M5R 2L7
Canada
416-960-8383; fax: 416-968-1017
Graeme Gibson has been running birding trips to Cuba since 1984. Trips are led by a Cuban ornithologist, and each has a maximum of fifteen participants.

Harper and Hallett   Birding
697 Darlington Road, N.E.
Atlanta, GA 30305
404-233-3974
Birdwatching tours to Alaska, Florida, Montana, and California; also pelagic trips from Gloucester, Massachusetts. Some trips are run for the American Birding Association.

Hawk, I'm Your Sister   Canoeing
P.O. Box 9109
Santa Fe, NM 87504-9109
505-984-2268
Wilderness canoe trips to the Everglades and other U.S. destinations. Some trips are for women only, offering participants "a safe, supportive, noncompetitive environment." Low-impact camping, small groups.

HF Holidays   General
Imperial House, Edgeware Road
Colindale, London NW9 5AL
United Kingdom
081-905-9558; fax: 081-205-0506
HF began operations in 1913, offering walking tours. Today they own (or lease) nineteen country houses in Britain and Europe where participants are based. "Nature Rambles" and other natural history programs are offered at various centers.

High Desert Museum   General
59800 South Highway 97   Educational
Bend, OR 97702
503-382-4754
The museum offers a variety of natural history field excursions ranging from three to ten days. All trips are led by museum staff and other experts.

Himalaya Trekking and Wilderness Expeditions Hiking
1900 Eighth Street
Berkeley, CA 94710
800-777-8735; fax: 510-644-1777
Mostly offer cultural treks, but they also have a few natural history trips. The company is concerned about the ecological problems of the Himalayas. Costs of trips include a donation to Nepal's Annapurna Conservation Project, and funds are matched locally. Small groups lessen the impact on the environment.

Holbrook Travel General
3540 N.W. 13 Street
Gainesville, FL 32609
800-377-7111
A travel agency that specializes in natural history vacations. For every traveler booking a trip through Holbrook to a rain forest destination, Holbrook will contribute $50 to the SOS Rain Forest Project. The goal of the project "is to purchase and preserve an area of tropical rain forest in the state of Rondonia, Brazil, which contains the richest diversity of plants, birds, and butterfly species on Earth." Many of Holbrook's trips are led by specialist guides.

Inca Floats General
1311 63 Street
Emeryville, CA 94608
510-420-1550; fax: 510-420-0947
In business since 1976, Inca Floats specializes in trips to the Galápagos. Trips depart every week of the year, all on small boats.

Inland Bird Tours Birding
94 Hunter Street
Deniliquin, NSW 2710
Australia
058-813378
Birding tours led by Philip Maher, an environmental consultant. Mr. Maher has been conducting a banding study of Plains-wanderers, a rare and endemic Australian bird, for the past decade. He is an accomplished naturalist, and is also knowledgeable about the mammals, reptiles, and plants of his country. People like birding with Maher: "My two days and one night with Phil was one of the finest out-of-door experiences I have ever had," said Tom Arny, a U.S. birder.

Innerasia Expeditions   **Hiking**
2627 Lombard Street   **Cultural**
San Francisco, CA 94123
800-777-8183; fax: 415-346-5535
Mostly cultural trekking, often rigorous, but some natural history trips are offered.

International Expeditions   **General**
One Environs Park
Helena, AL 35080
800-633-4734
A wide variety of trips to many popular natural history destinations. Some trips are
run for the Nature Conservancy. International Expeditions also runs rain forest
workshops in Peru and Costa Rica; some sessions are for educators. They are also
connected with the nonprofit Amazon Center for Environmental Education
(ACEER).

International Journeys   **General**
11595 Kelly Road
Fort Myers, FL 33908
800-622-6525
Trips to the Amazon and the Galápagos, accompanied by a biologist. The company contributes to environmental organizations.

International Oceanographic Foundation   **General**
P.O. Box 499900
Miami, FL 33149-9900
305-361-4697; fax: 305-361-9306
A variety of trips, some aboard such ships as the M.V. *Sea Bird,* the M.V. *Sea Lion,*
and the M.S. *Polaris.* IOF staff accompany the trips.

International Research Expeditions   **Research**
140 University Drive
Menlo Park, CA 94025
415-323-4228
Research trips involving botany, ornithology, oceanography, and zoology, among
other subjects. Most projects are ongoing, and teams work for one- or two-week
sessions. Contributions cover food and lodging and are tax-deductible. Field conditions vary from camping to first-class hotels.

International Zoological Expeditions   **General**
210 Washington Street   **Birding**
Sherborn, MA 01770   **Snorkeling**
508-655-1461
IZE has been specializing in natural history trips to Belize since 1972.

Intersea Research   **Whale watching**
P.O. Box 1667 Research
Friday Harbor, WA 98250
206-378-5980; fax: 206-378-5911
Research trips to study whales: summer trips to Alaska, winter ones to Hawaii. Small groups (ten to fourteen participants) accompanied by research scientists.

Inuit Adventures   **General**
19950 Clark Graham   **Cultural**
Baie d'Urfe, Quebec H9X 3R8
Canada
800-465-9474; fax: 514-457-4626
Inuit Adventures is a cooperative owned by the Inuit and the tourism development department of Quebec. Trips are run summer and winter to Arctic Quebec. Inuit guides lead all the trips. "It is our wish to promote sustainable economic development through our co-operatives by opening our land to travellers. As well, we want to preserve our cultural heritage and our connection to the environment on which we depend, by sharing them with others."

Joseph Van Os
(see TravelWild)

Journeys   **General**
4011 Jackson Road   **Animal safaris**
Ann Arbor, MI 48103   **Families**
800-255-8735; fax: 313-665-2945
Journeys and its partner company, Wildland Adventures, have formed an affiliate organization, the Earth Preservation Fund, which sponsors conservation and community development projects in host countries. Projects funded by EPF include clean-up treks in Nepal, poaching information reward programs in Africa, and contributions to the Caribbean Conservation Corporation in Costa Rica. Additionally, all participants on African safaris automatically become members of a local environmental preservation organization in the countries they visit. A wide variety of trips is offered to practically every corner of the globe; most have a natural history focus.

King Bird Tours   **Birding**
P.O. Box 196, Planetarium Station
New York, NY 10024
212-866-7923

The Asia specialists since 1980. Ben King pioneered birding travel to Asia. Concern for the environment is a top priority for King Bird Tours: "The only way eco-tourism can work is for people to make money from tourists who want to see nature as it ought to be." Tours visit India, Indonesia, Malaysia, the Philippines, China, and Siberia; itineraries vary slightly from year to year.

   Ben leads many of the tours himself, but some trips are led by local field naturalists. Most notable among these is Dennis Yong, in Malaysia. Dennis owns and runs the only Malaysian natural history travel company, Kingfisher Tours. His knowledge of field natural history—especially bird songs and calls—is legendary.

Labrador Scenic   **General**
Box 11
North West River, Labrador AOP 1MO
Canada
709-497-8326

Wilderness tours of Labrador, locally owned and operated. All trips are fully guided.

Learn at Leisure   **Educational**
University of Nottingham   **General**
14 Shakespeare Street
Nottingham NG1 4FJ
United Kingdom
602-483838; fax: 602-472977

Specialists in educational travel for over two decades. Maximum of twenty participants, usually with two leaders. Courses are held in Britain (at the Gibraltar Point Field Station, Horncastle College, and other localities) and abroad. A full range of programs is offered: botany, birdwatching, general natural history, and cultural programs as well.

Lemur Tours   **General**
2562 Noriega Street, #203
San Francisco, CA 94122
800-735-3687; fax: 415-681-6274

Specializing in trips to Madagascar, Lemur Tours is the only Malagasy-American tour operator in the United States. Custom and package tours offered.

Lost World Adventures   General
1189 Autumn Ridge Drive
Marietta, GA 30066
800-999-0558; fax: 404-977-3095

Lost World specializes in trips to Venezuela—from a birding trip to the llanos to a diving expedition off the Caribbean coast to hiking in the Tepuis. The company supports Venezuelan conservation organizations such as the Venezuelan Audubon Society, and uses local guides. We had a first-rate experience with Lost World, staying and birding at a ranch in the llanos, Doña Barbara. Other people we've met who used this company were equally satisfied with their trips and guides.

Marin Discoveries   General
11 First Street   Handicapped
Corte Madera, CA 94925   Learning
415-927-0410   Families

A varied program of one-day and weekend educational and natural history programs. Subjects include earthquakes, botany, animal tracking, and whale watching.
    Some trips are designed for the handicapped; others are suitable for families.

Massachusetts Audubon Society   General
Lincoln, MA 01773   Birding
800-289-9504   Research

An affiliate of the National Audubon Society, Massachusetts Audubon runs an extensive travel program. All trips are accompanied by naturalists and/or ornithologists. Some trips are cruises aboard such vessels as the M.S. *Polaris*. Massachusetts Audubon is also the coordinator for the Caribbean Conservation Corporation's program "Turtles of Tortuguero," a famous research project that has been ongoing since 1954. The CCC is a nonprofit conservation organization that operates the Green Turtle Research Station in Tortuguero, Costa Rica. Volunteers help with nesting and hatchling research on Leatherbacks and Green Sea Turtle tagging. Costs related to the research program are tax-deductible.

Michael Snow   Birding
Apartado 73   Butterflies
7200 Siquirres
Costa Rica
(no telephone)

Mr. Snow guides birders in Costa Rica; he also operates a lodge and private reserve—Viveros Salsipuedes. Trips visit a variety of national parks and wildlife reserves, and are customized for the client(s). Groups of up to ten can be accommodated. Says Mr. Snow, "My main field of expertise is bird identification, either by sight or by ear, and I can identify most butterflies on the wing, at least down to the genus level."

Mingan Island Cetacean Study   **Whale watching**
285 Green   **Research**
St.-Lambert, Quebec J4P 1T3
Canada
514-465-9176
MICS is a nonprofit research organization involved in marine mammal studies, education, and conservation. Research sessions with whales in Canada (summer) and in Baja California (winter).

Monarch Tours   **General**
P.O. Box 890
Belconnen, ACT 2616
Australia
062-591686; fax: 062-417465
Wildlife tours of Australia. All Monarch guides are Australians who have traveled extensively in their country and know the land and its flora and fauna. Groups are limited to twenty.

Motmot Nature Tours   **Birding**
101 West Upland Road
Ithaca, NY 14850-1415
607-257-1616
Small groups (ten to twelve participants, one or two leaders), leisurely pace, staying at each location for several days. Guides are frequently local experts or well-known authors. Motmot has been in business since 1972, and many of their clients are repeats. They act as the U.S. agent for Birds and Birders, a Dutch company.

Mountain Travel/Sobek   **General**
6420 Fairmount Avenue   **Hiking**
El Cerrito, CA 94530   **River rafting**
800-227-2384
An adventure tour company, but some trips have a natural history emphasis. Average group size is about ten. Leaders include both local and U.S. guides. On trips to remote areas, a physician goes along. "Eager to bring about positive change, we work with many nonprofit organizations to design trips that address issues such as tropical deforestation, endangered species and cultures, energy, and the preservation of pristine rivers and wilderness areas. . . . The 'People of the Rain Forest' environmental trip is run in conjunction with Rainforest Action Network."

National Audubon Society
613 Riverside Road
Greenwich, CT 06831
203-869-2017

Ecology
Educational

Ecology camps and workshops—all over the United States, and some international. The first Audubon camp in Maine was founded over fifty years ago. According to early naturalist Millicent Todd Bingham, "Hog Island has become a center from which radiates new ideas and new enthusiasm for the preservation of our whole heritage of natural resources." Field studies range from geology and marine life to birds, mammals, plants, insects, astronomy, and renewable energy. You'll be in the company of distinguished naturalists and fellow students who share your interest in nature. College credit is available.

National Wildlife Federation
1400 Sixteenth Street, NW
Washington, DC 20036-2266
800-245-5484

Families
Children
Educational

Conservation summits and outdoor discovery programs in four U.S. locations. Also three programs for young people: wildlife camp (ages nine to thirteen); leadership training for teens (ages fourteen to seventeen); and teen adventure (ages fourteen to seventeen). Designed to help you discover the natural world, the summits are held in some of our most spectacular areas. Extensive nature programs fascinate all ages. Already inexpensive, there are even lower rates for children and teens.

Natural Habitat Wildlife Adventures
One Sussex Station
Sussex, NJ 07461
800-543-8917

Polar Bears
Marine mammals
General

Best known for their pioneering Seal Watch program, Natural Habitat now watches Polar Bears (in Churchill), whales (in Baja), and primates (in Africa), among other trips.

Brian Davies, the founder, began Seal Watch in 1967 to save the Harp Seals—a real example of ecotourism in action! His idea was that if tourists came to take pictures of the "whitecoats," it might help to keep them from being clubbed to death for their pelts; that is, they'd be worth more alive. And, indeed, his dream has become a reality: Hundreds of tourists visit the floating ice fields in the Gulf of St. Lawrence, wielding video cameras, not clubs. The trips are run by Natural Habitat Adventures at the request of the International Fund for Animal Welfare, a nonprofit organization founded by Mr. Davies.

Nature Expeditions International　　　　　　　　　　　　　　**General**
P.O. Box 11496
Eugene, OR 97440
800-869-0639

"Education to promote conservation is a cornerstone of NEI's operating philosophy. In past years, NEI has donated nearly $40,000 to endow scholarships to graduates in biology, natural history, or anthropology . . . NEI also provides donations to education and conservation organizations. . . . most recently the Oregon Natural Resource Council for work involving the Northwest's ancient forests." NEI combines ecotourism, learning, and adventure. Trips are led by experienced field naturalists; most are limited to sixteen participants. Destinations include North, South, and Central America; Africa; and Oceania.

Naturetrek　　　　　　　　　　　　　　　　　　　　**Botany**
Chautara　　　　　　　　　　　　　　　　　　　　　　**Birding**
Bighton, Nr. Alresford
Hampshire SO24 9RB
United Kingdom
0962-733051; fax: 0962-733368

Naturetrek began operations in 1986 and now travels around the globe. All tours are led by at least one U.K. expert, and small groups are the rule. Most trips require a good deal of walking and generally move at a slow pace so that participants have time to see and explore the wildlife of an area. Detailed predeparture packs are sent to every client. Be advised that Naturetrek "strongly condemns the collecting of any specimen from the natural world. Our holidays provide the opportunity to watch and photograph wildlife only; not to disturb it!"

Nature's Touch　　　　　　　　　　　　　　　　　**Canoeing**
P.O. Box 514
Sequim, WA 98382
800-872-2163

Canoe trips in Esperanza Inlet, Vancouver Island, British Columbia.

Nature World Explorations　　　　　　　　　　　　　**General**
11442 High Hay Drive　　　　　　　　　　　　　　　　**Birding**
Columbia, MD 21044
301-730-0877; fax: 301-964-0951

Company specializes in trips to Costa Rica. Trips are limited to sixteen participants, two leaders.

Navigations and Expeditions   General
P.O. Box 1432
Denver, CO 80201
800-336-9007

This is a small company that recently began offering trips on the Brazilian Amazon, leaving from Manaus. Emphasis is on low-impact wildlife observation and understanding of the Amazon ecosystem. Travel is via locally owned wooden riverboat; food is typical of the region. Participants sleep on deck in hammocks, the way Caboclo (river people) do. Trips are limited to twelve people, with two leaders. According to the company's president and founder, Larry Mott, his trips "are about Brazil and its people as much as about the jungle. We offer a unique opportunity to know and enjoy the river and rain forest in a manner that will place you in contact with the people who live and work in the region." N & E's program bypasses the traditional tourism infrastructure; over 40 percent of its ecotourist dollars are spent in Brazil. The company also actively discourages the local variety of ecoexploitation—that of kidnapping jungle animals for photo sessions with tourists.

New Jersey Audubon Society   General
Rancocas Nature Center
Mt. Holly, NJ 08060
609-261-2495

NJAS has been conducting domestic and foreign nature-study trips since 1976. Destinations differ from year to year, but have included Trinidad and Tobago, the Rio Grande Valley (Texas), Southeast Arizona, Alaska, and the Galápagos. Well-known field naturalists and authors are among the trip leaders.

New York Botanical Garden   Botany
Bronx, NY 10458
212-220-8647

Different destinations from year to year; recent trips have gone to the Amazon, Venezuela, and Trinidad and Tobago. There is also ongoing research in the rain forest of French Guiana. NYBG botanists accompany the tours.

North Star Tours   General
Box 520
Churchill, Manitoba R0B OE0,
Canada
800-665-0690; fax: 204-675-2852

A local company offering photography, birding, and whale-watching trips in

Churchill. Scuba diving in the Churchill River estuary is also offered. All trips are led by local guides.

OBServ   Birding
3901 Trimble Road
Nashville, TN 37215
615-292-2739
Birding tours—mostly weekends—to various "hot spots" (Big Bend), or after special birds (Black Rail).

Oceanic Society Expeditions   Whale watching
Fort Mason Center, Building E   Research
San Francisco, CA 94123   Snorkeling
800-326-7491; fax: 415-474-3395
The travel affiliate for Friends of the Earth and the Environmental Policy Institute, also associated with the California Academy of Sciences, OSE is committed to the environment and practices ethical tourism. They have offered nature journeys since 1973. Professional (U.S.) naturalists lead all trips; "whenever possible, local guides join the group to offer a valuable resident's perspective." Groups average fourteen to eighteen participants.

Osprey Wildlife Expeditions   General
27 Strathalbyn Road   Educational
Aldgate, South Australia 5154
Australia
08-370-9337
This company was established in 1984, and organizes educational and research trips all over Australia. Research projects involve marine mammals. Cultural trips are also offered. Local guides are experienced naturalists; some speak aboriginal languages as well.

Outback Expeditions   Kayaking
P.O. Box 16343
Seattle, WA 98116
206-932-7012; fax: 206-935-1213
In business since 1985, Outback wishes to provide clients with "a wilderness experience that supports the natural balance of the surrounding habitat" and enables them to "enjoy a feeling of oneness with nature, the water, and their surroundings." Low-impact camping and small groups. All trips are guided; safety precautions are taken.

Outer Edge Expeditions
45500 Pontaic Trail
Walled Lake, MI 48390
800-322-5235; fax: 313-624-5140

Marine mammals
General

Outer Edge provides adventurous expeditions from Australia to Alaska. Small groups (two to ten people); experienced leaders. "We contribute a portion of the proceeds to local conservation and research projects in the area of the expedition."

Overseas Adventure Travel   **General**
349 Broadway
Cambridge, MA 02139
800-221-0814; fax: 617-876-0455

Mostly adventure travel, but some natural history trips as well. Has trips for singles, and some low-budget trips. Uses U.S. and local guides. "We are pioneers in ecotourism. We choose itineraries that will minimize the effect of our presence on the land . . . practicing scrupulous waste disposal and fuel-use restrictions. . . . And because we are firmly established in the place we visit, we remain sensitive to the subtleties of culture and lifestyle of the people who live there."

Pacific Exploration Company   **Hiking**
Box 3042
Santa Barbara, CA 93130
805-687-7282; fax: 805-569-0722

The company was founded in 1977, and since then has been specializing in nature and hiking trips to Australia and New Zealand. Custom itineraries.

Pacific Queen   **Whale watching**
2838 Garrison Street
San Diego, CA 92106
619-221-8500

Whale-watching trips from San Diego to Baja, some run jointly with natural history museums.

Perry Mason Safaris   **Animal safaris**
Box 1643
Darien, CT 06820-1643
203-838-1345

Custom safaris to Kenya. "The most important part of any safari is a knowledgeable guide. . . . Preserving the environment is foremost on our list. Unfortunately, there are not enough people that are aware of how important this is. Tourism is one of the main ways to save the wildlife of Kenya. It not only brings in revenue but keeps the poaching down. This is perhaps the reason we only use professional guides, not just driver-guides. A professional guide is much more aware of his surroundings and knows whom to address if there are positive changes to be made."

Princeton Nature Tours　　　　　　　　　　　　　　　　General
282 Western Way
Princeton, NJ 08540
609-683-1111
Various natural history trips run for colleges, universities, and nonprofit groups.

Quark Expeditions　　　　　　　　　　　　　　　　　　General
980 Post Road
Darien, CT 06820
800-356-5699; fax: 203-655-6623
The company was founded in 1985, and is now affiliated with Adventure Network International, known for its pioneering non-cruise trips to The Ice. Quark offers a variety of trips to Antarctica, a Galápagos dive trip, and an expedition down the Amazon, among other destinations. Uses U.S. and Australian guides; leadership is of the highest caliber. Pretrip information is very detailed, and a competent office staff is on hand to answer questions.

Questers Worldwide Nature Tours　　　　　　　　　　General
257 Park Avenue South
New York, NY 10010
800-468-8668; fax: 212-473-1078
Offers a wide variety of natural history tours to the Americas, Asia, Africa, and Australasia. In business since 1973; many repeat clients. All accommodations are first-class; maximum of twenty participants.

Russian Nature Tours　　　　　　　　　　　　　　　　Birding
57 Fore Street
Kingsbridge, South Devon, TQ7 1PG
United Kingdom
0548-856437; fax: 0548-857537
"Russian Nature Tours is a company created by naturalists of Russia and Lithuania. . . . The principal leadership of the company is in the hands of Dr. Algirdas J. Knystautas, the well-known Soviet naturalist. . . . We guarantee you a completely fresh and unrivalled look at the wildlife and birds of the world's largest country. . . . We will be happy to share our love and passion to [sic] everybody who belongs to the ever-growing army of environmentally aware people around the world." Based in England, the company travels to Russia (including Siberia and Central Asia) and Ukraine. All trips are limited to twelve to fourteen participants and have two leaders.

Scripps Aquarium
University of California, San Diego
La Jolla, CA 92093-0207
619-534-8665

Diving

A variety of natural history and snorkeling trips run for members of the aquarium. Two or three trips a year; recent destinations have included Baja, Hawaii, and Fiji.

Sea Quest
600 Corporate Drive, Suite 410
Fort Lauderdale, FL 33334
800-854-8999

General

Luxury cruises, some with a natural history emphasis, aboard the M.S. *Frontier Spirit.*

See & Sea
50 Francisco Street, Suite 205
San Francisco, CA 94133
800-348-9778; fax: 415-434-3409

Diving
Seniors

See & Sea has been offering diving trips to reefs and wrecks around the world since 1965. Today these trips are live-aboards on a variety of vessels. Many trips are accompanied by professional underwater photographers. Private charters also available.

Shearwater Adventures
P.O. Box 3961
Harare
Zimbabwe
735712; fax: 735716

Canoeing
River running
Hiking

Operating since 1981, Shearwater Adventures' area of expertise is adventure travel. All trips are in Zimbabwe. Both the walking safaris and the river trips offer participants the opportunity to see big game. All trips are fully guided.

Shearwater Journeys
P.O. Box 145
Soquel, CA 95073
408-688-1990

Whale watching
Birding

Pelagic trips into Monterey Bay in search of seabirds and marine mammals. All are accompanied by experienced naturalists. Environmental education is a part of each trip, and participants are kept up-to-date about the fate of the oceans. Of particular concern are drift nets and ocean dumping.

Sierra Club
730 Polk Street
San Francisco, CA 94109
415-923-5630

Hiking
Service
River running

The Sierra Club practically invented natural history vacations—their first outing was in 1901. "Since then the Outing Program has been growing, educating, and fostering a love of nature in generations of club members by letting the mountains, forests, and rivers speak to their hearts. . . . Inner City Outings . . . provide wilderness and environmental education opportunities for people who wouldn't otherwise have them—urban youths, senior citizens, and physically disabled persons." A wide range of hiking, camping, river, and service trips is offered each year, both to U.S. and foreign destinations. Trips are open to members only.

Smithsonian Institution
Research Expedition Program
490 L'Enfant Plaza S.W., Suite 4210
Washington, DC 20560
202-287-3210; fax: 202-287-3244

Research

Research projects that offer you the opportunity to work alongside Smithsonian scientists. Projects vary from year to year, but recent ones have included volcano study in Costa Rica and the biology of the Desert Tortoise in Nevada.

Smithsonian Institution
National Associates
1100 Jefferson Drive S.W., Room 3045
Washington, DC 20560

General
Cultural

A variety of study tours—some environmental, some cultural, some a combination. Recent destinations include Arizona, the Channel Islands and Santa Barbara, and forests of the Pacific Northwest. All tours are accompanied by knowledgeable guides and are for associates only.

Sourdough Outfitters
Beetles, AK 99726
800-288-8293, 209-638-6828 (winter)

Canoeing
Hiking

Trips to the backcountry of northern Alaska. Sourdough was founded in 1973, and their guides are experts, very knowledgeable about the botany, bird and animal life, and geology of the Brooks Range. Many repeat clients.

Southern Heritage Tours
P.O. Box 22, Waikari
Christchurch
New Zealand
03-314-4393; fax: 03-314-4137

General
Birding
Botany
Geology

Southern Heritage Tours was started by Rodney and Shirley Russ in 1985. Rodney is a trained ornithologist and has worked for the New Zealand Wildlife Service as an Endangered Species Officer. All programs are focused on New Zealand and its offshore and outlying islands. All itineraries are fully researched, and clients each receive detailed pretrip background information. Guides are of the highest caliber and are experienced field naturalists; Rodney guides many of the trips himself. Southern Heritage Tours offers the most comprehensive New Zealand program, and they're a local operator.

Southwind Adventures
P.O. Box 621057
Littleton, CO 80162
303-972-0701; fax: 303-972-0708

General

Southwind offers a variety of trips to several South American destinations. "Our travelers are gently encouraged toward understanding and awareness of environmental issues through predeparture discussions of topics such as Outdoor Travel Ethics. . . . In addition, we actively support local conservation efforts through donations to organizations and groups working in the areas that we visit." They use local guides. One of their goals is to provide opportunities for their in-country staff to improve their leadership skills, so each season they send one of their top guides to Outward Bound. Private, customized trips can be arranged.

Special Expeditions
7 Elm Street
Westfield, NJ 07090
800-348-2358; fax: 908-654-0098

General
Animal safaris

Luxury cruises aboard the M.V. *Sea Lion,* M.V. *Sea Bird,* and M.S. *Polaris* to a variety of destinations including Alaska, Baja, Belize, and Costa Rica. Other first-class trips include tented safaris to Africa. Experienced naturalists accompany all trips. Many of the cruises are run for natural history museums and organizations.

Special Interest Tours and Travel
134 West 26 Street, Suite 903A
New York, NY 10001
800-525-6772; fax: 212-627-1807

Animal safaris

The company travels to Africa—Tanzania, Kenya, and Botswana. These are traditional safaris, with morning and afternoon game drives. Low-cost camping trips are also offered.

Sue's Safaris   **Animal safaris**
P.O. Box 2171
Rancho Palos Verdes, CA 90274
800-541-2011; fax: 213-544-1502
"Sue's Safaris has a philosophy and a policy of conservation. We provide our clients with information and behavioral guidelines to make you more aware of the world around you and more responsive to the need for appropriate behavior when traveling in environmentally sensitive areas, so as to minimize any impact on that environment and its wildlife. Environmentally sensitive travel is particularly important when visiting Africa."

Sunbird   **Birding**
P.O. Box 76
Sandy, Bedfordshire SG19 1DF
United Kingdom
0767-682969
A birding company (the British affiliate of Wings), operating since 1978. Sunbird offers tours to Europe, the Middle East, Africa, Asia, and Australia. Many of their trips are the same as Wings'. In addition, Sunbirder "Events" are offered. These are package holidays, guided or not, as you choose. Small groups—ten to fourteen participants, with one or two leaders—are the rule.

Sunny Land Expeditions   **Hiking**
166 Main Street   **Kayaking**
Hackensack, NJ 07601   **Cultural**
800-783-7839; fax: 201-487-1546
Trips in the Amazon and Eastern Europe. Mostly adventure travel, but some trips have a natural history emphasis. Amazon trips are run by CanoAndes, founded in 1981. Local guides are employed. Eastern European trips tend to be more culturally oriented, but many involve hiking and kayaking.

Swan Hellenic   **General**
581 Boylston Street
Boston, MA 02116
800-426-5492
A famous cultural travel company, Swan Hellenic also offers some natural history trips. All are luxurious, first-class, and expensive. Trips are escorted by a tour manager and a guest lecturer, who is a specialist in her or his field.

Tamu Safaris
P.O. Box 247
West Chesterfield, NH 03466
800-766-9199

Animal safaris
Birding
General

Founded in 1987, this small, personalized company offers about eight trips to Africa each year. Trips are limited to sixteen participants, so that "the negative impact of tourism [can] be prevented. . . . In addition, Tamu Safaris promotes the direct employment of indigenous African peoples . . . and supports grassroots community development projects to spur local growth.

Tatra Mountain Recreation
12 Dover Road
New Britain, CT 06050-0757
203-229-8481

Hiking

Mostly hiking in the Tatra Mountains of Poland and the Czech Republic. Company has been operating since 1983. Uses U.S. and local guides.

Temptress Cruises
1600 N.W. LeJeune Road, Suite 301
Miami, FL 33126
800-336-8423; fax: 305-871-2657

General

Natural history cruises to the national parks of Costa Rica. Several naturalist guides accompany the trips.

The Nature Conservancy
1815 North Lynn Street
Arlington, VA 22209
703-841-5300

General

Domestic natural history trips are run by local field offices; overseas trips are run by Geostar and International Expeditions. There is a tremendous variety: birding in Alaska; ecology study in California; animal tracking in Montana; and botany in Oregon. International programs include trips to the Amazon, the Galápagos, and Costa Rica, among other destinations. Conservancy representatives accompany all trips. Costs include a charitable contribution to TNC. Small groups only, usually about twelve.

Trans Niugini Tours/Unirep
850 Colorado Boulevard, Suite 105
Los Angeles, CA 90041
800-521-7242; fax: 213-256-0647

General
Cultural

Local tour operator; developed wilderness lodges (Karawari and Ambua) and the "floating lodge," the *Sepik Spirit,* a boat that takes clients down the middle Sepik and Blackwater rivers. Cultural sites are visited as well. Both Karawari and Ambua lodges are well-known birding spots.

TraveLearn   **Educational**
P.O. Box 315
Lakeville, PA 18438
800-235-9114
Educational natural history and cultural travel to many popular destinations, including the Galápagos, Costa Rica, and Australia. Many trips are run for universities. College faculty escorts and in-country specialists accompany the trips; local guides are used.

TravelWild   **Photography**
P.O. Box 655   **Polar Bears**
Vashon Island, WA 98070   **General**
800-368-0077
A well-established company (formerly named for the founder, Joseph Van Os) that pioneered wildlife photography trips, now offers natural history trips as well. In addition to the Polar Bear spectacular in Churchill each fall, TravelWild visits wintering Monarch Butterflies in Mexico and Bald Eagles in Alaska, among many other destinations. U.S. guides and photographers accompany the trips. "Our trips embrace a holistic approach to nature."

Tundra Buggy Tours   **Polar Bears**
P.O. Box 662
Churchill, Manitoba ROB OEO
Canada
204-675-2121
Trips on the Tundra Buggies in and around Churchill to see Polar Bears in the fall and flowers and birds in the spring and summer. The buggies were designed to have a low impact on the fragile tundra, and the tours get you up close to the bears without harassing them.

Turtle Tours   **General**
9446 Quail Trail, Box 1147   **Cultural**
Carefree, AZ 85377
602-488-3688
Combination cultural–natural history trips to Africa. Also trips to South America.

University Research Expeditions Program   **Research**
University of California
Berkeley, CA 94720
510-642-6586

"For fifteen years UREP has been inviting the public to join the scientific community in exploring the wonders of planet Earth. . . . Single issues addressed by UREP teams have *global* consequences. Halting the deforestation of the world's rain forests ultimately benefits trees in our own backyard." Costs cover food and lodging and include a contribution to the project; they are tax-deductible. "The 1992 UREP catalog was printed on recycled paper. As a result, 30 trees, 12,600 gallons of water, and 7,383 kilowatts of energy were saved."

Victor Emanuel Nature Tours (VENT)   **Birding**
P.O. Box 33008   **Children**
Austin, TX 78764
800-328-8368; fax: 512-328-2919

VENT has been taking clients birdwatching since 1975; they now offer over a hundred birding and natural history tours worldwide. "VENT has an absolute commitment to conservation. We have been a leader in the field of ecotourism, organizing tours in support of conservation. . . . Many of our tour leaders play significant roles in the conservation movement. . . . Hand in hand with conservation is education. In association with the American Birding Association, VENT has pioneered the establishment of birding camps for young people. . . . From VENT's inception we have believed that a birding tour involves more than the accumulation of a long list. It involves experiencing the natural world and learning more about it." VENT contributes money to Conservation International's El Triunfo project (El Triunfo is a preserve in southern Mexico).

Most tours are limited to sixteen participants and have two leaders. VENT's leaders are among the most renowned experts in their areas of specialization. Several (Steve Hilty, Robert Ridgely, and Ted Parker, for instance) are authors of important books and articles, and some (Ted Parker and Maurice Rumboll) have described new species to science. Generally, U.S. guides are used, sometimes with local backups. Our experience with VENT has always been of the highest quality. Indeed, everyone we've spoken to has been pleased with their VENT tour.

Voyagers International   **General**
P.O. Box 915   **Photography**
Ithaca, NY 14851
800-633-0299; fax: 607-257-3699

Voyagers has been running natural history trips worldwide since 1982. In addition to trips for nonprofit organizations (museums, universities, and zoological societies), they have their own schedule of nature and photography trips. "All trips are designed to be culturally and environmentally sensitive—what is now termed eco-tourism. . . . We support local economies by using host-country tour operators and guides. We actively assist in fund-raising for many conservation organizations in the countries in which we operate." Small groups (ten to twelve) help to maintain low-impact, low-profile travel. Most tours are general, but some specialize in photography, birding, botany. African trips are largely animal safaris. Voyagers is a member and supporter of the East African Wild Life Society and the African Wildlife Foundation.

Wilderness Travel   General
801 Allston Way   Cultural
Berkeley, CA 94710
800-247-6700

In business since 1978. Many trips are adventure travel or combination cultural-natural history. Offers over a hundred trips on five continents. Maximum of sixteen participants on all trips. "There is an undeniable fragility to our wonderful planet. . . . Cultures and ecosystems are increasingly threatened by our own actions and abuse. And with each passing day, tourism becomes more of a factor in the global condition—either as a contributor to cultural and environmental exploitation or as a positive force for increased awareness and change. . . . As the world turns 'green,' you'll find that at Wilderness Travel it's not a new color. . . . Our adventures actively promote cultural preservation, conservation, and environmental protection."

Wildland Adventures
(see Journeys)

Wildlife Conservation Society   General
217 East 85 Street
New York, NY 10028
212-879-2588; fax: 212-879-6295

Trips run by Members Afield International for the Society. Recent destinations include Africa, Australia, Antarctica, and Belize, among others. Trips are frequently accompanied by curators.

Wings   Birding
P.O. Box 31930
Tucson, AZ 85751
602-749-1967; fax: 602-749-3175

Wings has been offering birdwatching trips since 1973, when, as Northeast Birding, they offered trips to New England and eastern Canada. They now offer trips worldwide, some in partnership with Sunbird. Groups are small, usually fourteen to sixteen participants, with one or two leaders. Leadership varies from excellent to fair. Notable leaders include Rich Stallcup and Jon Dunn, among others. Mostly U.S. guides, some in-country ornithologists. Many repeat clients.

Wonderbird Tours   **Birding**
P.O. Box 2015   **Butterflies**
New York, NY 10159   **Research**
212-727-0780; fax: 212-645-0402

A variety of tours, mostly to the Canadian Atlantic provinces and Caribbean. Leaders include authors of field guides and professional photographers.

Woodstar Tours   **Birding**
908 South Massachusetts Avenue   **Cultural**
DeLand, FL 32724
904-736-0327

Incorporated in 1987. "We wish to contribute to conservation by working with ground operators who spend money amongst locals in the destination countries and contribute to responsible conservation organizations. Indirectly some of the monies paid by clients find their way to [in-country conservation organizations], although the expenditures for local lodging, meals, and guides is much more significant in terms of the objective of making ecotourism a viable alternative to deforestation, mineral exploitation, hunting, and other forms of environmental degradation." Uses only local guides.

World Nature Tours   **Birding**
P.O. Box 693   **Botany**
Silver Spring, MD 20918
301-593-2522

Trips look at all aspects of natural history of the places they visit, with emphasis on the birds, flowers, and mammals. Small groups.

World Wildlife Fund   **General**
1250 Twenty-fourth Street, N.W.
Washington, DC 20037

WWF is a conservation organization, not a tour operator, but they do have an extensive travel program for their members. Recent destinations include the Galápagos, Kenya, Alaska, and India. A WWF representative accompanies all trips.

Zegrahm Expeditions
1414 Dexter Avenue N.
Seattle, WA 98109
206-285-4000; fax: 206-285-5037

General
Birding
Diving

"We believe expedition yachts and small ships to be one of the best methods of environmentally responsible travel." Zegrahm's founders are active members of the Ecotourism Society, and helped to develop the Antarctica Visitor and Tour Operator Guidelines (page 143). Zegrahm is affiliated with Eco Expeditions, a company founded by Peter Harrison and Shirley Metz. Guides (for both Eco Expeditions and Zegrahm) are naturalists, professional photographers, and authors.

RESOURCES

RECOMMENDED READING

Tour operators often send a list of recommended books along with other pretrip information. You'll enjoy your trip more if you familiarize yourself, even if only generally, with the flora and fauna of your destination. If you're avid about your subject—birds, plants, rocks, or whatever—be sure you have the appropriate field guide.

Generally, travel books do not contain much information on naturalist subjects. A few publishers, however, have begun offering books on nature travel. The APA Insight Guides to wildlife—currently available for Southeast Asia, India, The Amazon Basin, and East Africa—are excellent. Also good are the Outdoor Traveler's Guides (for Australia, Canada, the Caribbean), published by Stewart, Tabori & Chang.

For the United States, the Audubon Society Field Guides to Natural Places (Mid-Atlantic-Coastal, Mid-Atlantic-Inland, Northeast-Inland, and Northeast-Coastal) explain what you'll see at parks and nature reserves in each area; the books are published by Pantheon. Similarly, the Sierra Club Guides to the National Parks, published by Stewart, Tabori & Chang, describe the history and environments of the country's parks.

REFERENCES CITED IN TEXT

Adams, Douglas, and Mark Carwardine. *Last Chance to See.* New York: Harmony Books, 1990.

Bangs, Richard, and Christian Kallen. *Islands of Fire, Islands of Spice.* San Francisco: Sierra Club Books, 1988.

Grunfeld, Frederic V. *Wild Spain.* New York: Prentice Hall, 1988.

Nolting, Mark. *African Safari: The Complete Travel Guide to Ten Top Game Viewing Countries.* Pompano Beach, Fla.: Global Travel Publishers, 1987.

Whelan, Tensie, ed. *Nature Tourism.* Washington, DC: Island Press, 1991.

World Resources Institute. *1992 Information Please Environmental Almanac.* Boston: Houghton Mifflin, 1991.

ENVIRONMENTAL AND ECOTOURISM ORGANIZATIONS

Adventure Travel Society
6551 S. Revere Parkway (Suite 160)
Englewood, CO 80111
303-649-9016

American Birding Association, Inc.
P.O. Box 6599
Colorado Springs, CO 80934
(800) 835-2473

Birdlife International (formerly ICBP)
32 Cambridge Road
Girton, Cambridge CB3 OPJ
United Kingdom
0223-277318

Conservation International
1015 18th Street
Suite 1000
Washington, DC 20036
202-429-5660

Ecotourism Society
P.O. Box 755
North Bennington, VT 05257
802-447-2121

Environmental Defense Fund
1616 P Street, N.W.
Washington, DC 20036
202-387-3500

Friends of the Earth
218 D Street, S.E.
Washington, DC 20003
202-544-2600

Greenpeace
1436 U Street, N.W.
Washington, DC 20009
202-462-1177

National Audubon Society
700 Broadway
New York, NY 10003
212-979-3000

National Wildlife Federation
1400 16th Street N.W.
Washington, DC 20036
202-797-6800

Nature Conservancy
1815 North Lynn Street
Arlington, VA 22209
703-841-5300

Oceanites
2378 Route 97
Cooksville, MD 21723

Programme for Belize
P.O. Box 1088
Vineyard Haven, MA 02568
800-343-8009

Rainforest Action Network
466 Green Street, Suite 300
San Francisco, CA 94133
415-398-4404

Wildlife Conservation Society
2300 Southern Boulevard
Bronx, New York 10460
718-220-5121

The Wilderness Society
1400 Eye Street, N.W.
Washington, DC 20005
202-842-3400

World Resources Institute
1709 New York Avenue, N.W.
Washington, DC 20006
202-638-6300

World Wildlife Fund
Conservation Foundation
1250 24th Street, N.W.
Washington, DC 20037
202-293-4800

GEOGRAPHICAL INDEX

TRIP INDEX

The following is a geographical listing of special interest trips. General interest trips are not indexed, since they focus on several aspects of natural history simultaneously. Some interests, such as astronomy and herpetology, seem to be underrepresented, but they are frequently included in a general interest or research trip. And while many trips are not specifically designed for families, we have found that families are usually welcomed.